THE READING CONTEXT

THE READING CONTEXT

Developing College Reading Skills

Dorothy U. Seyler
Northern Virginia Community College

Allyn and Bacon
Boston   London   Toronto   Sydney   Tokyo   Singapore

Vice President, Publisher, Humanities: Joseph Opiela
Editorial Assistant: Kate Tolini
Marketing Manager: Lisa Kimball
Editorial Production Service: Elm Street Publishing Services, Inc.
Manufacturing Buyer: Megan Cochran
Cover Administrator: Linda Knowles

Library of Congress Cataloging-in-Publication Data

Seyler, Dorothy U.
    The reading context : developing college reading skills / Dorothy
U. Seyler.
        p.   cm.
    Includes bibliographical references and index.
    ISBN 0-205-18545-2
    1. Reading (Higher education)   2. Reading (Higher education)—
Problems, exercises, etc.   I. Title.
LB2365.R4S39   1996
428.4′071′1—dc20   96-7816
                                                          CIP

Printed in the United States of America
10 9 8 7 6 5 4 3 2 1   01 00 99 98 97 96

CONTENTS

Preface   xi

■ **CHAPTER 1**

The Reading Context   1

Your Reading Profile   3

The Engaged Reader   4

    Commitment   5   Concentration   6   Cognition (and Metacognition)   9

The Reading Process   10

    What Is Reading?   11   The Role of Vocabulary   12   Connecting and Predicting in Reading   13   The Reading Context   15

Selection 1   *Lester A. Lefton,* "Learning to Learn"   17

Selection 2   *Douglas Colligan,* "The Light Stuff"   20

■ **CHAPTER 2**

Reading Actively   26

Why Have a Reading Strategy?   26

Prepare—Read—Respond: How the Parts Connect   27

Prepare   28

    Identify the Author and the Work   28   Establish Purpose in Reading   32   Preread: William Barklow, "Hippo Talk"   33   What Do I Already Know?   38   What Will I Learn from Reading?   41

Read   42

    Write   42   Guidelines for Annotating   43   An Example of Annotating: Lester A. Lefton, "The Discovery of Short-Term Memory" and "Long-Term Memory: Focus on Retrieval"   43   Monitor   45   Guidelines for Fixing Comprehension   47

Respond: Reflect and Review   48

    Reflect   48   Questions to Aid Reflection   49   Review   50

Selection 1   *Lester A. Lefton,* "Hypnosis"   51

Selection 2   *Edward J. Tarbuck and Frederick K. Lutgens,* "The Nature of Scientific Inquiry"   56

Selection 3.   *Robert J. Samuelson,* "The Triumph of the Psycho-Fact"   61

■ **CHAPTER 3**

Concentrating on Main Ideas 67

The Role of Previous Knowledge 68

Identifying the Topic 69

Understanding Main Ideas 71

Identifying a Paragraph's Topic Sentence 75 Placement of the Topic Sentence 75 Paragraphs with an Implied Main Idea 80

Distinguishing among Supporting Details 83

Identifying Main Ideas in Longer Passages 89

Thomas A. Bailey and David M. Kennedy, "Jeffersonian Idealism and Idealists" 91 Turley Mings, "The New Industrial Revolution" 93

Selection 1 *Robert E. Ricklefs*, "The Behavior of the Baboon Has Evolved in a Social Context" 95

Selection 2 *Dianne Hales and Dr. Robert Hales,* "Does Your Body-Talk Do You In?" 100

Selection 3 *James M. Henslin,* "The Amish—*Gemeinschaft* Community in a *Gesellschaft* Society" 105

■ **CHAPTER 4**

Building Word Power 111

Context Clues 112

Definitions 113 Examples 114 Comparison and Contrast 116

Learning from Word Parts: Prefixes, Roots, Suffixes 120

Common Prefixes 120 Common Roots 122 Suffixes 123

Using the Dictionary 125

Glossaries 126 Pocket Dictionaries 126 Spelling-Only Dictionaries 126 Desk Dictionaries 126 The Thesaurus 127 Unabridged and Subject-Area Dictionaries 127

Information Found in Desk Dictionaries 128

Information on the English Language 128 Charts and Tables 128 Pronunciation Guides 128 Foreign Language Terms, Famous People, Mythological Figures, Place Names, Figures and Diagrams 129

What Each Entry Contains 130

Strategies for Learning New Words 134

Using Vocabulary Cards 135 Using New Words 137

Some Important Words from Various Disciplines 137

Selection 1 *Sydney J. Harris,* "Opposing Principles Help Balance Society" 138

Selection 2 *Lester A. Lefton,* "What Is Prejudice?" 142
Selection 3 *Roger L. Welsch,* "Belly Up to the Bar: This Round's on Me" 148

■ **CHAPTER 5**

Recognizing a Writer's Structures and Strategies 153

Listing 154
   Signal Words for Listing 155
Examples 156
   Signal Words for Examples 157
Definition 158
   Signal Words for Definitions 159
Ordering: Chronology and Process 161
   Signal Words for Ordering 161
Comparison and Contrast 163
   Signal Words for Comparison and Contrast 164
Cause and Effect 166
   Signal Words for Cause and Effect 168
Problem/Solution 169
   Signal Words for Problem/Solution 170
Mixed Patterns 176
Selection 1 *Stephen E. Lucas,* "Differences Between Public Speaking and
             Conversation" 178
Selection 2 *Thomas H. Kean,* "The Crisis Coming to Campus" 183
Selection 3 *James M. Henslin,* "The Effects of the Automobile" 187

■ **CHAPTER 6**

Writing Strategies to Reinforce Reading 194

Why Write? 195
Highlighting/Underlining 195
   Guidelines for Highlighting/Underlining 197
Annotating 197
   Guidelines for Annotating 198
Outlining 200
   Guidelines for Outlining 202
Mapping 206
   Guidelines for Mapping 207

Note Taking 208

  Paraphrasing 209 Guidelines for Paraphrasing 210 Note Taking: The Cornell Method 211 Guidelines for the Cornell Method 212

Summary 213

  James M. Henslin, "A New World Order?" 214 Guidelines for Summary 215 Jackson J. Spielvogel, "The Witchcraft Craze" 216

Selection 1 *Turley Mings*, "Private Participation in Public Education" 219

Selection 2 *Aaron Copland*, "How We Listen to Music" 222

Selection 3 *Charles Krauthammer*, "Painless 'Patriotism'" 229

■ **CHAPTER 7**

Reading for College Classes 235

Scanning 236

  Guidelines for Scanning 236 Daniel J. Curran and Claire M. Renzetti, "Global Insights" 240

Skimming 241

  Guidelines for Skimming 243 Julie Anthony, "The Fit Player" 244 Postlethwait, Hopson, and Veres, "Sexually Transmitted Disease: A Growing Concern" 246

Reading Graphics 248

Applying Reading Skills to a Textbook Chapter 258

  Tom L. McKnight, "Preface," Essentials of Physical Geography *258 Chapter 9: "The Biosphere" 261 "The Tropical Rainforest" 263*

Selection 1 *Tom L. McKnight*, "Rainforest Removal" 264

Selection 2 *Mark A. Norell, Eugene S. Gaffney, and Lowell Dingus,* "How Large Were the Biggest Dinosaurs?" 270

Selection 3 *Carl Sagan*, "What TV Could Do for America" 274

■ **CHAPTER 8**

Studying for College Classes 281

Preparing for Class 281

Participating in Class 282

Strategies for Retention 285

Preparing for Testing 287

  Preparing for Short-Answer Forms of Testing 288 John H. Postlethwait et al., "Homo sapiens" 289

Essay Tests   293

    Jackson J. Spielvogel, "The Reformation in England"   295

Selection 1 *Vincent Ryan Ruggiero, "The Basis of Moral Judgment"   299*

Selection 2 *J. Ross Eshleman , Barbara G. Cashion, and Laurence A. Basirico,*
    "Legalization of Drugs"   305

Selection 3 *Abigail Trafford, "The Unheeding Addict"   311*

■ **CHAPTER 9**

Reading Expressive Writing   317

Characteristics of Expressive Writing   318

Connotation   319

Sentence Style   321

Figurative Language   322

Reading Descriptive Essays   325

Reading Narrative Essays   330

Reading Fiction   334

    Narrative Structure   334   Character   335   Point of View   336   Style and Tone   337   Chopin, "The Story of an Hour"   337

Reading Poetry   340

    Herrick, "To Daffodils"   342   Hughes, "Dream Deferred"   344 Lowell, "Taxi"   345   Housman, "Is My Team Ploughing"   346

Selection 1 *Tracy Kidder, "Mrs. Zajac"   348*

Selection 2 *James Thurber, "The Secret Life of Walter Mitty"   353*

Selection 3 *Isaac Asimov, "Science and the Sense of Wonder"   360*

■ **CHAPTER 10**

Reading—and Thinking—Critically   366

Characteristics of the Critical Reader   368

Distinguishing Fact from Opinion   370

    "Just" an Opinion   370   Personal Preferences   371   Judgments   371 Inferences   371   Guidelines for Evaluating Inferences   373

Recognizing Your Biases   376

The Writer's Stance   377

    Attitude   378   Tone   381   Hyperbole, Understatement, and Irony   382 Dave Barry, "Unplugged"   383

Evaluating Arguments and Taking a Stand   387

Recognizing Logical Fallacies   387   Taking a Stand   390   Ernest van den Haag, from "The Ultimate Punishment: A Defense"   391   Anthony G. Amsterdam, from "Capital Punishment"   392

Selection 1   *Ellen Goodman, "Stranger-Danger"*   394
Selection 2   *Molly Ivins, "Ban the Things. Ban Them All; Nuts to Guns"*   398
Selection 3   *Lester C. Thurow, "Why Women Are Paid Less Than Men"*   403

■ **CHAPTER 11**

Living and Working in the Twenty-First Century   409

Rebecca J. Donatelle and Lorraine G. Davis, "Environmental Health" (Chapter 22 from Access to Health)   410

Sarah James and Floyd Peterson, "At Risk in Alaska: Our Salmon, Our Eagles"   421

Amy E. Schwartz, "Visions of the On-Line University—in 3-D"   423

Richard D. Kahlenberg, "Affirmative Action by Class"   425

William Raspberry, "Will Our Future Be Workable?"   427

Michael Barone, "The New America"   429

Jill Ker Conway, "Women, Children, and Ethics"   434

Glossary   *440*

Index   *447*

PREFACE

Reading can be fun! Reading should engage us: teach us something new, make us think, stir our feelings. *The Reading Context* seeks to engage you, the student, in the reading process. It is also designed to improve your reading skills, but that goal is sadly limited if you are not also turned on to reading. So, be forewarned; this book's goal is to change your attitude toward reading—as well as change your reading strategies.

The Reading Context is shaped by several concepts. First is the idea of reading in context, not just reading words on the page. To get meaning from those words, readers need to know about the author and type of work they are reading. They also need to know their purpose in reading. Second is the idea of active reading. Reading is not a passive activity of "receiving" information but an engagement with the text that generates meaning. Additionally, *The Reading Context* stresses the importance of being aware of the reading process *during* the process and consciously using strategies to aid comprehension and, hence, pleasure in reading.

The text's eleven chapters can be seen as forming three sections. Chapters 1 through 4 comprise the "nuts and bolts" strategies for reading. They introduce the idea of the reading context and active reading. Chapter 2 presents active reading as a three-step process: Prepare, Read, Respond. Students can work with this process and instructors will find it is quite similar to SQ3R and other reading strategies. Chapter 3 focuses on reading for main ideas, and Chapter 4 presents strategies for vocabulary building. Material in Chapter 4 on context clues, word parts, and the dictionary can be taught as a unit, or instructors can fit various sections into their own teaching plans.

Chapters 5 through 8 constitute the text's second section. In these chapters you examine an author's use of writing strategies as aids to comprehension and develop your own writing-to-learn strategies. Additionally, Chapter 7 introduces skimming and scanning as alternative reading strategies and guides you through textbook reading, including the reading of graphics. Chapter 8 concludes this section by helping you prepare for class and for exams.

Chapters 9 through 11 provide opportunities to read more widely, to study expressive and persuasive writing, and to explore a variety of works in a casebook on living and working in the twenty-first century. Although the "Questions for Discussion and Reflection" that follow all the end-of-chapter reading selections are designed to develop critical thinking skills, Chapters 9 through 11 are especially concerned with the enhancing of critical thinking. Here you are encouraged to evaluate what you read, to apply it to your own life and experiences, to ponder the issues raised, and to take a stand on the issues. In its focus on critical thinking, *The Reading Context* reinforces the concept of active reading in a specific context.

In *The Reading Context,* you will find clear explanations supported by many examples. You will have many opportunities to practice the skills explained in each chapter in exercises that you can complete within the text. In addition, there are longer reading selections at the end of each chapter that will hold your interest while representing the kinds of material you will meet in college assignments—material that ranges across the curriculum from geology to health, from history to sociology. Reading with understanding and retaining information and ideas from reading are essential skills for success in college courses, in the workplace, and in our personal lives. *The Reading Context* provides a "tool kit" for those students ready to develop their reading skills.

Fortunately for both authors and their readers, no book is prepared alone. Many colleagues and friends have helped me think more clearly about how we read and how we learn. To all of them I am grateful. In particular, I would like to thank Evonne Jones, Barbara Wilan, Pam Leggat, and Pat Hodgdon for lending me their books and sharing with me their ideas about the teaching of reading. And I can never complete a textbook without calling on the support of the library's reference staff, specifically Marion Delmore and Ruth Stratton. I also want to thank my most important first reader, my daughter Ruth. Additionally I would like to acknowledge the support and guidance of my editor, Joe Opiela. The following reviewers have also contributed many good suggestions throughout the development of this text: Rosann Cook, Purdue University–Calumet; Janet Elder, Richland College; Elaine M. Fitzpatrick, Massasoit Community College; Eric Hibbison, John Sargeant Reynolds Community College; Pamela Leggat, Northern Virginia Community College; Richard F. Malena, Phoenix College; Jack Scanlon, Triton Community College; Ellen Gage Searles, Mohawk Valley Community College; and Nancy E. Smith, Florida Community College at Jacksonville.

THE READING CONTEXT

CHAPTER 1

The Reading Context

In this chapter you will learn:

- To evaluate your reading profile

- The roles of commitment, concentration, and cognition in reading success

- Specific strategies for improving concentration

- What reading is

- Key characteristics of the reading context

Have you ever attended a party to watch the NCAA college basketball playoffs? If you have, you know that not all the partygoers have the same knowledge of the game. Some do not know much about basketball. Others enjoy watching the contest and cheering for their favorite team. But if you ask them why their team lost, their answer may simply be the other team was better. Their answer doesn't offer much insight into the game. Finally, there are the viewers who watch intently and speak a strange language; they talk of "three-point baskets" and "presses," offering commentary on what is happening throughout the game.

If we look at our basketball partygoers in another way, we can see other differences. Some at the party show little interest in the game. They enjoy the beer and chips. They may even retreat to the kitchen for conversation that is not about basketball. If we took a survey in the kitchen we would learn that most do not have much information about the game. Lacking knowledge, they quickly lose interest and turn their attention to something else. A second group at the party does show some interest in the game because their favorite team is playing. But if we were to take a picture of the partygoers sitting around the TV, we could identify these mildly interested folks in the photograph. One is busy eating a ham sandwich. Another is talking to the person sitting next to him. Also in the snapshot are those showing great interest in the game. They are leaning forward in their chairs. One is eating a pretzel without taking her eyes off the TV screen. Another is talking and gesturing while watching, just like a TV commentator.

Now, why has this chapter begun with a discussion of people watching basketball? If you are asking yourself this question, you are on track to becoming a good reader. In the space below, answer the question we have raised, and another one as well.

 ## Exercise 1-1 Thinking about a Writer's Strategy

Answer each question in the space provided before continuing to read.

1. What, if any, connection do you see between the subject of this chapter and the opening discussion of a basketball party?

   _____

   _____

   _____

2. Why might a writer choose to write something that doesn't seem at first to be directly connected to the topic?

   _____

   _____

   _____

Let's look first at answers to the second question. Some students use the lines above as a place to express their frustration with writers. They complain that "there is no good reason to write on another topic" or "writers do this to confuse readers." Perhaps you wrote an answer similar to one of these. Sometimes we do get frustrated when we fail to see a connection, when we do not understand what a writer is doing.

One way to get rid of the frustration is to recognize the advantages that writers find in an indirect approach. Perhaps you responded to the question by listing some of the advantages: (1) an example or comparison can help explain a complicated idea; (2) the indirect approach can be an attention getter that will engage the reader; (3) the indirect approach can be clever, amusing, fun. These are good reasons to take an indirect approach to developing a topic.

Now the first question. Did you see a connection? Is it possible to make an *analogy* (a comparison noting several similarities between two items, usually to explain one of the items) between watching a basketball game and reading? There are several points about reading that can be made, if we think about the comparison.

First, we can conclude that the various groups of partygoers are not "seeing" the same game. Those who understand how the game is played are experiencing a different game than are those who do not know much about basketball. Similarly, what a reader brings to a reading situation does much to shape the reading context. Your knowledge and experience make a difference not just in how easy or hard the reading task is, but also in what you understand from the reading. Second, the different degrees of interest shown in the game teach us something about reading. Those who show their interest by watching intently, engaged in what is happening, will be much more knowledgeable about the game. They are the ones you would want to ask for a summary of the game. Similarly, the more engaged you are in any reading task, the more you will remember from your reading. If you read a bit, then look out the window, you will not remember very much from the reading. Those who *concentrate* get more out of any experience than those whose attention wanders.

Finally, what about the folks in the kitchen? They are not experiencing the game at all, even though they are at the party. It seems that people often lose interest in those subjects they do not know much about. Sometimes people even ridicule what they do not understand. ("Who cares how many times they execute a fast break!") This is a rather sad approach. Why not watch the game and ask questions to learn more? They might discover a new interest; they will at least know more about a topic that interests their friends. Of course, as a student you cannot afford to lack interest. If you think your history text is "boring," you will find yourself failing history. Your role as a student is to *be interested*—to learn as much as you can from your reading. You cannot—to use our analogy again—hang out in the kitchen!

■ YOUR READING PROFILE

A reader's knowledge, interests, and attitudes greatly affect any reading experience. They are part of the reading context. Remember that the reader creates the reading context. You *choose* to pick up the work and turn the page, just as some of our partygoers choose to watch the game. Since the reader is so important a part of the reading context, we need to become acquainted with ourselves as readers. The following exercise will help you examine your reading habits and attitudes.

EXERCISE 1-2 Your Reading Profile

Mark T (true) or F (false) in the space provided after each statement. The goal is self-awareness, so answer truthfully.

		T	F
1.	In my leisure time, I usually choose to watch TV rather than read.	___	___
2.	I mostly read newspapers or magazines.	___	___
3.	My favorite place to read is on my bed.	___	___
4.	I enjoy reading novels but not textbooks.	___	___
5.	I usually read late at night.	___	___
6.	I rarely find time to read the newspaper.	___	___
7.	I usually have music or the TV on when I read for my courses.	___	___
8.	I would like to be a better reader.	___	___
9.	Reading bores me.	___	___
10.	I enjoy reading about new subjects.	___	___
11.	Reading is difficult for me.	___	___
12.	I would be a better reader if I had a larger vocabulary.	___	___
13.	I am taking this course so that I can read faster.	___	___
14.	Good reading skills are necessary for success in college and the workplace.	___	___

The first seven statements give you information about your reading habits. Study your answers to those seven first. What did you discover? How often do you read? Do you read when and where you can concentrate? The next seven statements ask you to think about your attitudes toward reading. Look over your responses to those statements. Do you like to read? Do you think reading skills are important? In answering these questions, rate yourself on each of the following scales. Circle the ratings that are right for you.

	Poor	Average	Good	Very Good
Reading Habits	1	2	3	4
Reading Attitudes	1	2	3	4

■ THE ENGAGED READER

What is your reading profile? Is there room for improvement? The ideal reading profile is the profile of the *engaged reader*. The *engaged reader* gets top marks for each of the **"3Cs": commitment, concentration, and cognition.** The following chart sums up the idea of the 3Cs.

The 3Cs of the Engaged Reader

Commitment: An *active* desire to read well and benefit from reading. Attitude matters.

Concentration: *Active* attention to reading, using specific strategies for concentration.

Cognition: *Active* use of language and reasoning skills to follow the writer's ideas.

Commitment

The fact that you are taking a reading course and using this text is an indication of commitment on your part to improve your reading skills. Signing up for the class is a good first step, but it is only a first step. This course on your schedule will not make you a better reader. Only *you* can improve your reading skills. Reading is a skill, just like driving a car or playing a sport. You improve any skill with the same three ingredients: a desire to improve, some good instruction or advice, and practice, practice, practice! This text and your instructor will offer you good advice and many opportunities for practice. If you seize the opportunity, because your commitment to improve is strong, then you will succeed in your goal.

Unfortunately, commitment is not something that you either have or don't have. Instead, there are degrees of commitment. Students tell teachers that they are *really* committed to doing well in school; employees tell bosses that they are *really* committed to succeeding in their jobs. Still, some students and some employees do not do well. Commitment must show itself each day in the way that time and energy and thought are used to produce success. Your commitment to improve reading skills will be measured in how much more time you spend reading—and in how often you turn off the TV or turn down the stereo. Commitment needs to show itself in action.

The degree to which you are committed to improving reading skills may be tied to your immediate college goals and long-term career goals. Why are you in college? What are your plans and dreams for the future? Use the following exercise to reflect on your goals.

EXERCISE 1-3

I. List 5 to 8 reasons why you are attending college. Try to be honest and thorough, including reasons such as "making new friends."

_____

_____

_____

_____

II. Analyze your list and then comment on your reasons for attending college. For example, does your list emphasize career goals or short-term goals of having fun?

_____

_____

_____

_____

Can your college and career goals be used to strengthen your commitment to improved reading skills? If you have strong goals for intellectual and personal growth, try reflecting on them when you become anxious or frustrated by all of the required reading for your courses. Let your goals serve as "commitment boosters." If your analysis has revealed a lack of serious goals, then perhaps you should begin by reflecting on the depth of your commitment to the rigors of college work. You may want to schedule an appointment with a counselor to discuss your reasons for attending college or to explore career possibilities.

Attitude does matter. It's okay to say that reading is difficult for you at times. It's not okay to begin each reading assignment by saying "This is boring" or "I hate reading biology." Negative feelings, whether expressed to others or thought to yourself, get in the way of positive actions.

Students sometimes have negative attitudes toward particular reading assignments because they do not find the course or subject matter interesting. But if they—or you—need to be entertained to find motivation for a course, there is a commitment problem. Rethink your reasons for taking the course—and for attending college—and then decide that you will do well and get the course behind you. If you cannot always make a positive statement, at least try to break the habit of negative thoughts.

Concentration

Concentration is also an essential trait of the engaged reader. If you do not concentrate well when you read, then achieving greater concentration will be a necessary step to improving your reading skills. The desire to be more focused is, of course, part of the equation, but desire alone won't do the job. Concentration, like commitment, requires action. Here are some specific steps that you can take to improve your concentration when you read.

Steps to Improved Concentration: Before You Begin Reading

1. *Reduce external distractions.* Find a quiet room. Turn off the television. Either turn off the stereo or turn it down and choose "quiet" background music. Select a comfortable chair, but avoid stretching out on a bed or couch. Stretching out invites the body—and the mind—to relax. If your dorm or house is rarely quiet, then read in the library. Select an individual desk in one of the library's quiet zones, not a large table in the busy reference section.

2. *Select appropriate times.* Do not read late at night or when you are very tired. If you must study late, save work that requires writing as well as reading, such as completing homework exercises or lab reports. If you are alert in the morning, read before attending classes, or read in the library or your room between classes.

3. *Announce your intentions.* Let roommates or family members know that you will be reading and do not wish to be disturbed. Ask friends not to call or come by during designated study times. Post a "Do Not Disturb" sign on your door. Then ignore those who try to interrupt in spite of your efforts. (If they refuse to get the message, show them this page of your text!)

4. *Set up a work plan.* Respect your reading as serious work by planning the time you will spend on each reading project. If thinking through your schedule doesn't keep you focused, then write out a schedule. For example: 30 minutes for history, 30 minutes for biology, 10-minute break, 45 minutes for English. Most experts advise shifting subjects rather than devoting several hours to only one. However, you do need to read in logical units: an entire short story, a complete chapter or several related sections of a chapter. If you read only a few pages at one sitting, you will probably have to reread them when you return to the work. This approach does not use your time efficiently.

5. *Free your mind.* Try to free your mind from the distractions of nagging details that may be hard to keep from your thoughts while you are reading. Return library books after class, before you come home to read, or decide that you will take them the next day. Set aside a time to pay bills, exercise, make phone calls. Keep a scratch pad handy for making shopping lists or writing other reminders to yourself. Many people like to maintain daily "To Do" lists or work sheets. The idea is to list all of the tasks needing action on a given day, carry the list with you, and cross through each task as it is completed. Often these lists contain more than can be done in one day. Check your progress as the day moves along and make certain to complete the tasks that must be finished that day. (For example, completing a paper due the next day.) List the unfinished tasks at the beginning of a new work sheet for the next day. Organize your life. Put it in writing. Then, when you pick up a book, focus on the reading, not on other parts of your life.

6. *Keep your body in shape.* Will power is a strong force, giving us the strength to carry on in difficult times. But will power alone cannot sustain us indefinitely. Eventually, if the body is being abused—too little sleep, poor nutrition, not

enough exercise—the body will say "enough," usually in the form of a cold or flu, sometimes with more serious ailments. So, get adequate sleep. Eat properly, and that means, beginning with breakfast, plenty of fruits and vegetables, proteins and carbohydrates. (A candy bar is *not* a fruit!) Schedule time for exercise. You will be more productive the rest of the day if you get at least 30 minutes of aerobic exercise every day.

Steps to Improved Concentration: While You Are Reading

1. *Think positively.* It is impossible to overstate the importance of attitude. Try to turn to each reading assignment with some enthusiasm. Anticipate what you may learn from the reading. Observe the progress you are making through a long, difficult textbook. Be proud of your accomplishment.

2. *Activate your memory.* As you begin to read, think about what you already know about the topic. If you are going to read a chapter of biology, think first about last week's reading and class work. How will the new chapter connect with or add to what you have already learned? If you are reading articles for a research project, think about the other sources you have read and how you might use the material in these articles for your paper. Creating a learning context will help you concentrate through the reading.

3. *Read actively to keep focused.* Strategies for active reading will be discussed in detail in Chapter 2. The process of reading actively is important enough to have its own chapter. To summarize briefly, reading actively includes asking questions; marking the work as you read (taking notes and/or summarizing or mapping the work); and then connecting what you are learning with the knowledge that you already have. Reading with a pencil in hand will keep you involved in the activity.

4. *Take breaks.* You may find that you concentrate better if you take a short break from reading every hour or so. Reading should not be physical torture. Even if you are reading in the library, you may want to get up and stretch and relax your body for a minute or two before getting back to work. In your own home or dorm, you can get something to eat or drink. Make certain, though, that your breaks come at logical places to stop in the reading and that your breaks do not last longer than your reading periods.

5. *Monitor your lapses in concentration.* When your attention wanders from the reading, try to understand why this has happened. If you are thinking about errands that you need to run, or if you are getting sleepy, then you have not attended to the necessary steps for concentration prior to reading. Resolve to follow more faithfully the steps listed above so that you can study efficiently. If your attention wanders to other topics, to what you have been studying in psychology class, for example, then it may be useful to put down the history text and do your psychology reading first. (Of course, if you are studying history for a test the next day, you do not have the luxury of shifting your reading around.) If you are getting frustrated by

the difficulty of the material, then you will need to give yourself a "commitment booster." Remind yourself that the course is a requirement for your major—and then get back to work.

If, however, you have taken your eyes off the page in order to think about what you are reading, that's not really a break in concentration. You may want to write down your thoughts; they may be the source of useful comments or questions you offer in class the next day. Tune in to yourself; the better you know yourself, the more effectively you can direct your reading and study time. Use the following exercise to improve your understanding of concentration difficulties.

EXERCISE 1-4 Thinking about Concentration Problems

I. Either as a class exercise or on your own, brainstorm about possible reasons for poor concentration. List as many reasons as you can for a student's problems with concentration.

_____

_____

_____

*II. From the list above, make a list of **your** reasons for concentration lapses. Then list specific steps you can take to cope with these problems. Draw on the suggestions in this chapter or others that occur to you.*

Your Concentration Problems   **Your Solutions**

_____   _____

_____   _____

_____   _____

_____   _____

Cognition (and Metacognition)

If you are committed to improving reading skills, and if you adopt strategies for concentrating while you read, then you will be able to use your cognitive abilities to their fullest to comprehend what you read. *Cognition* refers to both what you know or perceive and the process of knowing or learning. So your cognitive abilities refer to, among other skills, your ability to read with understanding and to follow the development of ideas in a written passage.

Much of the time you read and reason "automatically." That is, you are not aware of how you are using your skills; you just do it. This approach works well—until you face many pages of difficult reading material. Often with a simple task, of any kind, you indicate how easy it is by saying, "I can do this without even thinking." When given a more demanding job, however, you need to think about how to complete it. This is the time for *metacognition.*

Metacognition is made up, as you can see, of two words, "meta" and "cognition." We have already defined cognition. "Meta," a Greek word, means "beyond" or "behind" or "above." The suggestion is of a higher or more general level of cognition, or what stands behind cognition. In other words, metacognition refers to the knowledge of cognition, to knowing what you know and how you know it—to understanding the process of knowing.

Think of an athlete in action, a tennis player, for example. When the opponent isn't very good, our tennis player can go on "automatic pilot," can simply play without really thinking about how he is playing. Sometimes we talk about a player being "in the zone," playing so effortlessly that it seems instinctive. But the play is not at all instinctive. It is the result of much instruction and practice that has produced such a high level of learning that it *seems* instinctive rather than learned.

Suppose we turn to another tennis match. In this one, the player has lost the first set. Can she possibly win? Not if she continues to play the same way. You may know the expression: "always change a losing strategy." This player will have to think about ways to change her game in order to win. She will have to consciously plan and use new strategies. This will be hard work, but if she can win, the victory will be especially satisfying.

If you said to yourself, as you were reading the last two paragraphs, "Here is another analogy to sports, and it's used to explain metacognition," then you were using metacognition. You were not merely reading and understanding the passage; you were aware of the process of reading and understanding. When you understand the reading process, you can learn to monitor your reading comprehension and then take action to apply different strategies when comprehension does not come easily. Think of metacognition as the ability to stand "outside" the activity of reading and thinking so that you can see *how* it works, *when* it isn't working well, and *what* to do to make it work better. Knowledge puts you in control of the process.

■ THE READING PROCESS

Do you remember learning your first language? Probably not, or at least not in much detail. You may remember being corrected when you said "He goed" instead of "He went." With little memory of the process—perhaps with little help from parents who were not especially talkative—you still had a fairly sophisticated command of your native language by the age of five.

Humans seem to come equipped to learn a language. Still, language has to be learned; it isn't already in the brain. What language would each brain be programmed for? A baby born to Mexican parents but then adopted by Irish Americans will learn English, not Spanish. A child born to an American father (who speaks only English to him) and a French mother (who speaks only French to her son) will become bilingual. Occasionally we read of a youngster who spent most of the first five years locked in a closet (or something equally awful). Such children are language deficient. It seems, then, that language learning requires a social context, but each brain comes with the equipment for developing this highly complex skill in a relatively short period of time.

We know that oral language came first, and then various forms of writing were created later. And of course writing had to be invented before there were works to read. Since some people have, with little or no help, taught themselves to read, we may conclude that reading skill is closely connected to general language skills. Just as preschoolers learn language by sorting and storing information gained through practice with language and some guidance from adults, we later learn to read by sorting and storing information about the squiggly marks on the page, with guidance and encouragement from teachers. We learn that the various shapes represent or stand for words, the meaningful sounds of our oral language. Reading, because it contains another layer of symbols, is a more complex activity than speaking.

We also know that the brain is a highly complex instrument with interconnecting parts that together are the source of our cognitive abilities. For example, to read you must first process the visual information on the page. Some people who have difficulty reading may be having difficulty with the visual processing of the symbols on the page. They have trouble seeing the difference between, for example, "bad" and "bed." Others may know all the letters in the word but do not know the meaning of the word; their problem is one of vocabulary. Language acquisition and the reading process are both complex activities.

What Is Reading?

Reading is the process of obtaining or constructing meaning from a word or clusters of words. This statement gives us three ideas about reading. First, meaning is found in "clusters of words," not necessarily in complete sentences. In some contexts fragments, including just a word or two, express meaning. Look, for example, at the following three "sentences."

The thief stole Michael's book bag. And his keys. His wallet, too.

The first statement is a complete sentence, but "and his keys" is a fragment. By itself—without the context of the previous sentence, it would not offer a reader much meaning. "What about his keys?" we ask. And, "whose keys"? In this context, however, the cluster of words has meaning. So does "His wallet, too." We learn that Michael no longer has his book bag, his keys, or his wallet. We learn that all three items were taken from Michael by someone unknown to him, someone who intends to keep the items. We know all of this if we know the meanings of the words *thief* and *stolen,* and if we see how the second and third statements build on the first one.

The second idea about reading in the definition above is that reading involves getting meaning from the words. Reading does not refer to the ability to say the sounds that the words represent. It doesn't mean knowing the definitions of the words on the page. It means understanding what ideas or information or feelings the words, put together in the particular pattern chosen by the writer, convey. This definition tells us that if we are not getting a message, then we are not reading. Think of it this way: reading is a cognitive activity. You read with your brain.

Finally, we need to consider the two verbs *obtaining* and *constructing.* Both verbs have been used because the experts who study reading do not agree on which verb should be used. Some would say that the meaning is in the words as they are put together in particular patterns. The task of the reader is to *obtain* the meaning that the writer seeks to convey. But others argue that meaning is really *constructed* by the reader and that skill in reading depends upon the reader's ability to connect the material to what the reader already knows in order to make meaning out of a passage. Both ideas are useful in helping you understand reading. On the one hand, readers do strive to understand or *obtain* the writer's meaning. On the other hand, readers must use their knowledge of vocabulary and grammatical structures to process the passage, to *construct* meaning from the words on the page.

The Role of Vocabulary

Because you need to use your knowledge of words it follows that the larger your vocabulary the more you can read—and the more easily you will read. To illustrate, how difficult is the following passage for you?

> The series of somites that came to lie on each side of the notochord shortly after gastrulation now differentiate into three kinds of cells: (1) sclerotome cells, which later form skeletal elements; (2) dermatome cells, which become part of the developing skin; and (3) myotome cells, which form most of the musculature.
>
> Helena Curtis, *Biology,* 4th ed. Worth, 1983.

For many readers who are not scientists, this sentence is a challenge to understand. Why? To answer the question, go back and underline each word that you do not know. The reason for difficulty becomes clear: there are just too many words that are unfamiliar. How do you expand your vocabulary to make reading easier? By reading. Adults add to their vocabularies primarily from their reading. The more you read, the easier reading becomes.

Connecting and Predicting in Reading

Experienced readers do not need to look at every word in a passage to construct meaning. Your brain has a record of many sentence patterns as well as knowledge about various subjects. The information you already have allows you to comprehend a passage without reading every word. Because you seek meaning, you will make sense of incomplete statements, as you did with the three statements about the thief. You automatically attached the two fragments—about Michael's wallet and keys—to the previous sentence so that they would make sense.

Readers can also predict what will come next—in a sentence, a paragraph, or a longer work. In fact, active reading involves making predictions. Drawing on your knowledge of the patterns or structures of writing, you start to anticipate the rest of the sentence. For example, suppose you were to read the following:

> Instead of using a pen or a typewriter, today's students usually do their papers _____

What would you predict the rest of the sentence to say? Answer this question by working the following brief exercise.

EXERCISE 1-5 Predicting in Reading

Circle any statement that could complete the sentence and then explain why the others would not work.

a. in the library.
b. on a computer.
c. while listening to music.
d. which is a good thing.

_____

_____

_____

Only one of the four statements can fit into the sentence. "D" adds a new thought without completing the first idea in the sentence. Although the other three all "sound" as if they could fit, "a" and "c" do not fit logically. For the sentence to make a meaningful statement, it must tell us what *tool* students now use to do their written work. Where they work or what else they do while working are ideas that fail to complete the contrast pattern started in the sentence. Your knowledge of today's students would help you to predict the sentence's concluding point.

You can also predict what you will read in longer passages. If a paragraph begins with the sentence "There are three good reasons to participate in the political process," you should anticipate that the rest of the paragraph will state and develop those three reasons. You would be a frustrated reader if you found that only two reasons were discussed in the paragraph.

In the following exercise, see how well you can predict what will follow. Look for patterns established by the writer to guide you.

 EXERCISE 1-6 Predicting in Longer Passages

Use a piece of paper to cover the lines of the following passage and then uncover one line at a time, as you read. Each time that you come to a question, answer it, keeping the rest of the passage still covered. If you look ahead, you will not benefit from this exercise.

Sociologists Paul Lazarsfeld and Jeffrey Reitz (1989) divide sociology into three phases.

What will the rest of this paragraph be about?

_____

_____

First, . . . when sociology began it was indistinguishable from attempts to reform society. The primary concern of early sociologists was to make the world a better place. The point of analyzing social conditions was to use the information to improve social life. Albion Small, one of the first presidents of the American Sociological Society (1912–1913), said that the primary reason for the existence of sociology was its "practical application to the improvement of social life." Sociologists, he said, should use science to gain knowledge and then use that knowledge to "realize visions" (Fritz 1989). This first phase of sociology lasted until the 1920s.

What will the next paragraph be about?

_____

_____

During the second phase, it became the goal of sociologists to establish sociology as a respected field of knowledge. To this end, sociologists sought to develop **pure** or **basic sociology,** that is, research and theory aimed at making discoveries about life in human groups, but not at making changes in those groups. This goal was soon achieved, and within a generation sociology was incorporated into almost every college and university curriculum in the United States.

How will this paragraph end?

_____

_____

World War II marked the end of this phase.

What will the next paragraph be about?

_____

_____

During the third and current phase, there has been an attempt to merge sociological knowledge and practical work. . . .

James M. Henslin, *Sociology,* 2nd ed. Allyn & Bacon, 1995.

The Reading Context

In the reading process, the reader is an active participant. Figure 1.1 illustrates the reading context, a context in which the writer and the written work are significant but incomplete without the reader. The diagram also illustrates the idea that the reader brings much to the work, including knowledge and the cognitive skills needed to construct meaning.

Readers bring knowledge and experience, as well as values, beliefs, and biases, to the reading experience. Knowledge about the topic or experience relevant to the topic aid the reading process. What a reader knows about the writer and understands about the particular written work is part of the background knowledge that can make a difference in how a work is read and understood. Before reading, you will want to think about each element in the reading con-

■ **FIGURE 1.1**

The Reading Context

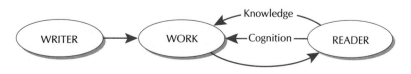

text. What do you know about the writer, or what can you learn, that may help you understand the writer's purpose, approach, or perspective on the topic? What kind of work are you about to read? Is it a textbook, a novel, a sports magazine? What do you expect the work to contain, and how do you expect it to be put together? Reflect on yourself as well. What do you already know about the topic? What attitudes toward the writer or the subject do you bring to the reading context? Through reflection you activate the knowledge that you have and find out what questions you need to answer.

Think back to the statements about Michael's stolen book bag, wallet, and keys. Let's put those statements in a reading context. Suppose that you read those sentences in a letter from your mother. Further, suppose that Michael is your brother. Now think how much more you "know" from reading those sentences than you did when you first read them in this chapter. Because you "know" Michael well, you can imagine how he is feeling about the loss of his belongings. You can also "hear" your mother's tone of voice through the words on the page; you know if she is really upset by the circumstances, or just reporting news from home. And because this is a family matter, you are not just receiving information from the words; you also have feelings in response to what you have read. Because of what you bring to the reading context, you construct a far more complex meaning out of the words than the rest of us would.

Perhaps you "know" that your mother frequently exaggerates and turns minor problems into crises. You also know that your brother is rather careless with things. Because of your knowledge, you may question the accuracy of the statements. Evaluating what we read is another way that readers actively participate in the reading context. Remember: not everything in print is accurate or true. This statement applies to textbooks and newspaper articles, not just to "letters from home."

Many ideas about reading have been presented in this chapter. The following list summarizes key ideas for you.

The Reading Context

1. To improve reading skills, you need commitment.
2. To read with understanding, you need to concentrate.
3. Reading is a cognitive activity. You read to construct meaning from words.
4. Cognitive skills such as reading can be improved through the use of metacognition.
5. Wide reading expands knowledge and vocabulary.
6. Experienced readers get the idea from passages that are not fully developed.
7. Active reading involves predicting what will come next.

8. Experienced readers use their previous knowledge and cognitive skills to understand what they read.
9. Not every statement in print is accurate or true, so readers must question and evaluate what they read.

Before beginning to read the following selections, commit to practicing what you have learned in this chapter. Review guidelines for concentration and put them into practice. Try to predict what is coming next as you read. After reading, check your comprehension, complete the vocabulary study, and reflect on the questions for discussion.

Selection 1 · Learning To Learn

by **Lester A. Lefton**

The following is an excerpt from *Psychology* (5th ed., Allyn & Bacon, 1995). Professor Lefton has taught undergraduate and graduate courses in psychology for more than twenty years at the University of South Carolina.

1   Most college seniors believe they are much better students now than they were as first-year students. What makes the difference? How do students learn to learn better? Today, educators and cognitive researchers are focusing on how information is learned, as opposed to what is learned. To learn new information, students generate hypotheses, make interpretations, make predictions, and revise earlier ideas. They are active learners (Wittrock, 1987).

2   Human beings learn how to learn; they learn special strategies for special topics, and they devise general rules that depend on their goals (McKeachie, 1988). The techniques for learning foreign languages differ from those needed to learn mathematics. Are there general cognitive techniques that students can use to learn better? McKeachie, Pintrich, and Lin (1985) have argued that lack of effective learning strategies is a major cause of low achievement by university students. They conducted a study to see whether grades would improve overall when rote learning, repetition, and memorization were replaced by more efficient cognitive strategies.

3   To help students become better learners, McKeachie, Pintrich, and Lin developed a course on learning to learn; it provided practical suggestions for studying and a theoretical basis for understanding learning. It made students aware of the processes used in learning and remembering. This awareness (thinking about thinking, learning about learning) is called *metacognition.* Learning-skills practice, development of motivation, and development of a positive attitude were also included. Among specific

topics were learning from lectures, learning from textbooks, test taking, self-monitoring, reduction of test anxiety, discovering personal learning styles, and learning through such traditional strategies as SQ3R plus (Survey, Question, Read, Recite, Review, *plus* write and reflect). The course focused on learning in general, not on specific courses such as history or chemistry. The goal was to develop generalized strategies to facilitate learning.

4   The voluntary learning-to-learn course attracted 180 students. They were tested at the beginning and end of the semester, and their test scores were compared with those of control groups enrolled in other psychology classes. Various measures were used to assess whether the course had any impact on SAT scores, reading test scores, anxiety test scores, and especially academic grades.

5   The results showed that the learning-to-learn students made gains in a number of areas, including grades and motivation. In later semesters, the students continued to improve. This straightforward study tells an important story about psychology in general and about learning psychology in particular. First, it shows that psychologists are engaged in activities that help people, not just in esoteric laboratory studies. Second, it shows a shift in emphasis from studies of learning specific facts or of specific stimuli and responses to studies of learning strategies. Third, it shows that research into thought processes can lead to more effective thought and, subsequently, to high levels of motivation. Last, this simple study shows that people can be taught to be more efficient learners.

6   McKeachie, Pintrich, and Lin argued: "The cognitive approach has generated a richer, deeper analysis of what goes on in learning and memory, increasing our understanding and improving our ability to facilitate retrieval and use of learning. . . . We need to be aware of several kinds of outcomes—not just *how much knowledge* was learned, but *what kinds of learning* took place" (p. 602). Students can better grasp history, chemistry, or economics if they understand *how* to go about studying these topics. Law, psychology, and medicine require different learning strategies. After we learn how to learn, the differences become obvious; indeed, some researchers think of creativity as a metacognitive process involving thinking about our own thoughts (Pesut, 1990). Individuals can learn to learn, reason, and make better choices across a variety of domains (Larrick, Morgan, & Nisbett, 1990).

Comprehension Check ·

Finish each of the following sentences by adding a word or phrase that best completes the idea.

1. College students become better students because _____

_____ .

2. Thinking about the processes of thinking and learning is known as _____

_____ .

3. The learning-to-learn course stressed the importance of a _____

_____ .

4. Creativity can be defined as a process of _____

_____ .

5. Different subjects require different _____

_____ .

Expanding Vocabulary

Match each word in the left column with its definition in the right column by placing the correct letter in the space next to each word.

_____ hypotheses (1)   a. make easier

_____ theoretical (3)   b. judge or evaluate

_____ facilitate (3, 6)   c. the process of obtaining knowledge from memory

_____ assess (4)   d. conjectures or assumptions given to explain a situation, event, or behavior

_____ retrieval (6)   e. areas of study

_____ domains (6)   f. based on principles or ideas

For Discussion and Reflection

1. Has this analysis of "learning-to-learn" convinced you that "people can be taught to be more efficient learners"? If so, why? If not, why not?

2. The learning-to-learn students improved in several areas of learning. In what, if any, skill areas do you need improvement? What strategies could you use in your current reading course to work on those skills?

3. In paragraph 6 one definition of *creativity* is offered. How would you define the term? Try to include specific examples of creativity.

4. The selection says that different strategies are needed to learn different subjects. In a group with classmates or on your own, make a list of the strategies that would be best for learning a subject that you are taking or plan to take.

Selection 2   The Light Stuff

by **Douglas Colligan**

Douglas Colligan is an editor for *Reader's Digest* and the author of many articles on science and medicine. In "The Light Stuff" (published in the February/March 1982 issue of *Technology Illustrated*) Colligan explains how NASA scientists have solved many of the problems facing humans in a weightless environment.

1   Probably not since Christopher Columbus worried about skidding off the edge of the earth have humans had to face such an awesome unknown as surviving, let alone living, in space. An almost total vacuum, an environment where temperatures of objects can routinely glide from 250 degrees Fahrenheit below zero to 250 degrees above, a world where gravity is practically nonexistent, space has hardly seemed inviting. Yet little by little scientists have learned, first, how to get air-breathing, gravity-bred earthlings out to space and back without killing them and, later on, how to get them to settle in and actually enjoy outer space.

2   Getting a human back alive is largely a matter of packaging: wrapping an astronaut in a cocoon of simulated earth atmosphere. That problem was solved on the Mercury space flights and later refined with the Gemini and Apollo missions. Much trickier is how to cope with all the weird challenges posed by the absence of gravity. If, as some visionaries project, humans are to live and work in space, making peace with zero gravity is vital.

3   As a result, over the years of space flight, including the Skylab missions in 1973 and 1974 and culminating with the space shuttle, there has evolved a whole zero-g technology. Earthbound engineers and designers have begun to give present and future astronauts the components of a world custom-built for weightlessness.

4   Much of the attention, naturally, is on outfitting the body for weightlessness. Living in space, not just commuting through it on the way to the moon, has some strange effects on the human form, as NASA found out during the Skylab mission, when three crews of astronauts lived in zero-g for one, two, and three months. Joe Kosmo, NASA engineer and space-suit expert, recalls one curious discovery: "During flights the men had trouble getting into their space suits." They complained they were too tight. No one knew what to make of the complaint. Suits were custom-tailored, and each was meticulously checked before the launch. Once the astronauts got back to earth the mystery cleared up. The astronauts were taller than when they left earth, sometimes by as much as two inches.

5   In-flight growth, NASA calls it. In weightlessness the spinal column becomes loose and stretches. With no gravity to compress the soft disks between the spinal bones, bodies expand and grow, at least temporarily. To compensate for this, suits now issued to space-shuttle astronauts are designed to grow with their wearers. Both the legs and sleeves of the suits have laced-in inserts to let out the suit a little when needed.

6   Zero-g bodies change shape as well as length. The body's fluids tend to migrate away from the lower half to the torso and head. As a result astronauts find they have skinnier feet and narrower waists and slightly larger chests and shoulders. Because of this, the standard-issue uniform for shuttle occupants has a jacket with elasticized pleats built in to expand with the body.

7   Of course, this fluid drift is reversed, with a vengeance, once the weightless person returns to earth's gravity. The sudden drop of fluid to the lower part of the body is so violent that anyone not prepared for it would black out. For that reason, astronauts have been routinely wearing what are called antigravity pants when they dress for reentry. Very simply, the pants are a pair of inflatable leggings that can be pumped to apply pressure to the lower body and minimize the fluid shock. The danger of blackout is very real, as Dr. Joseph Kerwin of the first Skylab crew found out. He had only partially inflated his suit before reentry and almost fainted. "Surprised the tar out of me," he later admitted.

8   Putting food into the weightless body has always been a special challenge for NASA. For a while no one was sure if a human could eat normally in zero-g. There were those who worried that when John Glenn made the first American around-the-world space flight he wouldn't be able to swallow his food in weightlessness and would choke to death. Once Glenn returned to earth, his stomach full, his throat clear, extraterrestrial meal planning began in earnest. Space meals have progressed from such items as gelatin-coated coconut cubes and peanut cubes to complete heat-and-serve meals on board Skylab and the space shuttle.

9   Space meals are not prepared so much as assembled. All the food is precooked and is either canned, dehydrated, or packed in aluminum-backed plastic envelopes called flex pouches. Because it's impossible to pour water in zero gravity (it congeals into silvery balls that drift around in a spacecraft), dehydrated food is revived by squirting water through a needle into the sealed plastic pouches. Each pouch has a flexible plastic top that lets the cook knead the water into the dried food. Liquids are drunk through a straw with a clamp attached to keep the straw pinched shut when not in use. All are in containers shaped to fit neatly into a compartmentalized and magnetized food tray, where they are anchored in place by Velcro tape.

10   Weightlessness affects not only how the food is packaged, but also what kind of food is inside. Even without gravity, it is possible to eat some foods off an open plate with a fork or spoon. Meals with sauces or gravies work especially well because they tend to stick to the plate and not float away. The Skylab astronauts, who tested out many space meals, found some were disasters. In one report to earth, the first crew crossed chili off their eating schedule. Every time they opened a container of it, there was an explosion of food: "Great gobbets of chili go flying all over; it's bad news."

11   Other adaptations to weightless eating include items like liquid salt and pepper. Ordinary crystals and granules are practically impossible to get out of shakers, and when something does come out, it tends not to hit

the food but drift away in midair. Eating utensils are also made smaller because, in a gravity-free dining area, food sticks to the bottom as well as the top of the utensil. To keep an astronaut from spooning up more than he can chew, NASA provides utensils about three-fourths the size of what we use here on earth.

12   Even taste is affected by zero-g. "Body fluids migrate to your upper body, and you end up with engorged tissue around the nasal passages and ear," explains Gerald Carr, who was commander of the third and longest (84 days) Skylab mission. "You carry with you a constant state of nasal and head congestion in a weightless environment. It feels pretty much like you have a cold all the time." As with any head cold, the sense of taste and smell are numbed. To counter this some of the Skylab crews brought up spices and Tabasco sauce to jazz up the food, and shuttle crews will find barbecue and hot sauces in their meal packets.

13   And, of course, there is the matter of personal hygiene in zero-g, a great source of wonderment to earthlings. Using the toilet is much more of an adventure than here on earth. The toilet in the space shuttle has a footrest, handholds, and a seat belt to hold the user in position. The lack of gravity is solved by a suction fan. Fans are also used in water drains when astronauts wash. Getting clean is complicated by the fact that water is hard to contain in space. Using Skylab's shower, basically a collapsible cloth cylinder, was a time-consuming chore. To wash up, bathers squirted their bodies with a water gun. That turned out to be a messy design. For every astronaut scrubbing up, another would have to stand by with a vacuum cleaner to suck the escaping water globules out of the air. Designer Larry Bell, who has been working on the plans for a space village for NASA at the University of Houston's School of Architecture, says a better design would be what he calls a "human car wash" or "human dishwasher" approach, in which the bather goes inside a sealed box, is sprayed with water, and is later completely air-dried.

14   Sleeping in space, on the other hand, is a relatively simple affair. At bedtime the astronaut steps into a bag anchored vertically or horizontally to a firm surface, zips the bag up from toe to chest, and, after connecting a waist strap around the bag, tucks both arms under the strap to keep them from flailing around during sleep. Without gravity, sleepers can rest anywhere. Mattresses and pillows are unnecessary, since there's no reason for a body to sink into them; a padded board suffices. In the shuttle the sleeping area has what looks like a two-level bunk bed. One person sleeps on the top, a second on the bottom, and a third underneath the bottom bunk facing the floor. Only in zero gravity could you fit three persons this way into a two-person bed.

15   But even sleeping can have odd complications. Anyone sleeping in weightlessness is in danger of suffering from the clouds of carbon dioxide-laden air exhaled during the night. On Skylab a fan kept a steady floor-to-ceiling current of air flowing by the sleepers' mouths. One astronaut, Charles Conrad, got so annoyed by this breeze constantly blowing up his

nose that he once turned his sleeping bag upside down and tried to rest that way. (It would have worked except for the fact that the air then blew into his sleeping bag, billowing it out.)

16   With little resistance to struggle against, the human body tends to lose muscle tone in weightlessness. Exercise regimens are usually prescribed for the longer space flights. Skylab astronauts kept in shape by riding a stationary bicycle exerciser and walking on an ingenious treadmill. It was nothing more than a large sheet of Teflon with some elastic bungee cords. To exercise, an astronaut would anchor himself to a spot on the floor with the cords and walk on the slippery Teflon in his socks. There will be no room for a bicycle exerciser on the shuttle, but it will be carrying a Teflon treadmill.

17   One problem weightless astronauts can encounter when exercising is that, without fans blowing directly on them, the air heated by their bodies tends to hover nearby. And perspiration doesn't dry but sticks to their skin in ever-thickening layers. The Skylab crews discovered this the hard way and rigged up a fan by the bicycle to help evaporate the sweat. That, however, blew the perspiration off their bodies in sheets, which then had to be vacuumed out of the air.

18   There is hardly a part of day-to-day space living that doesn't require some zero-g forethought. Standing still is impossible, for example. Astronauts in the shuttle attach suction-cup soles to their shoes to keep them anchored. Without some means of fixing people in place, Newton's third law of motion—for every action there is an equal and opposite reaction—can conjure bizarre results from even simple actions. When trying to unscrew a bolt, astronaut William Pogue neglected to anchor himself; when he turned the screwdriver, he suddenly found his body corkscrewing through the air. Without some sort of brace, even a motion like bending over can send someone into a somersault. As a way of eliminating these problems, NASA has packed aboard the shuttle handholds with suction cups for use almost anywhere.

19   And because no one can truly sit down in the earthbound sense, furniture has to be redesigned to suit the zero-g stoop, a quasi-fetal slouch the human body naturally adopts when there is no gravity. The space crews on Skylab complained that many of the tables and control panels were too low and too hard to use. To remain seated at a 90-degree angle, weightless people must tense their stomach muscles constantly. Skylab astronauts finally removed a chair from one console because it was practically impossible to use. In deference to this, the shuttle has removable working and eating tables that are about a foot higher than an earth table, and their metal surfaces accommodate magnetic paperweights and magnetic food trays.

20   How well this kind of technology helps people adjust to a world where notions like up, down, heavy, and light take on new meaning is difficult to say. What is known is that astronauts do become totally acclimated to zero gravity. In *A House in Space*, a description of the Skylab experience, author Henry Cooper, Jr., tells the story of astronaut Jack Lousma shaving

one morning after his return to earth. Letting go of a can of shaving cream while it was poised in midair, Lousma was genuinely surprised when it fell straight to the floor.

21   Fellow Skylab veteran Gerald Carr chuckled when he heard the story. "Yeah, I had the same problem," he recalled. "It's surprisingly natural to become what I call a three-dimensional person, one who can move in all three dimensions. It quickly gets to the point where it is no bother." Carr may be screening out memories of hour-long shower preparations and 3-D flotsam drifting through the cabin, but it's clear that with the proper equipment, zero-g living can be enjoyed rather than just survived.

Comprehension Check ·

Finish each of the following sentences by filling in a word or phrase that best completes the idea.

1. Zero-g means _____ .

2. The biggest challenge to humans in outer space is finding ways to function

   in a _____ environment.

3. Because astronauts _____ in weightlessness,

   their suits are made to _____ .

4. _____ is used to hold food containers onto food trays.

5. Forks and spoons used in space are made _____ because

   food _____ .

6. Foods are harder to taste in space because increased fluids in the upper

   body lead to nasal and head _____ .

7. In zero-g bunk beds hold _____ people.

8. The space shuttle carries a _____ to provide exercise for
   astronauts.

9. Because _____ is impossible, the astronauts use suction
   cups to anchor themselves.

Expanding Vocabulary ·

Match each word in the left column with its definition in the right column by placing the correct letter in the space next to each word.

_____ cocoon (2)   a. exactlingly

_____ components (3)   b. regulated plans to maintain health

_____ meticulously (4)   c. clever

_____ migrate (6)   d. elements

_____ regimens (16)   e. a drooping of the head and shoulders

_____ ingenious (16)   f. a protective covering

_____ deference (19)   g. accustomed to a new environment

_____ acclimated (20)   h. to go from one region to another

Analysis of Content and Strategies

1. Why did the author choose "The Light Stuff" as his title? How does it connect to his subject? _____

   _____

   _____

2. Does the title suggest anything else to you? Can you connect it to another work? _____

   _____

3. How would you explain, to a second-grade class, the way the toilet works on the space shuttle? _____

   _____

   _____

For Discussion and Reflection

1. The author's descriptions help readers see what life in weightlessness is like. If you were going to prepare some drawings to show to the second-grade class, what would be one drawing you would make? Describe it in words.

2. Why are we going into space? What can we gain from our explorations?

3. Should we continue the space program? Are the gains worth the costs?

4. Would you like to work at a space station? Why or why not?

CHAPTER 2

Reading Actively

In this chapter you will learn:

- Why you need a reading strategy

- The steps in the Prepare—Read—Respond strategy

- How to prepare to read a selection

- How to activate your knowledge as part of reading

- How to read actively

- How to monitor your reading comprehension

- Why you need to reflect and review after reading

In Chapter 1 you learned about the important role of the 3Cs—commitment, concentration, and cognition—in reading success. Taken together, they lead to *active* engagement in reading. In addition, when examining the reading context, you learned of the important role of the reader. So, Chapter 1 has already introduced you to the idea of active reading. Chapter 2 will put the ideas into practice. It will explain the specific steps in an active reading strategy and give you opportunities to "groove" your new strategy.

■ WHY HAVE A READING STRATEGY?

Why have a plan or strategy at all? Why not just pick up the book, read a number of pages, and then put the book down? This rather simple process may work well enough for pleasure reading, but it is not a successful system when the goal is to learn from reading. A strategy—almost any strategy—for reading is probably better than no system because a strategy encourages readers to be aware of the act of reading. It encourages the use of metacognition. A good reading strategy is one that guides you to prepare before reading, to read in ways that will improve comprehension, and then to respond in ways that help fulfill your reading purpose. If you follow the three-phase plan of **PREPARE— READ—RESPOND,** you will become a better reader.

■ PREPARE—READ—RESPOND: HOW THE PARTS CONNECT

The diagram in Figure 2.1 shows how the steps in this plan divide into three stages: before reading, during reading, and after reading. The several activities included under **PREPARE** are preliminary steps; they prepare you to read with understanding and purpose. Then, as you **READ,** you need to mark the text as a support to the reading process, and you need to continually monitor comprehension. Finally, you need to **RESPOND:** reflecting on what you have read will make the reading more meaningful to you, and you will remember the material better if you both reflect on and review your reading.

■ FIGURE 2.1

STEPS IN YOUR READING STRATEGY

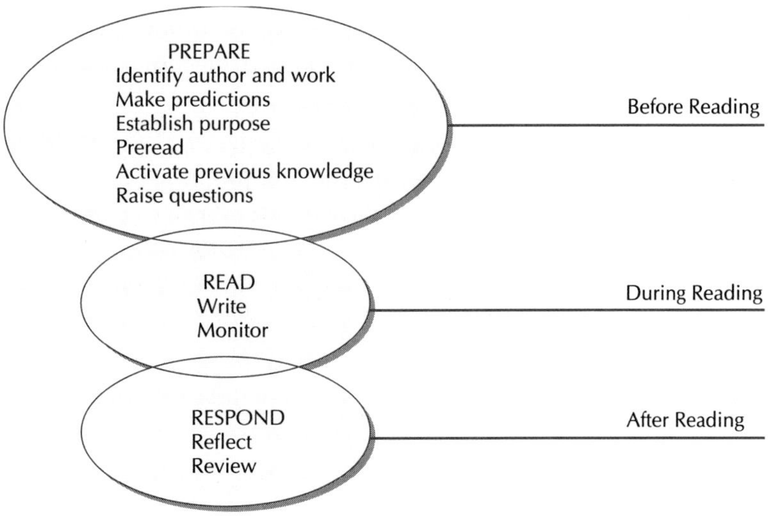

PREPARE
Identify author and work
Make predictions
Establish purpose
Preread
Activate previous knowledge
Raise questions

Before Reading

READ
Write
Monitor

During Reading

RESPOND
Reflect
Review

After Reading

Notice, though, that the first and third circles in the diagram overlap and shade into the middle circle. The diagram tells us that the steps do not fall neatly into three stages. You may continue to question as you read, and you may want to stop reading from time to time to reflect on what you have already covered. Additionally, with a difficult text, you may need to review subsections of the material rather than waiting until you have completed a reading assignment. Understand that your plan includes a series of activities that are essentially performed in three stages but recognize that the stages also overlap and together create an ongoing, interconnected process.

■ PREPARE

Most readers prepare in some way before they begin to read even if they would not describe it as preparing. You probably do not select a novel to read without having heard, perhaps from a friend, that it is a good book. You choose a magazine—on fashion or sports or news—because you are already interested in the topics covered. When facing new material, as you will in your course work and on the job, you need to prepare consciously and in specific ways to get the most out of your reading.

To prepare successfully, you will probably need to go through each of the following steps:

1. identify the author and the work
2. make predictions about the work
3. establish your purpose in reading
4. preread the material
5. activate your previous knowledge about the topic
6. raise questions about the material

Although this list seems so long that you are wondering if there will be time to actually read the work, you will find that you can move through most of these steps fairly quickly. You will also discover that as you become a more accomplished reader, the time for preparing will be reduced. There are two reasons for this: (1) you will not have to think about the steps because they will have become a habit and (2) you will have more knowledge of the subjects you are reading about and more knowledge about books in general. When you actively prepare to read, you are thinking about the *reading context*. You are learning about the *author*, the *work*, and the *reader*.

Identify the Author and the Work

You need to begin by first learning all you can about the author or authors of the reading material. Identifying doesn't mean just noting the author's name but also answering these questions: What are the writer's credentials and why might this writer choose to write this work? A writer's credentials include the person's education, position, or experiences, the facts that explain why this person's writing on this subject has been published. Identifying a writer's qualifications for writing is a first step to understanding where the writer "is coming from" and to evaluating the work.

How do you learn about writers? In most books there is an "About the Author" page that provides the author's credentials, and sometimes a picture as well. In textbooks, you will often find that the college where the author teaches is given immediately after the name on the title page. (Find and study the material about the author of your reading text just to see what kind of information is included.)

We also know the authors of most articles and essays, short stories and poems. Editorials are one exception. Newspaper and magazine editorials are written by one of the top editors but are considered to be the views of the entire editorial staff. Magazine (but not newspaper) articles are usually followed by a brief biography of the author. In the article "Hippo Talk" (on page 35), for example, we learn that the author William Barklow is "a professor of biology at Framingham State College in Framingham, Massachusetts," and that he has also studied the "call of loons in Maine." We learn that he has a position in the academic community and that the "language" of animals is his special area of study.

If information about the author does not accompany the work, then ask your instructor or a librarian how you might learn something about the writer. You always want to think about whose words you are reading—because they do come from somebody, somebody who has an individual identity just as you do.

Readers need to begin not by reading but by looking—literally looking at the work and then thinking about what kind of work they are about to read. The type of work contributes significantly to the reading context, so you do not want to read without first seeing what it is that you are about to study. Different types of works have different purposes and different *conventions*, or ways of presenting the material.

One kind of knowledge that skilled readers bring to their reading is the knowledge of the conventions of style and purpose and presentation that can be expected of various types of written material. Picture, for example, one of your college textbooks. It is probably a large book, with chapters divided into many subsections. It has many graphics: pictures, charts, diagrams. It may also have "boxes," brief essays set off from the text either by lines to form a box or by use of color on the paper where the essay appears. Do not skip over these essays; they are often the basis for class discussions or papers. The boxes are related to the chapter topic but are not a direct part of the information the authors need to provide in the chapter. The boxes usually present applications of the information in the chapter, or raise controversial issues. For example, one box in an educational psychology text debates the success of the Head Start Program.

The straight text and the "boxes" in a textbook often represent different purposes in writing. That is why they are separated. The primary purpose of a textbook is to *explain*. We can categorize this writing as *expository*. If the boxed essays take a position on an issue, or even if they raise issues for reflection or class debate, they begin to move away from expository writing to *persuasive* writing. Persuasive writers want, of course, to persuade readers to see issues their way. A similar distinction is made between the newspaper's news articles and its editorials. The editorials are always placed on a separate page, along with letters to the editors and across from essays of opinion. The purpose of the editorials and the letters and the columnists' essays is to persuade readers to each author's views. Newspaper readers need to know the difference; they need to expect ideas and reasons but not lots of details in the persuasive pieces. The details are in the straight news articles.

Into which category do we put the newspaper articles labeled "News Analysis"? The purpose of these articles is to explore some current event in greater depth, to examine causes and effects perhaps. Is this expository or persuasive writing? To be accurate, we need to place it somewhere in the middle. The purpose seems to be to explain, but obviously there can be many disagreements about the causes of the 1995 Oklahoma terrorist bombing, for example.

How do you know when you are going to read a poem? By the way it looks on the page. Poems are "set up" differently than prose. How do you know when the work is a novel? A novel uses *narration*; that is, it tells a story. But narration is also used in nonfiction works, including histories, biographies, and narrative essays. Sometimes, then, a work can be identified by its purpose (to explain, to persuade), but sometimes it is better identified by the writing strategy that is used, such as narration or description. If you are going to read a novel, you anticipate an interesting, fictional story. There will be events in which characters are involved, and probably some of the story will be told through dialogue among the characters. If you turn to your history text, you can anticipate that some narration will be used to recreate events of the past. You also know that the author's purpose is expository, so you can expect both many facts and explanations of the causes and effects of key events.

Prepare to read by identifying both the author and the work. Predict as much as you can about the work's subject, purpose, and ways of presentation. The following exercise offers practice in this process.

 ## Exercise 2-1 Identifying the Type of Work

Answer the questions for each of the works cited below, providing as much information as you can. The first one has been done for you.

1. "Hippo Talk," by William Barklow, a professor of biology at Framingham State College. The article is a "box" in a longer article ("Fluctuating Fortunes of the River Horse") that was published in *Natural History* magazine.

What type of work is this?

A short essay on one part of the hippo's life. It will be serious.

Based on knowledge of the author and title of the work, what can you predict about purpose and format or writing style?

It will be expository and give details from the professor's research.

2. *Foundations of College Chemistry* by Morris Hein and Susan Arena, both professors at Mount San Antonio College.
   What type of work is this?

   _____

   _____

   Based on knowledge of the authors and title of the work, what can you predict about purpose and format or writing style?

   _____

   _____

3. *Marriage and Family in Transition.* Edited by John N. Edwards and David H. Demo of the Sociology Department at Virginia Polytechnic Institute.
   What type of work is this?

   _____

   _____

   Based on knowledge of the authors and title of the work, what can you predict about purpose and format or writing style?

   _____

   _____

4. *Hamlet* by William Shakespeare. (1594–1616)
   What type of work is this?

   _____

   _____

Based on knowledge of the author and title of the work, what can you predict about purpose and format or writing style?

_____

_____

5. *Russia 2010: And What It Means for the World* by Daniel Yergin (Ph.D.) and Thane Gustafson (Ph.D.), president and director of the international consulting firm Cambridge Energy Research Associates.
What type of work is this?

_____

_____

Based on knowledge of the authors and title of the work, what can you predict about purpose and format or writing style?

_____

_____

6. "Hate Crimes and Free Speech." Editorial. *Washington Post*.
What type of work is this?

_____

_____

What do you anticipate based on your knowledge of the author?

_____

_____

What format or elements of presentation do you anticipate?

_____

_____

Establish Purpose in Reading

Usually when we know why we want to do something, we get more out of the activity. Aimless wandering, for example, is less satisfying than a walk for aerobic exercise, or sightseeing, or to bird watch. The same is true of reading.

Different reading tasks have different purposes. You need to be able to answer the questions "Why am I reading this?" and "What do I expect to learn from this material?"

The best way to answer these questions for assigned readings is to review the specifics of the assignment as part of your preparation. Are you to read and answer the study questions at the end of the chapter? Are you reading in preparation for a class lecture? Or class discussion? If your assignment includes answering questions on the reading, then read the questions *before* reading the material. The best way to prepare for a lecture class is to read and annotate the assigned reading and list questions you have on the material. If the lecture does not clear up your confusion, you can ask the questions you have listed. Your lecture notes should help direct your review of the reading. If you are in a discussion class, then you need to complete all steps to active reading. Your review and reflection will help you participate in class.

There are of course reading purposes other than those directly connected to studying in a course. You may read novels for pleasure; you may read the newspaper to keep informed on current public policy issues. You will find all reading opportunities more pleasurable, because they are more meaningful, if you prepare before reading and reflect after reading. As you reflect on reading not directly connected to course work, ask yourself how what you have read might connect to what you are studying. The relationships developed in the novel may suggest questions that you can raise in your psychology class; a current debate in Congress covered in the newspaper may parallel a similar conflict from the past discussed in your history text. Make all your reading purposeful in some way and you will have more fun reading.

Preread

Perhaps you are now beginning to see the value of some preparation before reading. But, why preread the work? Prereading allows you to see what elements the work contains and how they are put together. It gives you a chance to preview both content and the author's strategies for development. Additionally, prereading extends your preliminary knowledge of a work. This will help your comprehension when you are ready to read the material in its entirety. Prereading will vary somewhat depending on the material. The following guidelines are organized by type of work.

Prereading a Novel

Nothing is gained by reading parts of a narrative out of order. Your prereading of a novel, therefore, will include only identifying the type of work and predicting based on what you know about the author or have heard or read about the novel. **Note:** If the novel is part of an anthology or if you are using a scholarly edition of the novel, be sure to read the editor's introduction before beginning the novel.

Prereading a Nonfiction Book

There is much more to look over in most nonfiction books, especially textbooks. Take a few minutes to preview an entire book before preparing to read the first chapter or section. Only by examining the whole piece will you understand how the parts fit together. Before reading any nonfiction book, including your textbooks, preread by examining each of the following parts:

1. The *title* and *subtitle.* Sometimes titles that may be misleading are clarified by their subtitles. The title of Hans Klingel's article "Fluctuating Fortunes of the River Horse" is explained in the subtitle: "As water levels fall, so does the lot of the hippopotamus."

2. The *preface* or *introduction.* Here the author explains the book's focus and scope and usually presents some key ideas that underlie his or her approach to the book's subject. Read the entire preface or introduction.

3. The *table of contents* provides chapter titles and major headings within chapters. Study this information to get an idea of the specific topics covered.

4. *Appendices,* when included, often contain statistical information or other specifics that support the text's discussion. You should know what is available to you in the appendices in case you need to turn to the material while reading the book. Note, for example, if the work contains a *glossary*, a list of key terms and their definitions.

5. *Notes* and *bibliography* mark the scholarly nature of the book. If you are reading for a research paper, you will want to use the references as a guide to other sources on your topic.

Prereading a Chapter

After completing the steps to previewing an entire book, be sure to remember to preread each chapter or major section before reading it fully. You should be able to complete the following in only a few minutes. Do not linger; push yourself through the prereading stage, keeping in mind that this is only one step in your reading strategy.

1. Read the chapter's *title* and *objectives*, if objectives are stated at the beginning. (Objectives, sometimes presented as questions that the chapter will answer, are quite common in textbooks.)

2. Read the *opening paragraph*. This is especially important if the chapter does not state objectives.

3. Read the first sentence of each paragraph.

4. As you preread, note *major headings, subheadings,* and *words in italics or bold* face.

5. Also, note any use of *graphics*: diagrams, charts, pictures. Take a few seconds to glance at each one. They will help you become familiar with the chapter's subject matter.

6. Read the chapter *summary* (or *conclusion*) at the end, if there is one. Look over any *review questions* or *exercises* at the end of the chapter. These will give you a good idea of what you are supposed to learn from reading the chapter.

Prereading an Article

How you preread an article will depend in part on the type of article. When you identify the type of article, you will know which of the following steps to take to complete your prereading. Whatever the type of article, your prereading should take only a few minutes.

1. Read the *title*, and the *subtitle*, if there is one.
2. Read the *abstract*, a summary paragraph that follows the title, if there is one. (Abstracts usually accompany scholarly articles in the sciences and social sciences.)
3. Read the entire opening paragraph.
4. Skim the article for *headings*, *subheadings*, and *words in italics* or *bold face*. Scholarly articles, especially in the sciences and social sciences, frequently use these same features as textbooks. Essays in popular magazines and newspaper columns may use these strategies.
5. Read the first sentence of each paragraph from the second paragraph to the end.

Even though prereading is designed to be a quick and incomplete look at the material, you may be surprised to discover just how much you learn about the subject from this step in your preparation. The reason you pick up information from prereading is that you are reading the key parts of the work. The following exercise will show you the benefits of prereading.

 EXERCISE 2-2 Prereading

Read only the shaded parts of the following "box" essay from the article on the hippopotamus. Then complete the comprehension exercise. Do not look back at the selection. The idea is to see how well you comprehend just from prereading.

Hippo Talk
by **William Barklow**

1   Much of hippo social life takes place when the animals are completely underwater, and—as work that my students and I have been conducting in Tanzania's Ruaha National Park reveals—a submerged hippo can produce an impressive array of underwater sounds.

2   Some sounds—grunts, growls, and screams—are underwater versions of noises hippos make when their heads are out of the water. Some are

quite loud: I recorded one underwater scream at 115 decibels. Often the only signs of such intense vocalizations are the fountains of water that erupt as air exhaled by the hippos hits the surface. Sometimes—such as when the vocalizing hippo is not far below the surface—this air forms a bubble that explodes at the surface with an infrasonic thud. After producing such a bubble blast, a hippo may rise to the surface and, keeping its head low and its ears forward, direct an aggressive stare at a nearby subordinate.

3   Other hippo sounds are produced only underwater and without any noticeable expiration of air. One of these—the most common sound made by hippos—is a simple croak. Given most often when calves and sub-adults are playing near their mothers, this call is probably used to maintain contact in murky water.

4   Hippos also produce a variety of high-pitched underwater whines. Some are similar to notes in humpback whale songs, while others (for example, a sustained note of unvarying pitch and lasting a full five seconds) are unlike anything I have heard before.

5   For me, the most intriguing of the hippos' underwater sounds are the various types of clicks they make, usually in a series. These "click trains" bring to mind similar sounds of cetaceans (whales and dolphins) and pinnipeds (seals, sea lions, and walruses). Dolphins and other toothed whales use their clicks in echolocation as they navigate and search for food. (The function of pinniped clicking is unresolved.) Most hippos live in environments where echolocation would certainly be useful: the waters of African lakes and rivers are usually clouded with silt and strewn with boulders and other obstructions. So far, however, there is no evidence that hippos echolocate. I, for one, have never heard hippos click as they move, sometimes for hundreds of feet at a time, beneath the water surface.

6   All hippo clicks that I have been able to correlate with behavior of any kind have been given during social interactions. At the Toledo Zoo's large hippo pool (one of the few places with clear enough water to watch submerged hippos), I once watched a male and female perform a mating dance as graceful and balletic as that of the animated hippos in Walt Disney's *Fantasia*. Part of this ritual involved a gentle clashing of their huge lower canines and incisors. A sound recording showed the clashes to be identical to a click category recorded in the field. Perhaps some of the clicks, then, are associated with courtship. Other clicks, like some whines, may play a role in the frequent jostling for position that is part of the hippo social scene.

7   The effort to decipher the meaning of all these grunts, screams, croaks, clicks, and whines is just beginning. And underwater sounds are only part of the hippos' system of communication; other sounds transmit above and below water simultaneously. To fully understand these "amphibious" sounds, we will need to learn more about how hippos hear. I suspect that they can hear in air and water at the same time, and I hope one day to determine whether a big bull hippo, after growling aggressively below the surface, can then listen for the amphibious screams of his intimidated neighbors.

Comprehension Check ·

Answer the following with a, b, c, or d to indicate the phrase that best completes each statement. Then answer the question that follows.

_____ 1. William Barklow's knowledge of hippo talk has been obtained primarily from
   a. books
   b. on-site studies in Yellowstone National Park
   c. on-site studies in Ruaha National Park
   d. his students

_____ 2. Hippos live
   a. near water
   b. only under water
   c. near other large animals
   d. both under water and on land

_____ 3. Some grunts, growls, and screams are sounds hippos make
   a. both on land and under water
   b. only on land
   c. only under water
   d. only when they are frightened

_____ 4. Some sounds made only under water are produced
   a. without any movement
   b. when no one is around
   c. without seeming to let out any air
   d. when it rains

_____ 5. The underwater clicking sounds seem to correlate with
   a. social interaction
   b. dolphin sounds
   c. a desire to be alone
   d. a desire to fight

_____ 6. Hippo talk is
   a. well understood by scientists
   b. of no interest to scientists
   c. not being studied by scientists
   d. just now being studied by scientists

_____ 7. The sounds most interesting to the author are
   a. the hippo's grunts
   b. the hippo's clicks
   c. the whines of dolphins
   d. the sounds made above the water

Question: What additional information do you anticipate learning from reading the entire article?

_____

_____

What Do I Already Know?

Did you do better than you expected on the comprehension quiz following "Hippo Talk"? If so, are you convinced of the wisdom of prereading? Can your success be explained in part by an interest in animals or by some previous knowledge of hippos? Studies have shown that knowledge of the topic does more than general reading skill to raise scores on reading tests. An interest in learning about new subjects also helps. What the reader brings to the reading context really matters. The more you know, the better you read. It's that simple—and that challenging, because the best way to know a great deal about many subjects is to read. If this sounds like a "Catch-22," do not despair. You are building your store of knowledge—including, now, some new information about the ways hippos talk to one another.

You may actually know more about a topic than you think you do. If you can apply the knowledge you already have, you will read with greater comprehension—even of material that, on the whole, is new to you.

How do you activate your knowledge? Some readers do this by reflecting on the subject before and during their reading. Others may be better off if they do their activating on paper. Pushing yourself to jot down some information or ideas related to the subject will ensure an active use of your knowledge.

There are several ways to write notes to yourself. You may *freewrite* on the topic for a few minutes, creating a loosely organized paragraph. You may prefer instead to *brainstorm*, to list points, probably in incomplete sentences. A third possibility, particularly useful with subject matter that is quite new to you, is to *ask questions*. Here are examples of each approach used in response to a chapter title from a textbook on public speaking.

What Do I Already Know About: "Ethics and Public Speaking"?

Freewrite Response

I've not thought about public speaking before as either ethical or unethical. I guess this has something to do with honesty. I suppose you could be dishonest in a speech just as in a paper, so the chapter may talk about avoiding stealing ideas. It might also talk about telling the truth in your speech—not lying to people.

Brainstorm Response

1. Honesty—be truthful, don't lie in your speech
2. Don't take others' ideas—note sources
3. Use your own words
4. Don't yell at people or call them names in your speech

Question Response

1. Will this chapter tell me to be honest? Will it tell me how?
2. Will it discuss plagiarism?
3. Are there other ethical issues in giving speeches that I haven't thought of?

Now look at the primary and secondary headings in the chapter to see how activating your knowledge before reading can be useful.

CHAPTER 2   ETHICS AND PUBLIC SPEAKING

THE IMPORTANCE OF ETHICS

GUIDELINES FOR ETHICAL SPEAKING

  Make Sure Your Goals Are Ethically Sound
  Be Fully Prepared for Each Speech
  Be Honest in What You Say
  Avoid Name-Calling and Other Forms of Abusive Language
  Put Ethical Principles into Practice

PLAGIARISM

  Global Plagiarism
  Patchwork Plagiarism
  Incremental Plagiarism

GUIDELINES FOR ETHICAL LISTENING

  Be Courteous and Attentive
  Avoid Prejudging the Speaker
  Maintain the Free and Open Expression of Ideas

Stephen E. Lucas, *The Art of Public Speaking*, 5th ed., 1995.

Each response to the question "What do I already know," though different in form, has picked up on the idea of being honest in what you say in the speech and in not plagiarizing, stealing words or ideas from someone else. On the other hand, our imaginary reader did not anticipate two interesting topics in this chapter: (1) the idea that not being prepared is unethical and (2) the entire section on the ethics of listening to speeches. However, if our reader combined pre-reading the entire chapter with activating knowledge on the ethics of public speaking, then he or she would be prepared to read about these new ideas. And, presumably, our reader would be eager to read the chapter in anticipation of both expanding existing knowledge and being challenged to consider some new information and ethical concepts.

Practice discovering what you already know by working the following exercise.

Exercise 2-3 What Do I Already Know?

I. Using each of the three methods illustrated above, activate your knowledge of the following topic from a sociology text: "Problems in U.S. Education and Their Solutions."

Freewrite Response: _____

_____

_____

Brainstorm Response: _____

_____

_____

Question Response: _____

_____

_____

II. Select the strategy that works best for you to activate your knowledge of each of the following chapter or section titles.

a. "Health in the United States: A Nation of Contrasts" (from *Social Problems: Society in Crisis*)

_____

_____

_____

b. "How Congress Works" (from *American Government: Roots and Reform*)

_____

_____

_____

c. "Subatomic Parts of the Atom" (from *Foundations of College Chemistry*)

_____

_____

_____

What Will I Learn from Reading?

You may have discovered that you chose to use questions to activate knowledge when you felt that you knew little about the subject. When your knowledge is limited, you can still become an active reader by thinking about what you will learn from each work you read. As you preread material, ask yourself what you will be learning by turning titles and headings into questions. So, instead of just reading the section heading "Problems in U.S. Education and Their Solutions," generate questions, such as:

What are the problems in U.S. education today?

What are some solutions to these problems?

Or, instead of merely reading "Health in the United States: A Nation of Contrasts," ask yourself:

What health issues will be examined?

What are the contrasts in health in the U.S.?

As you ask these questions, others may occur to you to aid in anticipating the material: Will contrasts be established within the country? Perhaps between different groups, such as by age or gender or regions of the country? Will contrasts be made with other nations?

Turning headings into questions prepares you to expect to learn specific information and alerts you, as well, to possible patterns of organization. Strategies that help readers push through the material, actively searching for answers to questions will improve reading comprehension.

EXERCISE 2-4 Turning Headings into Questions

Turn each of the following titles or section headings into one or more questions.

1. "The Information Processing Model of Memory" (from Woolfolk's *Educational Psychology*)

   _____

   _____

2. "Computer Crime" (from Fuller and Manning's *Computers and Information Processing*)

   _____

   _____

3. "Disorders Associated with the Immune System" (from Curtis's *Biology*)

   _____

   _____

4. "Dinosaurs and Drifting Continents" (from *Natural History* by Sereno).

   _____

   _____

■ READ

The second step in your reading strategy has three closely connected phases: reading, writing, and monitoring comprehension. In this chapter we will examine only the second and third phases of the reading step. The rest of the text provides specific instruction in ways to become a more skilled reader. This chapter focuses on all the other steps in your reading plan, on every part of the reading process except the actual reading of the material. But of course you have been reading all along; it's the other steps to becoming an active reader that you need to become acquainted with and to practice.

Write

Writing during the reading stage is so important that an entire chapter (Chapter 6) is devoted to exploring several different ways of responding to reading by writing. Since this chapter presents an overview of the entire reading process, it will introduce only one, but probably the most frequently used, writing strategy.

Studies have shown that writing is an essential aid to reading comprehension. First, the more senses you engage during reading, the more likely you are to maintain concentration and be an active reader. Second, writing forces you to make distinctions, to generalize, to note what is important. In short, it forces you to think about the material, to read with your brain.

One useful writing strategy is to **annotate,** that is, to mark up the text, underlining and making notes in the margin. Now, before you say to yourself that you cannot mark up books, let's stop and think about this. Of course you cannot annotate library materials, but you can annotate your textbooks, photocopied articles that you are using for a research paper, and both fiction and nonfiction books that you own. What have you gained by keeping your texts spotless if you end up not doing well in the course? For those works that cannot be written in, other kinds of writing strategies can be used. But you will want to learn how to annotate and to use this writing strategy "day in and day out," both in school and on the job.

Guidelines for Annotating

1. After you read a section, underline key sentences (or the important parts of sentences). Underline what seems to be the most important idea in each paragraph.
2. Remember: underlining is designed to highlight by contrast. Underlining just about every sentence misses the point.
3. When you look up a word's definition, write the definition in the margin next to the word.
4. Distinguish between ideas and examples by writing "ex." in the margin next to an example. If a writer provides a series of examples (or points or reasons), label them as examples (or points or reasons) and then number each one in the margin.
5. Draw arrows to connect example to idea. Draw pictures to illustrate concepts.
6. Make whatever other notes in the margins that will help you stay engaged as you read and serve as guides to review.

An Example of Annotating

As you read the following selection, an excerpt from Lester A. Lefton's *Psychology* (5th ed., Allyn & Bacon, 1995), observe the usefulness of the annotations and the extent of reader involvement they show. As you read, add your own marginal notes.

The Discovery of Short-Term Memory

key researchers

Researchers had been studying memory and retrieval for decades, but it was not until 1959 that Lloyd and Margaret Peterson presented evidence for the existence of short-term memory. The (Petersons) asked subjects to recall a three-consonant sequence, such as *xbd*, after varying time intervals. During a time that ranged from no delay to 18 seconds, the subjects were required to count backwards by threes. The aim of counting backwards was to prevent the subjects from repeating or rehearsing the sequence. The Petersons wanted to examine recall when rehearsal was not possible. As the interval between presentation and recall increased, accuracy of recall decreased. The Petersons interpreted this result as evidence for the existence of short-term memory.

topic

Petersons' experiment

Petersons' conc. about s-t mem.

process of putting information into storage

3 storage characteristics

The storage of information in sensory memory is temporary; the information is either lost through decay or transferred to the second stage—short-term memory. In short-term memory, semipermanent storage exists; information is actively processed—further (encoded) and stored for a bit longer (about 20 to 30 seconds). At this stage, people rehearse important information to make sure they will remember it; if they do not rehearse, the information will be lost. Thousands of research studies have been done on the components and characteristics of storage in short-term memory. They focus on the importance of duration, capacity, and rehearsal.

rehearse or lose it

EXERCISE 2-5 Annotating a Selection

Read the following excerpt, another selection on memory from Lefton's Psychology, *and, using the guidelines given above, annotate the selection. Compare your work with classmates and discuss any differences.*

Long-Term Memory: Focus on Retrieval

1   Information such as names, faces, dates, places, smells, and events—both important and trivial—can be found in a relatively permanent form in **long-term memory.** The duration of information in long-term memory is indefinite; much of it lasts a lifetime. The capacity for long-term memory is seemingly infinite; the more information we acquire, the easier it is to acquire information. Using the library analogy again, we

can say that long-term memory includes all the books in the library's permanent collection.

2   The information that is typically encoded and stored in long-term memory either is important (a friend's birthday, for example) or is used frequently (your telephone number, for example). Maintaining information in long-term memory often involves rehearsal or repetition, but sometimes an important event is immediately etched into long-term memory (Schmidt, 1991).

3   Several types of information are stored in long-term memory. For example, a person may remember the words to a Springsteen song, the meaning of the word *sanguine*, and how to operate a compact disc player. Each of these types of information seems to be stored and called on in a different way. Psychologists therefore split long-term memory into two types: procedural and declarative.

4   **Procedural memory** is memory for the perceptual, motor, and cognitive skills or habits required to complete a task. Learning how to drive an automobile, wash dishes, or swim involves a series of steps that include perceptual, motor, and cognitive skills—and thus procedural memory. Acquiring such skills is usually time-consuming and difficult at first; but once the skills are learned, they are relatively permanent. The encoding and retrieval of procedural information are indirect; the pieces of information are not stored together and must be assembled (Richardson-Klavehn & Bjork, 1988).

5   **Declarative memory** is memory for specific facts, such as Bill Clinton was elected President in 1992 or Neil Armstrong was accompanied to the moon by Edwin Aldrin and Michael Collins. The memory is established quickly, and the information is more likely to be forgotten over time than is the information in procedural memory. It is easier to examine declarative memory than procedural memory, since people can quickly relate a specific fact but have more trouble explaining how to do something such as swimming.

Monitor

As you read and interact with the material by annotating (or using some other type of written response to reading), you also need to be thinking about how well you are reading. That is, are you comprehending? And if not, what are you going to do to fix the problem?

Some ideas that we established in Chapter 1 are relevant to the monitoring step in the reading process. First, to read is to obtain meaning, not just to look at words. Second, when you are both reading and thinking about how you are reading, you are using metacogniton. You are participating in the process of making meaning from the material while, at the same time, you are able to stand outside the process and monitor how well the process is working. When monitoring your own performance, you can step in and redirect or refocus your attention as problems arise. As an active reader, you are both player and coach.

Monitoring progress in an activity is not a new experience. We often talk to ourselves to organize the day, set up a new lab experiment, or contemplate a move in chess. On the other hand, we perform many activities—driving the car on familiar streets, swimming across the pool—without consciously guiding our actions. When reading complex material or material that you must learn thoroughly, you will want to direct your behavior in a purposeful way.

What are some clues that are warnings of trouble with reading? First, here are some behavior clues to watch for:

You find yourself gazing out the window.

You start to think about plans for later.

You take a second break in only ten minutes.

You realize that you are frowning as you read.

Can you think of other behavior clues? What do these actions tell you? First, that you have lost concentration. Second, that you are struggling with reading comprehension.

Now think about the conversations we have with ourselves that signal problems. What do the following verbal clues tell you?

"I've just read three pages, but I don't know what I've read."

"None of this makes any sense to me."

"I'll never understand this stuff!"

Can you think of other verbal clues?

If you are monitoring the process, you can tell from these actions and statements that all is not going well. The first step to monitoring is recognizing—or admitting—that just continuing to turn pages will not accomplish the needed understanding.

The next step is to find some way to remove the reading difficulty so that you can once again make progress. The reasons for lapses in comprehension will vary among readers, so the solutions have to vary as well. Here are some suggestions for fixing comprehension problems.

Guidelines for Fixing Comprehension

1. *Monitor your concentration.* Your problem may be the result of a loss of concentration. Review the guidelines for concentration in Chapter 1 and respond appropriately. (For example, move from your noisy room to a quiet place to complete the reading.)

2. *Redo the steps to active reading.* Perhaps you forgot to prepare and just plunged into the reading, only to find yourself confused. If so, go back and preview the material, define your purpose, and activate your previous knowledge.

3. *Connect the material to previous reading.* If your comprehension problems are occurring in the middle of a section or chapter of a textbook, go back and review the material in the previous section or chapter. If you are struggling with the material in a textbook, you may need to review in some depth to activate your knowledge before moving forward.

4. *Fill in the gaps.* A specific section or passage may be causing you trouble because there are key words that you do not know. If you cannot determine meaning from the context, you will have to obtain the relevant definitions before continuing to read. Perhaps the definitions are to be found in a previous section of the text. Find them and copy the definitions into the margin. Next, try the text's glossary, if there is one. Finally, turn to your dictionary for definitions.

5. *Reread the material.* Understand and accept that some material is difficult and may require a second reading for full comprehension. Be sure to include writing as you read.

6. *Go to additional sources for help.* If, after trying the remedies listed above, you are still confused, you may need to find help outside the reading material itself. Try the library for other, simpler books on the subject, perhaps encyclopedias or a text designed for a lower-level course. If your library can't help, ask your instructor to recommend other books or study guides. Additionally, find a classmate to study with or obtain a college-sponsored tutor.

EXERCISE 2-6 Monitoring Reading Comprehension

Read the following selection, monitoring your comprehension. Then list the strategies you would use to fix any comprehension problems you had or that you think other readers might have. Compare your list with classmates.

Other compounds are not purely ionic but involve electron sharing between atoms. In these covalent compounds, it is not possible to associate a measurable charge with a particular atom. In a purely artificial way, we define the formal charge to be the charge an atom would have if electrons were divided exactly equally between the two atoms that share them. In other words, when the bonding is covalent, we simply assume that it is *perfectly* covalent (equal sharing). If the result is a Lewis structure with large positive or negative formal charges on atoms, then there is something wrong. The artificial assignment of formal charge is a check for consistency because, in a true covalent compound, the atoms should not be highly charged. If they turn out to be that way in our representation, we either look for a new Lewis structure or predict that the compound will not be stable. Formal charge also allows conclusions about the nature of bonding. A C—N single bond, for example, has a different length, bond strength, and reactivity from a C=N double bond, so the choice of the best Lewis structure (based on formal charge) is often a very useful guide to molecular properties.

Oxtoby, Nachtrieb, and Freeman, Chemistry: Science of Change,
2nd ed. Saunders College Publishing, 1994.

_____

_____

_____

_____

_____

■ RESPOND: REFLECT AND REVIEW

Just as important as preparing before you read is responding to what you have read. To fulfill your purpose in reading and get the most out of your reading, you need to both reflect and review.

Reflect

Some readers like to reflect as they read, stopping from time to time to have a conversation with themselves about the significance of the material for them. (Remember the overlapping circles in Figure 2.1.) Others prefer to complete an article, a chapter, or a poem and then reflect on the work as a whole. Whichever process works best for you is a good process, so long as you do reflect on the reading.

Psychologists studying the memory process have found that the most difficult material to commit to and maintain in long-term memory is material that seems random or disconnected from anything else. Random numbers or lists of words, for example, are difficult to remember. If you can connect what you are reading to something in your life, the material will not seem random. By relating the information and ideas to something important, you greatly improve your chances of remembering what you have read.

Instructors are often frustrated by students who insist that they have read an assignment but who cannot answer questions or engage in a discussion about the assignment. When instructors show their frustration it is not because they fail to believe students but because they cannot understand why students have such trouble remembering material that is so fascinating to the instructors. But the information in the assignment is material that instructors both value highly and use repeatedly. They have connected the material to their work and related it to other information that is a part of their field of study. They "know it cold." By contrast, students may be introduced to the material for the first time; students may also have neglected to reflect on how the information connects to their course of study, much less to their personal lives.

Take, for example, information about memory. For psychologist Lester Lefton, a discussion of short- and long-term memory (see pages 44 and 45) is vitally important to the understanding of how we function as humans, his field of study. But surely we do not all have to be psychologists to be interested in how our memories function. Just wanting to understand how your brain functions ought to be reason enough to reflect on the passages in this chapter on memory and relate their ideas to your life.

Time for reflection is not time for daydreaming about Friday's date. You do want to keep focused on the task of understanding what you are reading. To keep focused, you may need to ask yourself some specific questions. On the other hand, do not close out the possibility of serendipity, of making connections and having insights that are profound and truly important to you. You may find that if you develop the habit of reflecting on your reading as a way to improving reading skills, you will become a more reflective person, and this new dimension to your life will bring you pleasure.

What kinds of questions can you ask yourself to aid reflection? Here are some general questions that can be applied to many kinds of written works.

Questions to Aid Reflection

- How does the selection connect to the course? Why has the instructor assigned (or recommended) it?
- How does this chapter (or section) connect to previously studied material in the text and in class? Does it add to or qualify previous material?
- How does this literary work connect to the ways we are studying literature? Does it connect chronologically? Or as a type of literature? Or, what elements of literature does it illustrate?

- How does this work relate to other courses I'm taking? Are there chronological connections (U.S. history and a survey of American literature)? Philosophical connections (literary naturalism and evolutionary theory in biology)? Subject-matter connections (psychology and sociology; management and speech; calculus and physics)?
- How can I use this information in my career? How will it make me better trained? Or better informed? Or more understanding of people I'll be working with?
- How does this material help me better understand myself? My family relationships? People who are different from me? The physical universe or natural world of which I am a part? How do I feel about this new knowledge? Does it change my outlook on life, my values or attitudes?

EXERCISE 2-7 Reflecting on What You Read

Select either "Hippo Talk" (p. 35) or the two excerpts on memory (p. 44 and p. 45). Reread the selection you choose and then reflect on its connections with your other courses, your career plans, and your learning about life. Write some of your reflections in the space below.

_____

_____

_____

_____

_____

Review

Although Reflect and Review are listed as separate steps in your reading strategy, in fact the time you spend reflecting is also time spent reviewing. Reviewing what you have read can take a variety of forms. What is critical is that you review *immediately* and then *periodically*.

The appropriate time for your first review is *immediately* after you finish reading. Not after you have dinner or return from another class. Even though you may be pleased to have completed a long reading assignment and feel as though you have finished a major task, you must resist celebrating until you have taken time for the post-reading steps of reflecting and reviewing. Studies show that immediate review is the best way to ensure remembering. To take this idea into a social setting: if you want to remember the names of people introduced to you, repeat their names when you greet them. This repetition is known as *rehearsing*. After repeating the names during your greeting, say them to yourself several times, and then use them again in conversation. Chances are good that you will remember the names.

Observe that you reviewed the names immediately and then periodically thereafter. Even with an immediate review, some material will not be remembered unless you continue to go over it. You are wise to review several times between your first reading and a test date, rather than reviewing all at once just before the exam. When studying for your courses, one good strategy is to review what you have most recently read before reading further. So, review Chapter 1 before reading Chapter 2, review Chapter 2 before reading Chapter 3, and so on. Each time you "relearn" the material, you remember more of it.

Your immediate review may include several strategies. First, redo the prereading step: read the headings, words in boldface, diagrams, the opening paragraph, and the first sentence of the remaining paragraphs as a way of rehearsing key ideas. Second, look over your annotations—the lines you've underlined and notes you've put in the margin. Third, answer the questions that you generated as part of your prereading, or, if you are reading a textbook, answer the discussion or review questions in the text. Finally, integrate reflection with reviewing. Now, practice your Prepare-Read-Respond strategy on the following selections.

Selection 1   Hypnosis

by **Lester A. Lefton**

The following is an excerpt from *Psychology* (5th ed., Allyn & Bacon, 1995). Professor Lefton has taught undergraduate and graduate courses in psychology for more than twenty years at the University of South Carolina.

Prepare

1. From what you know about the author and the selection, what can you predict about purpose and format or style?

   _____

   _____

2. State briefly what you expect to read about. _____

   _____

   _____

3. What do you already know about the topic? Respond using *one* of the methods described in the chapter.

_____

_____

4. What is your purpose in reading? _____

_____

5. Preread the selection. (Read the opening paragraph and the first sentence of the rest of the paragraphs; note headings and words in **bold** or *italic* type.) After prereading, answer the following with either a T (true) or F (false).

		T	F
a.	Hypnotized people do not know where they are.	___	___
b.	Barber does not believe that hypnosis works.	___	___
c.	Hypnosis has not been used to reduce pain.	___	___
d.	Hypnosis has been used in psychotherapy.	___	___

6. Read and annotate the selection. Then complete the comprehension and vocabulary checks that follow and respond to the questions for discussion and reflection.

1   "You are falling asleep. Your eyelids are becoming heavy. The strain on your eyes is becoming greater and greater. Your muscles are relaxing. You are feeling sleepier and sleepier. You are feeling very relaxed."

2   These instructions are typical of those used in *hypnotic induction*—the process used in hypnosis. **Hypnosis** is an altered state of consciousness brought about by procedures that induce a trance. The generally accepted view of hypnosis is that hypnotized individuals are in a semimystical state of consciousness and no longer have control over their behavior. They are aware of their surroundings and are conscious, but their level of awareness and responses to others are altered. A person's willingness to follow unconventional instructions given by the hypnotist, such as to make funny noises, is called *hypnotic susceptibility* or *suggestibility*. Most people can be hypnotized to some extent (Hilgard, 1965). Children between 7 and 14 are the most susceptible; those who daydream are also especially susceptible (Hoyt et al., 1989).

3   *Effects of Hypnosis.* People who have been hypnotized report that they know they have been hypnotized and are aware of their surroundings.

Some report being in a special, almost mystical state; and most report a sense of time distortion (K. S. Bowers, 1979). One time distortion effect of hypnosis is **age regression**—the ability to report details about an experience that took place many years earlier or to act and feel like a child. Because few studies that report age regression during hypnosis have been controlled for accuracy of recall, the authenticity of age regression has been questioned (Nash, 1987). *Heightened memory* is another effect of hypnosis. Evidence indicates that hypnosis helps subjects recall information (e.g., McConkey & Kinoshita, 1988). However, techniques that do not involve hypnosis may work just as well for this purpose.

4   In a study by Putnam (1979), hypnotized and nonhypnotized subjects were asked to recall events they had seen earlier on a videotape. Hypnotized subjects made more errors when answering leading questions than did nonhypnotized subjects. Putnam suggests that hypnotized subjects not only make more errors (misrecollection) but also mistakenly believe that their memories are accurate (McConkey & Kinoshita, 1988). Results from such studies have led researchers to question the use of hypnosis in courtroom settings; in fact, some states do not allow the testimony of hypnotized subjects as evidence (Sanders & Simmons, 1983; M. C. Smith, 1983).

5   Hypnosis is also used for pain reduction. In a case reported by E. F. Siegel (1979), hypnosis successfully reduced lower-leg pain in a woman who had undergone an above-the-knee amputation. (The phenomenon of pain in a part of the body that no longer exists is called *phantom pain*; it occurs in some amputees.) Hypnosis has also been used to reduce pain from heat, pressure, and childbirth (Harmon, Hynan, & Tyre, 1990). Few studies of pain management, however, are conducted with adequate experimental rigor. Critics of hypnosis note that most patients show signs of pain even when hypnotized. Also, in many cases, analgesic drugs (pain relievers) are used along with the hypnotism. Some researchers (especially Barber, considered next) challenge the ability of hypnosis to reduce pain, reasoning that relaxation and a subject's positive attitude and lowered anxiety account for reported reductions in pain.

6   ***Challenges to Hypnosis.*** Theodore Xenophon Barber, one of the major skeptics of traditional theories of hypnotism, contends that the concepts of hypnosis and the hypnotic trance are meaningless and misleading. According to Barber, behaviors of hypnotized subjects are no different from behaviors of subjects willing to think about and imagine themes suggested to them. If subjects' attitudes toward a situation lead them to expect certain effects, those effects will be more likely to occur. Barber's approach is called the *cognitive-behavioral viewpoint* (Barber, Spanos, & Chaves, 1974).

7   Barber's studies show that subjects given task-motivating instructions perform similarly to subjects undergoing hypnotic induction. Typically, more than half of the subjects in experimental groups showed

responsiveness to task suggestions, in contrast to 16 percent in the control groups, which were given no special instructions. From the results, Barber has concluded that task-motivating instructions are almost as effective as hypnotic induction procedures in increasing subjects' responsiveness to task suggestions.

8   Barber's studies have received support from other research. Salzberg and DePiano (1980), for example, found that hypnosis did not facilitate performance any more than task-motivating instructions did. In fact, they argued that, for cognitive tasks, task-motivating instructions are more effective than hypnosis. The evidence showing that hypnosislike effects can be achieved in various ways (e.g., Bryant & McConkey, 1989) does not mean that psychologists must discard the concept or use of hypnosis. It simply means they should reconsider traditional assumptions.

9   Hypnosis continues to be widely used as an aid in psychotherapy. Most clients report that it is a pleasant experience. Therapists assert that in some cases it can (1) help focus a client's energy on a specific topic, (2) aid memory, and (3) help a child cope with the aftereffects of child abuse. Many therapists use hypnosis to help patients relax, enhance their memory, reduce stress and anxiety, lose weight, and stop smoking (e.g., Somer, 1990). Some psychologists assert that hypnosis can be a formidable aid to help athletes concentrate (Morgan, 1992). Research into the process and effects of hypnosis continues, with an emphasis on defining critical variables in hypnosis itself and in the subjects who are the most and the least easily hypnotized (e.g., Nilsson, 1990) and on ascertaining potential negative effects (e.g., Owens et al., 1989).

Comprehension Check .

Answer the following with a, b, c, or d to indicate the phrase that best completes each statement.

_____ 1. The general view is that hypnosis produces

    a. a state of sleep
    b. happiness
    c. a semimystical state
    d. boredom

_____ 2. "Hypnotic susceptibility" refers to a hypnotized person's

    a. willingness to do unconventional things
    b. willingness to daydream
    c. willingness to sleep
    d. willingness to ignore the hypnotist

_____ 3. People under hypnosis are

    a. unaware of their surroundings
    b. more aware of their surroundings

    c. less susceptible to illness

    d. more susceptible to illness

____ 4. The experience of age regression when under hypnosis has been

    a. questioned by researchers

    b. shown to occur every time

    c. shown to make subjects happy

    d. outlawed

____ 5. Hypnotized people usually believe that their

    a. memories are distorted

    b. youth is restored

    c. youth is lost

    d. memories are accurate

Answer the following with a T (true) or F (false).

	T	F
6. Critics dispute the power of hypnosis to reduce pain.	___	___
7. Therapists believe that hypnosis can help memory.	___	___
8. Therapists do not use hypnosis to help patients quit smoking.	___	___
9. Barber does not believe that hypnosis improves performance.	___	___

Expanding Vocabulary

Match each word in the left column with its definition in the right column by placing the correct letter in the space next to each word.

____ induce (2)	a. asserts or claims
____ susceptible (2)	b. great or powerful
____ skeptics (6)	c. capable of being affected
____ contends (6)	d. make easier
____ facilitate (8)	e. differences
____ formidable (9)	f. to bring out
____ variables (9)	g. doubters or questioners

Analysis of Content and Strategies

1. Explain why court testimony of hypnotized subjects is not allowed in some states.

2. Explain Barber's challenges to hypnosis. _____

_____

_____

3. Why are children and those who daydream most susceptible to hypnosis?

_____

For Discussion and Reflection

1. What were your views of hypnosis prior to reading this selection? Has the selection changed your thinking in any way? If so, how?

2. Are you interested in being hypnotized? Why or why not?

3. Is it a good idea to try to bring back memories of childhood—by hypnosis or any other means? Why or why not?

Selection 2   The Nature of Scientific Inquiry

by **Edward J. Tarbuck** and **Frederick K. Lutgens**

The following is an excerpt from *The Earth: An Introduction to Physical Geology* (4th ed., Macmillan, 1993). The authors are professors of geology at Illinois Central College.

Vocabulary Alert

This selection uses the following two scientific terms:

plate tectonics: theory that the earth's outer shell is made up of separate plates whose movements cause volcanoes and earthquakes

laws of thermodynamics: laws that relate to the function of heat (or energy). The first law states that in all processes the total amount of energy remains constant. The second law states that all natural processes move toward disorder or breaking down.

Prepare

1. From what you know about the author and the selection, what can you predict about purpose and format or style?

_____

_____

2. State briefly what you expect to read about. _____

_____

3. What do you already know about the topic? Respond using *one* of the methods described in the chapter. _____

_____

_____

4. What is your purpose in reading? _____

_____

5. Preread the selection. (Read the opening paragraph and the first sentence of the rest of the paragraphs; note headings and words in **bold** or *italic* type.) After prereading, answer the following with either a T (true) or F (false).

	T	**F**
a. Scientists believe that the natural world operates in consistent and predictable ways.	___	___
b. Scientists are satisfied gathering facts.	___	___
c. A hypothesis can never become a theory.	___	___
d. The scientific method is the making up of laws of science.	___	___

6. Read and annotate the selection. Then complete the comprehension and vocabulary checks that follow and respond to the questions for reflection.

1   As members of a modern society, we are constantly reminded of the significant benefits derived from scientific investigations. What exactly is the nature of this inquiry?

2   All science is based on the assumption that the natural world behaves in a consistent and predictable manner. This implies that the physical laws which govern the smallest atomic particles also operate in the largest, most distant galaxies. Evidence for the existence of these underlying patterns can be found in the physical world as well as the biological world. For example, the same biochemical processes and the same genetic codes that are found in bacterial cells are also found in human cells. The overall goal of science is to discover the underlying patterns in the natural world and then to use this knowledge to make predictions about what should or should not be expected to happen given certain facts or circumstances.

3   The development of new scientific knowledge involves some basic, logical processes that are universally accepted. To determine what is occurring in the natural world, scientists collect scientific *facts* through observation and measurement. These data are essential to science and

serve as the springboard for the development of scientific theories and laws.

4   Once a set of scientific facts (or principles) that describe a natural phenomenon are gathered, investigators try to explain how or why things happen in the manner observed. They can do this by constructing a tentative (or untested) explanation, which we call a scientific **hypothesis.** Often several hypotheses are advanced to explain the same factual evidence. For example, there are currently five major hypotheses that have been proposed to explain the origin of the earth's moon. Until recently, the most widely held hypothesis argued that the moon and the earth formed simultaneously from the same cloud of nebular dust and gases. A newer hypothesis suggests that a Mars-sized body impacted the earth, thereby ejecting a huge quantity of material into earth orbit that eventually accumulated into the moon. Both hypotheses will be submitted to rigorous testing that will undoubtedly result in the modification or rejection of one, or perhaps both, of these proposals. The history of science is littered with discarded hypotheses. One of the best known is the idea that the earth was at the center of the universe, a proposal that was supported by the apparent daily motion of the sun, moon, and stars around the earth.

5   When a hypothesis has survived extensive scrutiny and when competing hypotheses have been eliminated, a hypothesis may be elevated to the status of a scientific **theory.** A scientific theory is a well-tested and widely accepted view that scientists agree best explains certain observable facts. However, scientific theories, like scientific hypotheses, are accepted only provisionally. It is always possible that a theory which has withstood previous testing may eventually be disproven. As theories survive more testing, they are regarded with higher levels of confidence. Theories that have withstood extensive testing, as for example, the theory of plate tectonics or the theory of evolution, are held with a very high degree of confidence.

6   Some concepts in science are formulated into scientific laws. A scientific **law** is a generalization about the behavior of nature from which there has been no known deviation after numerous observations or experiments. Scientific laws are generally narrower in scope than theories and can usually be expressed mathematically. Examples include Newton's laws of motion and the laws of thermodynamics. Scientific laws describe what happens in nature, but they do not explain how or why things happen this way. Also, unlike hypotheses, which are inventions of the mind to explain scientific facts, scientific laws are based on observations and measurements and thus are rarely overthrown or seriously modified. Nevertheless, even scientific laws are not necessarily "perpetual truths." As the mathematician Jacob Bronowski so ably stated, "Science is a great many things, but in the end they all return to this: Science is the acceptance of what works and the rejection of what does not."

7   The processes just described, in which scientists gather facts through observations and formulate scientific hypotheses, theories, and laws, is called the *scientific method.* Contrary to popular belief, the scientific method is not

a standard recipe that scientists apply in a routine manner to unravel the secrets of our natural world. Neither is this process a haphazard one. Some scientific knowledge is gained through the following steps: (1) the collection of scientific facts through observation and measurement; (2) the development of a working hypothesis to explain these facts; (3) construction of experiments to test the hypothesis; and (4) the acceptance, modification, or rejection of the hypothesis based on extensive testing. Other scientific discoveries represent purely theoretical ideas, which stood up to extensive examination. Still other scientific advancements have been made when a totally unexpected happening occurred during an experiment. These so-called serendipitous discoveries are more than pure luck; for as Louis Pasteur said, "In the field of observation, chance favors only the prepared mind." Since scientific knowledge is acquired through several avenues, it might be best to describe the nature of scientific inquiry as the *methods* of science, rather than *the* scientific method.

■ Comprehension Check ·

Finish each of the following sentences by filling in a word or phrase that best completes the idea.

1. Scientific inquiry operates on the assumption that the natural world is

   _____.

2. One basic goal of science is to discover _____ in nature.

3. The second basic goal of science is to make _____ about what will happen in particular circumstances.

4. A scientific hypothesis is a _____

   _____ .

5. A scientific theory is more widely accepted than a _____ .

Answer the following with a T (true) or F (false).

	T	F
6. Several hypotheses may be presented to account for a related collection of scientific facts.	___	___
7. Scientific laws explain why things happen in nature.	___	___
8. Evolution is a widely accepted scientific theory.	___	___
9. Scientific laws are often expressed mathematically.	___	___
10. The scientific method involves only observation and experimentation, not theoretical work.	___	___

Expanding Vocabulary

Match each word in the left column with its definition in the right column by placing the correct letter in the space next to each word.

_____ nebular (4)   a. based on reason rather than experiment

_____ simultaneously (5)   b. variation from the norm

_____ provisionally (5)   c. luminous

_____ deviation (6)   d. at the same time

_____ theoretical (7)   e. tentatively

Analysis of Content and Strategies

1. Many people use the word *theory* somewhat differently than scientists. What is usually meant by the word?

   _____

   How do scientists use the word? _____

   _____

2. Near the end of paragraph 7, the authors quote the scientist Louis Pasteur. Explain the meaning of Pasteur's statement.

   _____

   _____

3. Explain why a geology text would include this section in its opening chapter.

   _____

   _____

For Discussion and Reflection

1. What is the most important new idea in this selection for you? Why is it important?

2. Prior to reading this selection, did your idea of the scientific method include the three processes explained by the authors? If not, what one/ones are new to you? Why is it important to understand the several "*methods* of science"?

Selection 3 ■ **The Triumph of the Psycho-Fact: If We Feel It's True, Then It Is—Even If It Isn't**

by **Robert J. Samuelson**

Journalist Samuelson is a syndicated columnist whose articles appear weekly in many newspapers and biweekly in *Newsweek* magazine. He usually writes about economics and culture. The following article appeared in *Newsweek* on May 9, 1994.

Prepare

1. From what you know about the author and the selection, what can you predict about purpose and format or style?

   _____

   _____

2. State briefly what you expect to read about. _____

   _____

3. What do you already know about the topic? Respond using *one* of the methods described in the chapter.

   _____

   _____

4. What is your purpose in reading? _____

   _____

5. Preread the selection. (Read the opening paragraph and the first sentence of the rest of the paragraphs; note headings and words in **bold** or *italic* type and tables.) After prereading, answer the following with either a T (true) or F (false).

	T	F
a. Psycho-facts are supported with evidence.	____	____
b. Journalists help create psycho-facts.	____	____
c. Regulations created to regulate psycho-facts waste money.	____	____
d. Information is not necessary for good judgment.	____	____

6. Read and annotate the selection. Then complete the comprehension and vocabulary checks that follow and respond to the questions for reflection.

1   We live in a world of real dangers and imagined fears. The dangers are often low and falling, while the fears are high and rising. We are hounded by what I call "psycho-facts": beliefs that, though not supported by hard evidence, are taken as real because their constant repetition changes the way we experience life. We feel assaulted by rising crime, increasing health hazards, falling living standards and a worsening environment. These are all psycho-facts. The underlying conditions aren't true, but we feel they are and, therefore, they become so.

2   Journalists—trafficking in the sensational and the simplistic—are heavily implicated in the explosion of psycho-facts. But so are politicians, policy advocates and promoters of various causes and life-styles. Rarely does any of us deliberately lie. However, we do peddle incomplete or selective information that inspires misleading exaggerations or unwarranted inferences. People begin to feel that something's wrong, and this new sensation becomes an irrefutable fact or (worse) the basis for a misguided policy.

3   Crime? Yes, there's long been too much of it. But the best surveys do not show that it's dramatically worsened. Indeed, some victimization rates have dropped. The household-burglary rate declined by 42 percent between 1973 and 1991. The number of annual murders has fluctuated between 20,000 and 26,000 since 1980; the major increase occurred in the 1960s, when the number doubled. A Gallup poll reports that 86 percent of the respondents haven't been victims of violent crime. By contrast, our consciousness of crime—fanned by local TV news—has risen.

4   "Are We Scaring Ourselves to Death?" asks ABC correspondent John Stossel on a recent network special exploring these issues. The answer is yes. But psycho-facts are seductive precisely because they are often plausible. We've been told for years, for example, that our living standards are dropping, and this became a big Clinton theme in 1992. It isn't really so. Over any extended period, our living standards have risen. In the past 25 years, median family income is up by about one-fifth. But the rise is much slower than we expected and so slow that it's often imperceptible or nonexistent in any one year. We don't feel it.

5   Health, safety and environmental hazards inspire similar misconceptions. Suppose an experiment shows that substance X causes cancer—at some dosage in some animal. We're soon worried that everything we eat or breathe is giving us cancer or heart disease. We feel that identifiable risks should be avoidable risks. We act as if there's a constitutional right to immortality and that anything that raises risk should be outlawed. Our goal is a risk-free society, and this fosters many outsize fears.

6   Lots of theoretical dangers (like asbestos or plane crashes) aren't large practical dangers. The easiest way to grasp this is to glance at the adjoining table. It compares relative risks of dying. What's worth remembering

is that roughly 2.2 million Americans die every year. With about 260 million Americans, this means that in a crude arithmetic sense the average risk of dying is about 1 in 118 (2.2 million goes into 260 million 118 times). Now obviously, the old die in much greater numbers than the young. Still, the general risk of dying from natural causes or unavoidable accidents is much greater than the specific danger of many hazardous substances or jobs. (The table shows both.)

The Odds of Dying

Every year, nearly 1 in 100 of us dies. The dangers from high-profile risks such as asbestos and plane crashes are relatively small.

For everyone
1 in 118

For those 35 to 44 years old
1 in 437

For police on the job
1 in 4,500

For women giving birth
1 in 9,100

From airplane crashes
1 in 167,000

From lightning
1 in 2 million

From asbestos in schools
1 in 11 million

Source: Robert Mitchell, Clark University

---

7   Alarmists will point out that all the specific risks of dying create the overall risk of dying. True. But no matter how much we reduce any specific risk, we'll still die from something, and many specific risks aren't very threatening. In the ABC program, Stossel tweaks Ralph Nader for seeing danger almost everywhere: hot dogs have too much fat; airplanes aren't adequately maintained; coffee has caffeine; rugs collect dust and cause indoor pollution. "Life is preparedness—the old Boy Scout motto, be prepared," Nader says. The trouble is that if you spend all your life preparing, you may miss out on living.

8   Of course, we should take sensible personal precautions and enact prudent safety and environmental regulations. But they should be sensible

and prudent. We should not overreact to every ghoulish incident or conceivable danger. The abduction and murder of Polly Klaas late last year was horrifying, but so was the kidnapping of the Lindbergh child in 1932. Cloistering children in generally safe neighborhoods is not a sensible reaction. The old, too, often senselessly barricade themselves indoors against imagined crime. We "give up some freedom," as Stossel says.

9   Likewise, misguided regulations based on exaggerated risk can waste lots of money. The asbestos panic was a costly mistake, as federal Judge Stephen Breyer shows in a new book, "Breaking the Vicious Circle: Toward Effective Risk Regulation." Leaving asbestos in buildings poses almost no hazard; removing it increases the danger by putting asbestos particles into the air. Breyer cites a toxic-waste case in which the company objected to the final cleanup. The site was already so clean that children could eat some dirt 70 days a year without significant harm. Why do more? "There were no dirt-eating children playing in the area," he writes, "for it was a swamp."

10   The standard retort is: A rich country like ours can afford absolute safety. No we can't. Regulatory costs raise prices or taxes. Our incomes are lower than they might be. That's okay if we receive lots of benefits—much cleaner air or healthier food. But it's not okay if the benefits are trivial or nonexistent.

11   Good judgment requires good information. Every imagined danger or adverse social trend is not as ghastly as it seems. Consciousness-raising can be truth-lowering. We fall prey to our fears and fantasies. We create synthetic truths from a blend of genuine evidence, popular prejudice and mass anxiety. Psycho-facts are not real facts. We should try to tell the difference.

■ Comprehension Check ·

Finish each of the following sentences by filling in a word or phrase that best completes the idea.

1. Psycho-facts are beliefs that are _____ by evidence.

2. Samuelson blames several groups of people for spreading psycho-facts, including

   _____ .

3. Many of our fears are the result of our desire for a world without _____

   _____ .

4. The odds of dying from lightning are _____

   _____ .

5. Samuelson believes that we are overreacting to _____

_____

Answer the following with a T (true) or F (false).

	T	**F**
6. Although statistics do not show an increase in crime, many people believe that violent crime has increased.	___	___
7. Samuelson opposes safety regulations.	___	___
8. Journalists and television help create mass anxiety.	___	___
9. Our country can afford and should want to pay for absolute safety.	___	___
10. America's standard of living has declined in the past twenty-five years.	___	___

Expanding Vocabulary

Match each word in the left column with its definition in the right column by placing the correct letter in the space next to each word.

_____ trafficking (2)   a. withdrawing from life

_____ inferences (2)   b. changed position

_____ fluctuated (3)   c. believable

_____ plausible (4)   d. sensible or cautious

_____ tweaks (7)   e. dealing in

_____ enact (8)   f. teases

_____ prudent (8)   g. conclusions reached from evidence

_____ cloistering (8)   h. make a statute or law

Analysis of Content and Strategies

1. Samuelson has coined the term "psycho-fact." What are some of his examples of psycho-facts?

_____

_____

2. What makes his term an effective label? _____

_____

3. What are the sources or causes of people's fears? _____

_____

_____

4. Are there other sources you would add to Samuelson's?

_____

For Discussion and Reflection

1. Can you add to Samuelson's list of psycho-facts? How do you know that your items are not real facts?

2. Do you agree with Samuelson that many people are afraid of dangers that are not as serious as those people believe? Why or why not?

3. Have you been believing in some of Samuelson's psycho-facts? (Consider, for example, the table on the odds of dying.) If so, has he changed your views on any of your fears? Why or why not?

CHAPTER 3

Concentrating on Main Ideas

In this chapter you will learn:

■ To identify a paragraph's topic

■ To understand the main idea in paragraphs

■ To recognize supporting details

■ To understand the main idea (thesis) in longer selections

Have you ever tried to tell a joke only to have your listener not laugh? The listener just "didn't get it." This is a frustrating experience for you as well as for your listener. A joke makes a point. We laugh when we "get it." If there is no laughter, the meaning of the joke has not been understood. (Or, it is a very bad joke!) And what is more distressing than trying to explain a joke to someone who did not understand it the first time through. Repeating the details will not do much good if the listener doesn't understand what they *mean*.

Consider the cartoon shown in Figure 3.1. What makes it funny? What is the point or idea developed through the frames? What different meanings of the word *stand* help to make the joke? Briefly explain the joke in the space below.

_____

_____

_____

_____

_____

FIGURE 3.1

Source: Reprinted with special permission of King Features Syndicate

Just as we need to understand the idea of a joke or cartoon to see what is funny, so we need to read for the main idea to "get the point" of what we read. Details, examples, reasons: they lose much of their value if we fail to see what they add up to, what they *mean.*

■ THE ROLE OF PREVIOUS KNOWLEDGE

Many jokes and cartoons are topical; they refer to someone or some event recently in the news. Such jokes will fail to amuse those who are unfamiliar with the news story. As you learned in Chapter 2, the knowledge you bring to your reading does much to shape the reading context. Those who are familiar with the topic will read the material more easily and with greater comprehension than those who know little or nothing about the topic. Knowledgeable readers readily identify main ideas, see how the parts fit together, and predict what is coming. They are able to "push through" the material.

Readers with little knowledge of the topic need to use all the strategies of active reading to aid their understanding. Review in your mind the prereading steps. What are they designed to accomplish? They help you create a comfortable reading context for new or difficult material. Activating existing knowledge and prereading the selection help readers create a context similar to those more familiar with the topic.

When you plunge into relatively unfamiliar or difficult material, comprehending rests upon your ability to identify the topic, recognize main ideas, and see how supporting details develop the main ideas. Instead of just reading words, you need to organize those words into clusters of meaning. You need both to find the general point in the details and see how the details explain the general point.

Some readers are better than others at stating the main idea or general point of a passage. They seem to just naturally think at a general level, but they may have trouble remembering details from their reading. Others are good at the details, but they sometimes have trouble expressing the point of the details. Over lunch with friends, one person observes that professional athletes make too much money. Another responds: "Oh, you mean that Michael Jordan was overpaid." The first one is thinking about professional athletes *in general.* The other understands the idea best if it is expressed in the *example* of Michael Jordan. Reflect for a moment on this conversation. Are you more likely to think in general or specific terms? And when you read, are you better at remembering the general points or supporting details? If you lean one way or the other, then when you read make a conscious effort to work on that part of the process that is less natural for you. If you are reading to learn—as you are when studying a textbook, for example—you need to learn the details (the parts of the atom) as well as the general ideas (how atoms and molecules explain the behavior of matter in the natural world). In other reading contexts you may not need to recall all of the details, but you will be expected to know the main ideas.

■ IDENTIFYING THE TOPIC

One useful way to come to an understanding of the main idea in a passage is to start by identifying the topic, the subject under discussion. Identifying the topic requires a generalization about the material; it answers the question: what is the passage about? If I talk about apples and strawberries and grapefruit and peaches, what am I talking about? The four specifics are all fruit. My topic, then, is fruit; fruit is the general category into which my four specific examples can be placed.

EXERCISE 3-1 Practice in Generalizing

For each of the lists below state the general idea that includes the specific items. The first list has been done for you.

Details	Generalization
1. pens, pencils, chalk, crayons	*writing instruments*
2. football, hockey, tennis, skiing	_____
3. chemistry, botany, geology, physics	_____
4. novels, plays, poems, short stories	_____
5. Bush, Reagan, Carter, Clinton	_____

When responding to the fifth list of details in the exercise, did you put down "presidents" or "recent presidents"? The first answer is not wrong, but the second answer is better. Why? Because it is more precise. When identifying the topic of a passage, try to make it general enough to cover the material in the passage but not so general that the label could apply to many passages. Remember that the topic is what unifies the specific details in the passage.

Read the following paragraph from a history of Western civilization.

> Beginning in the late tenth century, many new cities or towns were founded, particularly in northern Europe. Usually, a group of merchants established a settlement near some fortified stronghold, such as a castle or monastery. Castles were particularly favored since they were usually located along major routes of transportation or at the intersection of two such trade routes; the lords of the castle also offered protection. If the settlement prospered and expanded, new walls were built to protect it.
>
> Jackson J. Spielvogel, *Western Civilization*

What is this paragraph about? The opening sentence tells us that it is about "cities or towns" in the "tenth century" in "Europe." But, is it about *all* towns in tenth-century Europe? No, as the opening sentence announces, it is about the *founding* of *new* towns. The rest of the paragraph contains specific details about how (by merchants) and where (near castles and trade or transportation routes) the new towns were established. The paragraph's topic: the founding of towns in tenth-century Europe.

The following exercise offers practice in identifying topics.

 EXERCISE 3-2 Identifying the Topic

For each of the following paragraphs, state the paragraph's topic in the space provided.

1. The mass media are expensive to set up and operate. The equipment and facilities require major investment. Meeting the payroll requires a bankroll. Print media must buy paper by the ton. Broadcasters have gigantic electricity bills to pump their messages through the ether.

   John Vivian, *The Media of Mass Communications*

   Topic: _____

2. The soil and climate of New England encouraged a diversified agriculture and industry. Staple products like tobacco did not flourish, as in the South. Black slavery, although tried, could not exist profitably on small farms, especially where the surest crop was stones. No broad, fertile hinterland, comparable to that of the South, beckoned men inland. The

mountains ran fairly close to the shore, and the rivers were generally short and rapid.

Bailey and Kennedy, *The American Pageant: A History of the Republic*

Topic: _____

3. We live in an age of statistics. Day in and day out we are bombarded with a staggering array of numbers: Billy Joel has sold over 50 million albums; 12 percent of American children under the age of eighteen suffer from some form of psychological illness; France produces almost 2 billion gallons of wine every year; the literacy rate of Iraq is 71 percent; Americans consume more than 700 million pounds of peanut butter annually.

Stephen E. Lucas, *The Art of Public Speaking*

Topic: _____

4. It may be difficult for some of us—particularly those who may have heard or seen him only in his later years—to realize what a great instrumentalist and important American musician Louis Armstrong was. His influence is everywhere. Anyone, anywhere in the world, in any musical idiom, who writes for trumpet is inevitably influenced by what Louis Armstrong and his progeny have shown can be done with the instrument—not only in terms of extending its range, but also in the variety of mutes, half-valve effects, and the like, that have expanded its timbral potential. All of our jazz, real and popularized, is different because of him, and our popular singers of all kinds are deeply in his debt.

Joseph Machlis, *The Enjoyment of Music*

Topic: _____

■ UNDERSTANDING MAIN IDEAS

Identifying the topic of a passage is a good first step to understanding the idea or point of the passage, but it isn't quite the same thing. The topic answers the question: What is the passage about? The *main idea* answers the question: What does the writer have to say about the topic? Topics are like titles to books or articles; they announce the work's subject. The main idea is the central point of the work. Main ideas are what writers assert about their subjects.

Let's go back to the topic *fruit* to illustrate. My supporting details are: apples, strawberries, grapefruit, and peaches. My topic is fruit. What main idea could I assert about these details? There are many possibilities; here are two:

> Main idea #1: My favorite fruits are apples, strawberries, grapefruit, and peaches. (I could then develop a paragraph that explains why these are my favorites.)

> Main idea #2: Fruits should form a part of any healthy diet. (I could then explain the nutritional benefits of fruit, using my four fruits as examples.)

Do not be confused by the various terms used to discuss a work's main idea. Other terms include: controlling idea, key point, and thesis. Writing instructors most frequently use the term *thesis* to refer to a writer's main idea in a complete work, usually an essay. Reading instructors prefer the term *main idea* because it is more universal; that is, it can refer to the key point in a paragraph, a section of a textbook, an essay, or a longer work. Try to keep focused on your task without letting terminology confuse you. As a reader you need to understand the difference between a passage's topic and its main idea and be able to state, clearly, the main idea in any passage that you read.

Writers often give help to readers by using headings and subheadings and by following patterns of writing that are so widely used we call them *conventions of writing.* In most textbooks and many articles you will find major headings and subheadings. Announcing each section's topic, the headings let you concentrate on identifying the section's main idea. Additionally, the main idea of a paragraph is frequently stated in one sentence known as a *topic sentence.* (Even though it is called a "topic" sentence, it actually states the paragraph's main idea.) Look for these devices as aids to reading, but keep in mind that not all writers are so helpful.

> *Remember:* The topic is what the passage is about. The main idea is the writer's assertion about the topic. It is the general point to be understood from the passage; it is the "glue" that unifies the passage. Supporting details are the specifics that develop and explain the main idea. They may include examples, definitions, explanations, and reasons.

Here are specific steps you can take to identify main ideas.

Guidelines for Identifying Main Ideas

1. *Use headings.* Headings announce the section's topic. Often they are in **bold** type. Identifying the topic is the first step to recognizing the main idea.

2. *Ask questions.* If there are no headings, ask yourself: "What is this passage about?" to determine the topic. Then ask: "What does the writer assert—or want me to understand—about this topic?"

3. *List details.* If you are having trouble generalizing to recognize the topic, make a list of the details. Then ask: "what do these details have in common?"
4. *Look for general statements.* The main idea is a more general statement than the details that support it. Underline the most general statements and then ask: "Which statement best represents the main point of the passage?"
5. *State the main idea as a complete sentence.* To assure that you move from topic to main idea, make certain that you can state the main idea in a complete sentence. A word (fruit) or phrase (writing instruments) can state a topic, but only a complete sentence can make a point about the topic.

The following exercise will give you practice in recognizing the kinds of statements that announce topics, provide details, and state main ideas.

EXERCISE 3-3 Distinguishing Among Topics, Main Ideas, and Supporting Details.

For each cluster of statements identify the topic, the main idea, and the supporting detail. The first one has been completed for you.

I.

__*topic*__ Role of aristocratic women in medieval society

__*main idea*__ Aristocratic women had numerous opportunities for playing important roles.

__*detail*__ Keeping financial accounts, both for the household and the landed estate, alone required considerable financial knowledge.

Jackson J. Spielvogel, Western Civilization

II.

_____ There are two types of signals for transmitting data: analog and digital.

_____ Analog versus Digital Transmission

_____ With **analog transmission** the signals form a continuous wave pattern, as demonstrated by human speech.

Fuller and Manning, Computers and Information Processing

III.

_____   If you wish to feel greater calmness, behave in a calm way.

_____   **Act Calm to Feel Calm**

_____   Evidence suggests that you can bring on certain emotions by behaving as if you were feeling those emotions.
Beebe and Beebe, _Public Speaking: An Audience-Centered Approach_

IV.

_____   Ceramics employ a wide variety of chemical compounds, and useful ceramic bodies are nearly always mixtures of several compounds.

_____   **Silicate ceramics,** which include the traditional pots, dishes, and bricks, are made from aluminosilicate clay minerals.

_____   **Composition and Structure of Ceramics**
Oxtoby, Nachitrieb, and Freeman, _Chemistry: Science of Change_

V.

_____   **The Mass Media: Source of Powerful Symbols**

_____   Like females, the elderly are underrepresented on television, in advertisements, and in the most popular magazines.

_____   Just as the mass media help to shape our ideas of gender and relationships between men and women, so they also influence our ideas of the elderly.
James N. Heslin, _Sociology: A Down-To-Earth Approach_

VI.

_____   Organisms assimilate a wide variety of chemical elements.

_____   **Life requires inorganic nutrients.**

_____   After hydrogen, carbon, and oxygen, the elements required in greatest amount are nitrogen, phosphorus, sulfur, potassium, calcium, magnesium, and iron.
Robert E. Ricklefs, _Ecology_

Identifying a Paragraph's Topic Sentence

We have already noted that the main idea of a paragraph is often stated in one of the sentences, called the *topic sentence.* The rest of the paragraph contains supporting details that explain, develop, or illustrate the topic sentence in some way. See if you can identify the topic sentence and the supporting details in the following paragraph. Underline the topic sentence and circle the number of each sentence that contains a supporting detail.

> (1) Violence in college relationships seems to be manifested not only in dating behavior but also in the amount of acquaintance rape cases that occur on campuses. (2) Recent studies on acquaintance rape show that a high percentage of the female college population has suffered sexual victimization, usually by a person they previously knew. (3) For example, Rappaport and Burkhart (1984) found that more than 22% of all the freshman and sophomore women in their study had been forced to have sex against their will. (4) Koss (1985), in a national survey on relationships between men and women, reported that one-fourth of the women studied were victims of rape, and almost 90% of them knew their assailant.
>
> Aizerman and Kelley, "The Incidence of Violence and Acquaintance Rape
> in Dating Relationships Among College Men and Women"

Did you underline the first sentence? It announces the topic (violence in college relationships) and makes the assertion that this violence is evidenced in the amount of date rape in college relationships. Observe that sentences 2, 3, and 4 all provide support for the topic sentence or main idea. The second sentence is a generalization, but it is one drawn from many studies of college date rape. The third and fourth sentences then provide data from two studies as concrete evidence. Also note the signal words that announce specifics: "Recent studies," "For example," and "Koss . . . reported."

Placement of the Topic Sentence

You found, in the paragraph on violence, that the topic sentence is the first sentence in the paragraph. The most frequent placement of a stated topic sentence is as a paragraph's first sentence. Now you know why prereading involves reading headings, the opening paragraph, and the first sentence of each remaining paragraph of the selection. Headings and opening paragraphs announce a selection's topic; the opening paragraph may also contain a main idea statement; and the main idea of each paragraph is most commonly expressed in the first sentence. Your prereading of these parts will give you a good quick look at the work's key ideas.

Many reading and writing textbooks have adopted the practice of visualizing the shape of a paragraph based on the location of the topic sentence. If the topic sentence is considered the core or base of a paragraph, then the widest part of the triangle can be used to designate the topic sentence's placement, as shown in the diagram below.

Here is another example of a paragraph that begins with the main idea.

> *The television audience is not only the most heterogeneous public ever assembled but also the most nonselective.* Most viewers watch by the clock and not by the program. Viewing is a ritual governed by styles of life and time. Different kinds of programs serve the same basic formula designed to assemble viewers for the most profit and sell them at the least cost. The classifications of the print era with their relatively sharp differentiations between news, drama, documentary, and so on, do not apply as much to television. Heavy viewers watch more of everything. Different time and program segments complement and reinforce each other as they present aspects of the same symbolic world.
>
> Gerbner and Gross, "The Violent Face of Television and Its Lessons"

Another placement of the topic sentence is at the end of a paragraph. In this pattern, the topic sentence states what the details "add up to" or prove. An example of this pattern is shown in the paragraph following the diagram below.

> To meet their expenses, the mass media sell their product in two ways. Either they derive their income from selling a product directly to mass audiences, as do the movie, record and book industries, or they derive their income from advertisers who pay for the access to mass audiences that the media provide, as do newspapers, magazines, radio and television. *In short, the mass media operate in a capitalistic environment, and, with few exceptions, they are in business to make money.*
>
> John Vivian, *The Media of Mass Communications*

Although the first sentence sounds like a generalization that could be a topic sentence, the last sentence is more general. Note also the signal words "in short" to announce the paragraph's summary statement: the media are in business to make money.

Occasionally you will find the topic sentence in the middle of a paragraph. Often, with this placement, the writer begins with a transition from the previous paragraph or with several details to catch the reader's attention before stating the main idea. The topic sentence is then followed by additional details. The shape of this kind of paragraph looks like this:

Details

Main Idea

Details

Here is an example of this diamond-shaped pattern.

The average American preschooler watches more than twenty-seven hours of television per week. This might not be bad if these young children understood what they were watching. But they don't. Up through ages three and four, most children are unable to distinguish fact from fantasy on TV, and remain unable to do so despite adult coaching. *In the minds of young children, television is a source of entirely factual information regarding how the world works.* There are no limits to their credulity. To cite one example, an Indiana school board had to issue an advisory to young children that, no, there is no such thing as Teenage Mutant Ninja Turtles. Children had been crawling down storm drains looking for them.

Brandon S. Centerwall, "Television and Violent Crime"

The paragraph begins with a startling statistic—the number of hours per week that preschoolers watch television—and then moves to the even more distressing fact that these children do not know what they are watching. This idea, the paragraph's main idea, is then stated in a positive rather than negative structure: children believe that what they are watching factually recreates the real world. A specific example then follows to illustrate children's inability to distinguish between fact and fiction on TV.

One final placement pattern for a paragraph's topic sentence should be noted. In some paragraphs the topic sentence appears both at the beginning and the end of the passage. The writer repeats or, more accurately, restates the paragraph's main idea. Sometimes the restatement at the end complements or extends, in some way, the first statement of the main idea. Paragraphs with this structure provide a nice sense of completeness because the details are "wrapped within" the two statements of the main idea. An example of this pattern follows the diagram of its structure.

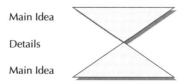

Main Idea

Details

Main Idea

Media-depicted violence scares far more people than it inspires to violence, and this, according to George Gerbner, a leading researcher on screen violence, leads some people to believe the world is more dangerous than it really is. Garbner calculates that 1 in 10 television characters is involved in violence in any given week. In real life, the chances are only about 1 in 100 per *year*. People who watch a lot of television, Gerbner found, see their own chances of being involved in violence nearer the distorted television level than their local crime statistics or even their own experience would suggest. *It seems that television violence leads people to think they are in far greater real-life jeopardy than they really are.*

John Vivian, The Media of Mass Communications

The following exercise will give you practice in stating the topic, identifying the main idea by locating the topic sentence, and recognizing details. If you have trouble, review the sample paragraphs and their various shapes and also use the guidelines for identifying main ideas (see pp. 72–73).

Exercise 3-4 Recognizing the Topic, Locating the Topic Sentence, and Stating Details

After reading each paragraph, state the topic, list the chief details, and then underline the paragraph's topic sentence.

1. Most of us pass through two stages in our attitudes toward statistical conclusions. At first we tend to accept them, and the interpretations placed on them, uncritically. In discussion or argument, we wilt the first time somebody quotes statistics, or even asserts that he has seen some. But then we are misled so often by skillful talkers and writers who deceive us with correct facts that we come to distrust statistics entirely, and assert that "statistics can prove anything"—implying, of course, that statistics can prove nothing.

Wallis and Roberts, Statistics: A New Approach

Topic: _____

Details: _____

_____

_____

_____

2. Today, most of the books that shape our culture are adapted to other media, which expands their influence. Magazine serialization put Henry Kissinger's memoirs in more hands than did the publisher of the book. More people have seen Carl Sagan on television than have read his

books. Stephen King thrillers sell spectacularly, especially in paperback, but more people see the movie renditions. Books have a trickle-down effect through other media, their impact being felt even by those who cannot or do not read them. Although people are more in touch with other mass media day to day, books are the heart of creating American culture and passing it on to new generations.

John Vivian, *The Media of Mass Communications*

Topic: _____

Details: _____

_____

_____

_____

3. It is hard to stretch a small vocabulary to make it do all the things that intelligent people require of words. It's like trying to plan a series of menus from the limited resources of a poverty-stricken, war-torn country compared to planning such a series in a prosperous, stable country. Words are one of our chief means of adjusting to all the situations of life. The better control we have over words, the more successful our adjustment is likely to be.

Bergen Evans, *The Word-A-Day Vocabulary Builder*

Topic: _____

Details: _____

_____

_____

_____

4. As the size of the listening audience increased, so too did the cost of air time. At the same time, however, radio's novelty began to wane. Audiences no longer granted the medium their uncritical attention. Consequently, to minimize cost and magnify audience attention, other means of audience enticement including music, song, and testimony from supporters were added to unadorned speeches. Campaigning politicians also turned from long messages to shorter ones. In 1928 the usual time

purchased by candidates was one hour. In 1980 the typical political message was thirty seconds long.

Kathleen Hall Jamieson, Packaging the Presidency: A History
and Criticism of Presidential Campaign Advertising

Topic: _____

Details: _____

_____

_____

_____

5. Many people find it helpful to define media by whether the thrust of their content is entertainment or information. By this definition, newspapers almost always are considered an information medium, and audio recording and movies are considered entertainment. As a medium, books both inform and entertain. So do television and radio, although some networks, stations and programs do more of one than the other. The same is true with magazines, with some titles geared more for informing, some for entertaining.

John Vivian, The Media of Mass Communications

Topic: _____

Details: _____

_____

_____

_____

Paragraphs with an Implied Main Idea

Some paragraphs contain details but no topic sentence. The details are not random. They are on the same topic, but the main idea that they support is implied rather than stated. We, the readers, must infer from the details the point to be understood. Inferring is not the same as guessing. Inferring means drawing a conclusion from evidence. The author expects us to be able to understand what the details add up to so that we can state the paragraph's main idea. Drawing inferences will be discussed at length in Chapter 9, but since we want to be thorough in examining the different placement patterns of the topic sentence, we need to include, in this discussion, the possibility of an implied rather than stated main idea. Paragraphs with an unstated topic sentence are often—but not exclusively—found in narrative and descriptive writing. Let's look at the following paragraph with an unstated main idea.

> When a colonial housewife went to the village well to draw water for her family, she saw friends, gathered gossip, shared the laughs and laments of her neighbors. When her great-great-granddaughter was blessed with running water, and no longer had to go to the well, this made life easier, but also less interesting. Electricity, mail delivery and the telephone removed more reasons for leaving the house. And now the climax of it all is Television.
>
> Daniel J. Boorstin, "Television: More Deeply Than We Suspect, It Has Changed All of Us"

The first question to ask is: "What is the paragraph about?" That is, what is the paragraph's topic? Here are three possibilities. Let's think about which best states the paragraph's topic.

1. The development of modern conveniences
2. The great achievement of television
3. The isolating nature of technological advances, especially television

If you focus on the paragraph's listing of new conveniences developed over time, you might select topic #1. If you focus on the word *climax* in the last sentence, you might select topic #2. But if you think carefully about the details and note such words as *shared* and *less interesting*, you recognize that the writer thinks something has been lost with the "advantages" of modern conveniences. When information comes to our homes, we do not have to leave them. We become isolated from our community. We conclude (infer from our study) that the best statement of topic is the third one.

What, then, is the paragraph's main idea? What does the writer want us to understand about the topic? Although there is more than one way to state the main idea, we might say this: *Although technological advances provide convenience, they unfortunately also separate us from others, from a sense of community.* The writer sees these conveniences as a mixed blessing at best. Since the paragraph ends with television, we can anticipate that the next paragraph will develop the idea that television is the most separating of all, even though it seems to bring the world into our living rooms.

The following exercise will give you practice in identifying the main idea when there is no stated topic sentence.

EXERCISE 3-5 Identifying the Main Idea When There Is an Unstated (Implied) Main Idea

After reading each paragraph, state the paragraph's topic, list key details, and then state the main idea.

1. The corner of the office where I work has no windows. The climate is what they call controlled. I can be there all day without knowing if it's hot or cold outside. I commute in a machine on pavement, following the

directions of red and green lights. My work day is determined by a clock that remains the same through all tides, moons and seasons.

Ellen Goodman, "Content to Be in My Place"

Topic: _____

Details: _____

_____

_____

_____

Main Idea: _____

_____

2. About $90 billion is spent annually in the United States on various media. Approximately $30 billion goes to books, newspapers, and magazines, while the remainder is spent on audio-visual media, such as records, compact discs, videotapes, and movies (U.S. Department of Commerce, 1991). In terms of time rather than dollars spent, however, television is undoubtedly the most popular public medium. More than 98 percent of U.S. households have at least one television; almost 69 percent have videocassette recorders, and 56 percent subscribe to cable television (U.S. Department of Commerce, 1991). It is estimated that average household viewing time is six hours per day (Staples and Jones, 1985).

Curran and Renzetti, *Social Problems*

Topic: _____

Details: _____

_____

_____

_____

Main Idea: _____

_____

3. In the war against tobacco, we do not expect help from the tobacco industry. If someone were to call upon the tobacco industry to cut back production as a matter of social conscience and concern for public health, we would regard that person as simple-minded, if not frankly deranged. Oddly enough, however, people have persistently assumed that the television industry is somehow different—that it is useful to appeal to its social conscience. This was true in 1969 when the National Commission on the Causes and Prevention of Violence published its recommendations for the television industry. It was equally true in 1989 when the U.S. Congress passed an anti-violence bill that granted television industry executives the authority to hold discussions on the issue of television violence without violating antitrust laws. Even before the law was passed, the four networks stated that there would be no substantive changes in their programming. They have been as good as their word.

Brandon S. Centerwall, "Television and Violent Crime"

Topic: _____

Details: _____

_____

_____

_____

Main Idea: _____

_____

■ DISTINGUISHING AMONG SUPPORTING DETAILS

So far in this chapter we have concentrated on identifying main ideas. To pursue this goal we have distinguished between a stated topic sentence and all supporting details. Not all details are alike, however. In many passages support can be divided between major and minor details. Think of the major details as providing the primary explanation and support for the main idea, and think of the minor details as providing support for, and examples of, the major details. The chart in Figure 3.2 illustrates the basic pattern of main idea and details.

As a reader you may delight in the minor details, especially if you learn best from specifics. These details are interesting or amusing or startling—and fun to remember. But usually it is the major details—the reasons, explanations, definitions—that you need to understand and remember, along with the main idea,

■ **FIGURE 3.2**

Basic Paragraph Structure

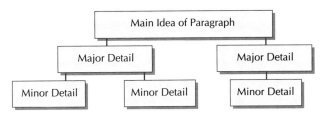

to really be in command of the material. It is important, then, to be able to distinguish between major and minor details.

The following paragraph on leadership illustrates the distinction between major details and less significant minor details.

topic sentence

Leadership is as much a question of timing as anything else. The leader must appear on the scene at a moment when people are looking for leadership, as Churchill did in 1940, as Roosevelt did in 1933, as Lenin did in 1917. And when he comes, he must offer a simple, eloquent message. *minor details*

major details

Michael Korda, "How to Be a Leader"

Observe how the paragraph has been annotated to identify its parts. The topic sentence (the paragraph's first sentence and the passage's main idea) has been underlined twice. The two major details in the paragraph have been underlined once. The first major detail extends the main idea: a leader must emerge when people are looking for leadership. The second major detail explains what the leader must do to become a leader, once he or she has appeared at the right time. The passage contains three minor details, the three specific examples of leaders from the past. Notice that Korda presents them in order going back in time. Notice also that they are part of a sentence that contains a major detail. How the material is organized into sentences is not the issue here. What matters is separating key ideas from examples of those ideas. Korda's essay is not about Churchill or Roosevelt or Lenin; it is about the characteristics of leadership. To illustrate his points, Korda brings in examples of historical figures he expects his readers to know.

Here is another paragraph to examine. After reading it, underline the topic sentence twice and all major details once.

No sure-fire formula for creating a best-selling record has yet been found. Producers have great faith in concert appearances by the artist and in massive publicity campaigns, but these ploys have proved to be neither infallible nor indispensable. Highly touted albums collect dust on dealers' shelves, while those of, for example, Carole King, who almost never concertizes and actively avoids publicity, disappear from stock with gratifying rapidity. Her album *Tapestry* averaged three million discs in annual sales for four straight years, making it the best-selling album since the advent of rock.

Edith Borroff and Marjory Irvin, *Music in Perspective*

Did you decide that the first sentence is the paragraph's topic sentence? The rest of the paragraph provides evidence to support the idea that no one has a guaranteed method for producing a best-selling record. The major details are found in the second and third sentences, excluding the reference to Carole King in the third sentence. The fourth sentence completes the specific King example and so belongs in the minor-detail category. To make the distinction, ask yourself, "Is this paragraph about making successful records or about Carole King?" Such a question helps you see that King is an example provided to illustrate the ideas in the second and third sentences.

 EXERCISE 3-6 Identifying the Main Idea and Major Details

After reading, state each paragraph's topic, the major details, and the main idea. Some of the paragraphs have a stated topic sentence (the main idea); some have an implied topic sentence.

1. Through argument we can examine our own thoughts and beliefs. Our opinions can be challenged, requiring us to justify them. As we continue to rebuke the challenge we may discover underlying assumptions we did not know we had. This can enable us to see the world with a broadened perspective by illuminating the values we hold. Suppose you and I were to share a box of ice cream. If I assert that ice cream "A" is better than ice cream "B," you could claim the opposite. I might then present justification for my opinion, that "A" has nuts and chunks of chocolate. When you reply that you prefer smooth ice cream, I realize that my definition of good ice cream is based on chunkiness. I now know that not everyone likes chunky ice cream. I then argue that "A" has the best flavor. You counter that "B" costs considerably less than "A." While I place more value on the quality of the ice cream, you place more value on its affordability. The more we argue back and forth, the more we learn about the values each of us has and how strongly we cling to them.

Thom Raybold, "Why Argue?"

Topic: _____

Major Details: _____

_____

_____

_____

Main Idea: _____

_____

2. The wonder of dinosaurs also is that they are an enigma seemingly beyond solution. Science has explained so much: the divisibility of atoms and the nature of subatomic particles; the decipherable code of heredity contained in DNA; the earth's restless crust; gravity, electromagnetism, and the age of the solar system. Science has identified hundreds of species of dinosaurs, assembling their bones and dating their time on earth, but so much about the lives of these strange and monstrous creatures defies explication. It is reassuringly human of scientists that, when it comes to dinosaurs, they can be just as stricken with puzzlement as the next person and find themselves with little more to work with than their imaginations. Yet they persist in their search for solutions to the riddle, knowing they will never fully succeed but believing they will learn something about the greater mysteries of life. This is the wonder of humans, their faith that there is much about dinosaurs worth knowing.

John Noble Wilford, *The Riddle of the Dinosaur*

Topic: _____

Major Details: _____

_____

_____

_____

Main Idea: _____

_____

3. To understand the circumstances confronting contemporary Native Americans, we must begin with the fact that their ancestors emigrated to North America between 20,000 and 30,000 years ago. By the time the Europeans started to arrive, there were at least 400 distinct tribes inhabiting the territory north of the Rio Grande, and they encompassed a wide variety of cultural types. There were the hunting and fishing groups of Alaska and the sub-Arctic regions, as well as the herding and farming societies of Arizona and New Mexico. Some tribes were egalitarian like the Hopi of the southwest, while still others, such as the Kwakiutl of the Pacific northwest, were highly stratified with both chiefs and slaves. And

there was a vast array of languages spoken—at least 161—derived from about a dozen language stocks "as disparate as English and Russian" (Kitano, 1985:135; Mohawk, 1992; Dorris, 1981; Price, 1981.)

Curran and Renzetti, *Social Problems*

Topic: _____

Major Details: _____

_____

_____

_____

Main Idea: _____

_____

4. Here is a clue to the question of why our performance in government is worse than in other activities: because government offers power, excites that lust for power, which is subject to emotional drives—to narcissism, fantasies of omnipotence, and other sources of folly. The lust for power, according to Tacitus, "is the most flagrant of all the passions" and cannot really be satisfied except by power over others. Business offers a kind of power but only to the very successful at the very top, and even they, in our day, have to lay it down. Fords and Du Ponts, Hearsts and Pulitzers nowadays are subdued, and the Rockefeller who most conspicuously wanted power sought it in government. Other activities—in sports, science, the professions, and the creative and performing arts—offer various satisfactions but not the opportunity for power. They may appeal to status seeking and, in the form of celebrity, offer crowd worship and limousines and recognition by headwaiters, but these are the trappings of power, not the essence. Of course, mistakes and stupidities occur in nongovernmental activities too, but since these affect fewer people, they are less noticeable than they are in public affairs. Government remains the paramount field of unwisdom because it is there that men seek power over others—and lose it over themselves.

Barbara W. Tuchman, "The Persistence of Unwisdom in Government"

Topic: _____

Major Details: _____

_____

_____

_____

Main Idea: _____

_____

5. Human beings are made up mostly of water, in roughly the same percentage as water is to the surface of the earth. Our tissues and membranes,
   our brains and hearts, our sweat and tears—all reflect the same recipe for
   life, in which efficient use is made of those ingredients available on the
   surface of the earth. We are 23 percent carbon, 2.6 percent nitrogen, 1.4
   percent calcium, 1.1 percent phosphorus, with tiny amounts of roughly
   three dozen other elements. But above all we are oxygen (61 percent) and
   hydrogen (10 percent), fused together in the unique molecular combination known as water, which makes up 71 percent of the human body.

   Al Gore, _Earth in the Balance_

Topic: _____

Major Details: _____

_____

_____

_____

Main Idea: _____

_____

6. Because water is dense, it provides considerable support for organisms
   that, after all, are themselves mostly water. But organisms also contain
   bone, proteins, dissolved salts, and other materials that are more dense
   than salt or freshwater. These would cause organisms to sink were it not
   for a variety of mechanisms that reduce their density or retard their rate
   of sinking. Many fish have a swim bladder, a small gas-filled structure
   whose size can be adjusted to make the density of the body equal to that
   of the surrounding water (Denton 1960). Some large kelps, a type of sea-
   weed found in shallow waters, have analogous gas-filled organs. The
   kelps are attached to the bottom by holdfasts, and gas-filled bulbs float
   their leaves to the sunlit surface water.

   Robert E. Ricklefs, _Ecology_

Topic: _____

Major Details: _____

_____

_____

_____

Main Idea: _____

_____

■ IDENTIFYING MAIN IDEAS IN LONGER PASSAGES

This chapter has focused on understanding the parts of a paragraph so that each paragraph's main idea can be recognized and understood. Although we rarely read just one paragraph at a time, we need to be comfortable with the paragraph unit, because paragraphs function as building blocks in the shaping of articles and books. Still, before completing this focus on identifying main ideas, you should apply what you have learned to longer passages.

You have seen that paragraphs are composed of sentences of varying significance. One sentence may state the main idea; several more develop major details; and one or more may provide interesting, but sometimes less significant, examples. If you are anticipating that longer selections will follow a similar pattern, you are on target—with some qualifications.

Most essays, articles, or editorials establish one main idea or thesis that is either stated or implied. The thesis is then developed and supported with levels of details that you have already observed in paragraphs. The only difference with the longer article is that a paragraph's main idea becomes a major detail in support of an essay's thesis. The result is a pattern of four, rather than three, levels of significance. The chart in Figure 3.3 illustrates the more complex structure of longer passages. Depending upon reading purpose, you may be content to concentrate only on the work's thesis and major details (the main idea of each paragraph). You still have to read each paragraph, though, because you do not know if the main idea will be stated or implied. If it is stated, you have to read to find it. If it is implied, you have to read to see what point the details make. The "minor" details are important because they teach us what the writer wants us to understand. They just may not need to be remembered—or learned—once they have served their purpose in the article.

Sections of textbook chapters may be viewed as short articles. As you have learned, the section heading announces the section's topic. Each section is usually unified around a controlling idea that is most likely presented in either the

■ **F**IGURE **3.3**

The Pattern of Ideas and Details in Longer Passages

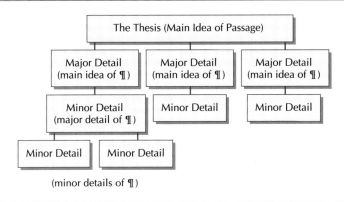

(minor details of ¶)

first or last paragraph (or in both places). If the similarity to articles holds up, you can then anticipate that the topic sentences of the other paragraphs present major details and that the remaining sentences present minor details that develop and illustrate the major details. All the details work together to support the section's main idea.

Sometimes textbook sections are not exactly like articles. A section may have two or three interrelated main ideas and have few, if any, minor details. If you think for a minute about the purpose of a textbook, you may understand why this difference can be found. The primary purpose of textbooks is to present information—a lot of information—about a subject. Articles, on the other hand, may combine information with persuasion, with the desire to have readers see a particular subject their way. The essayist may have a thesis and only two or three major details—reasons or explanations—to make that thesis convincing to readers. The textbook writer, on the other hand, has organized an enormous amount of information around a number of topics. You may find that most of the details within a section are important and need to be learned. Still, you want to read first for the main ideas and major details and see how these elements give structure to the material. You will remember more of the details once you see how they fit into each section's pattern of organization.

To practice with longer passages from textbooks, read the following section from *The American Pageant: A History of the Republic* (6th ed.) by Thomas A. Bailey and David M. Kennedy, both historians who have taught at Stanford University. Remember your reading strategy: prepare, read actively, and respond. Preview the selection by noting the heading and reading the topic sentences that have been underlined. Consider that your purpose is reading for your U.S. history course. As you read, add your own annotations to mark major details and think how you would state the section's main idea. Respond to the exercise that follows. Some parts of the exercise have been started for you.

Jeffersonian Idealism and Idealists

1   Leading the anti-Federalist forces was Thomas Jefferson. Lanky and re-laxed in appearance, lacking personal aggressiveness, weak-voiced, and unable to deliver a rabble-rousing speech, he became a master political organizer through his ability to lead men rather than drive them. His strongest appeal was to the middle class and to the underpriviledged—the "dirt" farmers, the laborers, the artisans, and the small shopkeepers.

2   Liberal-thinking Jefferson, with his aristocratic head set on a farmer's frame, was a bundle of inconsistencies. By one set of tests he should have been a Federalist, for he was a Virginia aristocrat and slaveowner who lived in an imposing hilltop mansion at Monticello. A so-called traitor to his upper class, Jefferson cherished uncommon sympathy for the common man, especially the downtrodden, the oppressed, and the persecuted. As he wrote in 1800, "I have sworn upon the altar of God eternal hostility against every form of tyranny over the mind of man."

3   Jeffersonian Republicans, or Democratic-Republicans, as they were called, demanded a weak central regime. They believed that the best government was the one that governed least. The bulk of the power, Jefferson argued, should be retained by the states. There the people, in intimate contact with local affairs, could keep a more vigilant eye on their public servants. Otherwise, a dictatorship might develop. Central authority—a kind of necessary evil—was to be kept at a minimum through a strict interpretation of the Constitution. The national debt, which Jefferson regarded as a curse illegitimately bequeathed to later generations, was to be paid off.

4   Jeffersonians, themselves primarily agrarians, insisted that there should be no special privileges for special classes, particularly manufacturers. Agriculture, to Jefferson, was the favored branch of the economy. He regarded farming as essentially ennobling; it kept men away from wicked cities, out in the sunshine and close to the sod—and God. Most of his followers naturally came from the agricultural South and Southwest.

5   Above all, Jefferson advocated the rule of the people. But he did not propose thrusting the ballot into the hands of *every* adult white male. He favored government *for* the people, but not by *all* the people—only by those men who were literate enough to inform themselves and wear the mantle of American citizenship worthily. Universal education would have to precede universal suffrage. The ignorant, he argued, were incapable of self-government. But he had profound faith in the reasonableness and teachableness of the masses, and in their collective wisdom when taught. His enduring appeal was to America's better self.

6   The open-minded Jefferson championed free speech, because without free speech the misdeeds of tyranny could not be exposed. He even went so far as to say that as between "a government without newspapers" and "newspapers without a government," he would choose the latter. No American statesman, except perhaps Lincoln, ever suffered more foul abuse from editorial pens; he might well have prayed for freedom *from* the Federalist press. Yet in 1801 he declared, "Error of opinion may be tolerated where reason is left free to combat it."

1. How does the heading announce the two topics covered in this section?

   _____

   _____

2. State one important minor detail in paragraph 1: _____

   _____

3. List two political positions held by Jeffersonian Republicans:

   1. *They wanted a weak central government.*_____

   2. _____

   _____

4. List four of Jefferson's political beliefs:

   1. *He was sympathetic to ordinary people and farmers.*_____

   2. _____

   3. _____

   4. _____

5. The authors include some details of Jefferson's appearance and personality. Do you think they would be important enough to learn for a test on the chapter? Why do you think the authors included these details?

   _____

6. Why do the writers say that Jefferson "was a bundle of inconsistencies"? Explain.

   _____

7. State the section's thesis (main idea) by completing the sentence started here: Jefferson and the Jeffersonians were idealists who believed

_____

Your study of this section reveals that many "minor" details in textbooks are actually important ideas that you will need to learn. For example, a student of U.S. history needs to know that Jefferson was an *agrarian*, someone who favored farmers.

The following exercise will give you additional practice with a longer passage. The reading is from *The Study of Economics* (5th ed.) by Turley Mings, a retired economics professor from San Jose State University.

 EXERCISE 3-7 **Identifying Main Ideas in Longer Passages**

Prepare and then read the following passage. As you annotate, underline each stated topic sentence. Then answer the questions that follow.

The New Industrial Revolution

1   The first Industrial Revolution was the second most important economic event in humankind's history, exceeded in significance only by the change from nomadic wandering to settled agriculture. We are now in the midst of a second Industrial Revolution, which also may have far-reaching effects. At the heart of this new revolution is a tiny piece of silicon, a "chip," less than the size of a fingernail. This chip is a microprocessor, which can do everything from controlling the shutter speed on a camera to weighing the cargo of a truck. When linked to input-output and programming units on separate chips, it forms the central processing unit (CPU) of a computer.

2   The public is most familiar with the uses of microprocessors in consumer goods such as pocket calculators, automobile controls, and personal computers, but it is their industrial applications that may ultimately have a greater impact on our lives. A Kansas City, Missouri, firm manufacturing air conditioning refrigeration systems for buildings formerly needed months of engineering work and production time to custom design and fabricate a system for a new building. Now it can do the job in a few weeks with only one-fourth the personnel formerly needed. It is able to do this through the use of CAD/CAM (computer-aided design/computer-aided manufacturing). CAD/CAM is to the second Industrial Revolution what the steam engine was to the first.

3   The biggest CAD project to date was the development of the Boeing 777, introduced in 1994. Previously, airplanes had been designed with the aid of physical mock-ups to ensure that the millions of parts fit together. With the 777, the fit was all done by means of an electronic mock-up on the computer.

4　　　The maximum use of CAD/CAM is the factory totally automated by computer-integrated manufacturing (CIM). What effect will CIM have on workers' jobs? Is the U.S. labor force going to be thrown out of work en masse? Will we see workers riot as they did when machines were installed in factories at the beginning of the Industrial Revolution? The answer to these questions is probably not. Just as the first Industrial Revolution was responsible for creating more jobs than the total number of workers employed when it began, this second revolution will very likely create more than enough new opportunities to offset the jobs eliminated. However, this technological revolution will radically alter the types of jobs available and most likely cause temporary dislocations. There will be jobs in the industries that produce the new equipment, jobs in operating and maintaining the equipment, and, most of all, jobs in a variety of new industries created by the reduction in costs due to CIM.

1. What is the section's topic? _____

_____

2. What invention has brought about a second Industrial Revolution?

_____

3. What is the topic sentence of paragraph 2? _____

_____

4. Give an example of a minor detail in paragraph 1 that you think is important enough to remember:

_____

5. Give an example of a minor detail in paragraph 1 that you find interesting but would probably not study for a test:

_____

6. What is the primary concern about the industrial use of CAD/CAM?

_____

7. How does the author respond to the fears associated with CIM? _____

_____

8. State the main idea or thesis of the section: _____

_____

| Selection I | **The Behavior of the Baboon Has Evolved in a Social Context** |

by **Robert E. Ricklefs**

The author of many scholarly articles, Dr. Ricklefs is a professor at the University of Pennsylvania. The following section is from his textbook *Ecology* published, in its third edition, in 1990.

Prepare

1. From what you know about the author and the selection, what can you predict about purpose and format or style?

   _____

   _____

2. State briefly what you expect to read about. _____

   _____

3. What do you already know about the topic? Respond using *one* of the methods described in Chapter 2.

   _____

   _____

4. Use the section heading to pose questions about the reading selection.

   _____

   _____

5. Preread the selection. Then read and annotate the selection. Finally, complete the comprehension and vocabulary checks that follow and answer the questions for discussion and reflection.

1   Social behavior has developed to different degrees in various animals, but nowhere has its study excited so much interest as in the subhuman primates, the closest relatives of man (Hinde 1983, Smuts et al. 1987). The social group consists of individuals of the same species, many of whom are closely related, upon whom the individual depends in part for its survival. The extent to which some animals have evolved in a social context

is demonstrated by their utter dependence upon the group for survival. Such is the case among the baboons of East Africa. In groups, these animals are avoided by all predators except lions; individual baboons, despite their strength and fearsome teeth, have very poor prospects. As a consequence of living in a social group, the individual adapts to an environment determined largely by the behavior of its group members. Whereas individual antagonism and avoidance are the general rules among nonsocial animals, group cohesiveness is absolutely necessary for the survival of such social animals as the baboon. This cohesiveness is promoted by the evolution of a high level of organization within the baboon troop.

2   Anthropologists S. L.Washburn and Irven DeVore (1961) studied baboons intensively at two localities in Kenya: a small park near Nairobi and the Amboseli Reserve at the foot of Mount Kilimanjaro. Months of careful observation revealed details of the social interactions among the baboons. For example, the troop, moving in an open savanna, has a spatial structure that reflects the roles of individuals (Figure 3–4). When resting in trees, baboons are normally safe from predators, but when they move across open grasslands without the immediate safety of trees, members of a troop assume an organized, defensive pattern. The less dominant adult males and some of the older juveniles occupy the periphery of the group. Females without infants and some of the older juveniles stay closer to the center. Females with infants and young juveniles, the most vulnerable members of the troop, move at the center with the dominant males. When the troop is threatened by a predator, the dominant males move into position between the center of the troop and the threat, while the rest of the baboons seek safety behind them. The importance of trees as potential escape routes is so great that baboons are not often found in areas lacking them, even if the habitat is otherwise perfectly suitable.

3   Interactions among individuals within the troop are many and diverse. The baboon has a strong tendency to stay with other baboons. Even within the troop, individuals form small, persistent friendship groups, within which there is much grooming and playing. Most baboons, particularly adult females, spend many hours each day grooming others that present themselves in the proper manner. To groom, one baboon parts the hair of the other with its hands and removes dirt, lice, ticks, and other objects with its hands and mouth. Grooming and play additionally strengthen the social bonds within the troop and promote its stability and cohesiveness.

4   Care of infant baboons is left to their mothers. The fathers' attentions are directed toward the well-being of the troop as a whole. After an infant has been weaned, its strong bond with its mother is replaced by looser associations within a play group of other juveniles. As young baboons reach adulthood, they enter the dominance hierarchy of the troop in which their position is determined by fighting, bluffing, and the relative rank of those with whom they associate most frequently. Several males may band together and enhance each other's position in the hierarchy, although

■ FIGURE 3.4

A moving troop of baboons. Females with infants riding on their backs are near the center, close to some large males. Small juveniles and young males are closer to the periphery of the troop.

individually they hold lower ranks. The position of an individual in the social hierarchy determines to some degree the amount of grooming it receives and its precedence over other baboons at a food and water source. Rank also extends privileges in mating with females.

5   The female is sexually receptive for about 1 week each month. At the beginning of her estrus cycle, a female often mates with the older juveniles and some of the subordinate males. But when she becomes fully fertile she mates only with the dominant males, who consequently sire most of the offspring in the troop. During the mating period, a male and female form what is called a consort pair for a few hours to several days; all other social functions are disrupted for them. Paired baboons generally move at the periphery of the troop, and the male can be extremely aggressive toward others. Baboons appear not to form long-lasting pair bonds, although lack of close association within the troop need not imply a weak social bond.

6   The baboon must cope with a wide range of behavioral interactions during its lifetime. The relationship between mother and infant, among individuals in a friendship or play group, among males in a dominance hierarchy or among those individuals that cooperate to defend their dominance rank, between the male and female in a consort pair—all produce a complex social environment.

7   Social adaptation does not occur independently of the physical and biotic environments (Crook 1970, Kummer 1971). Baboon troops in different habitats exhibit considerable variation in their social organization

(Stammbach 1987). For example, in the open savannas, an average-sized baboon troop, perhaps 40 individuals near Nairobi and 80 individuals in the Amboseli, may occupy a home range commonly of 2 to 6 square miles, but sometimes as large as 15 square miles (DeVore and Washburn 1964). In Uganda, the baboons inhabit forest or mixed forest-grassland where troops of 40 to 80 usually range over less than 2 square miles (Rowell 1967). In the Ugandan forests, the preferred food of the baboon, which is fruit, is much more plentiful than in the open savannas of Kenya. Thus the troops can satisfy their food needs in a smaller area.

8   The social organization within the troops of the two areas also differs in several important aspects. In the open savannas of Kenya, antagonistic interactions between individuals are more frequent than in Uganda. In the forest, an individual can go out of sight behind a bush until its antagonist "forgets" about the dispute between them. No such social escape exists on the open savannas. Forest baboons can fill their stomachs in an hour's feeding each day, whereas baboons of the open grasslands spend most of their time in search of food. Whereas grassland troops are often on the move, forest baboons are frequently engaged in grooming, playing, sitting, and drowsing. Because grassland baboons forage almost continuously, individuals interact less socially, and when they do they are more often antagonistic than are forest dwellers.

9   Hamadryas baboons, inhabiting the arid grassland at the southern edge of the Danakil Desert in Ethiopia, are organized at three social levels: (1) single males with several females and their offspring; (2) persistent bands of several of these single-male family groups; and (3) a larger troop composed of many bands (Kummer 1968, Dunbar 1983, Abegglen 1984; Figure 3–4). During the day, the hamadryas disperse to feed as small bands or single-male groups (Sigg and Stolba 1981). At dusk, they congregate in large numbers to sleep on cliffs, where they are protected from nocturnal predators. Before breaking up in the morning, the troop congregates near the roosting cliffs for a morning social hour, filled with grooming and, among infant and juvenile males, play. The gelada baboon, a cliff-roosting species of the Ethiopian highlands, forages in large groups when food is abundant but disperses into single-male groups during seasons of scarcity (Crook 1966, Dunbar 1983). In contrast to hamadryas, geladas do not appear to have distinct bands within the troop. The patas monkey of the dry grasslands of Uganda has an entirely different social structure, based solely on single-male groups that seldom meet and are rarely on friendly terms (Hall 1965). These studies, and others describing additional variations on the basic single-male groups, multi-male bands, and the larger troops of savanna-dwelling species, emphasize the role of the environment in determining social organization. The particular social structure itself influences adaptations of behavior that strengthen social bonds and both organize and facilitate social interactions.

Comprehension Check

Answer the following with a T (true) or F (false).

                          T   F

1. A baboon troop maintains cohesiveness by having little organization. ___ ___
2. Cohesiveness is strengthened by grooming and playing. ___ ___
3. Baboons do not establish rank or hierarchy. ___ ___
4. Social organization is not influenced by the demands of the environment. ___ ___
5. Baboons participate in only a few relationships in their lifetime. ___ ___
6. Grassland baboons are more antagonistic than forest-dwelling baboons. ___ ___

Expanding Vocabulary

Match each word in the left column with its definition in the right column by placing the correct letter in the space next to each word.

_____ predators (1)   a. grassland

_____ cohesiveness (1)   b. a ranking system

_____ savanna (2)   c. outside edge or boundary

_____ habitat (2)   d. make easier

_____ hierarchy (4)   e. unity

_____ periphery (5)   f. natural environment of an animal or plant

_____ biotic (7)   g. animals that capture and feed on other animals

_____ facilitate (9)   h. biological

Analysis of Content and Strategies

1. What is the selection's topic? _____

_____

2. What two sentences in paragraph 1, taken together, state the section's main idea or thesis?

_____

_____

_____

3. Which sentence in paragraph 3 is the topic sentence? _____

_____

4. State one minor detail in paragraph 7 that is interesting but not something you would be tested on.

_____

5. What idea is supported by the studies referred to in paragraph 9?

_____

■ **For Discussion and Reflection**

1. What idea in this section do you find most interesting? Why?

2. What parallels do you see between baboon and human social interaction? List as many as you can. Do you see any differences? List those as well.

3. What do you think we can learn from the study of subhuman primate behavior?

Selection 2   **Does Your Body-Talk Do You In?**

by **Dianne Hales** and **Dr. Robert Hales**

Dr. Hales, a psychiatrist, and Dianne Hales have co-authored *Caring for the Mind: The Comprehensive Guide to Mental Health* (1995). The following article appeared in *Parade* magazine on March 12, 1995.

■ **Prepare**

1. From what you know about the authors and the selection, what can you predict about purpose and format or style?

_____

_____

2. State briefly what you expect to read about. _____

_____

3. What do you already know about the topic? Respond using *one* of the methods described in Chapter 2.

_____

_____

_____

4. Use the title to pose questions about the reading selection.

_____

_____

5. Preread the selection. Then read and annotate the article. Finally, complete the comprehension and vocabulary checks that follow and answer the questions for discussion and reflection.

1   She extends only her fingers for a limp handshake. His grip could shatter bones. She looks down as she talks. His eyes lock onto the interviewer's unflinchingly.

2   Even though the two applicants are highly qualified, neither lands the job—not because of what they *say* but because of what they *do*. Her body language says she's timid; his says he's arrogant. "As much as 95 percent of communication is nonverbal," says Marilyn Maple, a professor of education at the University of Florida. "Body language is the oldest, most trusted language in the world."

3   **What body language can tell you.** Most nonverbal communication on the job centers on power. "In our culture, someone in power appears large, strong, with a relaxed posture," says Albert Mehrabian, a psychology professor at UCLA and author of *Silent Messages.* "People lower down look stiff and symmetrical."

4   Leaders signal superiority by sitting while others stand, leaning back in chairs and gesturing expansively. They also talk more, in louder voices, and interrupt others. Subordinates may lean forward and nod in agreement. Others may scratch their legs, twist watchbands—idiosyncratic ways of saying they're nervous or not interested.

5   Often there's a discrepancy between what someone says—that your job is secure, for instance—and what he or she does—jiggles a foot, perhaps, or avoids looking you in the eye. Which should you believe? What you see, say the experts, not what you hear. While words can be manipulated, gestures are a lot harder to control. Be suspicious of a speaker who barely moves. "People generally freeze up when they're lying," says Mehrabian.

6   **"Saying" it right.** "People can't see your credentials—they can only see you," says Lynn Pearl, the president of Executive Communication Inc., a

consulting company in Chicago. "That's why awareness of the nonverbal signals you send gives you a leg up."

7   One key to positive responses is posture. "Good posture identifies you as someone with something to say," Pearl explains. Stand tall, with flexed knees, and pull your rib cage up out of your waist.

8   Look directly at the people you address, no matter how many. "Eye contact is the most remembered element in forming an impression," says Nancy Austin of Capitola, Calif., a management consultant and co-author of *A Passion for Excellence.* But don't stare—five to seven seconds is the maximum for a meeting of the eyes.

9   For women, the greatest nonverbal challenge is demonstrating that they should be taken seriously. "Women in business have to appear more assertive just to be heard," says Donna Chevrier, an image consultant in Toronto. "Unfortunately, the body language they learn while growing up is almost apologetic. I tell women to try this assertiveness exercise in private: standing as if they owned a big mountain, with their legs open a bit and their hands on their hips."

10   In the workplace, a woman should put her hands on the arm rests of her chair rather than in her lap and not "glue" her legs together. Large gestures made from the elbow also are effective in projecting authority. If challenged, she should train herself not to back away but to hold her ground and maintain eye contact.

11   In today's sexually sensitive workplace, women should check innocent actions—such as "preening" moves, like brushing back hair, or "nervous" moves, like crossing and uncrossing legs—that can be misinterpreted as provocative.

12   And "a lot of good-hearted men are realizing that their old behavior isn't appropriate anymore," says Julian Fast, the author of *Subtexts: Making Body Language Work in the Workplace.* Pats, hugs and neck rubs are out. Similarly, a man shouldn't shake a woman's hand for more than a few seconds.

13   Any touching, by men or women, should be light, brief and in a neutral zone: the elbow or shoulder. Touching superiors of either sex is always taboo.

14   **Dos and don'ts.** Just as the right body language can make your words more effective, the wrong gestures can garble the message. Here are some non-verbal no-nos and their alternatives:

15   • *The Fig Leaf.* Speakers who clasp their hands in front of their groins look insecure. To project confidence, keep your arms loosely at your sides and use fluid gestures for emphasis.

16   • *The Terminator.* An unforgivably brutal handshake can crush any hope of a good impression. Also avoid The Fish Hand—a lifeless palm dangling from a limp wrist. To put your best hand forward, hold your fingers and thumb vertically, extend them directly, clasp well, then release.

17   • *The Space Invasion.* Americans feel most comfortable with a 3- to 6-foot "bubble" of space around them. Getting closer puts the other person on the defensive. Show respect for invisible personal boundaries.

18 • *The Roadblock.* Physical barriers—like folding your arms across your chest—indicate resistance. "Open" positions, with the torso exposed, convey a receptive attitude. Sit down and lean forward to give a kind impression.

19 • *The Pickpocket.* A man who keeps his hands in his pockets looks like he's hiding something. "After a while," observes Lynn Pearl, "people start to wonder what he's doing in there." To avoid such musings, keep your hands in sight.

20 • *The Pat on the Back.* It may seem to say "good job," but in fact it's patronizing. Better is a collegial squeeze of the upper arm at shoulder level.

21 • *The Fidgets.* "Comfort" gestures—rocking, stroking your leg, tugging on your ear—increase with stress. While you should try to control such nonverbal "noise," you don't have to straitjacket yourself. "Just make sure not to do anything in excess," says Pearl.

■ **Comprehension Check** ·

Answer the following with a, b, c, or d to indicate the phrase that best completes each statement.

_____ 1. Body language is language that should be
   a. ignored
   b. laughed at
   c. trusted
   d. exaggerated

_____ 2. Body language is a revealing form of
   a. nonverbal communication
   b. dance
   c. verbal communication
   d. interviewing

_____ 3. The body language of leaders includes
   a. standing stiffly
   b. nodding in agreement
   c. sleeping
   d. leaning back in chairs and gesturing

_____ 4. To be successful in business women need to practice
   a. standing on a mountain
   b. assertiveness
   c. being the boss
   d. back-slapping like men

_____ 5. Whether with one person or in a large group, it's important to
   a. stare hard at everyone
   b. always remain standing

     c. maintain eye contact

     d. keep your hands in your pockets

_____ 6. Gestures to avoid include

     a. a brief but firm handshake

     b. fluid gestures

     c. giving others enough space

     d. folding arms across the chest

Answer the following with a T (true) or F (false).

                                                   T   **F**

7. Gestures are usually more truthful than words.   ____ ____

8. Good posture is an important form of nonverbal communication.   ____ ____

9. In today's workplace, women need to avoid preening and men need to avoid pats and hugs.   ____ ____

10. Touching the boss will improve your chances for promotion.   ____ ____

Expanding Vocabulary

Match each work in the left column with its definition in the right column by placing the correct letter in the space next to each word.

_____ unflinchingly (1)	a.	primping
_____ symmetrical (3)	b.	personal mannerism
_____ idiosyncratic (4)	c.	arousing desires
_____ assertive (9)	d.	smooth
_____ preening (11)	e.	condescending
_____ provocative (11)	f.	without moving
_____ garble (14)	g.	behavior of colleagues
_____ fluid (15)	h.	forceful
_____ patronizing (20)	i.	distort
_____ collegial (20)	j.	perfectly balanced

Analysis of Content and Strategies

1. What is the essay's main idea? _____

_____

_____

2. The paragraphs in this essay are consistently shorter than in any other articles you have read in this chapter. What do the authors gain from this format?

_____

_____

3. The authors also quote many other people. What do they accomplish with this approach to developing their topic?

_____

_____

4. Why is eye contact so important? What nonverbal message is given by someone who won't "look you in the eye"?

_____

_____

For Discussion and Reflection

1. What are some of the reasons why women have trouble competing in an office? What are some strategies they can use to be successful in business?

2. Have you given thought to what you may be communicating nonverbally in the classroom? Think about your behavior, and think about what messages your professors are receiving. What, if any, useful changes in behavior might you make?

3. What advice would you give to other students regarding the do's and don't's of nonverbal communication in the classroom? Brainstorm on this issue as if you were planning to write an article, similar to the one you have just read, for the college newspaper.

Selection 3 | ## The Amish—*Gemeinschaft* Community in a *Gesellschaft* Society

by **James M. Henslin**

A professor of sociology at Southern Illinois University, James Henslin is the author of numerous books and articles that focus on his particular areas of interest. These include the sociology of ordinary life, deviance, and the homeless.

The boxed insert on the Amish is from his textbook *Sociology: A Down-To-Earth Approach* (2nd ed., 1995).

■   **Vocabulary Alert**

The two German words appearing in the title, now commonly used in sociological discussions of modern societies, were introduced by Ferdinand Tonnies in a study published in 1887. *Gemeinschaft* refers to an intimate society in which people know one another and have a feeling of togetherness. *Gesellschaft* refers to a society noted for impersonal relationships and individual goals achievement.

■   **Prepare**

1. From what you know about the author and the selection, what can you predict about purpose and format or style?

   _____

   _____

2. State briefly what you expect to read about. _____

   _____

3. What do you already know about the topic? Respond using *one* of the methods described in Chapter 2.

   _____

   _____

   _____

4. Use the title to pose questions about the reading selection. _____

   _____

5. Preread the selection. Then read and annotate the article. Finally, complete the comprehension and vocabulary checks that follow and answer the questions for discussion and reflection.

1   U.S. society exhibits all the characteristics Ferdinand Tönnies identified as those of a *Gesellschaft* society. Impersonal associations pervade everyday life. Local, state, and federal governments regulate many activities. Impersonal corporations hire people not based on long-term, meaningful

relationships, but on their value to the bottom line. Similarly, when it comes to firing workers, the bottom line takes precedence over personal relationships. And, perhaps even more significantly, millions of Americans do not even know their neighbors.

2   Within the United States, a handful of small communities exhibit characteristics that depart from those of the larger society. One such example is the Old Order Amish, followers of a sect that broke away from the Swiss-German Mennonite church in the late 1600s, settling in Pennsylvania around 1727. Today, more than 130,000 Old Order Amish live in the United States. The largest concentration, about 14,000, reside in Lancaster County, Pennsylvania. The Amish can also be found in about twenty other states and in Ontario, Canada, but 75 percent live in just three states: Pennsylvania, Ohio, and Indiana. The Amish, who believe that birth control is wrong, have doubled in size in just the past two decades.

3   To the nearly five million tourists that pass through Lancaster County each year, the quiet pastures and almost identical white farmhouses, simple barns, horse- or mule-drawn carts, and clothes flapping on lines to dry convey a sense of peace and wholeness reminiscent of another era. Although just sixty-five miles from Philadelphia, "Amish country" is a world away.

4   The Amish faith rests on separation from the world, taking Christ's Sermon on the Mount literally, and obedience to the church's teachings and leaders. This rejection of worldly concerns, Donald Kraybill writes in *The Riddle of Amish Culture,* "provides the foundation of such Amish values as humility, faithfulness, thrift, tradition, communal goals, joy of work, a slow-paced life, and trust in divine providence."

5   The village life that Tönnies identified as fostering *Gemeinschaft* communities—and which he correctly predicted was fast being lost to industrialization—is very much alive among the Amish. The Amish make their decisions in weekly meetings, where, by consensus, they follow a set of rules, or *Ordnung,* to guide their behavior. Religion and the discipline that it calls for are the glue that holds these communities together. Brotherly love and the welfare of the community are paramount values. Most Amish farm plots of one hundred acres or less, keeping their farms small so that horses can be used instead of tractors and neighbors can pitch in with the chores. In these ways, intimacy—a sense of community—is maintained.

6   The Amish are bound by many other communal ties, including language (a dialect of German known as Pennsylvania Dutch), a distinctive style of plain dress that has remained unchanged for almost three hundred years, and church-sponsored schools. Nearly all Amish marry, and divorce is forbidden. The family is a vital ingredient in Amish life; all major events take place in the home, including weddings and worship services, even births and funerals. Most Amish children attend church schools only until the age of 13. To go to school beyond the eighth grade would expose them to "worldly concerns" and give them information considered of no value to farm life. The Amish pay local, state, and fed-

eral taxes, but they pool their resources to fund their own welfare system, and therefore do not pay Social Security taxes. They won the right to be left out of the Social Security system only after drawn-out court battles. They believe that all violence is bad, even in personal self-defense, and register as conscientious objectors during times of war.

7   The Amish cannot resist all change, of course. Instead, they attempt to adapt to social change in ways that will cause the least harm to their core values. Because of the high cost of land due to urbanization, about 30 percent of married Amish men work at jobs other than farming, most in farm-related businesses, cottage industries, and woodworking trades. They go to great lengths to avoid leaving the home. The Amish believe that when the husband works away from the home, all aspects of life, from the marital relationship to the care of the children, seem to change—certainly an excellent sociological insight. They also believe that if a man receives a paycheck he will think that his work is of more value than his wife's. For the Amish, intimate, or *Gemeinschaft*, society is absolutely essential to their way of life.

Sources: Hostetler 1980; Kraybill 1989; Bender 1990; Jones 1990; Raymond 1990; Ruth 1990; Ziegenhals 1991; Kephart and Zellner 1994.

■ **Comprehension Check .**

Fill in each blank with the word or phrase that best completes the sentence.

1. The Old Order Amish represent Tonnies's _____ community.

2. About 14,000 Amish live in _____ Pennsylvania.

3. The Amish ride in _____ carts and

   farm using _____ rather than tractors.

4. The Amish make decisions collectively at _____ .

5. The Amish place a high value on _____

   and _____ .

6. For the Amish, most important events take place in the _____

   _____ .

7. Children go to church schools until they are _____ .

8. The Amish do not pay _____ taxes.

9. Most Amish men who do not farm still work near _____ .

10. The Amish oppose all _____ .

Expanding Vocabulary

Match each word in the left column with its definition in the right column by placing the correct letter in the space next to each word.

_____ pervade (1)   a. priority
_____ precedence (1)   b. shift from rural to city life
_____ reminiscent (2)   c. controlled by conscience
_____ consensus (5)   d. suggestive of something previously known
_____ paramount (5)   e. general agreement
_____ conscientious (6)   f. most important
_____ urbanization (7)   g. spread throughout

Analysis of Content And Strategies

1. What is the article's topic? _____

   _____

2. What is the main idea? What sentence in the article comes closest to stating the main idea?

   _____

   _____

3. What words make up the topic sentence in paragraph 6? _____

   _____

   _____

4. State two major details in paragraph 6. _____

   _____

   _____

5. Explain what the author means when he writes that "although just sixty-five miles from Philadelphia, 'Amish country' is a world away."

   _____

   _____

   _____

For Discussion and Reflection

1. In your view, what three or four details best support the idea that the Amish society is a *Gemeinschaft* community? Why did you pick those details?

2. Would you describe your home as the center of your life? If so, what have you gained from such a family life? If not, do you think you have missed something? That is, do the Amish have something in their lives that you would like to have?

3. Is *Gemeinschaft* possible today? What suggestions do you have for establishing a *Gemeinschaft* community?

CHAPTER 4

Building Word Power

In this chapter you will learn:

- How to understand the meanings of new words by using context clues

- What information can be found in a dictionary

- How to use a dictionary

- How to understand the meanings of new words by looking at their parts

- Strategies for expanding your vocabulary

Would you try to play tennis with some of the strings missing from your racquet? Probably not, but if you did, you would soon become frustrated. Trying to read without a good vocabulary is much the same. Your best efforts to use active reading strategies and to concentrate on main ideas will be frustrated if too many of the words are "missing."

Studies have shown a strong connection between school and work success and a good vocabulary. That's why key exams, such as the SAT's, contain sections on vocabulary. Let's face it; there is no argument to be made for a limited vocabulary. With a limited vocabulary, reading is difficult and without much pleasure. So, what must you do to build a good vocabulary? The answer is both simple and difficult: you must read. Most of us build on our basic vocabularies by reading. The answer seems to create a dilemma: how can you read easily with a limited vocabulary? But how can you improve your word power unless you read? This chapter will help by providing several strategies for vocabulary building.

You should view the following strategies as a series of steps to take each time you come across a new word or a word that seems to be used in a new way. First, you can examine the word's context for help, including looking for a definition provided by the writer. If the context offers little help, then examine the parts of the word to see if it is composed of smaller words, or word parts, that you recognize and from which you can infer the meaning of the new word. Many words, from automobile to autoinoculation, are composed of several words or word parts that you may know individually. Not all words can be taken apart, however, so you may need to turn to a dictionary for guidance. Finally, you need a plan for building your general vocabulary and for learning new terms in the courses you are taking.

■ CONTEXT CLUES

When reading about a subject new to you, or when reading material written in a complex style (both common situations in college courses), you will come across words that are unfamiliar, or only vaguely familiar. Fortunately you do not have to turn to the dictionary to look up each new word. Often you will find clues within the sentence or paragraph (the word's context) that help you understand what the unfamiliar word probably means. Suppose, for example, that you read:

> In response to the three speakers, the audience gave the most applause to the president's **oration.**

Perhaps *oration* is only somewhat familiar to you. If you think about how it is used in the sentence, though, you can feel comfortable that it is another word for speech and continue with your reading. How? The context tells you that the audience has listened to three *speeches* and liked the president's *speech (oration)* the best. The following exercise will show you that it is possible to get a good idea of a word's meaning from the context in which it appears.

 EXERCISE 4-1 Learning from the Context

Circle the letter of the word that comes closest to the meaning of the word in
bold type in each sentence.

1. Some elderly people live in such **abject** poverty that they go without meals.
   a. little
   b. objectionable
   c. miserable
   d. jaded
2. Feeling trapped when in crowds, Joe stayed on the **periphery** of the group.
   a. angle
   b. outside
   c. inside
   d. edge

3. After lecturing the defense lawyer, the judge told the prosecutor to continue with her **inquiry.**
   a. questioning
   b. lecture
   c. speech
   d. argument

4. Although **inept** at parties, George was a great football player.
   a. unskilled, awkward
   b. injured
   c. quiet
   d. noisy

5. After several months of struggling to be accepted, John finally felt that he had become an **integral** part of his office.
   a. excluded
   b. essential
   c. intellectual
   d. integer

6. The professor planned to **clarify** the concept by providing three or four examples.
   a. make essential
   b. challenge
   c. undercut
   d. make clear

How many of the underlined words could you have defined? For how many did you correctly identify a synonym in the exercise? Most people can understand more words in context than they can actually define. And writers help us, using several different strategies to clarify words in context.

Definitions

As you have discovered, textbooks and other assigned readings are filled with new terms, with the language of a field or discipline you are studying. Fortunately for students, the writers of these works often give definitions of key terms. Here are two examples.

> Energy passes from one organism to another along a particular food chain. A *food chain* is a sequence of organisms related to one another as prey and predator. The first is eaten by the second, the second by the third, and so on, in a series of *trophic levels*, or feeding levels.
>
> Helena Curtis, *Biology*

Two terms are defined in this passage. The first definition, for *food chain*, may be described as a formal definition. The purpose of the entire sentence is to state the meaning of the term. The third sentence continues the explanation of the term and then introduces a second term, *trophic levels.* This term is defined informally, in the phrase "or feeding levels." Formal definitions are easy to spot as you read. You need also to watch for the informal definition that appears after the term to be defined but is not the main point of the sentence. In the example, "trophic levels" is defined even though the purpose of the sentence is to illustrate the process of the food chain.

 EXERCISE 4-2 **Identifying the Passages that Define**

*In each of the following sentences, underline the words that provide a definition of the word or phrase in **bold type.***

1. **Advertising** is paid nonpersonal communication from an identified sponsor using mass media to persuade or influence an audience.

    Wells, Burnett, & Moriarty, *Advertising*

2. One of the properties of ecosystems is **productivity,** which is the total amount of energy converted to organic compounds in a given length of time.

    Helena Curtis, *Biology*

3. **Fossils,** the remains or traces of prehistoric life, were also essential to the development of the geologic time scale.

    Tarbuck and Lutgens, *The Earth*

4. A **corporate culture** consists of the shared values, norms, and practices communicated to and followed by those working for a firm.

    Evans and Berman, *Marketing*

5. The courts and Congress also have attempted to uphold the rights of **whistle blowers,** federal employees who publicly disclose waste or mismanagement in their agencies.

    O'Connor & Sabato, *American Government*

Examples

In addition to providing both formal and informal definitions of key terms, writers often clarify words by giving examples. For example, you may not know the term *malapropism* before reading this sentence:

> A frequent **malapropism** on student exams is the use of "conscious" when the writer means "conscience."

From the example, you may be able to conclude that a malapropism is an incorrect word accidently used instead of the word needed in the sentence. Here are two other examples of the strategy. After reading each sentence, give a brief definition or synonym for the word in **bold** type.

1. In Chopin's story, Mrs. Mallard's **epiphany** occurs in the few moments that she sits in her bedroom contemplating and then embracing the new, freer life she can have now that her husband is gone.

   _____

2. A writer's **diction** may range from the formality of Lincoln's "Gettysburg Address" to the current slang of rap artists.

   _____

From the first example, you may be able to conclude that an *epiphany* is a brief moment of new awareness or insight about life. From the second, you may understand that the term *diction* is a synonym of *word choice*. The type of language a writer generally uses is that writer's diction. Notice that neither example seeks to provide a definition of the underscored word, but the details given in each sentence provide clues to each term's meaning. Examples are sometimes introduced by such words as "for example," "such as," and "including."

EXERCISE 4-3 Understanding Words from Examples

*Read each of the following sentences and then write a definition or synonym for each of the words in **bold type**.*

1. Several **phobias,** including fear of heights, fear of flying, and fear of crowds, limited Michael's career opportunities as well as his social life.

   _____

2. Frequently wearing sweaters and carrying his own luggage, Jimmy Carter was known for his **unassuming** presidential style.

   _____

3. **Debilitating** diseases such as arthritis and adult-onset diabetes make growing old a challenge.

   _____

4. **Autocratic** rulers from Napoleon to Hitler have changed the course of history.

   _____

5. Working in the library and waiting tables at nearby restaurants are two popular methods for **augmenting** college scholarships.

   _____

6. The public's **apathy** regarding environmental problems can be seen in the continued destruction of rain forests and the polluting of rivers.

Comparison and Contrast

Comparison and contrast are widely-used strategies for organizing ideas. These methods can be used for an entire essay or for a sentence. As a reader you can employ your recognition of these patterns to understand the meaning of a word you do not know. Suppose you read the following sentence:

> All winter the trees in my neighborhood were bare, but now that spring is here they are adorned with new **foliage.**

If you do not know the word *foliage,* you can conclude from the contrast structure of the sentence that *foliage* must refer to the opposite of bare. The contrast of winter and spring also helps readers realize that *foliage* must refer to the leaves that have come out on the trees. Here is another example, this one from a textbook:

> To speak as if all soldiers (or doctors, or lawyers, or firefighters) are men is incorrect—just as it is **erroneous** to speak as if all elementary-school teachers (or secretaries, or nurses, or flight attendants) are women.
>
> Stephen Lucas, *The Art of Public Speaking*

Although the content of each half of the sentence contrasts (speaking as if some jobs belong only to men in the first half, and speaking as if some jobs belong only to women in the second half) the two halves are parallel in that the author asserts that each type of reference to jobs is incorrect—or *erroneous.* The words "just as" tell us that both kinds of speaking are incorrect, so we can conclude that the word *erroneous* also means incorrect.

Comparisons are often noted by use of "just as," "the same as," and "similarly." Contrasts are signaled by words such as "although," "but," "while," "yet," and "on the other hand."

EXERCISE 4-4 **Understanding Words from Comparison and Contrast**

*Read each of the following sentences and then write a definition or synonym for each of the words in **bold** type.*

1. Although Bob was quick to give up on difficult tasks, James remained **tenacious,** no matter how difficult the assignment.

---

2. Joan liked to talk about movies and sports, while Elizabeth preferred **esoteric** conversations about art and philosophy.

_____

3. The history teacher encouraged his students to **emulate** the leaders, scientists, and entrepreneurs of the past rather than trying to be like Michael Jordan.

_____

4. Rachel used to wear conservative, professional clothing, but now her clothes are **provocative.**

_____

5. Wouldn't it be nice if politicians spoke **candidly** about their views on the issues instead of saying what their advisors think the public wants to hear.

_____

6. John Keats's poem seemed clear and straightforward to the class, but Robert Frost's poem confused them with its **ambiguity.**

_____

The following exercise provides practice with sentences that use one of the strategies you have studied. You will need to recognize the type of context clue as well as define the word in bold type. Before completing this exercise on context clues, consider these few reminders:

1. Context clues help readers guess at the approximate meaning of words they may be unfamiliar with, but context clues do not give guaranteed answers.
2. Use context clues so that you can continue reading to the end of a section or work, but mark the words you have doubts about and look them up after you finish reading. Checking the words in a dictionary or glossary will help reinforce the learning of new words.
3. Studying the context for help with unfamiliar words will not always work. Sometimes you will have to stop reading to look up words you do not know.

 ## Exercise 4-5 Recognizing Context Clues

Read each of the following sentences and underline the words that provide a clue to the meaning of the word or phrase in **bold type.** Then write a definition or synonym for the word. Finally, write the definition from a dictionary that fits

the meaning of the word in that context. Compare your answer with the dictionary definition.

1. Sometimes it's easier to learn a new word by finding an **antonym** rather than a synonym for the word.

   Your definition: _____

   The dictionary definition: _____

   _____

2. Because hunting and gathering societies have no rulers, do not acquire possessions, and make most decisions as a group, they are the most **egalitarian.**

   Your definition: _____

   The dictionary definition: _____

   _____

3. Psychologists use the term **sublimation** to refer to the redirecting of unacceptable impulses into socially acceptable ones.

   Your definition: _____

   The dictionary definition: _____

   _____

4. It is illogical to try to challenge someone's ideas by attacking the person's character; it is also a **fallacy** to argue that there are only two solutions to a problem when there may be several.

   Your definition: _____

   The dictionary definition: _____

   _____

5. Although Art could beat Mark at chess, Ruth remained his **nemesis.**

   Your definition: _____

   The dictionary definition: _____

   _____

6. Often a word's **etymology** (word origin) helps us understand the word's meaning.

   Your definition: _____

   The dictionary definition: _____

   _____

7. Even if they do not **deter** girls from science classes, it is wrong for teachers to actively encourage only boys to take science.

   Your definition: _____

   The dictionary definition: _____

   _____

8. When he was expelled from college for cheating, his father told him he was a **discredit** to the family.

   Your definition: _____

   The dictionary definition: _____

   _____

9. Please **explicate,** that is, give a line-by-line explanation of, Shakespeare's "Sonnet 73."

   Your definition: _____

   The dictionary definition: _____

   _____

10. The professor was famous for his **caustic** remarks to students even though he always spoke kindly and without sarcasm to colleagues.

    Your definition: _____

    The dictionary definition: _____

    _____

■ LEARNING FROM WORD PARTS: PREFIXES, ROOTS, AND SUFFIXES

Suppose the context does not help you with a new word. You have a second option before turning to the dictionary. You can look at the word's parts. Consider the word *like*. Many words can be formed from it, including: *likely, likeness, likeable,* and *likeableness.* These four words have been made by adding different suffixes (endings) to the root (or base) word *like.* If we add the prefix "dis" to the beginning of the root *like,* we get still another word: *dislike.* And these five words, made from one root, one prefix, and four suffixes, are by no means all the words that can be made starting with the root *like.* In fact, it is useful to think of "families" of words, groups made out of the same root but different prefixes or suffixes or combinations of them. If you know one from a family, you may be able to understand the meaning of others in that "family."

There are good reasons to learn the most common prefixes and suffixes and to recognize the meanings of common roots. First, when you learn one new word, you know that you have actually learned several. Second, you can often figure out the meaning of a new word by recognizing its root and the prefix or suffix that has been used. For example, suppose you are not certain of the word *disclose.* If you recognize its two parts, the prefix "dis" and the root "close," and you know that "dis" means apart or away, then you can conclude that *disclose* means to remove or reverse or separate from "close." Thus the word means to open up or reveal, as in "He disclosed the truth at last."

Before beginning a study of word parts, remember these points: (1) not all words have a prefix or suffix; (2) some word parts change spelling in combination with other parts and so may be difficult to recognize; and (3) words can have more than one prefix, root, or suffix. In addition, as you study the following lists of common word parts and work the exercises remember: (1) you cannot learn every part at once and (2) you already are familiar with many on the lists. As you study, try to think of families of words even though you need only one to complete part of an exercise.

Common Prefixes (Word Parts Placed at the Beginning of Words)

Prefix	Meaning	Example	Your Example
ad	to, at, for	adequate	_____
anti	against	anticlimax	_____
circum	around	circumstance	_____
com/col/con	together, with	commit; connect	_____
contra	against	contravene	_____
de	away, from	deplete	_____
dis	apart, not	disappear	_____

Prefix	Meaning	Example	Your Example
ex	from, out of	example	_____
in/il/ir/im	in, into, not	inactive, illicit	_____
inter	between	interchange	_____
intro/intra	within, in	introspection	_____
mis	wrong	misprint	_____
mono	one	monologue	_____
non	not	nonconformist	_____
post	after	postgraduate	_____
pre	before	preserve	_____
pro	for	prohibit	_____
re	back, again	regain	_____
retro	backward	retrogression	_____
semi	half	semifinalist	_____
sub	under	subtotal	_____
super	above, extra	supernatural	_____
tele	far	telescope	_____
trans	across, over	transatlantic	_____
un	not	unsettled	_____

EXERCISE 4-6 Working with Prefixes

Fill in the blank with the appropriate prefix to make a word that fits the context of the sentence.

1. Jane spends some time each day in quiet _____spection.
2. The instructor asked students to _____view their notes for the next quiz.
3. He argued that the error was a _____take.
4. Mary left work early because she was _____well.
5. Please _____pone the meeting so that I can attend.
6. We must all help _____tect the environment.
7. After his nasty remarks, Jim was _____popular in the dorm.
8. The professor began to _____lect the exam.
9. Board members _____spired to block his election as company president.
10. Many of the world's rain forests are located in a _____ tropical climate.

Give a brief definition or a synonym for each of the following words or phrases.

1. irreversible _____

2. transcend _____

3. monopoly _____

4. disavow _____

5. subsistence _____

6. interpersonal _____

Common Roots (to Which Prefixes and/or Suffixes Are Added)

Root	Meaning	Example	Your Example
aqua	water	aquatic	_____
aster/astro	star	astronomy	_____
aud	hearing	audio	_____
auto	self	autograph	_____
bene	well, good	benefit	_____
bio	life	biology	_____
chron(o)	time	chronicle	_____
corp	body	corpse	_____
cred	belief	credence	_____
dict/dic	say, tell	dictate	_____
duc/duct	lead	conduct	_____
fact/fac	make, do	facsimile	_____
geo	earth	geographer	_____
graph/gram	write	telegram	_____
log/logo/logy	study, thought	anthropology	_____
micro	small	microfilm	_____
mit/miss	send	commit	_____
mort/mor	death	mortician	_____
path	feeling	empathy	_____
phob	fear	phobia	_____
phon/phono	sound	symphony	_____
poly	many	polygamy	_____
port	carry	transport	_____
psych	soul, mind	psychoanalysis	_____
script/scrib	write	scribble	_____
sen/sent	feel	sentimental	_____
spec/spect	look at	spectator	_____
terr/terre	land, earth	terrain	_____

Root	Meaning	Example	Your Example
ven/vent	come	convention	_____
vis/vid	see	visible	_____
voc	call	vocation	_____

 EXERCISE 4-7 **Working with Roots**

Fill in the blank with the appropriate root to make a word that fits the context of the sentence.

1. Because her story lacked _____ability, no one believed her.
2. Socio_____ is the study of humans in groups.
3. The math instructor drew a _____gon on the board.
4. After overloading her suitcase, Joan found that it was no longer _____able.
5. The _____acle of the circus elephants delighted the children.
6. The secretary prepared a tran_____ of the proceedings.
7. Some _____ologists emphasize modifying behavior whereas others want patients to explore their childhood experiences.
8. Although Michelle felt deeply, she found it hard to _____alize her feelings.
9. Some teenagers drive too fast, apparently believing that they are im_____al.
10. Those who like to explore caves must be comfortable in sub_____anean places.

Without using a dictionary, study word parts and then give a brief definition or a synonym for each of the following words.

1. benediction _____

2. astrophysicist _____

3. inaudible _____

4. phonograph _____

5. microbiology _____

6. chronology _____

Suffixes (Word Parts Placed at the End of Words)

When you add a suffix to a word, you may change its meaning, but more often you just change its part of speech and therefore how it is used in a sentence. *Act* is a word from which several new words can be made by adding suffixes: *actor, activity, action.* More typically, suffixes change the part of speech:

Michael *sympathized* with his sister. (verb)

Michael showed *sympathy* for his sister. (noun)

Michael has a *sympathetic* feeling for his sister. (adjective)

Michael spoke *sympathetically* to his sister. (adverb)

The following list groups suffixes by their general meaning or their effect when added to a word. For example, the adjective *kind* becomes a noun referring to the state of being kind when "ness" is added: *kindness.* When "er" is added to the verb *teach,* we have "one who" teaches, a *teacher.*

Common Suffixes

Suffixes meaning "one who":

Suffix	Example	Your Example
–ee	employee	_____
–eer	pamphleteer	_____
–er	manager	_____
–ist	tourist	_____
–or	sailor	_____

Suffixes meaning "referring to":

–al	seasonal	_____
–ship	ownership	_____
–hood	childhood	_____
–ward	backward	_____

Suffixes establishing a condition, doctrine, or quality:

–able/ible	believable	_____
–ance/ence	excellence	_____
–ic	angelic	_____
–ion/tion	election	_____
–ish	childish	_____
–ism	realism	_____
–ity	inferiority	_____
–ive	restive	_____
–less	worthless	_____
–ment	establishment	_____
–ness	meanness	_____
–ous	fabulous	_____

Suffix	Example	Your Example
–ty	fidelity	_____
–y	silky	_____

EXERCISE 4-8 Working with Suffixes

Fill in the blank with an appropriate suffix to make a word that fits the context of the sentence.

1. When John saw improve_____ in his tennis game, he began to practice harder.
2. Someone planning to become a doct_____ today has many specialties to choose among.
3. The union lead_____ rallied the factory work ___.
4. The train slowed at the crossing and then lurched for_____ .
5. Angela was fam_____ for putting together interesting parties.
6. If you study nineteenth-century literature, you will study romantic_____ .
7. In spite of the doctor's efforts, the patient grew less and less respon_____ .
8. Margaret refused to continue to work unless she was given part owner____ of the shop.
9. The cruel_____ and vicious_____ of the murders frightened the community.
10. After listening to the angry debate, Robert withdrew his mo_____ .

By adding suffixes, make two new words from each of the following words. Note: Sometimes you need to delete a letter before adding a suffix.

1. boy _____

2. capital _____

3. commune _____

4. operate _____

5. prevent _____

■ USING THE DICTIONARY

When neither context nor word parts help you with a word's meaning, you will need to turn to the dictionary. Actually, "the dictionary" is misleading because there are several different kinds of dictionaries.

Glossaries

The first "dictionary" you should turn to, when studying your textbooks, is the text's *glossary*. Not all texts contain a glossary, but many do, and these can be most helpful to students. The glossary is usually located at the back of the book, just before the index. A text's glossary is a better place for looking up a word's meanings than a dictionary for two reasons: (1) it is handier because it is in the same book that you are reading; and (2) the definition given will be appropriate for the word's use in the text—in that field of study. (Remember: many words have several meanings, only one of which fits the context of the work you are reading.) Words that appear several times in a section and in the text's glossary are words that you will need to learn for the course.

Pocket Dictionaries

For the study of words in works without glossaries, you will need at least one but probably two dictionaries of your own. Many students like to purchase a paperback dictionary because it is easiest to carry to class and to the library for study between classes. A "pocket" dictionary is a shorter version of a desk dictionary, so it will not include as many words or as much about each one, but it is relatively inexpensive and convenient.

Spelling-Only Dictionaries

Some students prefer to carry electronic spellers or very small "spelling only" dictionaries with them to class. These are wonderful tools for times when you write in class. (Most instructors will allow spelling-only tools for in-class work.) If you have problems with spelling, one of these "dictionaries" will be useful, but it cannot substitute for a dictionary with definitions and other information about language.

Desk Dictionaries

Even if you purchase a small dictionary or electronic speller, you should also buy a hardcover college or desk dictionary. Three good choices include:

The Random House College Dictionary
The American Heritage Dictionary of the English Language
Webster's New Collegiate Dictionary

Your college bookstore will stock at least one desk dictionary, and perhaps several from which you can choose. If your reading instructor does not require the hardcover desk dictionary, your writing instructor may, so you probably should go ahead and spend the twenty or more dollars to have the tools you need for college study. Yes, books are expensive—but they last a long time.

The Thesaurus

Another tool that many students "swear by" is a thesaurus, a dictionary of synonyms. A thesaurus lists together words that are similar in meaning. The most widely used, *Roget's Thesaurus*, is available in an inexpensive paperback version. A thesaurus can help you find a more appropriate or more effective word than the one that you can recall. For example, suppose you want to tell your friend at home about your new boyfriend and you write:

I just feel that we were supposed to come together.

The sentence does not give powerful expression to your feelings. If you look at the excerpt shown in Figure 4.1 for help, you will see several possibilities, including "destined," "fated," or "preordained."

A word of caution is in order regarding the helpfulness of a thesaurus. A thesaurus does not distinguish among the shades of meaning of words listed together. You would not want to write, for example, that you and your boyfriend were "doomed" to meet. "Destined" is a positive word, but "doomed" conveys negative feelings. So, do not select a word from the list unless you know the word and understand that it is appropriate to use in the context you have created for it. Also, you will need to learn how to use this tool. Words are not listed alphabetically. To find synonyms for a word, you must first look it up in the index of words at the back of the book and then turn to the section(s) listed for that word. As you can see from the excerpt, sections are numbered and are established around an idea or concept, such as "future events." The index directs you to a section number, not to a page number.

Unabridged and Subject-Area Dictionaries

Two other kinds of dictionaries may be important to you during your college years. Your library houses, in its reference collection, both complete or unabridged dictionaries and subject-area dictionaries. Most of the time a desk dictionary gives all the information about a word that you need, but sometimes

■ FIGURE 4.1

Excerpt from *Roget's Thesaurus*

> **152. FUTURE EVENTS–***N.* destiny, fatality, fate, lot, doom, fortune; future, future state; future existence, hereafter; next world to come; life to come; prospect.
> *V.* impend, hang over, threaten, loom, await, approach; foreordain, preordain; destine, predestine, doom.
> *Adj.* impending, destined; coming, in store, to come, instant, at hand, near, imminent; in the wind, in prospect.
> *Adv.* in time, in the long run; all in good time; eventually.

you need to check an unabridged dictionary for a rarely-used word not given in your smaller dictionary. Other times, you may need to consult a subject-area dictionary for the meaning of a word as it is used in a particular field of study. Most college libraries will own one or more unabridged dictionaries including the multi-volume *Oxford English Dictionary (OED)*, a gold-mine of information about how a word has changed meaning from one time to another. They will also own dictionaries for specific fields of study, dictionaries such as:

Dictionary of Classical Mythology
Dictionary of Film Terms
Dictionary of Genetics and Cell Biology

Check your library's reference collection for dictionaries in the subject areas you plan to study.

■ INFORMATION FOUND IN DESK DICTIONARIES

Although you will use your dictionary primarily to check the spelling of a word or to learn its meanings, you should be aware of the many kinds of information provided by a good desk dictionary.

Information on the English Language

Some desk dictionaries contain essays on the history of the English language and on dialects, and a chart of the Indo-European language family showing how languages are related to one another.

Charts and Tables

Some dictionaries include various charts and tables of information, including foreign alphabets, lists of symbols, and standard weights and measures (with U.S. and metric equivalents).

Pronunciation Guides

The way to reinforce the learning of new words is to use them in speech. To do this comfortably, you need confidence that you are pronouncing new words correctly. Your college dictionary provides a complete key to pronunciation in the front of the book and a briefer guide at the bottom of each right page (See Figure 4.2). The brief guide will usually be enough to help you understand each entry word's phonetic spelling (spelling the way the word sounds) that is provided immediately after a word's bold-type entry. For example, suppose your history instructor uses the term *coup d'etat*, a new term for you that means a sudden change in government, often by force. If you look up the word to learn how to pronounce it, you will find the phonetic spelling "ko͞o′ dā tä′." The phonetic spelling tells you that the "c" is the hard "k" sound, that the final "t" in "etat" is not pronounced, and that the first syllable is stressed slightly while the final syllable gets the primary stress or emphasis. The brief guide to pronunciation (Figure 4.2) tells you to pronounce the "oo" as in "boot," the first "a" as in "pay," and the second "a" as in "father." The two sources of information work together to help you pronounce the term correctly. Be sure to practice; say the word or term aloud several times and then use it in speech as soon as you can.

Foreign Language Terms, Famous People, Mythological Figures, Place Names, Figures, and Diagrams

The dictionary of words (the main part of any dictionary) includes some non-English words, proper nouns, and various figures and diagrams that illustrate some of the words. In this way the dictionary becomes a kind of encyclopedia in the range of information provided. You have just seen that a desk dictionary includes the French term *coup d'etat*. Other foreign terms you will find include the French terms *faux pas* and *bon jour* and the German term *Weltanschauung*. Words still considered "foreign" are entered in the dictionary in *italic* rather than **roman bold** type. When you see a word entered in italics, that means that you should underline it when you use it in writing.

Remember also that your dictionary is the first place to go to look up famous people mentioned in works you are reading, people from Aaron, the brother of Moses, to Zwingli, a Swiss Protestant reformer. Place names are also listed, including countries, cities, rivers, and mountain ranges. Gods and goddesses from various mythologies are often referred to by writers; you will find them in your dictionary as well, from Aphrodite, the Greek goddess of love and beauty, to Thor, the Scandinavian god of thunder. Often people and places and figures from mythology are not identified by writers; writers assume that readers will recognize the proper nouns they use. Whenever you do not recog-

■ **FIGURE 4.2**

Excerpt from *The American Heritage Dictionary of the English Language*

ă pat	oi **boy**
ā pay	ou **out**
âr care	ŏŏ **took**
ä father	ōō **boot**
ĕ pet	ŭ **cut**
ē be	ûr **urge**
ĭ pit	th **thin**
ī pie	*th* **this**
ir **pier**	hw **which**
ŏ pot	zh **vision**
ō toe	ə **about, item**
ô paw	♦ **regionalism**

Stress marks: ´ (primary)
´ (secondary), as in
dictionary (dĭk´ shə nĕr´ ē)

nize the person or place referred to, look it up. Understanding the reference could be important to understanding the passage, and you will expand your knowledge each time you open the dictionary.

■ WHAT EACH ENTRY CONTAINS

As the sample dictionary page illustrates (See Figure 4.3), each entry contains several types of information about each "ordinary" word. (Exceptions include proper nouns, for which some of the standard pieces of information do not apply.)

Note first the two words at the top of the sample page. The word on the left is the first entry on the page; the word on the right is the last entry on the page. Use these guide words as you flip through the dictionary to find the word you need. If you are searching for the word *like*, for example, then when you see the words "Ligurian Sea to Limburg" you know that *like* will be on that page somewhere between the two guide words. Here is a list of the typical items in each entry.

1. **The entry word in bold type,** providing the word's spelling (or most common spelling) and showing, by the use of dots, the word's syllables, thus: *lik•a•ble*. Plural forms of the word are given when not typical, as for *criterion*, whose plural is *criteria*.

2. **The word's phonetic spelling,** including stress marks for pronunciation, placed in parentheses, thus: (lī ́ kəbəl).

3. **The word's part (or parts) of speech.** The abbreviations used are: n. (noun), v. (verb), adj. (adjective), adv. (adverb), prep. (preposition), conj. (conjunction). When the word can be used in more than one part of speech, then each abbreviation is preceded by a bold-type dash: —adj.

4. **The word's definition(s).** If there is more than one definition, they are numbered and listed in order from the most to the least common usage. When necessary, restrictive labels for region (*Brit.*), time (*Obs.*—obsolete), subject (*Math, Music*), or level of usage (*Slang*) are used.

5. **Illustrations.** Some definitions are aided by the addition of a drawing, chart, or map.

6. **Word history.** The word's origin (etymology) is placed in square brackets and follows the definitions in some dictionaries; in others, the etymology comes immediately after the word's phonetic spelling. Many abbreviations are used in giving a word's origin; these abbreviations are identified in a chart in the opening pages of your dictionary.

7. **Synonyms.** (words similar in meaning) One or more synonyms are sometimes given, preceded by —**Syn.**

8. **Antonyms** (words opposite in meaning) are also given for some words, preceded by —**Ant.**

9. **Usage.** At times a section on usage is provided to give more information than can be conveyed by a usage label only. See the usage section accompanying the entry for *like*.

Li·gu'rian Sea', *n.* a part of the Mediterranean between Corsica and the NW coast of Italy.

lik·a·ble or **like·a·ble** (lī'kə bəl), *adj.* readily or easily liked; pleasing. [1720–30] —**lik'a·ble·ness, lik'a·bil'i·ty,** *n.*

Li·ka·si (li kä'sē), *n.* a city in S Zaire. 194,465. Formerly, **Jadotville.**

like[1] (līk), *adj.,* (*Poetic*) **lik·er, lik·est,** *prep., adv., conj., n., interj.* —*adj.* 1. of the same form, appearance, kind, character, amount, etc.: *I cannot remember a like instance.* 2. corresponding or agreeing in general or in some noticeable respect; similar; analogous: *drawing, painting, and like arts.* 3. bearing resemblance. 4. *Dial.* likely. —*prep.* 5. similarly to; in the manner characteristic of: *She works like a beaver.* 6. resembling; similar to: *Your necklace is like mine.* 7. characteristic of: *It would be like him to forget our appointment.* 8. as if there is promise of: indicative of: *It looks like rain.* 9. disposed or inclined to (usu. prec. by *feel*): *to feel like going to bed.* 10. used correlatively to indicate similarity through relationship): *like father, like son.* 11. (used to establish an intensity, often facetious, comparison): *ran like hell; sleeps like a log.* —*adv.* 12. nearly; approximately: *The house is more like 40 years old.* 13. *Informal.* likely or probably: *Like enough he'll come with us.* —*conj.* 14. in the same way as; just as; as: *It happened like that it would.* 15. as if: *He acted like he was afraid.* —*n.* 16. a similar or comparable person or thing, or persons or things; counterpart, match, or equal (usu. prec. by a possessive adjective or *the*): *No one has seen her like in a long time.* 17. kind; sort; type: silk (usu. prec. by a possessive adjective): *I despise toadies and their like.* 18. **the like,** something of a similar nature: *They grow oranges, lemons, and the like.* —*interj.* 19. *Informal.* (used preceding a WH-word, an answer to a question, or other information in a sentence on which the speaker wishes to focus attention): *Like, why didn't you write to me? The music was, like, really great.* 20. *Chiefly Brit. Informal.* (used following an adjective, phrase, or clause, usu. implying that the description or evaluation therein is the speaker's own characterization of the matter): *standing against the wall, looking tough, like.* —**Idiom.** 21. **like anything, blazes, crazy,** or **mad,** *Informal.* extremely; extensively: *I ran like crazy.* 22. **like to** or **liked to.** *Nonstandard.* was on the verge of or came close to (doing something): *The poor kid like to froze.* 23. **something like,** approximately the same as. 24. **the like** or **likes of,** the equal of. [1150–1200: ME *lic, lik* < ON *līkr.* reduced form of *glīkr;* see ALIKE] —**lik'er,** *n.* —**Usage.** LIKE[1] as a conjunction meaning "as, in the same way as" (*Many shoppers study the food ads like brokers study market reports*) or "as if" (*It looks like it will rain*) has been used for nearly 500 years and by many distinguished literary and intellectual figures. Since the mid-19th century there have been objections to these uses. Nevertheless, such uses are almost universal today in all but the most formal speech and writing, in which *as, as if,* and *as though* are more commonly used than LIKE: *The general accepted full responsibility for the incident, as any professional soldier would. Many of the bohemians lived as if (or as though) there were no tomorrow.* The strong strictures against the use of LIKE as a conjunction have resulted in the occasional hypercorrect use of *as* as a preposition where LIKE is idiomatic: *She looks like a sympathetic person.* See also AS.

like[2] (līk), *v.,* **liked, lik·ing,** *n.* —*v.t.* 1. to take pleasure in; find agreeable or congenial to one's taste: *to like opera.* 2. to regard with favor; have a kindly or friendly feeling for (a person, group, etc.). 3. to wish or want: *I'd like a piece of cake.* —*v.i.* 4. to feel inclined; wish: *Stay if you like.* 5. *Archaic.* to suit the tastes or wishes; please. —*n.* 6. Usu. **likes.** the things a person likes. [bef. 900: ME; OE *līcian,* c. OS *līkōn,* OHG *līhhēn,* ON *līka.* Go *leikan* to please; akin to ALIKE, LIKE[1]]

-like, a suffix use of LIKE[1] in the formation of adjectives: *childlike; lifelike.*

like·a·ble (lī'kə bəl), *adj.* LIKABLE.

like·li·hood (līk'lē hŏŏd') also **like'li·ness,** *n.* 1. the state of being likely or probable; probability. 2. a probability or chance of something. 3. *Archaic.* indication of a favorable end; promise. [1350–1400]

like·ly (līk'lē), *adj.,* **-li·er, -li·est,** *adv.* —*adj.* 1. probably or apparently destined (usu. fol. by an infinitive): *something not likely to happen.* 2. seeming like truth, fact, or certainty; reasonably to be believed or expected; believable: *a likely story.* 3. seeming to fulfill requirements or expectations; apparently suitable: *a likely place to live.* 4. showing promise of achievement or excellence; promising. —*adv.* 5. probably: *We will most likely stay home today.* [1250–1300; ME *likli* < ON *līkligr.* See LIKE[1], -LY] —**Usage.** LIKELY meaning "probably" is often preceded by a qualifying word: *The new system will quite likely increase profits.* Some usage guides maintain that such a qualifier must always be present. However, LIKELY without the qualifier is standard in all varieties of English: *The new system will likely increase profits.* See also APT, LIABLE.

like'-mind'ed, *adj.* having a similar or identical opinion, disposition, etc. [1520–30] —**like'-mind'ed·ly,** *adv.* —**like'-mind'ed·ness,** *n.*

lik·en (lī'kən), *v.t.* **-ened, -en·ing.** to represent as similar or like; compare: *to liken someone to a weasel.* [1275–1325]

like·ness (līk'nis), *n.* 1. a portrait; copy. 2. the state or fact of being like or similar. 3. the semblance or appearance of something; guise. [bef. 950: ME *līknesse,* OE *līcnes,* var. of *gelīcnes.* See ALIKE, -NESS]

like·wise (līk'wīz'), *adv.* 1. moreover; in addition; too. 2. in like manner; in the same way; similarly: *I'm tempted to do likewise.* [1400–50: late ME; earlier *in like wise* in a like way. See LIKE[1], WISE[1]]

lil·ied (lil'ēd), *adj.* 1. abounding in lilies. 2. *Archaic.* lilylike; white. [1605–15]

Lil·ith (lil'ith), *n.* 1. (in Semitic myth) a female demon dwelling in deserted places and attacking children. 2. (in Jewish folklore) Adam's first wife, before Eve was created.

Li·li·u·o·ka·la·ni (lē lē'ōō ō kä lä'nē), *n.* **Lydia Ka·me·ke·ha** (kä'me ke'hä), 1838–1917, last queen of the Hawaiian Islands 1891–93.

Lille (lēl), *n.* a city in N France. 177,218. Formerly, **Lisle.**

Lil·li·put (lil'i put', -pət), *n.* an imaginary country inhabited by people about 6 in. (15 cm) tall, described in Swift's *Gulliver's Travels* (1726).

Lil·li·pu·tian (lil'i pyōō'shən), *adj.* 1. extremely small; tiny; diminutive. 2. petty; trivial. —*n.* 3. an inhabitant of Lilliput. 4. a very small person. 5. a person who is narrow or petty in outlook. [1726]

Li·long·we (li lŏng'wä), *n.* the capital of Malawi, in the SW part. 186,800.

lilt (lilt), *n., v.,* **lilt·ed, lilt·ing.** —*n.* 1. rhythmic swing or cadence. 2. a lilting song or tune. —*v.i., v.t.* 3. to sing or play in a light, tripping, or rhythmic manner. [1300–50: ME *lulte;* pern. akin to D *lul* pipe, *lullen* to lull] —**lilt'ing·ly,** *adv.* —**lilt'ing·ness,** *n.*

lil·y (lil'ē), *n., pl.* **lil·ies,** *adj.* —*n.* 1. any scaly-bulbed plant of the genus *Lilium,* having showy, funnel-shaped or bell-shaped flowers. 2. the flower or the bulb of such a plant. 3. any of various related or similar plants or their flowers, as the mariposa lily or the calla lily. 4. FLEUR-DE-LIS (def. 1). —*adj.* 5. white as a lily: *her lily hands.* 6. delicately fair: *a lily maiden.* 7. pure; unsullied: *the lily truth.* 8. pale; fragile; weak. [bef. 1000: ME; OE *lilie* < L *lilium;* cf. Gk *leīron*] —**lil'y-like',** *adj.*

lil'y fam'i·ly, *n.* a family, Liliaceae, of nonwoody plants growing from bulbs, corms, rhizomes, or tubers, with narrow and parallel-veined, usu. basal leaves and often showy flowers: includes the true lily, tulip, trillium, hyacinth, asparagus, and aspidistra.

lil'y-liv'ered, *adj.* weak or lacking in courage; cowardly. [1595–1605]

lil'y of the val'ley, *n., pl.* **lilies of the valley.** a plant, *Convallaria majalis,* of the lily family, having an elongated cluster of small, drooping, bell-shaped, fragrant white flowers. [1555–65]

lil'y pad', *n.* the large, floating leaf of a water lily. [1805–15, *Amer.*]

lil'y-white', *adj.* 1. white as a lily. 2. pure; untouched by corruption or imperfection. 3. designating or pertaining to any faction or group opposing the inclusion of blacks in political or social life. [1275–1325]

Li·ma (lē'mə for 1; lī'mə for 2), *n.* 1. the capital of Peru, near the Pacific coast. 4,605,043. 2. a city in NW Ohio. 47,381.

li'ma bean' (lī'mə), *n.* 1. a bean, *Phaseolus limensis,* having a broad, flat, edible seed. 2. the seed. [1810–20; after LIMA, Peru]

lim·a·cine (lim'ə sin', -sīn, lī'mə-), *adj.* pertaining to or resembling a slug; sluglike. [1885–90; < L *līmāc-, s.* of *līmāx* slug; snail + -INE[1]]

lim·a·çon (lim'ə son'), *n.* a plane curve generated by the locus of a point on a line at a fixed distance from the point of intersection of the line with a fixed circle, as the line revolves about a point on the circumference of the circle. Equation: $r = a \cos\theta + b$. [1575–85; < F: lit., snail, OF, der. of *limaz* < L *līmācem,* acc. of *līmax* snail, slug]

$\theta = \pi/2$
$\theta = 0$
$OD = a$
$AB = BC = b$
$b < a$
limaçon

limb[1] (lim), *n., v.,* **limbed, limb·ing.** —*n.* 1. one of the paired bodily appendages of animals, used esp. for moving or grasping; a leg, arm, or wing. 2. a large or main branch of a tree. 3. a projecting part or member: *the four limbs of a cross.* 4. a person or thing regarded as a part, member, branch, offshoot, or scion of something. 5. *Informal.* a mischievous child; young scamp. —*v.t.* 6. to cut the limbs from (a felled tree). 7. to dismember. —**Idiom.** 8. **out on a limb,** in a risky or vulnerable situation. [bef. 900; ME, OE *lim;* akin to ON *limr* limb] —**limb'less,** *adj.*

limb[2] (lim), *n.* the graduated edge of a quadrant or similar instrument. [1350–1400; ME < L *limbus;* see LIMBUS, LIMBO[1]]

lim·bate (lim'bāt), *adj. Bot., Zool.* having a distinctive border or edging, esp. of a different color, as certain flowers. [1820–30; < LL *limbātus* bordered, edged. See LIMB[2], -ATE[1]]

limbed (limd), *adj.* having a specified number or kind of limbs (often used in combination): *a long-limbed dancer.* [1275–1325]

lim·ber[1] (lim'bər), *adj., v.,* **-bered, -ber·ing.** —*adj.* 1. characterized by ease in bending the body; supple; lithe. 2. bending readily; flexible; pliant. —*v.i.* 3. to make oneself limber (usu. fol. by *up*): *to limber up before the game.* —*v.t.* 4. to make (something) limber (usu. fol. by *up*). [1555–65; perh. akin to LIMB[1]] —**limb'er·ly,** *adv.* —**limb'er·ness,** *n.*

lim·ber[2] (lim'bər), *n.* the front part of the carriage for a horse-drawn field gun, to which the trails of the gun are attached. [1400–50; late ME *limo(ur* pole of a vehicle. See LIMB[2], -ER[1]]

lim·ber·neck (lim'bər nek'), *n.* a botulism of birds, esp. poultry, characterized by weakened neck muscles. [1905–10]

lim·bic (lim'bik), *adj.* pertaining to or of the nature of a limbus or border; marginal. [1880–85]

lim'bic sys'tem, *n.* a group of structures in the brain that include the hippocampus, olfactory bulbs, hypothalamus, and amygdala and are as-

The following two exercises will give you practice using your dictionary.

EXERCISE 4-9 Using the Dictionary

Answer the following questions about dictionary entries, using the sample page in Figure 4.3 as your source of information.

1. How many definitions are there for the word *like?* _____

2. In how many parts of speech can the word *like* be used? _____ Which part of speech use is still considered nonstandard by some? _____ Give an example of a sentence in which *like* is used in an "informal" way.

   _____

3. What is the source of the word *Lilliputian?* _____

   _____

4. Where is *Lima* located? _____

5. What is a synonym for *likewise?* _____

6. What is an archaic meaning of the word *lilied?* _____

   _____

7. What is the origin of the word *limacon?* _____

   _____

8. In the following sentence, which meaning of the word in italics is being used?

   Even though he had spent twenty years in the Senate, his reputation remained *lilywhite.*

   _____

   What word or phrase could be substituted for *lilywhite* in the above sentence?

   _____

9. When *likely* is used as an adverb, what word usually precedes it? _____

10. What kind of expression is *out on a limb?* _____

    _____

Exercise **4-10** **Using the Dictionary**

Use your desk dictionary to answer the following questions.

1. What is the meaning of *zeitgeist?* _____

   _____

   What is the origin of the word? _____

   Is the word considered a foreign term? _____ How do you know?

   _____

2. Who was Guy Fawkes? _____

   _____

3. What does *i.e.* stand for? _____

   What is the source of the abbreviation? _____

4. In the following sentence, "President Kennedy is famous for having *quar-antined* Cuba during the missile crisis," which definition of the italicized word is being used?

   _____

5. Where is Victoria Falls? _____

   _____

6. What is the difference in meaning in the words *sensual* and *sensuous?*

   _____

   _____

7. How many signs of the *zodiac* are there? _____ List three. _____

   _____

8. What is the preferred spelling of the past tense of *travel?* _____

9. What are the meanings of the words that combine to make the word *Tyran-nosaurus?*

   _____

What kind of animal is *Tyrannosaurus?* _____

When and where did it live? _____

_____

10. What is the origin of *ghetto?* _____

What is its older meaning? _____

What is its contemporary U.S. meaning? _____

■ STRATEGIES FOR LEARNING NEW WORDS

In this chapter you have explored a variety of ways for understanding the meanings of unfamiliar words. Responding to a word's context, studying word parts, and using dictionaries when necessary will help to make your reading easier and therefore more informative and more pleasurable. There is a difference, though, between having enough clues to a word's meaning to be able to go on reading and knowing the word so well that you can use it in speaking and writing. To really know a word, you have to *overlearn* it. Words that are truly a part of your vocabulary are words that you can use yourself and that you can get meaning from quickly as you read. How can you build a vocabulary that works for you? Here are useful steps you can take.

Guidelines for Learning New Words

1. **Intend to learn.** Only you can build your word power. Decide that it is time to make the effort to expand your vocabulary.

2. **Learn new words from this text.** Turn your intentions into action by studying all the new words in this chapter and those that are a part of each assigned reading selection's vocabulary section. Your instructor may select words from this chapter or from the "Expanding Vocabulary" lists for regular vocabulary quizzes. Begin by going back through this chapter and circling each word that is not now a part of your working vocabulary. (A process for overlearning those words follows this list.)

3. **Learn new words from general reading.** Just as you can build your word power by learning new words in this text, so you can identify and learn new words that you come across in your reading. Suppose you read the following sentence:

"Moreover, it is a distinctive feature of our civilization to be self-consciously aware of and inquisitive about cultures that are not our own."

Do you know the word *inquisitive*, or know it well enough to use it yourself? It was used in a newspaper article; it's probably a word you should have in your vocabulary. Circle the new words you come across and tear out the articles containing them so that, when you have time, you can include them in your vocabulary study. Or, record words to be studied in a notebook or on cards.

4. **Learn new words from your assigned college reading.** Much of the task of introductory courses in various fields of study is the learning of that field's terms and concepts. (This is why many textbooks have glossaries; the authors know that building vocabulary in that field is essential for beginning students.) *Intend* to learn these new words so that you will do well in your courses. Remember, too, that educated people use the language of the various fields of study in their conversation and writing. The language of your psychology course is found not only in psychology classrooms; it also appears in newspaper and magazine articles, in conferences between parents and teachers, and in conversations at the office. There is a long-term value in developing the vocabulary of a college-educated person. At the end of this chapter are lists of words associated with various fields of study. Draw from those lists words you do not know well and make them a part of your vocabulary study.

5. **Follow a plan for studying and overlearning new words to make them a part of your working vocabulary.** What follows is a popular strategy for overlearning words. It will help you expand your general vocabulary or learn terms for a course.

Using Vocabulary Cards

Instructors and students have long known that flash cards are useful for studying information that can be divided into small segments. You can make your own vocabulary cards for new words you intend to learn, whether these words come from this text, from your general reading, or from assigned readings. The process is the same. Here are the steps to follow.

1. Make one card for each new word you want to learn. Start the card when you come across a new word or later from the words you have circled in your reading.
2. Write the word on one side of the card. Then, find the meaning(s) of the word in your dictionary and write the definition(s) on the backside of the card. If you think you may have trouble pronouncing the word, add the word's phonetic spelling (found in the dictionary) to the front of the card.

3. You may want to include other useful information on each card, including the part of speech of the word, several members of the word's "family" (so that you can actually learn several words when learning one), examples or synonyms of the word, and a sentence in which you use the word. (Your instructor may require some or all of these elements.) Put words of the same family on the front of the card. Put all the other information on the back of the card. Figure 4.4 illustrates two sample vocabulary cards.

4. Find a few minutes each day to go through your cards, testing yourself. Look at the word on the front and say its definition to yourself. Also try to use it in a sentence. Then turn to the back of the card to see if you have defined and used the word correctly. If you do not know the word's definition, study the back side of the card again. Try to practice with a friend or classmate.

5. After you have practiced several times and think you have learned—really learned—some of the words, divide your stack of cards into two piles: those words you have learned and those you still need to work on. Continue to practice with the words you do not yet know.

6. Shuffle the cards after each practice so that you do not go through the words in the same order each time.

7. As you come across new words, add them to your stack and continue to sort out those cards for words you have learned. Every week or so, review

■ **FIGURE 4.4**

Sample Vocabulary Cards

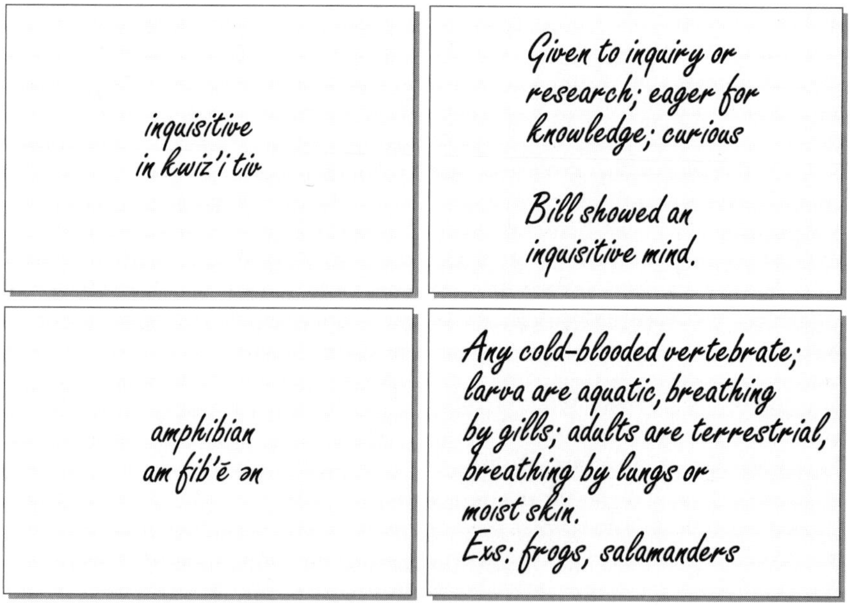

the cards for words you have learned, just to make sure that you continue to be comfortable with them. In your reviews, be sure to use each word in a sentence.

Using New Words

Remember that if you really know a word, you can use it in speech or in writing, not just respond to it when someone else uses it. So, to make new words a part of your vocabulary, you need to use them—and use them—every chance you get. Use the terms you are learning in class discussions and in papers or on quizzes. (If you are uncertain about usage or pronunciation, ask your instructor for guidance.) Use the words you are learning from other reading by talking about what you have read with friends. Then try to work in some of your new vocabulary when you write for this or other classes. Your expanded vocabulary will enable you to write with greater precision and vividness.

■ SOME IMPORTANT WORDS FROM VARIOUS DISCIPLINES

The following list contains some common terms from various fields of study. Those listed are ones frequently found in non-academic writing, such as newspapers and magazines. The list is also quite limited. You know, if you are taking a course in one of these disciplines, that you have already met many more new words than those listed here. Still, the list represents a good starting point for all college students, whatever subjects they choose to take. Make vocabulary cards for the words you do not yet know.

Business/Economics	**Social Sciences**	**Sciences**
affluent	cognition	black hole
aggregate	culture	density
consumer	demographics	ecosystem
deregulation	deviance	evolution
enterprise	egocentrism	gaseous
fiscal	gender	greenhouse effect
laissez-faire	meritocracy	organism
procurement	mores	primate
regressive tax	neurotic	species
scarcity	pathology	zygote

Government/History	**Philosophy/Religion**	**Literature/Arts**
anarchy	aesthetics	archetype
bureaucracy	asceticism	baroque
coalition	conscience	genre

Government/History	Philosophy/Religion	Literature/Arts
conservative	determinism	impressionism
devolution	ethics	icon
fascist	inherent	irony
gerrymandering	introspection	lyric
hegemony	meditation	metaphor
liberal	monotheism	narrative
Marxism	positivism	rhetoric
oligarchy	secular	symbol
parliament	theology	tragedy

Selection 1   Opposing Principles Help Balance Society

by **Sydney J. Harris**

Sydney Harris was both a drama critic and a columnist for the *Chicago Daily News.* His brief columns, covering a range of social, political, and philosophical issues, have been collected into several volumes, including *Clearing the Ground* (1986), in which the following essay appeared.

Prepare

1. From what you know about the author and the selection, what can you predict about purpose and format or style?

   _____

   _____

2. State briefly what you expect to read about. _____

   _____

3. What do you already know about the topic? Respond using *one* of the methods described in Chapter 2.

   _____

   _____

   _____

4. Use the title to pose questions about the reading selection. _____

_____

5. Preread the selection. Then read and annotate the essay. Finally, complete the comprehension and vocabulary checks that follow and answer the questions for discussion and reflection.

1   I devoutly wish we could get rid of two words in the popular lexicon: *liberal* and *conservative*. Both are beautiful and useful words in their origins, but now each is used (and misused) as an epithet by its political enemies.

2   *Liberal* means liberating—it implies more freedom, more openness, more flexibility, more humaneness, more willingness to change when change is called for.

3   *Conservative* means conserving—it implies preserving what is best and most valuable from the past, a decent respect for tradition, a reluctance to change merely for its own sake.

4   Both attributes, in a fruitful tension, are necessary for the welfare of any social order. Liberalism alone can degenerate into mere permissiveness and anarchy. Conservatism alone is prone to harden into reaction and repression. As Lord Acton brilliantly put it: "Every institution tends to fail by an excess of its own basic principle."

5   Yet, in the rhetoric of their opponents, both *liberal* and *conservative* have turned into dirty words. Liberals become "bleeding hearts"; conservatives want "to turn the clock back." But sometimes hearts *should* bleed; sometimes it would profit us to run the clock back if it is spinning too fast.

6   *Radical*, of course, has become the dirtiest of words, flung around carelessly and sometimes maliciously. Today it is usually applied to the left by the right—but the right is often as "radical" in its own way.

7   The word originally meant "going to the roots" and was a metaphor drawn from the radish, which grows underground. We still speak of "radical surgery," which is undertaken when lesser measures seem futile. The American Revolution, indeed, was a radical step taken to ensure a conservative government, when every other effort had failed.

8   Dorothy Thompson was right on target when she remarked that her ideal was to be "a radical as a thinker, a conservative as to program, and a liberal as to temper." In this way she hoped to combine the best and most productive in each attitude, while avoiding the pitfalls of each.

9   Society is like a pot of soup: It needs different, and contrasting, ingredients to give it body and flavor and lasting nourishment. It is compound, not simple; not like wine that drugs us, or caffeine that agitates us, but a blend to satisfy the most divergent palates.

10   Of course, this is an ideal, an impossible vision never to be fully realized in any given society. But it is what we should aim at, rather than promoting some brew that is to one taste alone. It may take another thousand years to get the recipe just right. The question is: Do we have the time?

Comprehension Check

Answer the following with a T (true) or F (false).

	T	F
1. Harris's main idea is that radical but not liberal views are needed by society.	___	___
2. The term *liberal* means anarchy.	___	___
3. The term *conservative* means preserving what is good from the past.	___	___
4. The meaning of the term *radical* comes from a comparison to radical surgery.	___	___
5. Dorothy Thompson (an American journalist) thought it was good to be a radical thinker.	___	___
6. Harris argues that a mix of viewpoints provides nourishment to society.	___	___
7. Conservatives can become radicals.	___	___
8. Any institution can destroy itself by excess.	___	___
9. The American Revolution was a conservative step to ensure a liberal government.	___	___

Expanding Vocabulary

Review the following words in their context and then write a brief definition or synonym for each word based on what you can learn from context clues.

lexicon (1) _____

epithet (1) _____

anarchy (4) _____

rhetoric (5) _____

maliciously (6) _____

agitates (9) _____

Write a brief definition or synonym for each of the following words after studying context clues and word parts.

degenerate (4) _____

repression (4) _____

pitfalls (8) _____

divergent (9) _____

Analysis of Content and Strategies

1. What is Harris's topic? _____

   Is it appropriate to say that Harris has two topics? Explain. _____

   _____

2. What is his thesis? State it in such a way that his two topics are united.

   _____

   _____

3. How, according to Harris, are the terms *liberal* and *conservative* misused and who misuses them?

   _____

   _____

4. Why is *radical* the dirtiest word of the three, and how is it most commonly misused?

   _____

   _____

5. When Harris writes that "society is like a pot of soup," what technique is he using?

   _____

   How does this technique help him to make his point?

   _____

   _____

Questions for Discussion and Reflection

1. What does Dorothy Thompson mean when she says she wants to be "a liberal as to temper"? How is she using the word *temper* in this context? (You may

need to study the various meanings of this word in your dictionary.) Do you agree with her? Why or why not?

2. Do you agree with Harris that a blend of differing attitudes is best for society? Why or why not?

3. Are there situations in our society today that should make our hearts bleed? Are there situations that should lead to wanting to turn back the clock? Be prepared to discuss these questions.

Selection 2   **What is Prejudice?**

by **Lester A. Lefton**

The following is an excerpt from *Psychology* (5th ed., Allyn & Bacon, 1994). Professor Lefton has taught undergraduate and graduate courses in psychology for more than twenty years at the University of South Carolina.

Preread

1. From what you know about the author and the selection, what can you predict about purpose and format or style?

_____

_____

2. State briefly what you expect to read about. _____

_____

3. What do you already know about the topic? Respond using one of the methods described in Chapter 2.

_____

_____

_____

4. Use the title to pose questions about the reading selection.

_____

5. Preread the selection. Then read and annotate the selection. Finally, complete the comprehension and vocabulary checks that follow and answer the questions for discussion and reflection.

1   **Prejudice** is a negative evaluation of an entire group of people that is typically based on unfavorable (and often wrong) ideas about the group. It is generally based on a small sample of experience, or even on no experience, with an individual from the group being evaluated. People sometimes develop prejudices because of stereotypes about others they do not know well. **Stereotypes** are fixed, overly simple (and often wrong) ideas, usually about traits, attitudes, and behaviors attributed to groups of people. Often, stereotypes are negative. People hold stereotyped ideas about Native Americans, Catholics, women, and mountain folk; the stereotypes can lead to prejudice. Stereotypes usually have a historical basis; for example, the idea that all African Americans are natural musicians or athletes probably stems from the fact that historically African Americans were barred from avenues of upward mobility except through the entertainment and sports industries.

2   Prejudice is an attitude. As we saw in chapter 16, an attitude is composed of a belief (all Xs are stupid), an emotional element (I hate those Xs), and often a behavior (I intend to keep those Xs out of my neighborhood). When prejudice is translated into behavior, it is called **discrimination**—behavior targeted at individuals or groups, with the aim of holding them apart and treating them differently. One widely held type of discrimination is *sexism*—prejudice based on gender; sexism involves accepting the strong and widely held beliefs of rigid gender role stereotyping. We examined gender role stereotyping in chapter 9, where we saw that gender differences tend to be small, when they exist at all. Overt discrimination based on gender is illegal; but it still exists, and many women's expectations for themselves are still based on their gender. Of course, not all people are sexist, but sexism remains a societal problem.

3   Sometimes people are prejudiced but do not show that attitude in behavior—that is, they do not discriminate. Merton (1949) referred to such individuals as *cautious bigots* (true bigots are prejudiced and discriminate). Also, sometimes people show *reverse discrimination*, bending over backward to treat an individual more positively than they should, solely to counter their own preexisting biases or stereotypes (Chidester, 1986). Thus, someone prejudiced toward African Americans may treat an African-American person oversolicitously and may evaluate the person favorably on the basis of standards different from those used for others. This too is discrimination.

4   A related concept is *tokenism*, in which prejudiced people engage in positive but trivial actions toward members of a group they dislike. A man may make a token gesture toward the women on his staff, or a manager may hire a token Hispanic American. By engaging in tokenism, a person

often attempts to put off more important actions, such as changing overall hiring practices. The trivial behavior justifies, in this person's mind, the idea that the person has done something for the disliked group. Tokenism has negative consequences for the self-esteem of the person it is applied to, and it perpetuates discrimination.

What Causes Prejudice?

5   The causes of prejudice cannot be tied to a single theory or explanation. Like so many other psychological phenomena, prejudice has multiple causes and can be examined within an individual, between individuals, within a group, or within society (Duckitt, 1992). We will consider four theories to explain prejudice: social learning theory, motivational theory, cognitive theory, and personality theory.

6   *Social Learning Theory.* According to social learning theory, children learn to be prejudiced; they watch parents, other relatives, and neighbors engaged in acts of discrimination, which often include stereotyped judgments and racial slurs; and then they incorporate those ideas into their own behavioral repertoire. After children have observed such behaviors, they are then reinforced (operant conditioning techniques) for exhibiting similar behaviors. Thus, through imitation and reinforcement, a prejudiced view is transmitted from parents to children, from one generation to the next.

7   *Motivational Theory.* We saw in chapter 10 that people are motivated to succeed, to get ahead, and to provide for basic as well as high-level emotional needs. If people are raised to compete against others for scarce resources, the competition can elicit negative views against competitors. Motivational theory thus asserts that individuals learn to dislike specific individuals (competitors) and then generalize that dislike to whole classes of similar individuals (races, religions, or colors). This helps make those groups of people (often seen as competitors) into scapegoats—such as the Jews in Nazi Germany, Japanese Americans during World War II, and blacks in South Africa today. Research with children, adolescents, and adults shows that people who are initially seen as friends or as neutral others are sometimes treated badly when turned into competitors. Competition for jobs among immigrants can also create prejudice, particularly in times of economic hardship.

8   *Cognitive Theory.* Cognitive theorists assert that people think about individuals and the groups they come from as a way of organizing the world. Recall from chapter 16 Cialdini's (1993) argument: There are so many events, circumstances, and changing variables in our lives that people cannot easily analyze all the relevant data. People thus devise mental shortcuts to help them make decisions. One of those shortcuts is to stereotype individuals and the groups they belong to—for example, all Hispanics, all homeless people, all men, all attorneys. By devising such shortcuts in thinking, people develop ideas about who is in an *in-group*—that is, who is a member of a group to which they belong or want to belong. People tend to see themselves and other members of an in-group in a favorable light.

9   As we saw in chapter 16, when judging other people, individuals make fundamental attribution errors. They assume that other people's behavior is caused by "internal dispositions"—which might not be true—and that other people are all alike (Judd & Park, 1988). They underestimate situational influences and overestimate dispositional influences on other people's behavior, and then they use those behaviors as evidence for their attitudes (prejudices). Thus, hostilities between Arabs and Israelis in the Middle East, Catholics and Protestants in Ireland, and blacks and whites in South Africa are perpetuated.

10   ***Personality Theory.*** Some psychologists assert that people develop prejudices because they have a prejudice-prone personality. Some personality tests examine the extent to which people are likely to be prejudiced. For example, one type of personality that appears to be prevalent is the *authoritarian personality.* Authoritarian people were fearful and anxious as children and may have been raised by cold, love-withholding parents who regularly used physical punishment. To gain control and mastery as adults, such individuals become aggressive and controlling over others. They see the world in absolutes—good versus bad, black versus white. They also tend to blame others for their problems and become prejudiced toward those people (Adorno et al., 1950). The relationship between personality and prejudice has its roots in psychoanalytic theory, but it is not widely accepted by many theorists who study prejudice today. However, the idea that some people have personality traits that lead them toward prejudice has guided some personality theory research.

Comprehension Check

Answer the following with a, b, c, or d to indicate the phrase that best completes each statement.

_____ 1. When people act on their prejudices, their behavior is called
   a. stereotyping.
   b. discrimination.
   c. tokenism.
   d. personality theory.

_____ 2. Cautious bigots are people who
   a. act on their authoritative personalities.
   b. act on their prejudices.
   c. act on their stereotypes.
   d. do not act on their prejudices.

_____ 3. Tokenism in hiring can result in
   a. a hiring freeze.
   b. not changing discriminatory practices.
   c. changing discriminatory practices.
   d. hiring in excess of need.

_____ 4. According to social learning theory, children learn prejudice through
  a. imitation and reinforcement from parents.
  b. reinforcement from other children.
  c. competition with other children.
  d. unloving parents.

_____ 5. According to cognitive theory, prejudice stems from stereotyping that is used to
  a. displace bad feelings.
  b. organize a company's hiring practices.
  c. imitate others in one's group.
  d. organize a complex world.

Fill in each blank with a word or phrase that best completes the sentence.

6. Treating a person from one group more favorably than people from other groups is _____ .

7. Prejudice may be caused by _____ for jobs, especially in difficult economic times.

8. Prejudice can result when people make errors in _____ ; that is, they assume that the behavior of others is caused by "internal dispositions" rather than possibly by the situation the others are in.

9. Some psychologists believe that people open to developing prejudice are those with _____ personalities.

10. Authoritarian personalities tend to see the world _____ and to _____ others for their problems.

Expanding Vocabulary

Review the following words in their context and then write a brief definition or synonym for each word based on what you can learn from context clues.

attributed (1) _____

expectations (2) _____

bigots (3) _____

phenomena (5) _____

slurs (6) _____

repertoire (6) _____

elicit (7) _____

scapegoats (7) _____

Write a brief definition or synonym for each of the following words after studying context clues and word parts.

reverse (3) _____

oversolicitously (3) _____

perpetuates (4) _____

dispositions (9) _____

Analysis of Content and Strategies

1. What is the author's purpose in this textbook section? That is, what does he seek to accomplish?

   _____

2. Explain the relationship between prejudice and discrimination. _____

   _____

3. Explain, in your own words, each of the four theories of prejudice formation.

   _____

   _____

   _____

   _____

Questions for Discussion and Reflection

1. Which of the four causes of prejudice, based on your experience and understanding of human behavior, make the most sense to you? Why? Are there any that do not seem reasonable to you? If so, why?

2. Are you prejudiced? If so, how do you account for your attitudes? Do you think you should work to eliminate those prejudices? Why or why not?

3. According to psychologists, differences between genders are slight, when they exist at all. Given the evidence, do you think sexism is ever justified? Why or why not?

4. What are some of the solutions to prejudice and to discrimination that you would propose?

Selection 3	Belly Up to the Bar: This Round's on Me

by **Roger L. Welsch**

In this article from *Natural History* magazine (April 1995), folklorist Welsch explores our culture's preference for what is square and shows how that preference is revealed in our buildings and dances and language itself.

Prepare

1. From what you know about the author and the selection, what can you predict about purpose and format or style?

   _____

   _____

2. State briefly what you expect to read about. _____

   _____

   _____

3. What do you already know about the topic? Respond using *one* of the methods described in Chapter 2.

   _____

   _____

   _____

4. Use the title to pose questions about the reading selection. _____

   _____

5. Preread the selection. Then read and annotate the selection. Finally, complete the comprehension and vocabulary checks that follow and answer the questions for discussion and reflection.

1   So why is squareness so dominant in American mainstream culture? Like people everywhere on this round earth, we presume that our way of living, our way of seeing things, our way of organizing, is obviously the most logical. Why do we shake hands firmly? Because a firm hand-

shake demonstrates honesty and trust, things like that. Why do we shake hands at all? Because, well, because that shows we're fair and square. There's that word again!

2 Contrarily, we throw "curve balls"—a double whammy—when we act erratically. "Going in circles" describes wasted time and frustration. If we want to suggest someone is crazy (or in modern parlance, "loopy"), we twirl a forefinger around an ear, as if a madman's problem is that his mind operates in circles. Yessir, he's a *screw*ball! Bad guys are "crooked"; good guys are "straight arrows."

3 I once asked an Omaha friend about the straight arrow metaphor for virtue; he laughed, saying this is a perfect example of how two peoples can see the same thing differently: "The white man sees only that an arrow goes to its target, not wavering from side to side; we Indians see an arrow's flight in its other dimension, as it rises from the bow and falls to its target."

4 Has an obsession with straight lines and right angles become a "straight" jacket that restricts our ability to see the world in other terms, to observe through the eyes of those who see the world in circles, arcs, and globes? What happens when we find ourselves in a culture where round is the rule; where, for example, it is not the cross that symbolizes religious understanding but the nested, curved commas that are yin and yang?

5 The late Lakota holy man Lame Deer, like many Native Americans, lived within a "round" culture and can give us some idea of the cross-cultural experience. He had explicit problems moving within the white man's square and straight world.

6 Why is my room square? Why are our buildings rectangular? Why are round beds not only peculiar but maybe even a little kinky? Why is a boxing "ring" square? (Ah, the wisdom of children with their round marbles and circled arena!)

7 I first became interested in the question of round versus square thirty years ago while examining Plains folk architecture. I was fascinated by the advantages of the Gothic barn roof as opposed to the gabled or hipped roof—less material, more open space, lines more suitable for piles of hay, more strength. I wondered why there weren't more Gothic roofs on barns. Maybe why there weren't *only* Gothic roofs.

8 There were also round barns, remarkable and beautiful—in part because their interiors are so open, so uncluttered by braces and supports. Round construction, it turns out, takes less material for the same amount of area and volume. It is stronger and more efficient, more attractive, more logical.

9 Also during my work with century-old barns, I encountered the original meaning and wisdom hidden in the expression "a square peg in a round hole." Today that phrase refers to someone (a square peg) who is out of tune with things around him (the round hole). Someone who is unqualified, who doesn't fit. Someone who makes things difficult.

10 Back in the days when heavy-framed barns were built by hand, however, the phrase had another meaning. Builders bored round holes in the gigantic beams of such barns and then, to be sure the buildings were solid

and secure for centuries, they drove into those round holes . . . square pegs. A square peg in a round hole was comparable to the hardy soul who refuses to go the easy route and thereby insures the strength of the union. But the original, structural meaning has been lost (so much so that some modern dictionaries offer "a round peg in a square hole" as an interchangeable alternative).

In 1970, at the age of 67, Lame Deer told ethnographer-biographer Richard Erdoes:

> To our way of thinking the Indians' symbol is the circle, the hoop. . . . The tipi was a ring in which people sat in a circle and all the families in the village were in turn circles within a larger circle, part of the larger hoop which was the seven campfires of the Sioux, representing one nation. The nation was only a part of the universe, in itself circular and made of the earth, which is round, of the sun, which is round, of the stars, which are round. . . . Our circle is timeless, flowing; it is new life emerging from death—life winning out over death.

11

> The white man's symbol is the square. Square is his house, his office buildings with walls that separate people from one another. Square is the door which keeps strangers out, the dollar bill, the jail. Square are the white man's gadgets—boxes, boxes, boxes and more boxes—TV sets, radios, washing machines, computers, cars. These all have corners and sharp edges—points in time, white man's time, with appointments, time clocks and rush hours—that's what the corners mean to me.

> —*Lame Deer, Seeker of Visions* (Simon and Schuster, 1972)

12   Is it any wonder that the Lakota and Omaha danced round dances while the pioneer favorite was the square dance?

13   Deploring governmental paternalism, historian Gilbert Fite recently wrote to *U.S. News and World Report* (January 9, 1995), "Congress should [abolish] reservations and bring [Indians] into the fullness of American life and society." Maybe, instead, we should open our gridlocked minds and give the mainstream a chance to enjoy the fullness of Native American life and society. After all, what goes around, comes around.

Comprehension Check ·

Fill in each blank with the word or phrase that best completes the sentence.

1. Mainstream American culture places a high value on _____ .

2. Many Native American cultures have lived in a _____ culture.

3. Evidence of our "square" culture can be found in our _____ .

4. The current expression "a square peg in a round hole" refers to someone who _____ .

5. When barns were built all by hand, square pegs were driven into round holes to make the barns _____ .

6. Lame Deer sees the circles of his culture as representing unity and

_____ .

7. The author suggests that those brought up in a "square" culture need to look at the world _____ .

8. We shake hands to show we can be _____ .

9. Round construction is _____ efficient than building square buildings.

Expanding Vocabulary

Review the following words in their context and then write a brief definition or synonym for each word based on what you can learn from context clues.

presume (1) _____

erratically (2) _____

parlance (2) _____

obsession (4) _____

explicit (5) _____

kinky (6) _____

gridlocked (13) _____

Write a brief definition or synonym for each of the following words after studying context clues and word parts.

contrarily (2) _____

ethnographer (10) _____

Deploring (13) _____

paternalism (13) _____

Analysis of Content and Strategies

1. What is Welsch's topic? _____

_____

2. What is the essay's thesis? _____

_____

3. Explain the source of the expression "a square peg in a round hole."

_____

4. Frequently, instead of making a statement, Welsch asks a question. What does he gain by this technique?

_____

Questions for Discussion and Reflection

1. Welsch wonders if we are so obsessed with "straight lines and right angles" that our obsession has become a "straight" jacket. In what way can our focus on "squareness" limit us?

2. If we are limited in how we see the world because of the ways we are taught in our culture, then what can be gained by learning about or experiencing other cultures?

3. If you are familiar with two cultures, think of ways that they differ in values, attitudes, simple expressions of beliefs. Does one set of views seem more "logical" to you than the other? If so, why?

4. Welsch gives examples of words and phrases that express cultural ideas and values. Can you think of other examples?

5. Welsch is implying that the way we use language shapes the way we see the world and the way we react to the world. Is this a new idea for you? If so, does it make sense? Why or why not?

CHAPTER 5

Recognizing A Writer's Structures and Strategies

In this chapter you will learn:

- The primary structures authors use to give order to their material

- To recognize signal words as guides to understanding a writer's structures and strategies

- To use a knowledge of structures to aid reading comprehension

- To read with understanding works that combine structures

In Chapter 3 you learned to distinguish between a work's main idea and the major and minor details that explain and illustrate the main idea. The pattern of main idea plus details is the dominant structure of good writing. Indeed, a work lacking a clear main idea, or one with details not connected to the main idea, is considered ineffective writing.

But there are other structures and strategies writers regularly use that you want to recognize when you read. Why? You can use your knowledge of structures to improve reading comprehension. Identifying a work's pattern helps readers understand the writer's purpose and remember the writer's ideas. Studies have shown that most of us have great difficulty remembering disconnected or random pieces of information. We do much better when we see how pieces fit together and give meaning to one another.

We also read more skillfully when we can predict what's coming next. Recognizing a work's structure or strategy allows us to anticipate what's coming and where, in general, the work is headed. For example, when we read in a history text that World War II was similar to World War I in several important ways, we can anticipate a comparison structure. The comparison structure is the appropriate one to accomplish the writer's purpose.

As you study the seven structures or strategies discussed in this chapter, keep two points in mind. First, most patterns are made clear to readers by particular words or phrases called *signal words*. The signal words commonly used to develop each structure will be listed; learn to recognize them. Second, identifying a particular structure is a means to an end (better comprehension), not an end in itself. So in the exercises you will need to do more than name the strategy used; you will also need to see how the key ideas fit into the strategy that has been used. Keep your goal in mind: greater control of the reading process.

■ LISTING

One of the simplest and handiest of patterns is the list. Sometimes the items are actually listed: indented and preceded by a numeral (1, 2, 3, etc.) or by bullets (•, •, •, etc.). You have seen lists in this text and probably in others as well. Lists are also presented within paragraphs and organized usually in one of three ways: (1) all of the items are listed in the first sentence and then each one is discussed in more detail in the sentences that follow; (2) one item at a time is introduced and each new item is announced by a signal word such as *second, in addition,* or *also*; (3) an opening sentence announces the number of items to be presented and then each one is explained in turn.

Whatever the particular strategy for introducing the list, a list tells us that all the items are equally important, unless the author signals that one item is more important. If we read, "Finally, and most importantly, salespeople must remember . . . ," then we know that the last item in the list is more important than the others. Usually, when you see a list, you need to learn all of the items. Here is an example.

topic sentence ———▶ Basically, human beings have affected the environment in three ways. The ① first factor is the natural growth of the human species. . . . The second element is the human appetite for natural materials. Coupled with increased population, this need for natural resources has reached a critical point where the depletion of certain goods is a distinct possibility. The ③ third element is the rapid development of technology, which generally has resulted in advances in the standard of living, but often at the cost of the natural environment.

Curran and Renzetti, Social Problems, 3rd ed.

Observe that this paragraph uses the approach of announcing the number of items in the opening sentence: there are *three* ways we have affected the environment. You should recognize that the first sentence is the paragraph's topic sentence. The paragraph has been annotated to indicate that three equal items have been listed.

Signal Words for Listing

The most common signal words to develop lists include:

also	first	last	next
and	furthermore	likewise	second
another	in addition	moreover	third
finally			

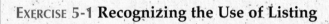

EXERCISE 5-1 Recognizing the Use of Listing

Read and annotate each of the following selections. Then complete the exercise that follows each selection.

I. Money serves three distinct functions. First, it serves as a *medium of exchange* in conducting transactions. It is much more efficient in facilitating the transfer of goods and services than a barter system would be. The second function of money is that it serves as a *unit of measurement.* Whether or not any transactions take place, the value of goods and services is measured in units of money. The unit of measurement within each country is the currency of that country. The unit of measurement in international transactions is quite often the U.S. dollar. Finally, money can be used as a *store of value.* During periods of rapidly rising prices, however, it does not serve this function well.

Turley Mings, The Study of Economics, 5th ed.

1. What is the paragraph's topic sentence? Underline it.
2. Briefly state each of the items listed in the paragraph:

   _____

   _____

   _____

3. List the signal words you find in the paragraph:

   _____

II. Four techniques used to "soften" hard water are distillation, chemical precipitation, ion exchange, and demineralization. In distillation the water is boiled, and the steam thus formed is condensed to a liquid again, leaving the minerals behind in the distilling vessel. . . .

   Calcium and magnesium ions are precipitated from hard water by adding sodium carbonate and lime. Insoluble calcium carbonate and magnesium hydroxide are precipitated and are removed by filtration or sedimentation.

In the ion-exchange method, used in many households, hard water is effectively softened as it is passed through a bed or tank of zeolite. Zeolite is a complex sodium aluminum silicate. In this process sodium ions replace objectionable calcium and magnesium ions, and the water is thereby softened. . . . The zeolite is regenerated by back-flushing with concentrated sodium chloride solution, reversing the foregoing reaction.

The sodium ions that are present in water softened either by chemical precipitation or by the zeolite process are not objectionable to most users of soft water.

In demineralization both cations and anions are removed by a two-stage ion-exchange system. Special synthetic organic resins are used in the ion-exchange beds. In the first stage metal cations are replaced by hydrogen and hydroxide ions. In the second stage anions are replaced by hydroxide ions. The hydrogen and hydroxide ions react, and essentially pure, mineral-free water leaves the second stage.

Hein and Arena, *Foundations of College Chemistry,* 5th ed.

1. What is the selection's topic sentence? Underline it.

2. Briefly explain each technique.

_____

_____

_____

3. What words or phrases announce each new technique? List them.

_____

_____

■ EXAMPLES

The use of examples is a strategy so common to good writing that we may not think of it as a strategy at all. But, even though providing examples is probably the most frequently used strategy, we still need to be alert to it as a particular choice writers make to develop their ideas.

The simplest pattern of presenting examples is to follow an idea with one example. The idea may be stated in one sentence or developed in several sentences, depending on the complexity of the idea. Then the example is given, and it, too, may take up one or several sentences. This pattern differs from listing because listing requires at least two items of equal importance. By contrast, writers don't need to give more than one example, and the example illustrates an idea, so it is not as important as the idea. Here is an example:

Main idea

> The aging U.S. population, geographic population shifts, and the satura-tion of many prime markets have resulted in various innovative retailing strategies. For (example) Limited Inc., which began by appealing to young, fashion-conscious women, now operates Lane Bryant for larger-sized women. Macy's has stores in Florida and California, to reduce the em-phasis on its Northeast base. Nontraditional locations, which have been underserved, are being used—Baskin-Robbins has outlets in U.S. Navy exchanges and Wendy's has an outlet in the Columbus, Ohio, Zoo.
>
> Evans and Berman, *Marketing,* 6th ed.

exs Limited/LB
Macy's location
Navy exs & Zoo
—new locations

There isn't any limit, of course, to the number of examples that may be given to develop one idea. We can imagine an entire section or a complete essay composed of a main idea and many examples. What we, as readers, need to rec-ognize is the difference between the ideas and the examples. Our primary task is to follow the discussion of ideas; examples help to explain those ideas and they add interest to the material. But, as you learned in Chapter 3, examples are details, and details may or may not need to be remembered. How important they are depends upon your purpose in reading. Examples can be very impor-tant in textbook reading for two reasons: (1) they help you learn difficult mate-rial and (2) you may be asked, on tests, to give an example of an idea or procedure. Be sure to note examples by writing "ex" in the margin as you an-notate your reading.

Signal Words for Examples

Examples are often introduced by one of two signal words:

for example   for instance

In many cases, however, no signal words are used. Examples are simply pre-sented without being labeled.

EXERCISE 5-2 Recognizing Examples

Read and annotate each of the following selections. Then complete the exercise that follows each selection.

I. The final player in the world of advertising is the collective variety of ser-vice organizations that assist advertisers, advertising agencies, and the media—the **vendors.** Members of this group are also referred to as free-lancers, consultants, and self-employed professionals. The list of possi-bilities is quite extensive and examples include freelance copywriters and graphic artists, photographers, music studios, computer service bureaus, printers, market researchers, direct-mail production houses, marketing consultants, telemarketers, and public relation consultants.

Wells, Burnett, and Moriarty, *Advertising: Principles and Practice*, 3rd ed.

1. What is the paragraph's topic sentence? Underline it.

2. How many examples are given? _____

3. List the signal words you find in the paragraph.

_____

II. The United States was a slow starter in the electronic field. It was not until the late sixties—almost two decades after the advent of musique concrete and synthesized sound—that any sizable number of electronic studios were in operation in the United States, although there was some early isolated activity on both coasts. Iconoclastic ventures took different forms in America, and the *enfant terrible* of the American avant-garde was John Cage (b. 1912). Always a rebel, he first attracted attention with his piano music of the 1930s, in which the piano was "prepared" by the insertion of nuts, bolts, screws, and other foreign objects between the strings, to produce overtone effects along with a certain jangle. He attacked the keyboard with his fingers, his forearm, and sometimes extraneous weapons as well.

Borroff and Irvin, *Music in Perspective*

1. What is the paragraph's topic sentence? State it.

_____

2. How many examples are given? _____ Briefly summarize the example(s).

_____

_____

3. How many signal words are used? _____

■ DEFINITION

As you have seen in this text, and as you have probably discovered in other courses, the defining of terms and concepts is a vital part of much writing. When we think of defining terms, we think particularly of textbooks, especially introductory texts, since so much of learning about a new subject is learning the vocabulary of that field of study. But the need to provide definitions is not limited to textbooks. When writing argumentative or persuasive essays, it is also important to define one's terms. Many arguments are actually over what a term means, or, in one writer's view, should mean. Think, for example, of the term *socialist*. Often in debates about political issues, someone will use the term as a negative label attached to an idea or a person, sometimes without really knowing what the term means. So, in many kinds of works we need to be alert to the use of definitions.

The structure of a formal definition requires placing the term in a category and then distinguishing it from other terms in that category. A *pen*, for example, can be defined as an instrument used for writing or drawing with ink. There are several kinds of writing instruments; a pen can be separated from other kinds (pencils, chalk) because it contains ink. When defining complex or debatable terms or concepts, writers often provide more than a one-sentence definition. They may give a brief history of the term, or contrast it with terms that are similar but not exactly the same, or give examples to illustrate the term. And they may develop the parts of their definition in any order; there is no required pattern, only various strategies used to fulfill the purpose of definition. Here, for instance, is a chemistry text's definition of *matter:*

exs

formal def.

The entire universe consists of matter and energy. Every day we come into contact with countless kinds of matter. Air, food, water, rocks, soil, glass, and this book are all different types of matter. Broadly defined, matter is *anything* that has mass and occupies space.

Hein and Arena, Foundations of College Chemistry, 5th ed.

Notice that the formal definition follows the examples in this paragraph.

Signal Words for Definitions

In textbooks the most obvious signal that a definition is coming is that the word to be defined is in **bold** or *italic* type. The signal is a visual one. Also look for the use of "that is" and "or" to introduce a definition:

Diction, that is, the writer's choice of language, . . .

Fossils, or the remains of prehistoric life, . . .

EXERCISE 5-3 Recognizing the Use of Definition

Read and annotate each of the following selections. Then complete the exercise that follows each selection.

I. **Cultural Lag** Ogburn coined the term **cultural lag** to describe the situation in which some elements of a culture adapt to an invention or discovery more rapidly than others. Technology, he suggested, usually changes first, followed by culture. The nine-month school year is an example. In the nineteenth century, the school year matched the technology of the time, which required that children work with their parents at the critical times of planting and harvesting. Current technology has eliminated the need for the school year to be so short, but the cultural form has lagged severely behind technology.

James M. Henslin, *Sociology*, 2nd ed.

1. Define the term **cultural lag** in your own words. _____

_____

2. What two strategies are used to define the term? _____

_____

3. What signals are used to indicate that a definition is being given? _____

_____

II. *Bureaucracy* is actually a term used to refer to any large, complex organization in which employees have specified responsibilities and work within a hierarchy of authority. The word *bureau* initially referred to the cloth covering of desks or writing tables used by seventeenth-century French government officials. Later, in the eighteenth century, the term "bureau" was coupled with the suffix *-cracy*, which long had been used to signify rule of government (as in *aristocracy*, *democracy*, or *theocracy*). In Britain, the bureaucracy is commonly referred to as the civil service or *Whitehall*, the name of the building in London that houses many government ministries. In looking at our government, when we refer to the bureaucracy and **bureaucrats**—employees of particular governmental agencies or units who possess expertise in certain issue areas—we mean the various departments, agencies, bureaus, offices, and other government units that administer our nation's laws and policies.

O'Connor and Sabato, *American Government:*
Roots and Reform, Brief Edition

1. Define the term *bureaucracy* in your own words. _____

_____

_____

2. List the strategies that are used to define the term.

_____

_____

3. What signals are used to indicate that a definition is being given? _____

■ ORDERING: CHRONOLOGY AND PROCESS

"Once upon a time . . ." The ordering of information in time sequence is familiar to us from the stories we have read. Chronological or time order is also found in histories and biographies, in works taking a historical look at some topic (such as the development of technology), and in explanations of how to do something (change a tire) or how a process is accomplished (how water is distilled). An advertising textbook may begin, for example, with a several-page history of advertising. In *American Government: Roots and Reform*, O'Connor and Sabato explain the three stages a bill must survive to become a law. Both textbooks use chronological order. Here is another example:

Main idea   Carbohydrate plays a prominent role in the global carbon cycle. Carbon
1st step   dioxide, water, and energy are combined in plants to form glucose; the
    plants may store the glucose in the polysaccharide starch. Then animals
2nd   or people eat the plants. In the body the liver and muscles may store the
3rd   glucose as the polysaccharide glycogen, but ultimately it becomes glucose
    again. The glucose delivers the sun's energy to fuel the body's activities.
4th   In the process, glucose breaks down to waste products, carbon dioxide
    and water, which are excreted. Later, these compounds are used again by
5th   plants as raw materials to make carbohydrate.

                            Sizer and Whitney, *Nutrition: Concepts and Controversies*

Observe that the passage announces that a cycle or process is being described. You want to annotate such a passage to emphasize the steps or stages that are explained.

When chronology is used to tell what happened or how something is accomplished, the success of the structure depends upon both completeness and accuracy in ordering the steps or stages. If long periods of time are not covered in a history text, or if steps are out of order in a process, then neither account is worth much. As readers studying material presented chronologically, we need to pay attention to the chronology. We need to learn not just what happened or what is done but also the order in which it happened or is done.

Signal Words for Ordering

The signal words for ordering include both "time" words and words denoting steps or stages. In addition, watch for the use of such words as *process, cycle, steps,* and *stages.* Here are key signal words for ordering:

after	first	last	second
before	following	next	then
finally	later	now	when

EXERCISE 5-4 Recognizing the Use of Ordering

Read and annotate each of the following selections. Then complete the exercise that follows each selection.

I. The first written messages were simply pictures relating familiar objects in some meaningful way—pictographs. Yet there were no images for much that was important in human life. What, for instance, was the image for sorrow or bravery? So from pictographs humans developed ideograms to represent more abstract ideas. An eye flowing with tears could represent sorrow, and a man with the head of a lion might be bravery.

The next leap occurred when the figures became independent of things or ideas and came to stand for spoken sounds. Written figures were free to lose all resemblance to actual objects. Some societies developed syllabic systems of writing in which several hundred signs corresponded to several hundred spoken sounds. Others discovered the much simpler alphabetic system, in which a handful of signs represented the basic sounds the human voice can make.

At first, ideas flowed only slightly faster when written than they had through speech. But as technologies evolved, humans embodied their thoughts in new ways: through the printing press, in Morse code, in electromagnetic waves bouncing through the atmosphere and in the binary language of computers.

Don Lago, "Symbols of Humankind"

1. What is the selection's topic? State it to indicate ordering or process.

_____

2. Briefly list the stages described. _____

_____

_____

_____

3. List the signal words that are used. _____

II. One way you can create money is to print it on a printing press in your basement. But if you were to do that you could get into a lot of trouble. A perfectly legal way you can create money, however, is to take out a loan at a bank. Imagine that you have decided that you will buy a computer that costs $1,200. You go to the bank for a loan, and if the bank approves your loan for $1,200, you sign a promissory note. The banker makes out a deposit slip to be credited to your demand deposit account, and you can then write a check to pay for the computer.

When the purchase is made and the computer dealer deposits your check in the bank, it is presented to your bank for payment. Your demand deposit account is decreased by the amount of the check. What has happened to your personal wealth? You now own a computer worth $1,200. You have also increased your liability by the amount of the loan ($1,200), so your personal wealth has not changed. Your assets and liabilities from this transaction are equal. But you have succeeded in increasing the money supply in the economy. That money is now in the computer dealer's checking account. When the computer dealer spends it, it will move to someone else's account.

Turley Mings, The Study of Economics, 5th ed.

1. What is the selection's topic? State it to indicate ordering or process.

_____

2. Briefly list the steps in the process. _____

_____

_____

_____

3. List the signal words that are used. _____

_____

■ COMPARISON AND CONTRAST

When we compare we examine similarities; when we contrast we examine differences. Writers use comparison and/or contrast structures because these structures help make sense of many topics. We can compare or contrast two schools, two movies, two jobs, two study methods. Writers select this structure for one of two reasons: (1) to explain their topic by comparing it to what may be more familiar to the reader; (2) to demonstrate that two items have important similarities or important differences. In the first instance, comparison is a strategy similar to providing examples; it illustrates the main idea. In the second instance, the comparison or contrast *is* the main idea.

Some writers examine both similarities and differences in their items, but more typically writers examine either one or the other. In fact, the comparison/contrast strategy is often signaled by an introduction such as: "In spite of some similarities, Item A (American schools, let's say) and Item B (Asian schools) are quite different." The similarities in this example are not important; the writer's purpose is to show how the items (American and Asian schools) differ. Consider the following example:

Contrast   *A*

To appreciate fully the distinction between aquatic and terrestrial environments, we should contrast the properties of water and air rather than those of water and earth. The density of water (about 800 times that of air) and its ability to dissolve gases and minerals largely determine the form and functioning of aquatic organisms. Water provides a complete medium for life. In contrast, both the atmosphere and the land make essential contributions to the environment of terrestrial life: air provides oxygen for respiration and carbon dioxide for photosynthesis, while soil is the source of water and minerals. Air offers less resistance to motion than does water, and thus constrains movement less, but it also offers less support against the pull of gravity.

← B

①

②

③

Robert E. Ricklefs, Ecology, 3rd ed.

When you recognize a comparison or contrast pattern, begin by labeling the two items being compared or contrasted. In the example above, the contrast is between *aquatic* (item A) and *terrestrial* (item B) environments (or between living in water and living on land). Then note the specific points of similarity or, in this case, contrast:

Item A (aquatic)	**Item B (terrestrial)**
1. water: high density	air much less dense
2. water: complete for life	land needed as well as air for life
3. water: more resistance but more support against gravity	air: less resistance but less support against gravity

Keep in mind that some points of similarity or difference may be implied rather than stated, or stated indirectly. That is, if I write that water is more dense than air, I have also "said" that air is less dense than water.

Signal Words for Comparison and Contrast

Signal words have two roles in developing the comparison or contrast pattern. Some words (or phrases) announce the use of the structure: "Comparing . . . views" or "The difference between . . . ," for example, announce the strategy that's coming. Other signal words *structure* the comparison or contrast. They indicate the shift from one item to the other.

both	however	likewise
but	in contrast	on the other hand
different	in the same way	similarly

EXERCISE 5-5 Recognizing the Use of Comparison and Contrast

Read and annotate each of the following selections and complete the exercise that follows each selection.

I. American teachers spend most of their time at school teaching. Among the Chicago elementary teachers we interviewed, just 7 percent of the sample of 112 teachers have only one or two preparations each day. None of the 65 Beijing teachers has more than two classes to prepare for each day. Classes might differ on different days, but generally the Beijing teachers in grades 1 to 3 teach reading, mathematics, and one other subject. After grade 4, they teach reading or mathematics and a second subject. High school teachers in Beijing typically teach only one subject two hours a day. The rest of their time is spent preparing for class, working with individual students, consulting with colleagues, and correcting papers. Even though they spend longer hours at school than American teachers, the schedules of Chinese and Japanese teachers allow them to enter the classroom with a level of energy and a degree of preparation seldom possible for American teachers.

Harold W. Stevenson, "Why Asian Students Still Outdistance Americans"

1. What two items are being contrasted? _____

_____

2. List the several points of difference. _____

_____

_____

_____

3. List the signal words that are used. _____

_____

II. Theorist *Marshall McLuhan* developed an innovative model to help explain the mass media. To McLuhan's thinking, books, magazines and newspapers were *hot media* because they require a high degree of thinking to use. To read a book, for example, you must immerse yourself to derive anything from it. The relationship between medium and user is intimate. The same is true with magazines and newspapers. McLuhan also considered movies a hot medium because they involve viewers so completely. Huge screens command the viewers' full attention, and sealed, darkened viewing rooms shut out distractions.

In contrast, McLuhan classified electronic media, especially television, as cool because they can be used with less intellectual involvement and hardly any effort. Although television has many of the sensory appeals of movies, including sight, motion and sound, it does not overwhelm viewers to the point that all else is pushed out of the immediate consciousness. When radio is heard merely as background noise, it does not require any listener involvement at all, and McLuhan would call it a *cool medium*. Radio is warmer, however, when it engages listeners' imaginations, as with radio drama.

John Vivian, *The Media of Mass Communications,* 3rd ed.

1. What are the two items being contrasted? _____

_____

2. Which media fit under Item A and which fit under Item B?

Item A   **Item B**

_____   _____

_____   _____

_____   _____

3. What are the points of difference? _____

_____

_____

4. List the signal words that are used. _____

_____

■ CAUSE AND EFFECT

One important way that we try to make sense of our world is to examine the *causes* of events or actions and to examine the *effects* of events or actions. We want to know what led to past events (Why did the Roman Empire collapse?), what is causing current situations (Why is there an increased fear of violence in our society?), and what will happen if we act in a particular way (Will reviewing periodically make me do better on tests?).

Cause/effect patterns can take several forms depending upon the writer's topic. First, a writer can explain how one cause produces one effect:

Cause   **Effect**
Dissolve zinc in sulfuric acid ——————▶ zinc sulfate forms

In many cases, one cause produces several effects:

Cause   **Effects**
                                                ——————▶ increase in sexist role stereotyping
television ◀——————————————————▶ decrease in time spent reading
                                                ——————▶ decrease in sensitivity to violence

In addition, several causes may work together to produce one effect:

Causes   **Effect**
less reading assigned ⟍
less writing assigned ————————————▶ lower SAT scores
dumbing down of textbooks ⟋

Finally, several causes may produce several effects:

Causes   **Effects**
improved reading skills ⟍   ⎰ better grades in courses
improved study skills ⟋ ————————▶   ⎱ more pleasure from school

These patterns of multiple causes and multiple effects remind us that rarely are there simple explanations in this complex world. When you recognize that a writer is discussing causes and effects, identify the particular pattern. Be sure that you understand which is the cause and which the effect and, then, be certain to note all the causes, or all the effects, that are listed. Let's look at this example.

Main idea
Greens did
not replace
p. parties

Although the Green movements and parties have played an important role in making people aware of ecological problems, they have by no means replaced the traditional political parties, as some political analysts in the mid-1980s forecast. For one thing, the coalitions that made up the Greens found it difficult to agree on all issues and tended to splinter into different cliques. Then, too, many of the founders of these movements, who often expressed a willingness to work with the traditional political parties, were ousted from leadership positions by fundamentalists unwilling to compromise their principles in any way. Finally, traditional political parties have co-opted the environmental issues of the Greens. By 1990, more and more European governments were beginning to sponsor projects to safeguard the environment and clean up the worst sources of pollution.

reasons:
 ①

②

 ③

Jackson J. Spielvogel, *Western Civilization*, 3rd ed.

First, what did (or did not) happen? Green (environmental) movements did not replace traditional parties in European politics. This is an effect—a negative effect—an expected event did not take place. Why not? Three causes are given, signaled by "For one thing," "Then, too," and "Finally." The Greens could not maintain their coalition, leaders who cooperated with traditional parties lost their positions, and traditional parties themselves embraced environmental issues.

Signal Words for Cause and Effect

The best indicators of course are the words *cause* and *effect*; you will find them in titles, section headings, and opening sentences. "Why" questions ("Why Women Are Paid Less Than Men") also announce that causes will be examined. Additionally, the following words and phrases signal cause/effect relationships.

as a result	due to	impact on
because	follows	therefore
changes	hence	thus
consequently		

Exercise 5-6 Recognizing the Use of Cause and Effect

Read and annotate each of the following selections and complete the exercise that follows each selection.

I. **Alcohol's Effects on the Brain** When alcohol flows to the brain, it first sedates the frontal lobe, the reasoning part. As the alcohol molecules diffuse into the cells of this lobe, they interfere with reasoning and judgment. With continued drinking, the speech and vision centers of the brain become sedated, and the area that governs reasoning becomes more incapacitated. Still more drinking affects the cells of the brain responsible for large-muscle control; at this point people under the influence stagger or weave when they try to walk. Finally the conscious brain becomes completely subdued, and the person passes out. This is fortunate because a higher dose would anesthetize the deepest brain centers that control breathing and heartbeat, causing death.

Sizer and Whitney, Nutrition: Concepts and Controversies, 6th ed.

1. State the topic of this passage so that a cause or effect pattern is indicated.

   _____

2. Briefly list the specific effects. _____

   _____

   _____

3. List the signal words that are used. _____

_____

II. When fossil fuels are burned in our homes, in our cars, or in our factories, two of the gases produced by the process are sulphur dioxide and nitrogen oxide. While other gases that result from burning of fossil fuels fall back to the earth, these two by-products enter the atmosphere to become two of the major pollutants responsible for the increased acidity of rainfall, commonly referred to as **acid rain.** More specifically, sulfur dioxide combines with oxygen and water in the atmosphere to form sulfuric acid and nitrogen oxide combines with water to form nitric acid. These acids return to the earth via rain and snow, which are at times as acidic as vinegar. Rain in some places is over 1,000 times more acidic than in the past. The major source of sulfur dioxide emissions is coal-burning power plants, many located in Midwestern states. The pollutants from these utilities are carried by the wind and clouds to the Northeastern states and Canada, raising the acidity in the rainfall in those areas. The major source of nitrogen oxide pollution in virtually all areas, however, is automobiles, although electrical utilities also emit nitrogen oxide and are the second major source of the pollutant.

Curran and Renzetti, *Social Problems* 3rd ed.

1. State the topic of this passage so that a cause or effect pattern is indicated.

_____

2. Briefly list the specific causes. _____

_____

_____

3. List the signal words that are used. _____

_____

■ PROBLEM/SOLUTION

A structure you should be alert to in both expository and persuasive writing is the problem/solution pattern. Many of today's textbooks explore problems in their subject area and present solutions that have been suggested and offer these for class discussion. The problem/solution pattern is also quite common in arguments over public policy issues.

The structure can have either two or three basic parts. The essay or textbook section begins by stating the problem under discussion: poverty, endangered species, or the budget deficit, for example. If the problem is well known by most readers, writers will not give too much space to introducing the problem. If the problem is new, or not properly understood, or not taken seriously, then writers may devote several paragraphs to explaining the problem.

In some uses of this structure, the second part is devoted to explaining the causes of the problem. If doing something to remove a cause is part of your solution, then you need to explain the cause first. (Hunger is caused by poverty. If you want to find solutions to hunger, you will need to find solutions to poverty.) If the causes are unknown, or no longer relevant to the solutions, then there is no section devoted to causes.

The third section (or second if causes are not discussed) presents the writer's solution(s). One solution may be presented, or several, depending on the problem and the writer's views on the issue. Because both problems and their solutions are complex, this structure is rarely found in one paragraph and is best illustrated in a section of several paragraphs. You have one example in the exercise that follows the material on signal words.

Signal Words for Problem/Solution Structures

Often the words *problem* and *solution* appear. Other words include:

answers   crisis   issues

 EXERCISE 5-7 Recognizing the Problem/Solution Strategy

Read and annotate the following selection and complete the exercise that follows.

Singles of all ages face problems concerning the purchasing, storing, and preparing of food. Whether the person is a student in a college dormitory, an elderly person in a retirement apartment, or a professional in an efficiency apartment, the problems of preparing nourishing meals are the same. Many college students live in dormitories, most without kitchens and freezers, and for them, purchasing and storage problems are compounded. Following is a collection of ideas gathered from single people who have devised answers to some of these problems.

Large packages of meat and vegetables are often suitable for a family of four or more, and even a head of lettuce can spoil before one person can use it all. Buy only what you will use. Don't be timid about asking the grocer to break open a family-sized package of wrapped meat or fresh vegetables. Look for bags of prepared salad greens to take the place of lettuce in both salads and sandwiches. Small-sized containers of food may be expensive, but it is also expensive to let the unused portion of a large-sized container spoil. Buy only three pieces of each kind of fresh fruit: a ripe one, a medium-ripe one, and a green one. Eat the first right away and the second soon, and let the last one ripen to eat days later. . . .

Buy fresh milk in the sizes best suited for you. If your grocer doesn't carry pints or quarts of milk, try a nearby convenience store. If you eat lunch in a cafeteria, try buying two pints of milk—one to drink and one to take home and store. . . .

Buy a loaf of bread and immediately store half, well wrapped, in the freezer (not the refrigerator, which will make it stale). Buy frozen vegetables in a bag, toss in a variety of herbs, and divide among single-serving containers. Vary your choices to prevent boredom.

For nutrition's sake, it is important to attend to loneliness at mealtimes; the person who is living alone must learn to connect food with socializing. Cook for yourself with the idea that you will invite guests, and make enough food so that you will have some left for a later meal. If you know an older person who eats alone, you can bet that person would love to join you for a meal now and then. Invite the person often.

Sizer and Whitney, *Nutrition: Concepts and Controversies*, 6th ed.

1. State the problem discussed in this passage. _____

_____

2. List two solutions you think are particularly important.

_____

_____

3. List the signal words that are used. _____

_____

EXERCISE 5-8 Distinguishing among Various Structures

Read, annotate, and then answer the questions that follow each of the selections. Part of your task in this exercise is to identify the structure or strategy used in each of the selections.

I. **Potential energy** is stored energy, or energy an object possesses due to its relative position. For example, a ball located 20 ft above the ground has more potential energy than when located 10 ft above the ground and will bounce higher when allowed to fall. Water backed up behind a dam represents potential energy that can be converted into useful work in the form of electrical or mechanical energy. Gasoline is a source of chemical potential energy. When gasoline burns (combines with oxygen), the heat released is associated with a decrease in potential energy. The new substances formed by burning have less chemical potential energy than the gasoline and oxygen did.

Hein and Arena, *Foundations of College Chemistry*, 5th ed.

1. What is the paragraph's topic sentence? Underline it.

2. What structure or strategy is used in this paragraph?_____

   _____

3. What techniques are used to develop the paragraph's strategy?

   _____

4. What signals are used in the paragraph? _____

   _____

II. SEX AND GENDER

An understanding of the difference between sex and gender is critical to the use of bias-free language.

Sex is biological: people with male genitals are male, and people with female genitals are female.

Gender is cultural: our notions of "masculine" tell us how we expect men to behave and our notions of "feminine" tell us how we expect women to behave. Words like *womanly/manly, tomboy/sissy, unfeminine/unmasculine* have nothing to do with the person's sex; they are culturally acquired, subjective concepts about character traits and expected behaviors that vary from one place to another, from one individual to another. . . .

Gender describes an individual's personal, legal, and social status without reference to genetic sex; gender is a subjective cultural attitude. Sex is an objective biological fact. Gender varies according to culture. Sex is a constant.

Rosalie Maggio, *The Dictionary of Bias-Free Usage:*
A Guide to Nondiscriminatory Language, 1991

1. What structure or strategy is used in this passage?

   _____

2. What is the main idea? State it so as to indicate the structure used.

   _____

   _____

3. List three points from the passage in a pattern that reveals the passage's structure.

_____

_____

_____

4. What signals are used? _____

_____

III. Most in-house agencies [advertising departments within companies] are found in retailing, for several reasons. First, retailers tend to operate under small profit margins and find they can save money by doing their own advertising. Second, retailers often receive a great many advertising materials either free or at a reduced cost from manufacturers and trade associations. Local media, for example, will provide creative and production assistance for free. Third, the timetable for retailing tends to be much tighter than that for national advertising. Retailers often create complete campaigns in hours, whereas advertising agencies may take weeks or months.

Wells, Burnett, & Moriarty, *Advertising: Principles and Practice,* 3rd ed.

1. What is the paragraph's topic sentence? Underline it.

2. What structure or strategy is used? _____

3. List three points from the paragraph in a pattern that reveals the paragraph's structure.

_____

_____

_____

4. What signals are used? _____

_____

IV. In addition to the massive erosional and depositional work carried on by Pleistocene (Ice-Age) glaciers, the ice sheets had other, sometimes profound, effects upon the landscape. For example, as the ice advanced and retreated, animals and plants were forced to migrate. This led to stresses that some organisms could not tolerate. Hence, a number of different plants and animals became extinct. Furthermore, many present-day stream courses bear little resemblance to their preglacial routes. The Missouri River once flowed northward toward Hudson Bay, while the Mississippi River followed a path through central Illinois and the head of the Ohio River reached only as far as Indiana. Other rivers that today carry only a trickle of water but nevertheless occupy broad channels are testimony to the fact that they once carried torrents of glacial meltwater.

Tarbuck and Lutgens, The Earth: An Introduction to Physical Geology, 4th ed.

1. What structure is used in this paragraph? _____

2. What is the main idea? State it so as to indicate the structure used.

   _____

3. List three points from the paragraph in a pattern that reveals the paragraph's structure.

   _____

   _____

   _____

4. What signals are used? _____

   _____

V. Population mobility offers openings for highly advertised international, national, or regional brands; retail chains and franchises; and major credit cards—among others. Their names are well known when consumers relocate and these names represent an assurance of quality. For example, Crest toothpaste, Heineken beer, British Airways, Honda, McDonald's, and Visa are recognized and successful worldwide, as well as throughout the United States. Macy's department stores do good business in Florida and California because a number of Northeasterners who were loyal customers have relocated there; yet, Macy's could not build a satisfactory customer following for its Missouri and Kansas stores and sold them.

Evans and Berman, Marketing, 6th ed.

1. What is the paragraph's topic sentence? Underline it.

2. What structure or strategy is used? _____

3. List three points from the paragraph in a pattern that reveals the paragraph's structure.

   _____

   _____

   _____

4. What signals are used? _____

   _____

VI. There is general agreement that the plague began in Europe when Genoese merchants brought it from the Middle East to the island of Sicily off the coast of southern Italy in October of 1347. It spread quickly, reaching southern Italy and southern France and Spain by the end of 1347. Usually, the diffusion of the black Death followed commercial trade routes. In 1348, the plague spread through France and the Low Countries and into Germany. By the end of that year, it had moved to England, which it ravaged in 1349. By the end of 1349, it had expanded to northern Europe and Scandinavia. Eastern Europe and Russia were affected by 1351, although mortality rates were never as high in eastern Europe as they were in western and central Europe.

   Jackson J. Spielvogel, *Western Civilization*, 2nd ed.

1. What structure is used in this paragraph? _____

2. What is the paragraph's topic? _____

3. List three points from the paragraph in a pattern that reveals the paragraph's structure.

   _____

   _____

   _____

4. What signals are used? _____

   _____

■ MIXED PATTERNS

You have already seen that more than one pattern can be used at a time in a given passage. Examples are often used to develop the definition of a word. The several effects of some event may be presented in a listing pattern, with signal words for listing used.

The longer the essay or textbook section, the more likely you are to find a mix of several patterns. As you read, try to recognize the primary structure. For example, observe that the example is given to develop the definition; in other words, the definition is the primary strategy in the passage.

Recognizing the primary structure will help you understand what the passage is about. If you observe a list, but don't see that it is a list of *effects*, you will miss the point of the passage. As you read the following example, try to recognize all of the strategies used but also decide which one is the primary strategy.

> There are three types of technology. The first is **primitive technology,** natural items that people have adapted for their use such as spears, clubs, and animal skins. Both hunting and gathering societies and pastoral and horticultural societies are based on primitive technology. Most technology of agricultural societies is also primitive, for it centers on harnessing animals to do work. The second type, **industrial technology,** corresponds roughly to industrial society. It uses machines powered by fuels instead of natural forces such as winds and rivers. The third type, **postindustrial technology,** centers on information, transportation, and communications. At the core of postindustrial technology is the microchip.
>
> James M. Henslin, *Sociology,* 2nd ed.

The opening sentence announces the paragraph's topic (types of technology) and signals the use of a list (three types). Examples are also used (spears, machines, the microchip) to illustrate each item in the list. But is either listing or providing examples the paragraph's primary purpose? Observe the use of **bold** type, often a visual signal of terms that will be defined. Isn't the primary strategy of the paragraph to define the three kinds of technology? Because three connected terms are defined together, a list is used. And examples are provided as a typical strategy in defining terms. You could also argue that a contrast structure is used, or at least implied, for the writer distinguishes among the three terms.

Remember that listing all of the patterns in use in a given selection is not your goal. Your goal is to understand the ideas and information provided and to recognize the writer's primary purpose so that you grasp what is most important in the passage. The following exercise and the readings that follow will give you more practice in using the writers' structures and strategies as guides to understanding.

EXERCISE 5-9 Recognizing and Learning from Mixed Patterns

Read, annotate, and then answer the questions that follow the selection.

By studying the rock cycle we may ascertain the origin of the three basic rock types and gain some insight into the role of various geologic processes in transforming one rock type into another. . . .

The first rock type, **igneous rock,** originates when molten material called **magma** cools and solidifies. This process, called **crystallization,** may occur either beneath the earth's surface or, following a volcanic eruption, at the surface. Initially, or shortly after forming, the earth's outer shell is believed to have been molten. As this molten material gradually cooled and crystallized, it generated a primitive crust that consisted entirely of igneous rocks.

If igneous rocks are exposed at the surface of the earth, they will undergo **weathering,** in which the day-in-and-day-out influences of the atmosphere slowly disintegrate and decompose rocks. The materials that result are often moved downslope by gravity before being picked up and transported by any of a number of erosional agents—running water, glaciers, wind, or waves. Eventually these particles and dissolved substances, called **sediment,** are deposited. Although most sediment ultimately comes to rest in the ocean, other sites of deposition include river floodplains, desert basins, swamps, and dunes. Next the sediments undergo **lithification,** a term meaning "conversion into rock." Sediment is usually lithified when compacted by the weight of overlying layers or when cemented as percolating water fills the pores with mineral matter. If the resulting **sedimentary rock** is buried deep within the earth and involved in the dynamics of mountain building, or intruded by a mass of magma, it will be subjected to great pressures and heat. The sedimentary rock will react to the changing environment and turn into the third rock type, **metamorphic rock.** When metamorphic rock is subjected to additional pressure changes or to still higher temperatures, it will melt, creating magma, which will eventually solidify as igneous rock.

Tarbuck and Lutgens, *The Earth: An Introduction to Physical Geology,* 4th ed.

1. What three strategies dominate this passage? _____

   _____

2. Which one of the three is the least important? _____

   _____

3. What, then, are the two primary purposes of this passage? Answer by completing each of the following statements so that the two strategies are indicated. The passage _____ three rock types. The passage _____ by which one rock becomes another type.

4. Briefly state, in your own words, how each rock type is formed.

_____

_____

_____

_____

_____

Selection 1 **Differences Between Public Speaking and Conversation**

Stephen E. Lucas

Stephen Lucas has been teaching communication arts at the University of Wisconsin at Madison since 1973. He directs the introductory course in public speaking and teaches a popular course on "The Rhetoric of Campaigns and Revolutions." This excerpt is from the fifth edition of Professor Lucas's textbook *The Art of Public Speaking*, published in 1995.

Prepare

1. From what you know about the author and the selection, what can you predict about purpose and format or style?

_____

_____

2. State briefly what you expect to read about. _____

_____

3. What do you already know about the topic? Respond using *one* of the methods described in Chapter 2.

_____

_____

_____

4. Use the title to pose questions about the reading selection. _____

_____

5. Preread the selection. Then read and annotate the article. Finally, complete the comprehension and vocabulary checks that follow and answer the questions for discussion and reflection.

1 Despite their many similarities, public speaking and everyday conversation are not identical. Let's consider an example in which casual conversation expanded gradually into a true—and vital—public speaking situation. Here the speaker originally had no intention of becoming a *public* speaker and had not trained formally for that role. She was forced to learn by trial and error—in circumstances where the outcome has affected one of the vital issues of our time:

2 Mary Fisher's life changed forever on July 17, 1991. Two weeks earlier, her ex-husband had called to say he had tested positive for the HIV virus. Now, as Fisher listened to her doctor, she learned that she, too, was HIV-positive.

3 Born into one of Detroit's most prominent families, Fisher was a successful artist, onetime television producer, and former staff assistant to President Gerald Ford. She was used to meeting challenges. But this was different. At the age of forty-three, the mother of two young sons, she felt a sense of shock "so great," she recalls, "that it took every ounce of energy for me to move."

4 For the next several months, Fisher wrestled with her grief and fear. In conversations with friends and family she wondered, "Why me?" and "What will happen to my children?" But as she came to terms with her condition, she also asked, "Can any good come out of this?" and "Is there anything I can do in the fight against AIDS?" Knowing that conversations with a few people would not solve the problem, in February 1992 she told her story to a reporter from the *Detroit Free Press*. The story made headline news and launched Fisher's career as an AIDS activist.

5 As Fisher moved more and more into the public eye, she found herself in many public speaking situations—from high-school auditoriums around

Detroit to the International AIDS Conference in Amsterdam. In the process, she had to adapt her conversational abilities to larger audiences and more structured occasions. The spontaneous give-and-take of conversation and informal interviews evolved into speeches prepared carefully in advance.

6   In April 1992 Fisher created the Family AIDS Network, a nonprofit organization devoted to expanding public understanding and resources in the battle against AIDS. Four months later, she presented a deeply moving speech at the Republican National Convention in Houston, Texas. The speech mesmerized delegates in the Astrodome and won the hearts of millions who saw it on television.

7   Again Fisher had to adapt—this time to the glare of national publicity. After Houston, her audience became the whole nation. Soon she was crisscrossing the land, speaking to church and community groups, health-care providers, educators, students, and government officials. Today she delivers about 75–80 speeches a year—not including radio, television, and newspaper interviews—to spread her message of awareness, compassion, and caring. She will continue, she says, as long as her health allows.

8   What a long road Mary Fisher has traveled in the past few years. If someone had asked her before July 17, 1991, "Do you see yourself as a major public speaker?" she would have laughed at the idea. Yet today she has become a compelling advocate for HIV-positive people of all ages, hues, and classes. Along the way, she has had to adapt to three major differences between conversation and public speaking:

9   **1.** *Public speaking is more highly structured.* It usually imposes strict time limitations on the speaker. In most cases, the situation does not allow listeners to interrupt with questions or commentary. The speaker must accomplish her or his purpose in the speech itself. In preparing the speech, the speaker must anticipate questions that might arise in the minds of listeners and answer them. Consequently, public speaking demands much more detailed planning and preparation than ordinary conversation.

10   **2.** *Public speaking requires more formal language.* Slang, jargon, and bad grammar have little place in public speeches. When Mary Fisher addressed the Republican National Convention, she didn't say, "We damn well better change our attitudes about people who are HIV-positive!" Instead, she delivered an eloquent appeal to "lift the shroud of silence which has been draped over the issue of HIV/AIDS." Despite the increasing informality of all aspects of American life, listeners usually react negatively to speakers who do not elevate and polish their language when addressing an audience. A speech is supposed to be "special."

11   **3.** *Public speaking requires a different method of delivery.* When conversing informally, most people talk quietly, interject stock phrases such as "you know" and "I mean," adopt a casual posture, and use what are called vocalized pauses ("uh," "er," "um"). Effective public speakers, however, adjust their voices to be heard clearly throughout the audience.

They assume a more erect posture. They avoid distracting mannerisms and verbal habits.

Comprehension Check

Answer the following with a T (true) or a F (false).

	T	**F**

1. When Mary Fisher knew she was HIV-positive, she was an accomplished speaker. ___ ___
2. Mary Fisher developed her speaking skills through trial and error. ___ ___
3. Mary Fisher's most famous speech was given at the 1992 Republican convention. ___ ___
4. Mary Fisher's experience shows that public speaking and ordinary conversation are quite similar. ___ ___
5. In both public speaking and informal conversation, people can interrupt and ask questions. ___ ___
6. Public speaking requires more preparation than informal conversation. ___ ___
7. Audiences expect speakers to elevate their language. ___ ___
8. Good public speakers stand and speak casually to help audiences relax. ___ ___
9. Good public speakers speak loudly enough to be heard by all the audience. ___ ___

Expanding Vocabulary

Match each word in the left column with its definition in the right column by placing the correct letter next to each word.

___ circumstances (1)	a. gradually developed
___ adapt (5) (8)	b. expect
___ evolved (5)	c. pretentious or unintelligible talk
___ mesmerized (6)	d. insert
___ anticipate (9)	e. conditions
___ jargon (10)	f. raise to a higher level
___ eloquent (10)	g. adjust
___ shroud (10)	h. spoken
___ elevate (10)	i. upright posture
___ interject (11)	j. kept spellbound
___ vocalized (11)	k. movingly expressive
___ erect (11)	l. cover or veil

Analysis of Content and Strategies

1. What is the selection's main idea? _____

   _____

   Where is it stated? _____

2. The wording of the main idea announces the passage's primary structure. What is that structure?

   _____

3. What two other structures or strategies are used by the author?

   _____

4. What signal word announces the second strategy used? _____

   What signal word announces the third strategy used? _____

   What visual signals are used to highlight each of these strategies?

   _____

5. Briefly state the three ways that conversation and public speaking differ.

   _____

   _____

   _____

For Discussion and Reflection

1. What do you think the author wanted to accomplish with his long example about Mary Fisher?

2. Were you interested in the story of Mary Fisher? Why or why not?

3. What two specific ideas in this passage about public speaking do you think are most important? Why did you choose these two?

4. In your view, what two characteristics of public speaking are the most difficult to produce? Why?

5. Are there any ideas in this selection that you could apply to your classes so that you could be more effective in discussions?

| Selection 2 | **The Crisis Coming to Campus** |

Thomas H. Kean

Thomas H. Kean is a former governor of New Jersey. He is currently the president of Drew University. His article appeared in the *Washington Post* on May 1, 1995 on the "op-ed" page, the page of columns of opinion opposite the editorial page.

■ Prepare

1. From what you know about the author and the selection, what can you predict about purpose and format or style?

   _____

   _____

2. State briefly what you expect to read about. _____

   _____

3. What do you already know about the topic? Respond using *one* of the methods described in Chapter 2.

   _____

   _____

   _____

4. Use the title to pose questions about the selection.

   _____

   _____

5. Preread the selection. Then read and annotate the article. Finally, complete the comprehension and vocabulary checks that follow and answer the questions for discussion and reflection.

1   Our nation is lurching toward what is arguably the gravest crisis in higher education in a generation. It is a crisis of access: The high cost of college is limiting quality higher education opportunities for all but the wealthiest

families. This crisis threatens more damage to campus diversity than all the high-profile battles in academia over race, gender and ethnicity.

2   That the United States sends more high school graduates to college than any other industrialized nation should not lull us to complacency. The continued willingness of students and families to incur an ever-growing mountain of debt partly masks the full impact of higher education's skyrocketing costs. But cracks in the facade are beginning to appear.

3   After decades of working to expand access to all students, our nation's commitment now seems to be more in word than in deed. Today, educational opportunities are increasingly sorted according to the type of school a student can afford. For low and moderate-income students, particularly minorities, the likely prospect of massive indebtedness often means reconsidering four-year college altogether. Nor are students the only ones reconsidering. Distressingly, some colleges, strapped for cash, have begun making admissions decisions based on a student's ability to pay rather the ability to benefit.

4   Students also know that college loans cannot pay all the bills, so they work part-time jobs. More than half of all full-time students work—an average of 25 hours a week—and there is growing evidence that it harms academic performance. Income, not merit, is increasingly determining the type of school students attend.

And this is only the beginning. T. Rowe Price recently estimated that a parent of a newborn today will have to invest more than $450 a month in high-yield stocks for the next 18 years to send a child to a private college.

5   As a university president, I see the impact every day. Students continually visit my office to tell me they no longer can afford to stay in school. Many are minorities, and an alarming number are middle-class. One described how her parents lost their home so they could keep paying the college bills. College presidents nationwide tell similar stories.

6   Ever since the G.I. Bill half a century ago, higher education has served as the great leveler in our country. But more and more it is becoming the great stratifier. Political and business leaders tell young people that education is the key to their—and our—futures. But the message to the students who visit my office is that the future is available only to those who can afford it.

7   This is not just an academic issue. At no other time in history has the possession of knowledge been so strong an indicator of economic wealth. It used to be that colleges and universities graduated people to manage capital. Now, we look to them to create capital. The health and vitality of colleges and universities cannot be separated from the health and vitality of our economy and society.

8   There is no magic wand to reverse this trend, but we must act soon. Unfortunately, the level of dialogue in Washington suggests that our political leadership has not yet come to grips with this crisis.

9   In the name of deficit-cutting, some proposals in Congress would burden already stretched students by increasing the cost of borrowing for school and eliminating some matching federal scholarship programs.

10   But even if Washington awakens to the problem, solving it will require more than tinkering with policy. Attitudes must also change. In recent years, higher education has mistakenly come to be viewed less as an investment and more as an expense. States with excellent public institutions, such as California and Virginia, focus more on downsizing and cutting state universities rather than improving them. The increasing reliance on student loans instead of grants suggests we are shifting the cost of education to future generations because we are not willing to pay the price today.

11   We must also ask hard questions of colleges and universities. Should our nation's investment in higher education undergo something similar to the restructuring corporate America has experienced the last 15 years? Do we lavish too much time and money on the top 10 percent of our institutions and not enough on improving the schools the majority of students attend? How can we use the new technologies to lower costs?

12   Debating these issues will be healthy, but it must be done in the context of enhancing—not diminishing—educational opportunity for all Americans. If we are to avoid becoming a nation of education haves and have-nots, we must address the looming access crisis now.

Comprehension Check ▪

Fill in the blank with the word or phrase that best completes the sentence.

1. The college crisis that concerns the author is a crisis of _____ .

2. More _____ in the United States go to college than in any other industrialized nation.

3. College costs continue to _____ .

4. Many potential students are having to choose colleges based on what they can _____ .

5. Over _____ percent of full-time college students work to help finance their schooling.

6. College graduates are essential to the society's _____ health.

7. Student loans, in contrast to grants, shift the cost of education to

_____ .

8. The author wants us to improve _____ for all Americans.

Expanding Vocabulary

Review the following words in their context and then write a brief definition or synonym for each word based on what you can learn from context clues.

access (1) (12) _____

academia (1) _____

incur (2) _____

facade (2) _____

strapped for (3) _____

vitality (7) _____

enhancing (12) _____

looming (12) _____

Write a brief definition or synonym for each of the following words after studying context clues and word parts.

complacency (2) _____

leveler (6) _____

stratifier (6) _____

downsizing (10) _____

Analysis of Content and Strategies

1. What is this essay's primary structure or strategy? _____

_____

2. What key idea is presented in paragraph 1? _____

_____

3. Which paragraphs are devoted to the first part of the essay's structure? _____ At what point does the author turn to the second

part of the essay? _____

4. What action does the author want to see? _____

_____

5. State the essay's thesis. _____

_____

_____

1. Do you agree that there is an access crisis in higher education? Why or why not?

2. Assuming that you agree that there is a problem, do you agree with the author's solutions? Is it appropriate to argue that starting a discussion about a problem is a good first step?

3. Would you like Kean to offer more detailed solutions? If so, do you have some suggestions for solving the problem?

Selection 3   **The Effects of the Automobile**

James M. Henslin

A professor of sociology at Southern Illinois University, James Henslin is the author of numerous books and articles that focus on his particular areas of interest. These include the sociology of ordinary life, deviance, and the homeless. The following is an excerpt from his textbook *Sociology: A Down-to-Earth Approach* (2nd ed., 1995).

1. From what you know about the author and the selection, what can you predict about purpose and format or style?

_____

_____

2. State briefly what you expect to read about. _____

_____

_____

3. What do you already know about the topic? Respond using *one* of the methods described in Chapter 2.

_____

_____

_____

4. Use the title to pose questions about the reading selection. _____

_____

5. Preread the selection. Then read and annotate the article. Finally, complete the comprehension and vocabulary checks that follow and answer the questions for discussion and reflection.

1   If we try to pick the single item that has had the greatest impact on social life in this century, among the many candidates the automobile and the microchip stand out, though it is still too early to judge the full effects of the latter technology. Let us look at some of the ways in which the automobile changed U.S. society.

2   **Displacement of Existing Technology**   The automobile gradually pushed aside the old technology, a replacement that began in earnest when Henry Ford began to mass-produce the Model T in 1908. People immediately found automobiles attractive (Flink 1990). They considered them cleaner, safer, more reliable, and more economical than horses. Cars also offered the appealing prospect of lower taxes, for no longer would the public have to pay to clean up the tons of horse manure that accumulated on the city streets each day. Humorous as it sounds now, it was even thought that automobiles would eliminate the cities' parking problems, for an automobile took up only half as much space as a horse and buggy.

3   The automobile also replaced a second technology. The United States had developed a vast system of urban transit, with electric streetcar lines radiating outward from the center of our cities. As the automobile became affordable and more dependable, Americans demonstrated a clear preference for the greater convenience of private transportation. Instead of walking to a streetcar and then having to wait in the cold and rain, people were able to travel directly from home on their own schedule.

4   **Effects on Cities**   The decline in the use of streetcars actually changed the shape of U.S. cities. Before the automobile, U.S. cities were web-shaped, for residences and businesses were located along the streetcar lines. Freed from having to live so close to the tracks, people filled in the areas between the "webs."

5   The automobile also stimulated mass suburbanization. Already in the 1920s, U.S. residents had begun to leave the city, for they found that they

could commute to work in the city from outlying areas where they bene-fitted from more room and fewer taxes (Preston 1979). Their departure significantly reduced the cities' tax base, thus contributing to many of the problems that U.S. cities experience today.

6   **Effects on Farm Life and Villages**   The automobile had a profound impact on farm life and villages. Prior to the 1920s, most farmers were iso-lated from the city. Because using horses for a trip to town was slow and cumbersome, they made such trips infrequently. By the 1920s, however, the popularity and low price of the Model T made the "Saturday trip to town" a standard event. There, farmers would market products, shop, and visit with friends. As a consequence, farm life was altered; for example, mail order catalogs stopped being the primary source of shopping, and ac-cess to better medical care and education improved (Flink 1990). Farmers were also able to travel to bigger towns, where they found a greater vari-ety of goods. As farmers began to use the nearby villages only for im-mediate needs, these flourishing centers of social and commercial life dried up.

7   **Changes in Architecture**   The automobile's effects on commercial ar-chitecture are clear—from the huge parking lots that decorate malls like necklaces to the drive-up windows of banks and restaurants. But the au-tomobile also fundamentally altered the architecture of U.S. homes (Flink 1990). Before the car, each home had a stable in the back where the family kept its buggy and horses. The stable was the logical place to shelter the family's first car, and it required no change in architecture. The change oc-curred in three steps. First, new homes were built with a detached garage located like the stable, at the back of the home. Second, as the automobile became a more essential part of the U.S. family, the garage was incorpo-rated into the home by moving it from the back to the front of the house, and connecting it by a breezeway. In the final step the breezeway was re-moved, and the garage integrated into the home so that Americans could enter their automobiles without even going outside.

8   **Changed Courtship Customs and Sexual Norms**   By the 1920s, the automobile was used extensively for dating, thereby removing children from the watchful eye of parents and undermining parental authority. The police began to receive complaints about "night riders" who parked their cars along country lanes, "doused their lights, and indulged in orgies" (Brilliant 1964). Automobiles became so popular for courtship that by the 1960s about 40 percent of marriage proposals took place in them (Flink 1990).

9   In 1925 Jewett introduced cars with a foldout bed, as did Nash in 1937. The Nash version became known as "the young man's model" (Flink 1990). Since the 1970s, mobile lovemaking has declined, partly because urban sprawl (itself due to the automobile) left fewer safe trysting spots, and partly because changed sexual norms made beds more accessible.

10   **Effects on Women's Roles**   The automobile may also lie at the heart of the changed role of women in U.S. society. To see how, we first need to

see what a woman's life was like before the automobile. Historian James Flink (1990) described it this way:

> Until the automobile revolution, in upper-middle-class households groceries were either ordered by phone and delivered to the door or picked up by domestic servants or the husband on his way home from work. Iceboxes provided only very limited space for the storage of perishable foods, so shopping at markets within walking distance of the home was a daily chore. The garden provided vegetables and fruits in season, which were home-canned for winter consumption. Bread, cakes, cookies, and pies were home-baked. Wardrobes contained many home-sewn garments.
>
> Mother supervised the household help and worked alongside them preparing meals, washing and ironing, and house cleaning. In her spare time she mended clothes, did decorative needlework, puttered in her flower garden, and pampered a brood of children. Generally, she made few family decisions and few forays alone outside the yard. She had little knowledge of family finances and the family budget. The role of the lower-middle-class housewife differed primarily in that far less of the household work was done by hired help, so that she was less a manager of other people's work, more herself a maid-of-all-work around the house.

11   Because automobiles required skill rather than strength, women were able to drive as well as men. This new mobility freed women physically from the narrow confines of the home. As Flink (1990) observed, the automobile changed women "from producers of food and clothing into consumers of national-brand canned goods, prepared foods, and ready-made clothes. The automobile permitted shopping at self-serve supermarkets outside the neighborhood and in combination with the electric refrigerator made buying food a weekly rather than a daily activity." When women began to do the shopping, they gained greater control over the family budget, and as their horizons extended beyond the confines of the home, they also gained different views of life.

12   In short, the automobile changed women's roles at home, including their relationship with their husbands, altered their attitudes, transformed their opportunities, and stimulated them to participate in areas of social life not connected with the home.

13   **In Sum**   With changes this extensive, it would not be inaccurate to say that the automobile also shifted basic values and changed the way we look at life. No longer isolated, women, teenagers, and farmers began to see the world differently. So did husbands and wives, whose marital relationship had also been altered. The automobile even transformed views of courtship, sexuality, and gender relations.

14   No one attributes such fundamental changes solely to the automobile, of course, for many other technological changes, as well as historical events,

occurred during this same period, each making its own contribution to social change. Even this brief overview of the social effects of the automobile, however, illustrates that technology is not merely an isolated tool but exerts a profound influence on social life.

Comprehension Check ·

Answer the following with a T (true) or F (false).

	T	F
1. People preferred cars to horses because cars would eliminate parking problems.	——	——
2. The automobile did not displace electric streetcars.	——	——
3. Because of cars, U.S. cities developed in web-shaped patterns.	——	——
4. Cars stimulated the suburban growth that has created problems for cities.	——	——
5. Cars brought farmers into nearby villages to shop, and those villages remained important social and commercial centers.	——	——
6. The car altered the architecture of U.S. homes by leading to garages attached to the houses.	——	——
7. Cars were used for dating, giving couples greater freedom.	——	——
8. Because of cars, women could shop in supermarkets, but they still found their social life at home.	——	——
9. Technology is an isolated tool having little effect on social life.	——	——

Expanding Vocabulary ·

Match each word in the left column with its definition in the right column by placing the correct letter next to each word.

_____ prospect (2)	a. ease, comfort
_____ eliminate (2)	b. separated from others
_____ radiating (3)	c. outlook
_____ convenience (3)	d. greatly
_____ isolated (6)	e. secret meeting
_____ cumbersome (6)	f. remove
_____ extensively (8)	g. borders or limits
_____ orgies (8)	h. gives credit to
_____ trysting (9)	i. proceeding outward from a central point
_____ confines (11)	j. wild parties
_____ attributes (14)	k. troublesome

Analysis of Content and Strategies

1. What is the selection's topic? _____

   _____

2. What is the selection's primary structure or strategy? _____

   _____

3. What gives you the answer to question 2? _____

   _____

4. List the major details in a pattern that reveals the essay's primary structure.

   _____

   _____

   _____

5. What other strategies does the author use? _____

   _____

6. What signals are used to mark each of the three strategies?

   _____

   _____

7. Briefly explain the series of changes in home architecture caused by the automobile.

   _____

   _____

   _____

   _____

For Discussion and Reflection

1. Which of the effects is the most startling to you—that is, the one you had not thought of as a result of the automobile? Does the author's explanation make the connection clear to you?

2. Which change do you think was the most significant for the twentieth century? Why?

3. Some of the changes were positive, but some, at least at the time, were negative. Which changes would you group as good? Which changes have had a negative effect on our society? Be prepared to defend your decisions.

CHAPTER 6

Writing Strategies
to Reinforce Reading

In this chapter you will learn:

- How writing reinforces reading comprehension

- How and when to highlight or underline

- How and when to annotate

- How and when to outline

- How and when to use mapping

- How and when to take notes

- How and when to write summaries

Many readers of the comics enjoy the comic strip character Cathy. Cathy has a job, friends and family, a dog—and problems. She's never quite ready to start her diet; she needs more time to get ready for a date; she tries really hard to get organized but still manages to have a desk piled high with unfinished work. Yes, we know Cathy; her difficulties are all too familiar. How do we get ourselves organized, disciplined, and directed to goals? These are good questions for both Cathy and college students. College students need answers to these questions if they are to cope with all the reading, writing, and learning required for success in their courses.

Students have been known to try to select their courses based on how much reading is involved. But let's face it: although some courses require more reading than others, most include a good bit of reading—reading from which you must learn complex information and ideas. The best approach is to take the courses you need and to develop effective strategies for handling the required reading. For most introductory courses you will have at least one textbook, some of which are more than 700 pages long. You may also have additional required readings, a book review to prepare, or readings for a research paper. To cope, you may need several specific strategies for reinforcing reading comprehension.

■ WHY WRITE?

Several points can be made to help you understand why writing as a part of active reading is so important. Remember that you do not read all materials the same way. Your purpose in reading and the difficulty of the material influence how you read. You are not going to be tested on this month's *Sport's Illustrated* or *People* magazine. You will be tested on the information in your textbook. And the level of difficulty varies between *People* and your texts. You don't have to study the articles in *People* to understand them; you may, by contrast, have to "work at" the material in a biology text.

Since you know that your purpose in reading your college texts is to become knowledgeable about the subject and prepare for testing in the course, the question then becomes how best to accomplish those goals. Studies have shown that students who mark their texts do better on exams than those who keep their books clean and new-looking. Studies have also shown that students who use one of the more detailed writing strategies, such as annotating or mapping, perform better than those who just highlight or underline their books. The evidence is in, and the message is clear: when reading to learn, learn by writing.

This chapter shows you five writing strategies (plus highlighting and underlining) to use to reinforce reading comprehension and to organize information that you want to learn. You have to decide what you want to learn, or how well you need to learn particular readings. Once you have decided on your purpose, you will also need to select the writing strategy best suited to you and to the particular reading context (your purpose in reading and the work to be read). No one of the strategies will be the best choice in every reading context, so become skilled in using several of these writing or marking tools.

■ HIGHLIGHTING/UNDERLINING

Highlighting is accomplished by marking over words or lines of text with colored pens designed for this use. The color calls attention to the marked material. In theory at least, one highlights only the key passages of any text.

Underlining serves much the same purpose of calling attention to key passages, in this case because the words or sections have been underscored with a pencil or pen. The goal of both strategies is to prepare the text for easier review of main ideas and as many of the supporting details as you need to learn.

Why use highlighting? Many students like to highlight their texts; are they doing something that will help their reading? First, highlighting helps you concentrate as you read. If you are going to mark the text, you will be paying more attention than if you have no pen in hand. In addition, highlighting, if done properly, requires readers to decide what is important—because that is what will be marked. Students seem partial to highlighting even though underlining produces the same results: increased concentration and a focus on main ideas. Many develop a complex system of several colors. The result may be a brightly colored page but not necessarily a good guide for review. The use of colored highlighting seems especially questionable with many of today's textbooks that use two or more colors and striking bold and italic type. Neat underlining of main ideas may be a better choice when you are reading a text that uses two or more colors. On the other hand, highlighting may be the better choice with a single-color text, particularly one in small print with lines close together, leaving little room for underlining.

Whether highlighting or underlining, you need to find the right balance between too little marking and too much. There is little point in holding a pen in your hand if you hardly ever use it. However, most who highlight or underline err in the other direction; they mark too much. Let's look at two versions of the passage on living in water and living on land that you studied in Chapter 5. Which version of underlining appears the most useful?

I. To appreciate fully the distinction between aquatic and terrestrial environments, we should contrast the properties of water and air rather than those of water and earth. The density of water (about 800 times that of air) and its ability to dissolve gases and minerals largely determine the form and functioning of aquatic organisms. Water provides a complete medium for life. In contrast, both the atmosphere and the land make essential contributions to the environment of terrestrial life: air provides oxygen for respiration and carbon dioxide for photosynthesis, while soil is the source of water and minerals. Air offers less resistance to motion than does water, and thus constrains movement less, but it also offers less support against the pull of gravity.

Robert E. Ricklefs, Ecology, 3rd ed.

II. To appreciate fully the distinction between aquatic and terrestrial environments, we should contrast the properties of water and air, rather than those of water and earth. The density of water (about 800 times that of air) and its ability to dissolve gases and minerals largely determine the form and functioning of aquatic organisms. Water provides a complete medium for life. In contrast, both the atmosphere and the land make essential contributions to the environment of terrestrial life: air provides oxygen for respiration and carbon dioxide for photosynthesis, while soil is the source of water and minerals. Air offers less resistance to motion

~~than does water~~, and thus constrains movement less, but it also offers ~~less support against the pull of gravity.~~

Robert E. Ricklefs, *Ecology*, 3rd ed.

You can see in the first example that almost every line of the paragraph has been underlined. This activity has not helped the reader concentrate on main ideas during the initial reading and will not offer much guidance for review. The underlining in the first version directs the student to reread almost the entire paragraph. In the second version, though, the underlining highlights the main differences between life in the water and life on land, as created by each environment. In the second version, the marking will aid, not hinder, review.

How do you avoid the tendency to underline or highlight too much of the text? If you mark as you read each sentence, you will probably mark too much. You may be wiser to read the entire paragraph first and then mark what is essential. Here are some guidelines for highlighting or underlining.

Guidelines for Highlighting/Underlining

1. Mark after reading a paragraph or section so that you can see what the main ideas are.

2. Resist marking too much. Remember that you want to focus on main ideas and major details that you need to learn.

3. Use your prereading as a guide. Read to answer the questions you have raised from titles and section headings. Mark the answers as you find them.

4. Use your knowledge of writing patterns as a guide to recognizing the section's main ideas and supporting details. For example, if the passage discusses several causes of the greenhouse effect, mark each cause when it is introduced.

ANNOTATING

Although highlighting or underlining is better than not marking your texts at all, these strategies are most effective when they are used as a part of annotating. You were introduced to annotating in Chapter 2 and have been practicing with readings in subsequent chapters. Let's briefly review this important strategy for learning from reading. Remember that annotating means adding your marks to the text, whatever marks will help you comprehend as you read and review for tests.

There is no one way to annotate a text because each reader's engagement with a text will be somewhat different. Also, you will vary your annotating depending on the type of work you are reading. With more difficult passages, for example, you may add questions to your underlining and other notations. When reading arguments, you may question the writer's evidence or note your reasons for disagreeing. Here are two examples of annotated passages, one from a textbook, one from a philosophical essay.

Atmos. makes life possible
What it does:

I. The Earth is different from other known planets in a variety of ways. One of the most notable differences is the presence around our planet of a substantial atmosphere with components and characteristics that are distinctive from those of other planetary atmospheres. It is our atmosphere that makes life possible on Earth. (1) It supplies most of the oxygen that animals must have to survive, as well as the carbon dioxide needed by (2) plants. (3) It helps maintain a water supply, which is essential to all living things. (4) It serves as an insulating blanket to ameliorate temperature extremes and thus provides a livable environment over most of the Earth. (5) It also shields the Earth from much of the sun's ultraviolet radiation, which otherwise would be fatal to most earthly life forms.

Tom L. McKnight, *Essentials of Physical Geography,* 1992

Greed? Perhaps survival instinct?

How do we balance greed and love?

II. The central conflict in our nature is the conflict between the selfish individual and the group. Nature gave us greed, a robust desire to maximize our personal winnings. Without greed we would not have survived at the individual level. But Nature also gave us love in its many varieties, love of wife and husband and children to help us survive at the family level, love of friends to help us survive at the cultural level, love of people in general to help us survive at the species level, love of nature to help us survive at the planetary level. Human beings cannot be human without a generous endowment of greed and love.

4 levels of survival possible by love

Do we love our planet enough to survive?

Freeman Dyson, *From Eros to Gaia,* 1992

These examples of annotation suggest the following guidelines for annotating, a more complete list than what was established in Chapter 2.

Guidelines for Annotating

1. After reading a paragraph or section, underline the parts of sentences that contain main ideas.
2. Remember that you highlight by contrast; do not underline too much.
3. When you look up a word's definition, write the definition in the margin next to the word.
4. Distinguish between ideas and examples by marking "ex" in the margin next to an example.

5. Note lists of points by numbering each one in the margin. Identify the type of list, such as a series of causes or steps in a process.

6. Do not just underline the essay's or section's thesis; label it "thesis." Label a paragraph's topic sentence. If the topic sentence is unstated, create one and write it in the margin.

7. Circle key terms and the names of important figures. (Not just the names of historical figures or characters in stories, but also important figures in science, such as Boyle in chemistry or Watson in psychology.)

8. Draw arrows to connect example to idea. Devise your own symbols and abbreviations.

9. Add your reactions and questions. Both keep you engaged in your reading and prepare you for class discussions and tests.

 EXERCISE 6-1 Annotating

Read and then annotate the following passages. Compare your annotations with classmates.

I. The cognitive and behavioral views differ in their assumptions about what is learned. In the cognitive view, knowledge is learned, and changes in knowledge make changes in behavior possible. In the behavioral view, the new behaviors themselves are learned (Shuell, 1986). Both behavioral and cognitive theorists believe reinforcement is important in learning but for different reasons. The strict behaviorist maintains that reinforcement strengthens responses; cognitive theorists see reinforcement as a source of feedback about what is likely to happen if behaviors are repeated.

Anita E. Woolfolk, *Educational Psychology,* 6th ed.

II. Silence, then, could be said to be the ultimate province of trust: it is the place where we trust ourselves to be alone, where we trust others to understand the things we do not say; where we trust a higher harmony to assert itself. We all know how treacherous are words, and how often we use them to paper over embarrassment, or emptiness, or fear of the larger spaces that silence brings. "Words, words, words" commit us to positions we do not really hold, the imperatives of chatter; words are what we use for lies, false promises and gossip. We babble with strangers; with intimates we can be silent. We "make conversation" when we are at a loss; we unmake it when we are alone, or with those so close to us that we can afford to be alone with them.

Pico Iyer, "The Eloquent Sounds of Silence"

■ OUTLINING

Annotating gives you the opportunity to respond to reading in two ways. It is both a main idea strategy and a personal response strategy. That is, you want to mark main ideas, but you can also raise questions and record reactions to what you read. Another main idea strategy is outlining. In fact, effective outlining depends upon your recognition of the relationships between main ideas and details.

When should you use outlining? Outlining is a good choice when:

- you cannot annotate because you do not own what you are reading,
- the text has such narrow margins that you cannot do much annotating,
- learning will be aided by your seeing how the material is organized.

If you have difficulty recognizing main ideas and seeing how the parts fit together, then you can benefit from the discipline of outlining.

The formal outline relies on a specific pattern of numbers and letters and indenting to show the relationship of ideas. Here is the pattern:

I. Main idea
   A. Supporting idea
   B. Supporting idea

II. Main idea
   A. Supporting idea
   B. Supporting idea
     1. Major detail
     2. Major detail
       a. Minor detail
       b. Minor detail
   C. Supporting idea

III. Main idea

Whenever you are required to hand in an outline, be certain to follow the formal pattern shown above.

Some writers are more organized than others. As a result, some works are easier to outline than others. At times, when you are outlining for yourself, you may find that relaxing the formal pattern a bit will help you prepare an informal outline that meets your study needs. Even when outlining informally, though, you want to show the relationships among ideas and details. If you do not use both major headings and subheadings, then you are going to end up with just a list of points that fails to show the work's pattern of development.

After reading the following passage, prepare an outline and then compare yours with the one that follows the passage.

Culture involves at least three components: what people think, what they do, and the material products they produce. Thus, mental processes, beliefs, knowledge, and values are parts of culture. Some anthropologists would define culture entirely as mental rules guiding behavior, although often wide divergence exists between the acknowledged rules for correct behavior and what people actually do. Consequently, some researchers pay most attention to human behavior and its material products. Culture also has several properties: It is shared, learned, symbolic, transmitted cross-generationally, adaptive, and integrated.

The shared aspect of culture means that it is a social phenomenon; idiosyncratic behavior is not cultural. Culture is learned, not biologically inherited, and involves arbitrarily assigned, symbolic meanings. For example, Americans are not born knowing that the color white means purity, and indeed this is not a universal cultural **symbol.** The human ability to assign arbitrary meaning to any object, behavior, or condition makes people enormously creative and readily distinguishes culture from animal behavior. People can teach animals to respond to cultural symbols, but animals do not create their own symbols. Furthermore, animals have the capability of limited tool manufacture and use, but human tool use is extensive enough to rank as qualitatively different and human tools often carry heavy symbolic meanings. The symbolic element of human language, especially speech, is again a vast qualitative expansion over animal communication systems. Speech is infinitely more productive and allows people to communicate about things that are remote in time and space.

John H. Bodley, Cultural Anthropology: Tribes, States, and the Global System

Understanding the meaning of the term *culture* is of course essential to the study of cultural anthropology. A student taking the course and using this text would want to be sure to learn most of the ideas in the passage above. You might outline the material this way:

Culture

I. Components of culture
   A. People's thoughts
      1. patterns of thinking
      2. beliefs   } Some anthropologists just focus on this part of culture
      3. knowledge
      4. values
   B. People's behavior
   C. What people make   } some think these are most important

II. Characteristics of culture
   A. Shared—social
   B. Learned—not genetic

C. Symbolic
   1. gives meanings to objects, behavior
   2. leads to creativity
      a. tool making & use
      b. language
D. Passed from one generation to next
E. Adaptive—can change
F. Integrated—unified

Observe that the outline follows the basic formal pattern, but that notes have been added about the differences of opinion among anthropologists regarding the elements of culture, an important idea in the study of anthropology. The following guidelines include both "rules" for formal outlines and advice for designing useful tools for learning.

Guidelines for Outlining

1. Items of the same level (e.g., A and B) are lined up evenly; use a ruler if necessary (or tab settings if you are typing).
2. Each subdivision needs at least two parts; that is, you cannot have an A without a B, or a 1 without a 2.
3. Any subsection can have more than two parts and some sections may not be divided at all.
4. Include a thesis statement or a statement of the topic at the top of the page.
5. Use your knowledge of writing patterns to help you distinguish between main ideas and supporting details. Pay attention to signal words that announce a list, or steps in a process, or other organizational strategies.
6. If you seem to be just making a list rather than an outline, look at what you have written and see how you can reorganize the material or if you need some headings under which to group points.
7. Add notes in the margin (of your study outline) when helpful.

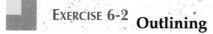

EXERCISE 6-2 **Outlining**

Read each of the following passages and then prepare an outline for each one. (Assume that you are studying these passages for a course.) Unless your instructor gives you other directions, make one a formal outline, the other an informal outline. You may want to annotate each passage first.

I. Sugars

Altogether, six sugar molecules are important in nutrition. Three are single sugars, or **monosaccharides.** The other three are the double sugars, or **disaccharides.** All of their chemical names end in *ose,* which means *sugar,* and while they all sound alike to the newcomer, they take on distinct characteristics to the nutrition enthusiast who quickly gets to know each individually.

The three monosaccharides are glucose, already described, **fructose,** and **galactose.** Fructose, or fruit sugar, the intensely sweet sugar of fruit, is made by rearranging the atoms in glucose molecules. Fructose occurs mostly in fruits; in honey; and as part of table sugar. Glucose and fructose are the most common monosaccharides in nature.

The other monosaccharide, galactose, has the same numbers and kinds of atoms, but they are arranged still differently. Galactose is one of the two single sugars bound together to form the pair that make up the sugar of milk. It does not occur free in nature; it is instead tied up in milk sugar until it is freed during digestion.

The three other sugars important in nutrition are disaccharides, linked pairs of single sugars. All three contain glucose. In **lactose,** the sugar of milk just mentioned, glucose is linked to galactose.

In malt sugar, or **maltose,** there are two glucose units. Maltose appears wherever starch is being broken down. It occurs in germinating seeds and arises during the fermentation process that yields alcohol. It also arises during the digestion of starch in the human body.

The last of the six sugars, **sucrose,** is the most familiar. It is table sugar, the product most people think of when they use the term *sugar.* In sucrose, fructose and glucose are bonded together. Table sugar is obtained by refining the juice from sugar beets or sugar cane, but sucrose also occurs naturally in many vegetables and fruits. It is as sweet as fruit sugar, because it too contains the sweet monosaccharide, fructose. It is of major importance in human nutrition.

Sizer and Whitney, *Nutrition: Concepts and Controversies*

_____

_____

_____

_____

_____

II. How a Bill Becomes a Law: The Textbook Way

A bill must survive three stages before it becomes a law. A bill may be killed during any of these stages; therefore, it is much easier to defeat a bill than it is to get one passed. The House and Senate have parallel processes, and often the same bill is introduced in each chamber at the same time.

Although a bill must be introduced by a member of Congress, it is often sponsored by a whole list of other members in an early effort to show support for the bill. Once introduced, the bill is sent to the clerk of the chamber, who gives it a number (for example, HR 1, or S 1—indicating House or Senate bill number one for the session). The bill is then printed, distributed, and sent to the appropriate committee for consideration.

The first stage of action takes place within the committee. The committee usually refers the bill to one of its subcommittees, which researches the bill and decides whether to hold hearings on it. The subcommittee hearings provide the opportunity for those on both sides of the issue to voice their opinions. Most of these hearings are now open to the public because of 1970s sunshine laws, which require open sessions. After the hearings, the bill is revised, and the subcommittee votes to approve or defeat the bill. If the subcommittee votes in favor of the bill, it is returned to the full committee, which then either rejects the bill or sends it to the House or Senate floor.

The second stage of action takes place on the House or Senate floor. Before the bill may be debated on the floor, it must be sent to the Rules Committee to be given a rule and a place on the calendar, or schedule. The rule given to the bill determines the limits on the floor debate and specifies what types of amendments, if any, may be attached. The calendar categorizes the bills. . . .

When the day arrives for floor debate, the House may choose to form a "Committee of the Whole" that allows the House to deliberate with the presence of only one hundred members to expedite consideration of the bill. This practice was borrowed from the British and used in the colonial legislatures as well. On the House floor the bill is debated, amendments are offered, and a vote is taken by the full House. If the bill survives, it is sent to the other chamber of Congress for consideration if it has not been considered there simultaneously.

Unlike the House, where debate is necessarily limited given the size of the body, bills may be held up by **filibusters** in the Senate. Filibusters, which allow for unlimited debate on a bill, grew out of the absence of rules to limit speech in the Senate and are often used to "talk a bill to death." . . . To end a filibuster, cloture must be invoked. To cut off debate, sixteen senators must first sign a motion for cloture. Then, a roll-call vote is taken. Two-thirds of the senators present—subsequent changes now require only sixty—must vote in the affirmative to end a filibuster. Each member of the Senate then can speak for one hour before debate is closed and the legislation on the floor is brought to a vote. If the other chamber approves a different version of the same bill, a conference committee is established to iron out the differences.

The third stage of action takes place within the conference commit-tee. The conference committee, whose members are from the original House and Senate committees, revises the bill and returns it to each chamber for a final vote. No changes or amendments are allowed at this stage. If the bill is passed it is sent to the president, who either signs it or vetoes it.

O'Connor and Sabato, *American Government: Roots and Reform*

_____

_____

_____

_____

_____

_____

_____

_____

_____

_____

_____

_____

_____

■ MAPPING

An alternative to outlining is mapping. Mapping is similar to outlining in that it records main ideas and shows the relationships between main ideas and supporting details. Mapping differs from outlining by using a visual pattern rather than numbers, letters, and indenting.

When should you use mapping? Whenever you might consider outlining, but you prefer a visual pattern. We know that some people understand material more easily when it is presented in drawings or diagrams. So, if you learn best this way, make your own diagrams to study from.

Although textbooks usually show maps that contain spokes coming out of a center circle, there really is no one right way to map information. Read the following paragraph on advertising and then observe how the information in this paragraph has been mapped in the two patterns shown in Figures 6.1 and 6.2.

■ FIGURE 6.1

Mapping

_____

Mapping

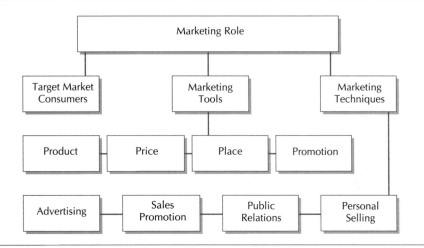

The Marketing Role. Marketing is the strategic process a business uses to satisfy consumer needs and wants through goods and services. The particular consumers at whom the company directs its marketing effort constitute the *target market*. The tools available to marketing include the product, its price, and the means used to deliver the product, or the place. Marketing also includes a mechanism for communicating this information to the consumer, which is called *marketing communication*, or promotion. These four tools are collectively referred to as the *marketing mix* or the *4 Ps*. Marketing communication is further broken down into four related communication techniques: advertising, sales promotion, public relations, and personal selling. Thus advertising is only one element in a company's overall marketing communication program, although it is the most visible.

Wells, Burnett, & Moriarty, *Advertising: Principles and Practice*, 3rd ed.

Experiment with different patterns. Find ones that you enjoy drawing, or think about ones that effectively show the relationship of ideas. For example, if you need to map the discussion of a process, think about using a flow chart map instead of spokes coming out of a center circle.

Guidelines for Mapping

1. Decide on the topic and write it, in a word or phrase, within a circle or box, either in the center of your paper or at the top.
2. Place each main idea on a line radiating out from the center circle (or in boxes attached to lines coming down from the top box).

3. Use as many levels of lines or boxes as needed to include the information you want to learn.

4. Try to draw your lines so that you can read each one without having to keep turning the paper around.

5. Give yourself enough room so that you can write out the information you need and read what you have written. For example, you may want to turn the paper to the side so that you have more space for your map.

6. Experiment with different patterns to find what works for you, or what best represents the pattern used in the material.

 EXERCISE 6-3 **Mapping**

On separate sheets of paper, prepare a map for each of the passages in Exercise 6-2. Either review each passage by looking over your annotations or use your outlines to help in mapping the material.

■ NOTE TAKING

There are times when annotating is not possible or when neither outlining nor mapping seems quite enough to help you learn from reading. At these times note taking may be the strategy to choose. When you take notes you may write more than with the other strategies you have studied. Sometimes you will write more than the original as you expand complex ideas in your own words in order to better understand them.

Note taking can be divided into *paraphrasing* and what is known as the *Cornell Method* of taking notes. When you paraphrase you restate the material in your own words, usually in complete sentences. The Cornell Method involves taking notes, either in sentences or phrases, on the right side of the page and then annotating the notes with key words placed down the left side of the page. When should you use one of these methods?

1. When you need to take down detailed information from reserve materials in the library. Paraphrasing can be used when taking notes for a research paper. The Cornell Method of notes may be effective when studying supplementary course materials.

2. When you are reading particularly complicated material that you need to study almost sentence by sentence to understand. Paraphrasing is the best writing strategy for making sense of difficult philosophical essays or complex poetry.

3. When you are studying complex material in your textbooks and feel that you need more help than annotating provides. The Cornell Method may

help you work through a detailed process or learn from a text that is almost entirely "straight words," with few section headings and other visual markers that give order to the material.

Let's look at each of these note taking strategies in turn.

Paraphrasing

A paraphrase is a restatement in your own words of some written material—a poem, a philosophical essay, a difficult section of a book. Your goal is to state the author's ideas accurately but in your own words, so a paraphrase calls for careful study of the original. Further, a paraphrase should not contain any words or phrases that add your opinion about the writer's ideas. Always one of the best ways to make sure that you understand some idea is to see if you can state it in your words.

Read, for example, the first four lines of a poem by Edna St. Vincent Millay and think how you would restate what they say.

Love is not all: it is not meat nor drink
Nor slumber nor a roof against the rain;
Nor yet a floating spar to men that sink
And rise and sink and rise and sink again;

Many students aid their reading of poetry by starting with a prose restatement. We can paraphrase the lines this way:

Love cannot take care of all our needs. It cannot provide food or shelter or help us sleep, or keep us from drowning.

Suppose that you were taking notes on Neil Postman's article on national news programs for a research paper. How would you paraphrase the following paragraph:

It is also believed that audiences are captivated by variety and repelled by complexity, which is why, during a typical thirty-minute show, there will be between fifteen and twenty "stories." Discounting time for commercials, promos for stories to come, and news readers' banter, this works out to an average of sixty seconds a story.

Suppose you prepared the following paraphrase:

Because it is believed that audiences like variety and dislike complexity, a typical thirty-minute show has between fifteen and twenty "stories." When you discount time for commercials, promos, and banter, this works out to about sixty seconds a story.

Is this a good paraphrase of Postman's passage? No, because it uses too many of Postman's words and ordering of ideas. Would you normally write "because it is believed" or "when you discount"? Probably not. Here is an equally accurate but also more honest paraphrase:

> A typical one-half hour news program covers 15 to 20 "stories." This means that each event gets covered in about sixty seconds—when commercials and announcements of what's coming are excluded. Apparently this is done because of the belief that viewers prefer brief coverage of many news items.

Observe that the language is simpler than Postman's but that the ideas are the same. Notice also that the order of Postman's ideas has been changed. The reason for brief treatment of many news items has been placed last. Reordering is acceptable when paraphrasing.

Guidelines for Paraphrasing

1. Read the passage through carefully before starting to paraphrase. (Often one sentence that is not clear by itself becomes clear as you read on.)
2. Check a dictionary for meanings of unfamiliar words. The dictionary may give you simpler language for the idea.
3. Paraphrase by idea, whether the idea is stated in a phrase or in several sentences; do not try to paraphrase word by word. Try to follow the development of ideas in the passage.
4. As you write each sentence of your paraphrase, do not look at the original passage. You want to show that you understand the ideas, not that you can just change a word here or there. Good advice for honest paraphrasing: Do not use more than *three* words in a row from the original.
5. You may find that changing the order of ideas will help you use your own wording.
6. After you have finished your paraphrase, compare it to the original to see if you are satisfied with the accuracy and completeness of your notes.

 EXERCISE 6-3   Paraphrasing

Read the following excerpt from Machiavelli's sixteenth-century essay The Prince, *an essay on politics and statecraft, and write a paraphrase of the excerpt. Do not include sentences on lions and foxes in your paraphrase. Instead, think about the human traits that Machiavelli has in mind when he compares princes to lions and foxes.*

> Everyone realizes how praiseworthy it is for a prince to honor his word and to be straightforward rather than crafty in his dealings; nonetheless

contemporary experience shows that princes who have achieved great things have been those who have given their word lightly, who have known how to trick men with their cunning, and who, in the end, have overcome those abiding by honest principles. . . .

So, as a prince is forced to know how to act like a beast, he must learn from the fox and the lion; because the lion is defenseless against traps and a fox is defenseless against wolves. Therefore one must be a fox in order to recognize traps, and a lion to frighten off wolves. Those who simply act like lions are stupid. So it follows that a prudent ruler cannot, and must not, honor his word when it places him at a disadvantage and when the reasons for which he made his promise no longer exist. If all men were good, this precept would not be good; but because men are wretched creatures who would not keep their word to you, you need not keep your word to them.

_____

_____

_____

_____

_____

_____

_____

_____

_____

_____

_____

_____

Note Taking: The Cornell Method

Note taking is, like outlining and mapping, a writing strategy that emphasizes main ideas and the supporting details that you need to learn in a course. Note taking usually means writing out more of the material than you would with outlining or mapping, but it is less complete and formal than paraphrasing. The Cornell Method is just a way of putting notes on paper so that you have an effective study tool when you finish. But since you are taking notes as a way to learn the material and have a convenient way to review the material, you probably should set up your notes the Cornell way. You always want to at least try strategies that you know have worked for other students.

Guidelines for the Cornell Method

1. Use 8½" by 11" lined paper that will fit into a three-ring notebook. With a ruler, draw a line from top to bottom on each page 2½" from the left margin.
2. Write your notes down the page in the 6" to the right of the line you have drawn. In the Cornell Method, the recommendation is to take notes in complete sentences, but you can modify this system and use incomplete sentences and phrases if you prefer.
3. After you finish taking notes—on a textbook chapter or supplementary readings—read through them, underlining key words.
4. Write the key words next to the notes on that topic in the 2½ inch space to the left of the vertical line you have drawn. Identifying the key words means that you are recognizing the various topics covered by your notes. Later you can use the key words, now placed down the left margin of the paper, as a way to review the notes before class or before tests.

Reread the paragraph on marketing (see p. 207) and then take notes on it using the Cornell Method. Compare your note taking to the sample page of notes that follows.

Notes on the Marketing Role

Marketing—def.	*Marketing—planned process to get goods and services to consumers.*
target market	*Consumers represent the target market.*
tools: 3	*Marketing tools include: product, price, & place.*
4th tool	*Promotion: Manner of communication.*
	4Ps—marketing mix
techniques—4	*4 communication techniques: advertising, sales promotion, public relations, personal selling*
advertising	*Advertising—most usable form of marketing.*

EXERCISE 6-4 Note Taking: The Cornell Method

Read the following passage and then prepare a page of notes using the Cornell Method.

According to the plate tectonics model, the earth's rigid outer shell, the lithosphere, is broken into several individual pieces called *plates*. Further, it is known that these rigid plates are slowly, but nevertheless continually, moving. This motion is believed to be driven by a thermal engine, the result of an unequal distribution of heat within the earth. As hot material gradually moves up from deep within the earth and spreads laterally, the plates are set in motion. Ultimately, this movement of the earth's lithospheric plates generates earthquakes, volcanic activity, and the deformation of large masses of rock into mountains.

Because each plate moves as a distinct unit, all interactions among plates occur along their boundaries. The first approximations of plate boundaries were made on the basis of earthquake and volcanic activity. Later work indicated the existence of three distinct types of plate boundaries, which are differentiated by the movement they exhibit. These are:

1. **Divergent boundaries**—zones where plates move apart, leaving a gap between them.
2. **Convergent boundaries**—zones where plates move together, causing one to go beneath the other, as happens when oceanic crust is involved; or where plates collide, which occurs when the leading edges are made of continental crust.
3. **Transform boundaries**—zones where plates slide past each other, scraping and deforming as they pass.

Tarbuck & Lutgens, *The Earth: An Introduction to Physical Geology,* 4th ed.

■ SUMMARY

The summary, one of the most important writing strategies, is a *brief* restatement of the main ideas of a work—a story, an article, or a chapter section, for example. Summaries are similar to paraphrases in that both *restate* the ideas in the original work but do not react to or comment on the original in any way. Summaries differ from paraphrases, though, because summaries *condense* the original whereas paraphrases are either about the same length or longer than the original. The primary purpose of a paraphrase is to clarify difficult material, but the primary purpose of a summary is to create a shortened version of the original that focuses on main ideas. A summary, then, is similar to an outline except that the format is different, for a summary is written in complete sentences and paragraphs.

Whenever you might make an outline or map you can write a summary. A summary makes a useful record for future study or helps you prepare for class discussions. You also want to practice writing summaries of your reading because you may have summary assignments in your courses. Instructors assign summaries because they are good measures of how carefully students have read and how well they have understood the writer's main ideas.

Read the following passage; then read the summary that follows and decide if it is condensed, clear, and accurate.

A New World Order?

The historical trend has been for states to grow larger and larger. Today, the embrace of capitalism and the worldwide flow of information, capital, and goods has rendered national boundaries increasingly meaningless (Robertson 1992; Toffler and Toffler 1993). Not only have the United States, Canada, and Mexico formed a North American free-trade zone (NAFTA), but 117 nations have made an agreement to slash tariffs globally (Davis and Ingrassia 1993). Most European countries have formed an economic and political unit (the European Union) that supersedes their national boundaries. Similarly, the United Nations, transcending national borders and moderating disputes between countries, can authorize the use of international force against individual nations—as it has done against North Korea in 1950, Iraq in 1990, and on a smaller scale, Somalia in 1993 and Bosnia in 1994.

Will this process continue . . . until there is but one state or empire, the earth itself, under the control of one leader? That is a possibility, perhaps deriving not only from these historical trends but also from a push by a powerful group of capitalists who profit from global free trade (Domhoff 1990). Although the trend is in full tilt, even if it continues we are unlikely to see its conclusion during our lifetimes, for national boundaries and national patriotism will die only a hard death. And as borders shift, as occurred with the breakup of the Soviet Union, previously unincorporated nations such as Lithuania and Azerbaijan demand their independence and the right to full statehood.

If such global political and economic unity does come about, it is fascinating to speculate on what type of government will result. If Hitler had had his way, his conquests would have resulted in world domination—by a world dictator and a world totalitarian regime based on racial identification. Fortunately, the tendency now is toward greater rights of citizens and greater political participation. If this trend continues—and it is a big "if"— and if a world order does emerge, the potential for human welfare is tremendous. If, however, we end up with totalitarianism, and the world's resources and people come under the control of a dictatorship or an oligarchy, the future for humanity could be extremely bleak.

James M. Henslin, Sociology, 2nd ed.

Summary #1

The passage questions if there will be a new world order. The trend has been for larger states, and now capitalism and worldwide communications make national boundaries much less important. Examples include NAFTA and the European Union. Also, U.N. forces have fought in many countries. Capitalists may create one state so they can make money. If unity does happen, it could result in a Hitler-like totalitarian government with a dictator. This would be terrible.

We can agree that the writer of this summary has read and understood parts of the passage. However, the summary contains details that should be removed, and it also needs some ideas added to be a clear and accurate restatement of the original. Sentences 3 and 4 should be eliminated as too specific while some coverage of the possible good results from a new world order need adding. These changes need to be made to create the balanced discussion in the original. The first summary suggests that the writer opposes any unified world state, believing that the result can only be bad. But that is not what the passage says. Here is an improved version:

Summary #2

The passage questions if there will be a new world order. The trend has been for larger states, and now global capitalism and worldwide communications seem to make national boundaries less important. Powerful capitalists may like to see a global state to enhance free trade, but historical trends and the desire of capitalists pull one way while patriotism and the desire of some groups for independent statehood pull against a global state. If global unity improved civil rights, that would be good. If global unity came about with a totalitarian government and a dictator, that would not be good. Global unity is not likely to happen in the near future.

The second version is only a bit longer than the first, but it is a much clearer and more accurate restatement of the original passage. From these summaries we can develop guidelines for summary writing.

Guidelines for Summary

1. Write in your own words, except for key terms that need to be included.
2. Begin with the topic or thesis and then add supporting ideas.
3. Write objectively; that is, do not include your opinion of the original passage. Be careful that your word choice does not distort the meaning of the original.
4. Do not include specific examples or descriptive details. Do include important definitions when appropriate.
5. Combine several ideas into one sentence as a way to condense the original.

EXERCISE 6-5 Summary

Read the following passage and then write a brief summary of the passage. Keep your summary under 100 words.

The Witchcraft Craze

1 Hysteria over witchcraft affected the lives of many Europeans in the sixteenth and seventeenth centuries. Witchcraft trials were prevalent in England, Scotland, Switzerland, Germany, some parts of France and the Low Countries, and even New England in America. As is evident from this list, the witchcraft craze affected both Catholic and Protestant countries.

2 Witchcraft was not a new phenomenon in the sixteenth and seventeenth centuries. Although its practice had been part of traditional village culture for centuries, the medieval church made it both sinister and dangerous when it began to connect witches to the activities of the Devil, thereby transforming witchcraft into a heresy that had to be extirpated. By the thirteenth century, after the creation of the Inquisition, some people were being accused of a variety of witchcraft practices and, following the biblical injunction, "Thou shalt not suffer a witch to live," were turned over to secular authorities for burning at the stake or hanging (in England).

3 The search for scapegoats to explain the disaster of the Black Death in the fourteenth century led to a rise in the persecution of people accused of sorcery. In a papal bull of 1484, Pope Innocent VIII made official the belief of the Catholic church in such pernicious practices. . . .

4 To combat these dangers, Innocent sent two Dominican monks, Jacob Sprenger and Heinrich Krämer, to Germany to investigate and root out the witches. Based on their findings, they wrote the *Malleus Maleficarum (The Hammer of the Witches)*, which until the eighteenth century remained one of the standard handbooks on the practices of witchcraft and the methods that could be used to discover and try witches.

5 What distinguished witchcraft in the sixteenth and seventeenth centuries from these previous developments was the increased number of trials and executions of presumed witches. Although estimates have varied widely, the most recent figures indicate that more than 100,000 people were prosecuted throughout Europe on charges of witchcraft. As more and more people were brought to trial, the fear of witches as well as the fear of being accused of witchcraft escalated to frightening proportions. Approximately 25 percent of the villages in the English county of Essex, for example, had at least one witchcraft trial in the sixteenth and seventeenth centuries. Although larger cities were affected first, the trials also spread to smaller towns and rural areas as the hysteria persisted well into the seventeenth century.

6 From an account of witch persecution in the German city of Trier, we get some glimpse of who the accused were: "Scarcely any of those who

were accused escaped punishment. Nor were there spared even the lead-ing men in the city of Trier." Although this statement makes it clear that the witchcraft trials had gone so far that even city officeholders were not immune from persecution, it also implies what is borne out in most witch-craft trials—that the common people were more likely to be accused of witchcraft. Indeed, where lists are given, those mentioned most often are milkmaids, peasant women, and servant girls. In the witchcraft trials of the sixteenth and seventeenth centuries, 80 percent of those accused were women, most of them single or widowed and many over fifty years old. Moreover, almost all victims belonged to the lower classes, the poor and propertyless.

7   The accused witches usually confessed to a number of practices. Many of their confessions were extracted by torture, greatly adding to the num-ber and intensity of activities mentioned. But even when people confessed voluntarily, certain practices stand out. Many said that they had sworn al-legiance to the devil and attended sabbats or nocturnal gatherings where they feasted, danced, and even copulated with the devil in sexual orgies. More common, however, were admissions of using evil incantations and special ointments and powders to wreak havoc on neighbors by killing their livestock, injuring their children, or raising storms to destroy their crops.

8   A number of contributing factors have been suggested to explain why the witchcraft craze became so widespread in the sixteenth and seven-teenth centuries. Religious uncertainties clearly played some part. Many witchcraft trials occurred in areas where Protestantism had been recently victorious or in regions, such as southwestern Germany, where Protes-tant–Catholic controversies still raged. As religious passions became in-flamed, accusations of being in league with the devil became common on both sides.

9   Recently, however, historians have emphasized the importance of so-cial conditions, especially the problems of a society in turmoil, in ex-plaining the witchcraft hysteria. At a time when the old communal values that stressed working together for the good of the community were dis-integrating before the onslaught of a new economic ethic that empha-sized that each person should look out for himself or herself, property owners became more fearful of the growing numbers of poor in their midst and transformed them psychologically into agents of the devil. Old women were particularly susceptible to suspicion. Many of them, no longer the recipients of the local charity available in traditional society, may even have tried to survive by selling herbs, potions, or secret re-medies for healing. When problems arose—and there were many in this crisis-laden period—these same people were the most likely scapegoats at hand.

10   By the mid-seventeenth century, the witchcraft hysteria began to subside. The destruction of the religious wars had at least forced people to accept a grudging toleration, causing religious passions to subside. Moreover, as

governments began to stabilize after the period of crisis, fewer magistrates were willing to accept the unsettling and divisive conditions generated by the trials of witches. Finally, by the end of the seventeenth and beginning of the eighteenth centuries, more and more educated people were questioning altogether their old attitudes toward religion and finding it especially contrary to reason to believe in the old view of a world haunted by evil spirits.

_____

_____

_____

_____

_____

_____

_____

_____

_____

_____

_____

_____

As you read and respond to the selections that follow, think about which writing strategy you would choose as the best way to learn the material in each selection. You may find that you have a favorite strategy that you want to use each time, but you may also discover that the best strategy for learning will vary from one selection to another. Your instructor may let you choose a writing strategy each time, or the instructor may require a specific strategy so that you practice with several. Your goal is to become skilled in all writing-to-learn methods so that you can be flexible in your studying.

| Selection 1 | **Private Participation in Public Education** |

Turley Mings

Turley Mings is Professor Emeritus of economics at San Jose State University. Dr. Mings taught the introductory course in economics at San Jose for thirty years and has also led many workshops on the teaching of economics. The following is from his text *The Study of Economics: Principles, Concepts, and Applications*, 5th ed., 1995.

■ Prepare

1. From what you know about the author and the selection, what can you predict about purpose and format or style?

   _____

   _____

2. State briefly what you expect to read about. _____

   _____

3. What do you already know about the topic? Respond using *one* of the methods described in Chapter 2.

   _____

   _____

   _____

4. Use the title to pose questions about the reading selection. _____

   _____

5. Preread the selection. Then read and annotate the article. Finally, complete the comprehension and vocabulary checks that follow and answer the questions for discussion and reflection.

1   Education is the most important collective good provided by state and local governments. It absorbs over one-third of all state and local government spending.

2   There is widespread concern over the condition of education in this country today. Over one-fourth of students drop out of school before graduation. Some 13% of the nation's 17-year-olds are functionally illiterate. Achievement tests given to students in 13 industrialized countries show American students rank 11th in chemistry, 9th in physics (for students who have taken 2 years of physics), and last in biology. Average Japanese 12th graders have a better command of mathematics than the top 5% of their American counterparts generally do.

3   This situation disturbs parents, educators, and politicians. It also disturbs leaders of American industry, who wonder where they are going to get the workers they need in coming years for their high-tech factories and offices. As an example, Baldor Electric Company installed a new manufacturing system at its Columbus, Mississippi, plant. Production was disrupted because, although computer-generated work orders clearly told employees *not* to weld motor shafts to rotors, they were welding them anyhow. Investigation turned up the fact that many of Baldor's employees simply couldn't read those orders. At a new Motorola factory that makes cellular phones in Schaumburg, Illinois, using highly automated equipment, just 25 out of 200 workers passed a basic skills test for jobs. Japanese automakers that have opened U.S. plants found that they have to hire college graduates to fill assembly jobs that would have been filled by high school graduates in Japan.

4   In coming years there will be a shortage of skilled labor at all levels. It was predicted that there would be a growth of 38% in job openings for technicians in the 1990s. The National Science Foundation estimates that the United States will experience a shortage of 700,000 scientists by the year 2010. Currently, more than half of the engineering Ph.D. degrees awarded in this country go to foreign nationals.

5   Concern over meeting the needs of American business for a competent labor force has led a number of companies and executives to get involved in the effort to improve education. In a 1990 *Fortune* magazine poll of its list of the 500 largest industrial corporations and the 500 largest service corporations, 98% of the companies responding contributed to public education. The principal form of assistance was contributing money (78% of the companies). Sizable percentages also provided students with summer jobs (76%), contributed materials or equipment to schools (64%), participated in school partnerships (48%), and encouraged employees to run for school boards (59%) or to tutor or teach (50%).

6   In the past, most corporate contributions have been at the college level, but businesses are increasingly getting involved in public education in the high schools and the lower grades. They have come to understand that worker competency in basic skills is as important to them as the contribution of the highly trained part of the labor force. Companies realize that they need to be part of the solution.

Comprehension Check

Fill in the blank with the word or phrase that best completes the sentence.

1. Over _____ of all state and local spending goes to education.

2. Problems in U.S. education concern _____ , _____ , and _____ .

3. Problems in U.S. education also concern _____ .

4. The United States can expect a _____ of skilled labor in the coming years.

5. More than 50 percent of engineering degrees awarded by U.S. colleges go to _____ .

6. In addition to giving money to improve education, companies are also providing _____ , _____ , and _____ .

7. Corporate involvement in education is now also at the _____ level.

Expanding Vocabulary

Review the following words in their context and then write a brief definition or synonym for each word based on what you can learn from context clues.

counterparts (2) _____

disrupted (3) _____

cellular (3) _____

automated (3) _____

foreign nationals (4) _____

Analysis of Content and Strategies

1. What is the section's topic? _____

_____

2. When you read "There is widespread concern over, . . ." what writing strategy can you identify or anticipate?

_____

3. What do the details in paragraph 2 contribute to developing the strategy?

_____

4. What do the examples in paragraph 3 contribute? _____

_____

What main idea do they support? _____

_____

5. How do paragraphs 5 and 6 contribute to the writing pattern? _____

_____

For Discussion and Reflection

1. Which one of the writing strategies would you choose to use to learn the material in this selection? Use that strategy to write to learn about this material.

2. Are you also concerned about U.S. education? If so, what concerns you the most? Why? If not, why are you not concerned?

3. What solutions would you propose to improve U.S. education?

Selection 2 | How We Listen to Music

Aaron Copland

The American composer Aaron Copland (1900–1990) is not only famous for his symphonies and ballets but also for his conducting. In addition he has written several books about music, including *What to Listen for in Music* (1939), from which the following excerpt is taken.

Vocabulary Alert

1. Copland refers to the following composers:
   Ludwig Beethoven, German composer, 1770–1827
   Igor Stravinsky, U.S. composer born in Russia, 1882–1971
   Peter Ilyich Tchaikovsky, Russian composer, 1840–1893
   Johann Sebastian Bach, German composer and organist, 1685–1750
   Wolfgang Amadeus Mozart, Austrian composer, 1756–1791
   Duke (Edward Kennedy) Ellington, U.S. jazz pianist, composer, and conductor, 1899–1974

2. Copland uses the following musical terms:
   fugue: a musical composition containing several themes developed by several voices or parts in turn

arpeggios: the soundings of the notes of a chord in rapid succession
    rather than at the same time
staccatos: notes played as a series of completely separate sounds rather
    than flowing into one another

Prepare

1. From what you know about the author and the selection, what can you predict about purpose and format or style?

    _____

    _____

2. State briefly what you expect to read about. _____

    _____

3. What do you already know about the topic? Respond using *one* of the methods described in Chapter 2.

    _____

    _____

    _____

4. Use the title to pose questions about the reading selection. _____

    _____

5. Preread the selection. Then read and annotate the article. Finally, complete the comprehension and vocabulary checks that follow and answer the questions for discussion and reflection.

1   We all listen to music according to our separate capacities. But, for the sake of analysis, the whole listening process may become clearer if we break it up into its component parts, so to speak. In a certain sense we all listen to music on three separate planes. For lack of a better terminology, one might name these: (1) the sensuous plane, (2) the expressive plane, (3) the sheerly musical plane. The only advantage to be gained from mechanically splitting up the listening process into these hypothetical planes is the clearer view to be had of the way in which we listen.

2   The simplest way of listening to music is to listen for the sheer pleasure of the musical sound itself. That is the sensuous plane. It is the plane on which we hear music without thinking, without considering it in any way.

One turns on the radio while doing something else and absentmindedly bathes in the sound. A kind of brainless but attractive state of mind is engendered by the mere sound appeal of the music.

3   You may be sitting in a room reading this book. Imagine one note struck on the piano. Immediately that one note is enough to change the atmosphere of the room—proving that the sound element in music is a powerful and mysterious agent, which it would be foolish to deride or belittle.

4   The surprising thing is that many people who consider themselves qualified music lovers abuse that plane in listening. They go to concerts in order to lose themselves. They use music as a consolation or an escape. They enter an ideal world where one doesn't have to think of the realities of everyday life. Of course they aren't thinking about the music either. Music allows them to leave it, and they go off to a place to dream, dreaming because of and apropos of the music yet never quite listening to it.

5   Yes, the sound appeal of music is a potent and primitive force, but you must not allow it to usurp a disproportionate share of your interest. The sensuous plane is an important one in music, a very important one, but it does not constitute the whole story.

6   There is no need to digress further on the sensuous plane. Its appeal to every normal human being is self-evident. There is, however, such a thing as becoming more sensitive to the different kinds of sound stuff as used by various composers. For all composers do not use that sound stuff in the same way. Don't get the idea that the value of music is commensurate with its sensuous appeal or that the loveliest sounding music is made by the greatest composer. If that were so, Ravel would be a greater creator than Beethoven. The point is that the sound element varies with each composer, that his usage of sound forms an integral part of his style and must be taken into account when listening. The reader can see, therefore, that a more conscious approach is valuable even on this primary plane of music listening.

7   The second plane on which music exists is what I have called the expressive one. Here, immediately, we tread on controversial ground. Composers have a way of shying away from any discussion of music's expressive side. Did not Stravinsky himself proclaim that this music was an "object," a "thing," with a life of its own, and with no other meaning than its own purely musical existence? This intransigent attitude of Stravinsky's may be due to the fact that so many people have tried to read different meanings into so many pieces. Heaven knows it is difficult enough to say precisely what it is that a piece of music means, to say it definitely, to say it finally so that everyone is satisfied with your explanation. But that should not lead one to the other extreme of denying to music the right to be "expressive."

8   My own belief is that all music has an expressive power, some more and some less, but that all music has a certain meaning behind the notes and that that meaning behind the notes constitutes, after all, what the piece

is saying, what the piece is about. The whole problem can be stated quite simply by asking, "Is there a meaning to music?" My answer to that would be, "Yes." And "Can you state in so many words what the meaning is?" My answer to that would be, "No." Therein lies the difficulty.

9   Simple-minded souls will never be satisfied with the answer to the second of these questions. They always want music to have a meaning, and the more concrete it is the better they like it. The more the music reminds them of a train, a storm, a funeral, or any other familiar conception the more expressive it appears to be to them. This popular idea of music's meaning—stimulated and abetted by the usual run of musical commentators—should be discouraged wherever and whenever it is met. One timid lady once confessed to me that she suspected something seriously lacking in her appreciation of music because of her inability to connect it with anything definite. That is getting the whole thing backward, of course.

10   Still, the question remains, How close should the intelligent music lover wish to come to pinning a definite meaning to any particular work? No closer than a general concept, I should say. Music expresses, at different moments, serenity or exuberance, regret or triumph, fury or delight. It expresses each of these moods, and many others, in a numberless variety of subtle shadings and differences. It may even express a state of meaning for which there exists no adequate word in any language. In that case, musicians often like to say that it has only a purely musical meaning. They sometimes go farther and say that *all* music has only a purely musical meaning. What they really mean is that no appropriate word can be found to express the music's meaning and that, even if it could, they do not feel the need of finding it.

11   But whatever the professional musician may hold, most musical novices still search for specific words with which to pin down their musical reactions. That is why they always find Tchaikovsky easier to "understand" than Beethoven. In the first place, it is easier to pin a meaning-word on a Tchaikovsky piece than on a Beethoven one. Much easier. Moreover, with the Russian composer, every time you come back to a piece of his it almost always says the same thing to you, whereas with Beethoven it is often quite difficult to put your finger right on what he is saying. And any musician will tell you that that is why Beethoven is the greater composer. Because music which always says the same thing to you will necessarily soon become dull music, but music whose meaning is slightly different with each hearing has a greater chance of remaining alive.

12   Listen, if you can, to the forty-eight fugue themes of Bach's *Well Tempered Clavichord*. Listen to each theme, one after another. You will soon realize that each theme mirrors a different world of feeling. You will also soon realize that the more beautiful a theme seems to you the harder it is to find any word that will describe it to your complete satisfaction. Yes, you will certainly know whether it is a gay theme or a sad one. You will be able, in other words, in your own mind, to draw a frame of emotional feeling around your theme. Now study the sad one a little closer. Try to

pin down the exact quality of its sadness. Is it pessimistically sad or resignedly sad; is it fatefully sad or smiling sad?

13   Let us suppose that you are fortunate and can describe to your own satisfaction in so many words the exact meaning of your chosen theme. There is still no guarantee that anyone else will be satisfied. Nor need they be. The important thing is that each one feel for himself the specific expressive quality of a theme or, similarly, an entire piece of music. And if it is a great work of art, don't expect it to mean exactly the same thing to you each time you return to it.

14   Themes or pieces need not express only one emotion, of course. Take such a theme as the first main one of the *Ninth Symphony*, for example. It is clearly made up of different elements. It does not say only one thing. Yet anyone hearing it immediately gets a feeling of strength, a feeling of power. It isn't a power that comes simply because the theme is played loudly. It is a power inherent in the theme itself. The extraordinary strength and vigor of the theme results in the listener's receiving an impression that a forceful statement has been made. But one should never try to boil it down to "the fateful hammer of life," etc. That is where the trouble begins. The musician, in his exasperation, says it means nothing but the notes themselves, whereas the nonprofessional is only too anxious to hang on to any explanation that gives him the illusion of getting closer to the music's meaning.

15   Now, perhaps, the reader will know better what I mean when I say that music does have an expressive meaning but that we cannot say in so many words what that meaning is.

16   The third plane on which music exists is the sheerly musical plane. Besides the pleasurable sound of music and the expressive feeling that it gives off, music does exist in terms of the notes themselves and of their manipulation. Most listeners are not sufficiently conscious of this third plane. . . .

17   Professional musicians, on the other hand, are, if anything, too conscious of the mere notes themselves. They often fall into the error of becoming so engrossed with their arpeggios and staccatos that they forget the deeper aspects of the music they are performing. But from the layman's standpoint, it is not so much a matter of getting over bad habits on the sheerly musical plane as of increasing one's awareness of what is going on, in so far as the notes are concerned.

18   When the man in the street listens to the "notes themselves" with any degree of concentration, he is most likely to make some mention of the melody. Either he hears a pretty melody or he does not, and he generally lets it go at that. Rhythm is likely to gain his attention next, particularly if it seems exciting. But harmony and tone color are generally taken for granted, if they are thought of consciously at all. As for music's having a definite form of some kind, that idea seems never to have occurred to him.

19   It is very important for all of us to become more alive to music on its sheerly musical plane. After all, an actual musical material is being used. The intelligent listener must be prepared to increase his awareness of the musical material and what happens to it. He must hear the melodies, the rhythms, the harmonies, the tone colors in a more conscious fashion. But above all he must, in order to follow the line of the composer's thought, know something of the principles of musical form. Listening to all of these elements is listening on the sheerly musical plane.

20   Let me repeat that I have split up mechanically the three separate planes on which we listen merely for the sake of greater clarity. Actually, we never listen on one or the other of these planes. What we do is to correlate them—listening in all three ways at the same time. It takes no mental effort, for we do it instinctively.

21   Perhaps an analogy with what happens to us when we visit the theater will make this instinctive correlation clearer. In the theater, you are aware of the actors and actresses, costumes and sets, sounds and movements. All these give one the sense that the theater is a pleasant place to be in. They constitute the sensuous plane in our theatrical reactions.

22   The expressive plane in the theater would be derived from the feeling that you get from what is happening on the stage. You are moved to pity, excitement, or gayety. It is this general feeling, generated aside from the particular words being spoken, a certain emotional something which exists on the stage, that is analogous to the expressive quality in music.

23   The plot and plot development are equivalent to our sheerly musical plane. The playwright creates and develops a character in just the same way that a composer creates and develops a theme. According to the degree of your awareness of the way in which the artist in either field handles his material will you become a more intelligent listener.

24   It is easy enough to see that the theatergoer never is conscious of any of these elements separately. He is aware of them all at the same time. The same is true of music listening. We simultaneously and without thinking listen on all three planes.

25   In a sense, the ideal listener is both inside and outside the music at the same moment, judging it and enjoying it, wishing it would go one way and watching it go another—almost like the composer at the moment he composes it; because in order to write his music, the composer must also be inside and outside his music, carried away by it and yet coldly critical of it. A subjective and objective attitude is implied in both creating and listening to music.

26   What the reader should strive for, then, is a more *active* kind of listening. Whether you listen to Mozart or Duke Ellington, you can deepen your understanding of music only by being a more conscious and aware listener—not someone who is just listening, but someone who is listening *for* something.

Comprehension Check ·

Fill in the blanks to complete each of the following statements.

1. The three listening planes are the _____ , _____ ,
   and the _____ .

2. The simplest plane is the _____ .

3. The appeal of the sensuous plane of music is that listeners can _____
   themselves in the music; they do not have to _____ .

4. Musicians pay _____ attention to the sheerly musical
   plane. Most listeners pay _____ attention to it.

Answer the following with a T (true) or F (false).

	T	F
5. Beethoven is a greater composer than Tchaikovsky.	___	___
6. A great piece of music always expresses the same feeling each time it is heard.	___	___
7. The best way to listen to music is to be conscious of the music, to be an active listener.	___	___
8. Listening to all three musical planes is similar to being aware of all the elements of a play produced in the theater.	___	___
9. We can listen to music on only one plane at a time.	___	___

Analysis of Content and Strategies

1. What kind of reader is Copland writing to? _____

   How do you know? _____

2. Copland discusses each musical plane separately, even though he says that
   we listen on all three planes at the same time. What does he gain by dividing listening into separate planes and explaining them one at a time?

   _____

   _____

3. List the writing patterns that Copland uses here. _____

   _____

   _____

4. Which do you think is the dominant pattern or strategy?

_____

Explain your choice. _____

_____

■ **For Discussion and Reflection**

1. Which one of the writing strategies would you choose to use to learn the material in this selection? Use that strategy to write to learn about this material.

2. On what plane do you usually listen to music? If you have not been responding to all three planes, do you find Copland's analysis of the ideal listening process to be helpful in explaining what you have been missing? Why or why not?

3. Copland describes the sensuous plane as brainless and says that people on this plane are not really listening to the music. If you usually listen on the sensuous plane, are you annoyed by the author's comments? Should you be annoyed? Explain your views.

4. The author develops a comparison between listening to music on all three planes and seeing a play performed. Can you think of another comparison that could be used?

Selection 3 **Painless "Patriotism"**

Charles Krauthammer

Psychiatrist Charles Krauthammer also studied political theory at Oxford University after graduating from Canada's McGill University. He has returned to political analysis as a syndicated columnist and regular participant on the political talk show _Inside Washington_. He has won a Pulitzer Prize for political commentary. The following column appeared June 30, 1995.

■ **Prepare**

1. From what you know about the author and the selection, what can you predict about purpose and format or style?

_____

_____

2. State briefly what you expect to read about. _____

_____

3. What do you already know about the subject? Respond using *one* of the methods described in Chapter 2.

_____

_____

4. Use the title to pose questions about the reading selection. _____

_____

5. Preread the selection. Then read and annotate the article. Finally, complete the comprehension and vocabulary checks that follow and answer the questions for discussion and reflection.

1   Responding smartly to the national flag-burning emergency—a grand total of, at most, five or six cases a year—the Republican-led House on Wednesday overwhelmingly approved a constitutional amendment to ban the scourge. This is the Republicans' rebuke to two Supreme Court rulings (in 1989 and 1990) that protected flag-burning. The court argued that flag-burning, however obnoxious it may be, is nothing if not a form of political expression, and the First Amendment, whatever its other limits, protects nothing if not political expression.

2   Faced with such incontrovertible logic—endorsed by the court's most conservative justice (Scalia)—House Republicans have decided to finesse the issue with brute force. They have the numbers. They'll try to change the Constitution. To prevent perhaps a half-dozen flag-burnings a year, they wish to produce the first alteration of the Bill of Rights in American history.

3   If this is conservatism, liberalism deserves a comeback. Indeed, President Clinton and congressional Democrats opposing the amendment deserve credit for resisting the cheap populism and easy patriotism fueling it. They are taking a principled stand that can do them no political good.

4   That is more than can be said for the state legislatures, 49 of which have already indicated their readiness to approve such an amendment as soon as they can get their hands on it. How would you like to be called soft on flag-burners in a 30-second spot at the next election? Only Senate heroism, a phenomenon as rare as a solar eclipse, can save us from this 28th Amendment—and it already has 55 Senate sponsors.

5   The amendment is not quite as bad as the one (one of 70 introduced by congressional Republicans this year) to ban retroactive tax increases, which amounts to a constitutional tantrum over Clinton's 1993 income tax

hike. But it is as small-minded. Even if there were an epidemic of flag-burning throughout the country, one could question whether it is really better to protect the physical flag rather than the freedoms it symbolizes. But there is no such epidemic. Why amend the Constitution for a non-problem?

6   Not that one should have such religious reverence for the Constitution that one never amends it. A large problem that threatens the country fundamentally may justify constitutional fixing. The balanced-budget amendment and the line-item veto are attempts to address structural defects in modern lawmaking (such as declining party loyalty and divided government) that threaten to engulf the country in debt.

7   One can argue about the wisdom of these particular constitutional corrections. One cannot argue about the magnitude of the problem they are meant to address. But flag-burning?

8   Nor is this the only instance of Republican high-handedness. Coming only a week after the defeat on a procedural maneuver of Henry Foster's nomination for surgeon general, it raises questions about the new majority's fast and loose dealing with the established ways of doing things.

9   True, the new majority aspires to be revolutionary, and much of what it wishes to wreck in the welfare state deserves wrecking. But there are established democratic practices it is wrecking along the way—wreckage it may one day come to regret.

10   Foster was stopped because the Senate raised the bar for his getting the job from 50 votes to 60. The Republicans threatened a filibuster, which could only be broken by 60 votes. The motion to break it got only 57.

11   This has been interpreted as 57 senators in favor of Foster. Not so. There were only 55. Sens. Nancy Kassebaum and Slade Gorton, who voted to break the filibuster, would have voted against Foster for the surgeon-generalship. But they thought that a presidential nominee deserved the straight up-and-down, 50-to-win ballot that Foster never got.

12   Kassebaum and Gorton are right. With the Foster nomination, Republicans have established a terrible precedent. Requiring nominees for high office to get not 50 but 60 votes is a bad way to run the country. Sixty votes should be required for something large. The filibuster is a useful instrument to ensure that major changes in the country's life enjoy not a bare but a supermajority, denoting some emerging national consensus.

13   Accordingly, large issues—impeachment, treaties, constitutional amendments, revolutionary social change (such as civil rights)—have required supermajorities. But the surgeon-generalship? An office with no power, to be occupied by a man who, if the revolution is as powerful as the Republicans pretend, had no more than a year and a half to serve anyway?

14   Republicans in Congress have the votes and the power. That they should use those votes and that power to raise the bar for presidential nominees and to punch a hole in the Bill of Rights is to trifle with the large for the sake of the small. Bad bargain, bad governance.

Comprehension Check

Answer each of the following with a T (true) or F (false).

	T	F
1. Republicans in the House of Representatives want to change the Constitution to prohibit flag-burning.	___	___
2. The author believes that a Constitutional amendment to the Bill of Rights is a good idea.	___	___
3. The author admires President Clinton for his stand against the proposed amendment.	___	___
4. State legislatures also oppose a flag-burning amendment.	___	___
5. To oppose the proposed amendment is smart politics.	___	___
6. Flag-burning is not a major problem in the U.S.	___	___
7. Changing procedures for approving presidential appointments is, in Krauthammer's view, destroying important democratic principles.	___	___
8. A filibuster threat can be stopped with a simple majority vote.	___	___
9. To approve treaties and constitutional amendments requires 60 votes in the Senate.	___	___
10. Republicans in Congress are not always using their power to govern wisely.	___	___

Expanding Vocabulary

Review each of the following words in their context and then write a brief definition or synonym for each word.

scourge (1) _____

obnoxious (1) _____

incontrovertible (2) _____

finesse (2) _____

epidemic (5) _____

engulf (6) _____

magnitude (7) _____

aspires (9) _____

filibuster (10) _____

precedent (12) _____

denoting (12) _____

Analyzing Content and Strategies

1. What is Krauthammer's subject? _____

_____

2. What *two* specific issues does he discuss? _____

_____

3. What do you think Krauthammer means by his title? Why is the word *Patriotism* in quotation marks?

_____

_____

4. State the essay's thesis. _____

_____

5. What are Krauthammer's reasons for opposing a constitutional amendment on flag burning?

_____

_____

6. What are Krauthammer's reasons for opposing a "super majority" vote on the surgeon-general?

_____

_____

7. Is Krauthammer supportive, in general, of the Republican agenda? How do you know?

_____

_____

_____

■   Questions for Discussion and Reflection

1. Are you in favor of or opposed to a Constitutional amendment prohibiting flag burning? Why or why not? Defend your position.
2. Do you think that Senate Republicans should have used the threat of a filibuster to reject the nomination of Dr. Foster as surgeon-general? Was their action fair and principled? Why or why not?
3. Assume that this article is one of several required supplementary readings for a course. Prepare a five to six sentence summary of the article.

CHAPTER 7

Reading For College Classes

In this chapter you will learn:

■ How and when to scan for information

■ How and when to skim reading material

■ How to read graphics

■ How to get the most out of textbook reading

You have been practicing active reading and can now support your "Prepare—Read—Respond" strategy with a focus on main ideas and by using writers' patterns to aid comprehension. In addition you are building vocabulary and, in Chapter 6, you learned several ways to use writing to aid comprehension. How else can you prepare yourself to be successful in your classes—and later in the workplace? This chapter brings together several strategies for reading efficiently and getting the most out of your texts. The chapter emphasizes the importance of:

1. Identifying each reading context, including understanding your purpose in reading
2. Selecting the best reading strategy for each context and purpose

Just as instructors use different strategies depending on what they are teaching, so readers need different strategies depending on *what* and *why* they are reading. In previous chapters, this text has stressed reading for full comprehension. Much of what you read for your classes must be thoroughly learned; you need to "know it cold." In some situations, though, you can speed up and still accomplish your purpose in reading. Two methods that you may use effectively in some situations are **scanning** and **skimming.**

■ SCANNING

Scanning involves searching written materials for a particular piece of information. Instead of reading the page, you let your eyes move quickly, searching for what you need. You scan when you look up a word in a dictionary, or a phone number in the telephone directory. You don't read all the definitions or all the names in the phone book; you scan for the particular word you need to define or for the name of the person you wish to call.

How can scanning help you read course materials more efficiently? You might scan your psychology text's table of contents to find the section on dreams that you want to reread. Better yet, scan the book's index for the pages on dreams. Or, having recently read the chapter on states of consciousness, you decide that you need to review the definition of *biofeedback.* You can scan the chapter to locate the discussion of the term. (You could also scan the glossary for the term's definition; that's a faster way to locate just the definition.)

Researchers regularly scan indexes and other reference tools in the library to find sources for their research papers. When you collect a stack of books and articles for a research project, you may find that some works may have just a table or chart of information that you want to use. You can scan to locate the table and then scan the table for the particular information you need. These are just some of the possible occasions for using scanning rather than reading as a tool for learning. What they all have in common is your need to locate specific information.

The process of scanning varies somewhat depending on the kind of material you are using. Regardless of the material's format, follow these basic guidelines for scanning:

Guidelines for Scanning

1. **Understand the organization of the material.** You cannot scan efficiently until you know how the work is put together. Is the material organized in columns? (dictionaries; tables) Is it alphabetical? (glossaries; indexes) Are there section headings and subheadings to guide you? (Most textbooks) Be clear about the organizational pattern before beginning your search.

2. **Keep focused on what you are looking for.** When scanning material in columns, search with your eyes in an organized way. Don't read; run your eyes down the columns of the index, looking first for the "d" section, then for the word *dreams.* When scanning prose materials, either focus on a key term or phrase (such as *biofeedback*), or pose a question and then scan to find the answer. Visualize the term *biofeedback,* hold it in your mind's eye so that you search only for that word and nothing else. To question, ask, for example, "what are the two contents of dreams that Freud identified?" Then scan the section on dreams looking for the clue word *Freud* to find the answer.

3. **Use whatever clues are available to speed your search.** Section headings are in large print, sometimes in color. Key terms are often in *italic* or **bold** type for easy spotting. At the top of each page of a dictionary are the words that begin and end that page. As you flip pages, look only at those identifying words until you find the page you need. For example, in my dictionary the word *scan* appears on the page that begins with **scam** and ends with **scare.**

4. **Confirm your information.** Scan aggressively, but once you think you have found what you are looking for, take time to confirm the information. Have you turned to the major section on dreams, or just to a brief mention of the word? Is it really *affect* that you want to spell correctly, or *effect*? Read the definition of the word to be sure. When looking for information in tables or charts, take time to understand how the information is presented so that you can word the information correctly when you use it.

When scanning prose materials, read a sentence or two before and after the sentence that seems to answer your question to be sure that you have not been misled. For instance, in the section on dreams, your scanning locates the terms **manifest content** and **latent content.** When you check the passage, you discover that the paragraph is labeled *Freudian Theory* and the sentence preceding the definitions reads: "Freud spoke about the manifest and the latent content of dreams." Yes, you have found what you were looking for.

The following exercises will give you practice in scanning different kinds of materials.

EXERCISE 7-1 Scanning Material in Columns

I. Assume that you need to locate several items in your text Patterns of Reflection. *Scan the book's index page shown in Figure 7.1 to answer the following questions. Try to complete the questions within 30 seconds.*

1. On what pages can you find a discussion of steps to active reading?

   _____

2. On what pages will you find "The Story of an Hour?" _____

3. Is Mrs. Zajac a person or the title of a work? _____

   _____ How do you know? _____

   _____

■ **FIGURE 7.1**

An Index Page from Dorothy U. Seyler, *Patterns of Reflection*, 2nd ed., 1995

Morrow, Lance, 4, 105–11
"Most Effective Deterrent to Crime,
    The," 384–88
"Mrs. Zajac," 3, 88–93
"My Backyard," 93–99
"My Father," 111–22

Narration, 39–40, 486
Norman, Liane Ellison, 130, 154–60

"On Friendship," 308–14
"On Reading and Becoming and
    Writer," 31–37
"Open Season on Koreans?" 181–85
Order, 83, 128–29, 169, 251–52, 486
Organization. *See* Order.
Orwell, George, 444–48

Paradox, 486
Part by part, 128–29, 487
Pastan, Linda, 160–61
"Pedestrian Students and High–
    Flying Squirrels," 154–60
Persistence of Memory, The, Ch. 3 insert
Peterson, Alan, 395, 429–33
Picasso, Pablo, Ch. 3 insert
"Playing Dumb," 272–80
Point of view, 41, 487
"Politicians of Silence," 400–04
"Population does Not Mean
    Progress," 416–20
"Population Means Progress, Not
    Poverty," 411–16
"Putting Your Job Interview into
    Rehearsal," 216–22
Process analysis, 210–12, 487
Purpose, 306, 487

Questions
    reporter's, 487
    rhetorical, 487

Raspberry, William, 384–88
Ravitch, Diane, 362–68, 390
Reading
    responses to, 3–4, 435–40
    steps to active, 5–7
Reading journal, 6–7, 9–11

Refutation, 395, 435, 487
Reich, Robert B., 285–95, 303
Reid, Alistair, 337–39, 344
"Relaxing Retreat, The," 122–25
Reynolds, Joseph, 9–12
Richman, Sheldon, 411–16
Rivers, Caryl, 185–90, 209
Rodriguez, Richard, 84–88
Rose, Mike, 40, 50–58
Rosenthal, A. M., 395, 400–04

Sakamoto, Nancy Masterson, 130–35
Samuelson, Robert J., 358–62, 390
Sarcasm, 487
Satire, 487
"Science and the Sense of Wonder,"
    437–38, 451–55
"Secret Life of Walter Mitty, The,"
    295–302
"Selecting the News: Interesting
    Stories," 268–72
Sentence
    complex, 484
    compound, 484
    simple, 487
Setting, 487
Simile, 129–30, 487
Smith, Adam, 369–73, 390
Sorovacu, Kiki, 339–43
Stanton, Elizabeth Cady, 455–58
"Stories the Public Has No Right to
    Know," 200–04
"Story of an Hour, The," 440–44
"Struggle to Be an All–American Girl,
    The," 42–46
Style, 17–21, 438–39, 487
Summary, 435–38, 487
Symbol, 170, 488
"Symbols of Humankind," 213–16
Synthesis, 436, 439–40

Tan, Amy, 99–104
"Teenagers in Dreamland," 358–62, 390
"Territorial Behavior," 252, 258–67
Theme, 488
Thesis, 252, 306, 488
Third of May, 1808, The, Ch. 3 insert
"Thirty Seconds," 170–77

II. *Assume that you are writing a research paper on costs of political campaigning. Scan Table 7.1 to answer the following questions. Try to complete the questions within 30 seconds.*

1. What percent of a typical candidate's funds is obtained from PACs?

_____

2. What is the single largest expenditure in the campaign budget?

_____

3. From what source does the candidate obtain about 3 percent of his or her funds?

_____

4. The table shows a typical budget for what kind of candidate?

_____

TABLE 7.1

Campaign for the U.S. Senate, 1992: A "Typical" Candidate's Budget of $2 Million

Funds from	Total $	% of Total
Political action committees (PACs)	$ 440,000	22%
Contributions from individuals	1,200,000	60
Political party	300,000	15
Candidate's own money (including family loans)	60,000	3
TOTAL	$2,000,000	100%
Are Spent On		
Television (and radio) advertising	$800,000	40%
Staff salaries and consultant fees	400,000	20
Polling	75,000	4
Print media (literature, mail, buttons, etc.)	60,000	3
Canvassing/get-out-the-vote efforts	125,000	6
Office rent, equipment, and travel	300,000	15
Fund-raising expenses	190,000	10
Legal and accounting services	50,000	2
TOTAL	$2,000,000	100%

From Karen O'Connor and Larry J. Sabato, *American Government: Roots and Reform,* 1994.

EXERCISE 7-2 Scanning Prose Materials

Assume that you are doing a research project for your social problems course on the problems in U. S. elections. Your textbook contains the box insert on election turnout shown in the following box. Scan the material to answer the three questions below. Do not read the passage; search aggressively just to answer the questions you have raised. Try to answer the questions within one minute.

1. What was the percentage of voter turnout in the 1988 U.S. presidential election?

   _____

2. What is the percentage of voter turnout in Japan? _____

3. What is the length of time of campaigns before an election in Britain?

   _____

Global Insights

Getting a Better Turnout: How Other Nations Run Their Elections

The voter turnout for the presidential election of 1988 was around 50 percent of those registered to vote. Some critics argue that the problem rests with the way U.S. elections are organized and the process of voter registration. Can changes be made to improve voter turnout? Here are the models used by some other countries that have produced better voter activity.

Italy—88.8 Percent Turnout

While voting is not compulsory, the system allows for the public disclosure of who votes and who does not. All parties receive campaign funding from the government. In addition, the government provides each party television time on state stations; time is allocated based on party membership. A party can purchase unlimited time on commercial television.

West Germany—84.4 Percent Turnout

Campaigning is limited to the ten-month period prior to election day. There is no limit on campaign spending and the primary sources of money are party members and the state. The parties are allocated paid television time on government stations; the amount of time is determined by the number of legislative seats held by the particular party.

Israel—79 Percent Turnout

In most cases, the duration of campaigns is between three and four months. Each of the parties is provided state campaign funds proportional to representative seats, but overall spending is not limited. Television time is also allocated according to the number of seats a party holds.

Britain—75 Percent Turnout

Once it is decided that an election will be called, campaigning is usually limited to a three-week period. In national elections, campaign spending is not limited and free radio and television time is provided based on the last election performance.

Japan—71.4 Percent Turnout

Virtually all citizens are registered voters, since at the age of twenty, those who register at ward offices for social benefits (including education) are automatically made eligible. There are strict guidelines on spending with the amount being determined by district size. All candidates are allocated five free six-minute television appearances and three six-minute segments on radio.

Source: Adapted from *New York Times,* 13 November 1988:E1, E3.

From Curran & Renzetti, *Social Problems,* 3rd ed., 1993.

■ SKIMMING

Skimming is a strategy for getting an overview of the ideas contained in a particular piece of writing. When you scan, you search for specific information; when you skim, you overlook specifics and seek to obtain just the "gist" or basic points of the piece. Skimming is like scanning, however, in two important ways. First, both strategies depend upon your understanding of the organization of the work and your ability to use that understanding to find key ideas. Second, both strategies are *alternatives* to the reading for full comprehension that you will use for most of your college reading. Neither strategy will produce success when you are reading to learn, but both can help you be more efficient with your reading time if you use them when appropriate.

When is skimming appropriate?

1. Skim some newspaper and magazine articles. Students are often too busy for extensive reading outside their required course work. Still, you want to have a general idea of current events and to keep up with a particular interest or hobby by checking out a weekly or monthly magazine. You can skim most of the paper or magazine, giving more time to one or two articles that especially interest you.

2. Skim some research materials. When doing a major research project, you will discover that some of the material becomes repetitive. When you have learned enough about your topic to recognize the repetition, start to skim articles, keeping your topic in mind and looking only for new information. Combining skimming and scanning with full reading will help you cover many relevant sources for your project.

3. Skim supplementary readings. Some instructors clearly establish that you will be tested on supplementary works on library reserve, but others announce that they want you to "look over" or "be familiar with" these readings. In the second situation, skimming can be used to produce a quick page or two of notes on the basics of each required reading. If, in the process, you find an article that seems especially interesting, or relevant to class discussion, you can stop to read that one more thoroughly. The box inserts in many textbooks can be included in this category of materials for skimming. Some instructors want students to know the boxed material; others want students to be familiar with the boxes but not study them in detail.

4. Skim to locate articles appropriate for a given assignment. Sometimes you may be asked to find an editorial that you disagree with and to write a paper challenging its argument, or you may be asked to respond to one article in a book of readings. There are many editorials in the papers each day, and maybe sixty or seventy articles in your reader; if you try to read each one thoroughly, you may never get around to choosing and writing your essay. Skim until you find a work that seems interesting and then read it more carefully to see if it will meet the assignment's requirements.

5. Skim sections of your textbooks that cover material you already know. If you have good recall of the parts of the atom from your high school chemistry class, then skim your college text's coverage of the atom, stopping only if you come to new material.

6. Skim to get an overview of a work *before* reading it carefully. As you study the guidelines for skimming given below, you will observe how similar they are to the guidelines for prereading a work (see Chapter 2).

7. Skim to review material *after* you have read it carefully. Some students prefer to review assigned chapters in addition to their notes on those chapters in preparation for testing. You may find that skimming, instead of a complete rereading, will jog your memory sufficiently to provide a review of the material.

In sum, there are three reasons to skim:

1. to preview before reading
2. to review after reading
3. to use instead of reading when a general familiarity with the work is all you need.

Guidelines for skimming vary somewhat depending on the type of work you are looking over and on how quick an overview you want. When skimming some books, for example, you may skip entire chapters, but when skimming a newspaper article, you may read the first three paragraphs fully and then skim the remaining paragraphs. How fast you skim will depend on the work and your purpose in skimming. The first three guidelines below apply to all skimming; the next three to particular types of works.

Guidelines for Skimming

1. **Establish your goal in skimming.** Know why you are skimming and how much of an overview of main ideas you need to obtain. Are you skimming an issue of *Sports Illustrated* for pleasure, or are you skimming supplementary readings that will be briefly discussed in class?

2. **Identify the type of work and study its organization.** We have already noted that you cannot locate main ideas unless you know how a work is put together. Identify the type of work, observe outward signs of organization such as headings, and try to anticipate, perhaps by thinking about the work's title, the work's primary writing pattern. (See Chapter 5.)

3. **Select the specific skimming strategy appropriate to the work and your purpose.** See below for more precise guidelines for different kinds of works.

4. **Skim newspaper articles** by reading the first one or two paragraphs and then let your eyes move quickly down the center of the narrow column. This process will let you see most words, so you can pause over any passages that are useful or interesting. Remember that key information comes at the beginning of newspaper articles, with supporting details added in later paragraphs. Exceptions to this structure are the editorials. For these, read the beginning paragraphs, skim the middle, and read the concluding paragraph.

5. **Skim popular magazine articles** by first reading the opening paragraph to see if it contains the main idea. If you do not find it there, read the second paragraph. (Popular articles often start with an attention-getter, frequently a specific example, and then move to the main idea.) Read headings, subheadings, and words in bold or italic type. Look over charts, pictures, and diagrams. Then "read" aggressively, letting your eyes glide over the words, noting repeated key terms, lists, or steps in a process. If you spot something that particularly interests you, stop to read it more thoroughly.

6. **For textbook prereading or reviewing and for nonfiction books and articles used for supplementary readings or research projects,** skim by following the guidelines for prereading in Chapter 2 (see pp. 34–35). Prereading guidelines involve reading those specific passages that are most likely to contain main ideas and key supporting ideas. For example, with works in this category, you should read the final paragraph, a place where main ideas are restated, conclusions are drawn, or applications are presented.

EXERCISE 7-3 **Practice in Skimming and Scanning**

I. While waiting to study with a friend in the library, you pick up the July 1995 issue of Tennis *magazine and see the following article. Skim it quickly and then answer the questions that follow.*

The Fit Player
By **Julie Anthony, Ph.D., Technical Advisory Panel**

The Truth about Power Foods

Recreational players who watch pros gulp down sports drinks, or chomp on bananas during changeovers, assume these "power" products help on-court performance. Often it's true: Proper nutrition will do wonders for your stamina and strength.

But don't be misled by the actions of the pros. They often eat or drink products for unique reasons. You must determine what works best for you. Let's closely examine the pros and cons of eight nutritional "power" products.

1. Bananas: These complex carbohydrates are healthy, provide energy and supply the body with potassium, one of the minerals lost in sweat. Potassium is crucial in maintaining hydration and muscle contraction. It makes sense that Michael Chang, who has been bothered by cramps during his career, often eats bananas during matches.

There's only one problem: The bananas Chang eats on court won't off-set cramps during his match. Bananas, like all complex carbohydrates, take four hours to metabolize. Chang eats bananas while on the court to help prevent cramping *following* the match. Bananas can help prevent cramps during tennis only if eaten prior to a match.

2. Water: The ultimate "power" food. Our bodies are made up of 55 percent water, so it's essential for all athletes to constantly replenish their systems with water. Athletes lose water through perspiration and respiration, which contributes to fatigue and loss of coordination. You should drink water early during play; if you only drink when you're thirsty, you're too late.

3. Starches: When starches break down into sugar in our systems, they become the fuel that makes us run. They're terrific pre-match meals if eaten at least four hours before playing. However, a plate of spaghetti with creamy alfredo sauce doesn't qualify as a carbohydrate-rich meal. It's now a high-fat and hard-to-digest meal. Fats delay the digestion process, meaning your food still may be floating around your system midway through the second set.

4. Honey: Ken Rosewall used to gulp tablespoons of honey while on the court. Today's pros turn to other simple carbohydrates (sugar) such as candy bars or soft drinks for energy. This quick energy rush is followed within 30 to 60 minutes by a drop in energy level.

Digesting a simple carbohydrate like honey is a bit like playing roulette. If you're about to begin a final-set tie-break, the risk is minimal. But if you don't know how long the match will continue, or how your body will react, you're taking quite a chance. Try the next "power" product instead.

5. Sports drinks and bars: These products are formulated in such a way to provide carbohydrates with only enough sugar to make the taste pleasant. The carbos help sustain energy during long matches; the low sugar content helps prevent a post-sugar-rush "crash."

The best drinks are made with a molecule called a glucose polymer, which allows the drink to pass through the stomach more easily and into the bloodstream faster. Sports bars should be low in fat (less than 10 grams), list whole foods (rolled oats, dried fruit) at the top of their ingredients list, and not taste too sweet, a sure sign of too much sugar.

6. Coffee: By releasing free fatty acids into the bloodstream, caffeine can enhance endurance. Cyclists and other endurance athletes have used coffee and caffeine tablets. However, I strongly recommend tennis players avoid using caffeine as a performance enhancer. The amount necessary for endurance levels to be boosted is high: about five mugfuls of coffee. That may be more disturbing than enduring!

7. Muscle-building and weight-loss supplements: There is no significant, credible research that shows these products can either help you lose weight or increase your strength. If you want to lose weight, you must expend more calories than you consume. If you want to get stronger, you must build more muscle.

8. Vitamins: While vitamins never can replace a healthy, balanced diet, there is plenty of substantial evidence to support supplementing your diet with vitamins. A multivitamin can help everyone, and women should take additional calcium and iron.

1. What is the subject of the article? _____

_____

2. What are four power foods discussed in the article? _____

_____

_____

3. Which is the ultimate power food? _____

4. Does proper nutrition contribute to increased stamina and strength?

_____

II. Return to "The Fit Player" and scan the article to answer the following question.

Are honey and candy bars good choices as power foods?

_____

III. Your biology instructor has announced that the textbook's boxes should be "looked over" but not learned in depth. Skim the following box on sexually transmitted diseases, underlining as you skim, and then respond with a T (True) or F (false) to the statements that follow.

	T	F
1. STD stands for *sexually transmitted diseases*.	___	___
2. STDs are not a serious medical problem.	___	___
3. The second most common STD is *herpes,* a virus affecting 20 million Americans.	___	___
4. The best-known STDs are *gonorrhea* and *syphilis*.	___	___
5. Condoms do not help to reduce the spread of sexually transmitted diseases.	___	___

Sexually Transmitted Disease: A Growing Concern

One consequence of America's sexual revolution during the 1970s and 1980s has been a dramatic rise in the incidence of *venereal diseases*—diseases of the genital tract and reproductive organs caused by bacteria and viruses. These diseases are part of the broader category of *sexually transmitted diseases (STDs)*—infectious diseases of any body region that can be passed to a partner through sexual contact. A person with multiple sex partners has a substantial risk of contracting a sexually transmitted disease. Over 10 million cases are treated each year in the United States. And if undetected or untreated, such diseases can led to severe complications.

The most common STD is *chlamydia,* an infection by the bacterium *Chlamydia trachomatis* picked up through sexual contact with an already infected person. A woman may have no symptoms of chlamydia at all, or she may experience pelvic pain, painful urination, vaginal discharge, fever, and swollen glands near the groin; a man may have a discharge from his penis or painful urination. The infection can be simply and effectively treated with antibiotics, but if undetected or untreated, it can lead to severe infection of the reproductive organs and even sterility. Because a person with chlamydia may have no symptoms, pregnant women can unknowingly pass the infection to their newborns. This STD, in fact, is the most common infection in newborns, with 100,000 cases per year.

The second most common STD is *herpes genitalis,* caused by the herpes simplex virus type 2 (HSV type 1 causes cold sores and fever blisters). At least 20 million Americans have herpes, and 300,000 to 500,000 new cases arise annually. The virus causes watery blisters to form around the genitalia; these break and form painful open sores that eventually heal. The virus can lie dormant for weeks, months, or years. Then, stimulated by sunlight, emotional stress, or sexual intercourse, the virus can break out once again and cause a new cycle of pustules and sores. Right now, there is no cure for herpes, and only partially effective antiviral drugs are available. If birth coincides with an active herpes phase in the mother, the newborn can suffer death or damage to the brain, liver or other organs.

The fastest-spreading, and in many ways most worrisome, STD is *venereal warts,* caused by the papilloma virus. These small, painless, cauliflower-like bumps grow around the sex organs, rectum, or mouth and are passed through skin-to-skin contact. Getting rid of the warts is usually no problem; they can be burned or frozen off or surgically removed. More ominously, however, researchers are finding that the papilloma virus (which can remain in the body even after the warts are removed) has been present in 90 percent of the cervical cancer tissues studied so far.

Perhaps the best-known STDs are *gonorrhea* and *syphillis.* Both are caused by microorganisms; both are contracted through sexual activity with an infected person; both can have mild initial symptoms (a discharge or painless sore) or no symptoms at all; and both can be successfully treated with antibiotics. As in chlamydia, failure to find and treat gonorrhea at an early stage can lead to severe infection of reproductive organs or sterility. Failure to treat syphilis can also result in widespread damage to the heart, eyes, and brain and can result in severe damage or death to an unborn child.

Other STDs include pubic lice (crabs), scabies (parasites that burrow under the skin), certain types of vaginal yeast infections, trichomonas (flagellated protists that infect the vagina or penis), and acquired immune deficiency syndrome (AIDS; see details in Chapter 22).

Clearly, sexually transmitted diseases have become a serious threat. Planned Parenthood recommends that sexually active adults (particularly those with numerous sex partners) use condoms to prevent the passing of infections; be alert to sores, bumps, discharges, painful urination, or pelvic pain; and get tested regularly for STDs. This is especially important before or during pregnancy.

From Postlethwait, Hopson, & Veres, *Biology! Bringing Science to Life,* McGraw, 1991.

IV. Return to the box on sexually transmitted diseases and scan the article to answer the following question.

Is there a cure for herpes? _____

■ READING GRAPHICS

Even though textbooks and many nonfiction books and articles are filled with tables, graphs, diagrams, maps, and pictures designed to aid the reader's study, many students ignore visuals, or at best give them only a quick glance. Both approaches are a mistake. Visuals serve three important purposes.

1. They are aids to learning, clarifying through a visual presentation material that is often difficult to follow in the text's discussion.
2. They provide information that may be referred to only briefly in the text.
3. They add interest, often dramatically so.

One reason you may have skipped over most visuals in the past is that you may be uncertain how to "read" a table or graph. The following discussion of the most common visuals will give you specific guidelines for getting the most learning from every part of your textbook. The exercises will give you practice "reading" the visuals.

How to Read Graphics

Graphics present a good bit of information in a relatively small space, usually less space than would be needed for a complete explanation in words. But words are also part of graphics, and actually appear in two places: (1) in the text, where you will almost always find a reference to each visual and (2) connected to the visual itself, above, below and even within the graphic representation.

You need to begin by paying close attention to the context in which the graphic is presented. Sometimes key ideas in the graphic will be summarized or analyzed in the text, and then the reader is referred to the visual by its figure number (for example: see Figure 7). In other works, most of the information in the chart or map or diagram can be found only in that visual. There is little textual discussion, just a referral to the appropriate figure. In either case, you should turn to the graphic at that point in your reading and study the visual until you understand it, and its connection with that part of the text. Remember that when the author writes "See Figure 7," the author wants you to look at Figure 7 at that point. When you study a graphic, follow these general guidelines. We will use Table 7.2 as the example to illustrate the guidelines; look at it several times as you read through the guidelines.

Guidelines for Reading Graphics

1. **Locate the particular graphic referred to in the text.** Tables are always labeled Tables; other graphics are labeled Figures, except for pictures, which are not labeled. Usually tables and figures are numbered by chapter (7) and then by the order in which they appear in the chapter (7.2).
2. **Read the title or heading of the graphic.** Think about what the visual will show you and note specific qualifiers of time or place. Table 7.2

will provide information about women in political office in the *United States* in 1993.

3. **Read any notes and the source, information that appears at the bottom of the graphic.** In the table we are studying, there is a general note listing the elected and appointed positions that are *not* included. The second note, (a), qualifies only the category of elected mayors. The source is the NWPC. Many textbooks contain diagrams and charts prepared just for that textbook. Pictures will have a brief description under them, followed by the name of the photographer or the organization owning the picture. Statistics based on census information should always reveal a source. Do not trust statistical information from unnamed sources!

4. **Read the headings for tables and graphs, the legend for maps.** Each column in a table will be labeled. A graph will label what is being shown on the vertical line and what is being shown on the horizontal line. A map's legend tells you the scale of the map and what the colors or shadings represent. This information tells you specifically what is included in the table, compared in the graph, or shown on the map. You cannot draw useful conclusions until you understand exactly what information you have been given. In Table 7.2, we are given the actual number (and the percent of the total) of women in the various national, state, and locally elected offices listed down the left column.

5. **Study the information.** Look at the numbers. Make comparisons. Observe trends. You might notice, to your surprise, that there are 1,517 women in state legislatures! That seems like a goodly number, until you check the percent column and discover that it is only 20 percent. What does that mean? It means that 80 percent of elected representatives to state houses are men.

6. **Draw conclusions.** Think about the information in several ways. First, what does the writer want to accomplish by including the graphic? Second, what is your reaction to the information provided? What, for example, can we conclude from Table 7.2? You might recognize that women have made considerable strides in political office at the local and state levels, but are not well represented at the national level. When you remember that women compose slightly more than 50 percent of the population, but only 6 percent of governors and 7 percent of U.S. senators are women, you have to wonder at the imbalance of representation. You might want to think about some of the causes for this imbalance.

Graphics provide information, raise questions, explain processes, make us think. Use this information in your course study. The following pages provide explanations and examples of typical graphics, with questions about each to aid your study.

TABLE 7.2

U.S. Women in Political Office, 1993

	Percentage and Number Held by Women	
	Percentage	**Number**
National Office		
U.S. Senate	7%	7
U.S. House of Representatives	11%	47
State Office		
Governors	6%	3
Attorneys general	16%	8
Secretaries of state	26%	13
Treasurers	38%	19
State auditors	10%	5
State legislature	20%	1,517
Local Office		
Mayors[a]	18%	175

Note: Does not include women elected to the judiciary, appointed to state cabinet–level positions, elected to executive posts by the legislature, or members of a university board of trustees.

[a]Of cities with a population over 30,000.

Source: National Women's Political Caucus, 1993.

Pictures and Photographs

You know the saying: "A picture is worth a thousand words." Fortunately for students, many textbooks contain a wealth of pictures that show what the authors are discussing and enliven the study of the material. History texts, for example, contain color reproductions of paintings of important figures, manuscripts, and old maps. These help students "reach back" to former times. On the title page of the chapter on the biosphere, part of which is included in this chapter, there is a wonderful photograph of the American bald eagle sitting in a nest with babies. Then, throughout the chapter, each large land ecosystem (biome) is shown in a photograph. You can both learn from and also enjoy these visuals.

Diagrams

Diagrams are drawings or illustrations that depict a concept or process or object under discussion. Textbooks in the sciences rely heavily on diagrams to (1) show and label the parts of subjects under discussion (plants, cells, the human skeleton, the arrangement of planets); and (2) represent processes that are not visible, or not readily so (the process of photosynthesis, or the process of sexual reproduction).

Questions on Figure 7.2

1. What are autotrophs? _____

_____

2. What are heterotrophs? _____

_____

3. How do heterotrophs fit into the carbon cycle? _____

_____

■ FIGURE 7.2

The Global Carbon Cycle
Vast amounts of carbon move through the air, soil, and water as photosynthe-
sizing autotrophs fix carbon dioxide into organic compounds, and heterotrophs
(along with nonliving combustion processes such as burning) break down those
compounds and once again release carbon dioxide.

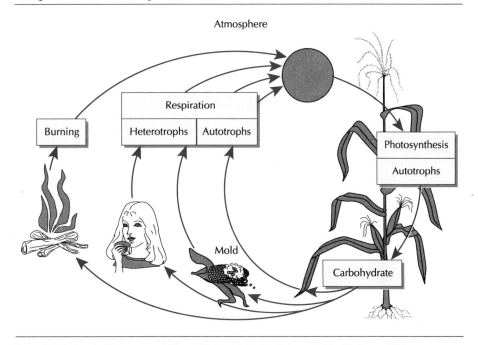

From Postlethwait; Hopson, and Veres, *Biology! Bringing Science to Life*, McGraw, 1991.

4. What is essential for photosynthesis? How is it depicted in the diagram?

_____

5. What is emphasized by placing the human figure in the diagram? _____

_____

Maps

Maps show geographical areas. Some maps show the entire surface of the Earth, that is, all land masses and oceans, bays, lakes, and rivers, to visually depict the world we live in. Others are topographical; they show differences in elevations and types of land mass, such as mountains and deserts. Most textbook maps, however, focus on one part of the world and reveal changes or trends—either to the earth itself or to the people living in that part of the world. You would expect to find many maps in history, geography, and geology textbooks, but don't be surprised to find them in texts in the social sciences as well.

Questions on Figure 7.3

1. What is the subject of the map? _____

_____

2. Clinton's electoral college votes came primarily from solid performance in what three parts of the country?

_____

3. In your opinion, what is the most startling information shown on this map?

_____

_____

4. If you were working for the Republicans, what advice would you give the presidential candidate for winning in 1996? Where should the candidate concentrate his or her attention?

_____

_____

■ FIGURE 7.3

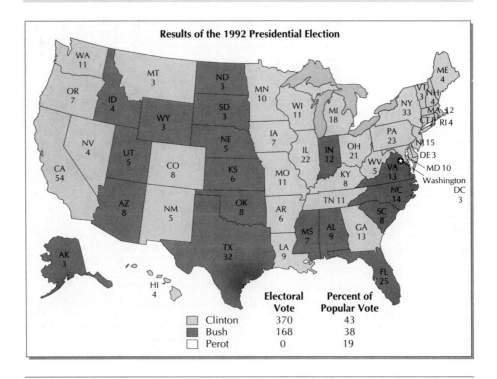

Results of the 1992 Presidential Election

	Electoral Vote	Percent of Popular Vote
Clinton	370	43
Bush	168	38
Perot	0	19

From O'Connor and Sabato, *American Government: Roots and Reform,* Allyn and Bacon, 1994.

Tables

As you have seen in Tables 7.1 and 7.2, a table presents information in columns on a given subject. By using columns, tables summarize and focus the information. In tables providing numbers, be certain that you understand how the numbers are represented. That is, are the numbers presented in the numerals actually showing, or do the numerals represent hundreds or thousands or millions? Or, are the numerals percentages rather than whole numbers?

Questions on Table 7.3

1. Which cities dropped out of the top 10 between 1950 and 1980? _____

_____

2. What do the dropouts have in common? _____

_____

TABLE 7.3

Population of World's 10 Largest Metropolitan Areas, 1950 and 1980, with Projections for 2000 (in Millions)

City	1950	City	1980	City	2000
New York	12.3	Tokyo	16.9	*Mexico City*	*25.6*
London	8.7	New York	15.6	*São Paulo*	*22.1*
Tokyo	6.7	*Mexico City*	*14.5*	Tokyo	19.0
Paris	5.4	*São Paulo*	*12.1*	*Shanghai*	*17.0*
Shanghai	*5.3*	*Shanghai*	*11.7*	New York	16.8
Buenos Aires	*5.0*	*Buenos Aires*	*9.9*	*Calcutta*	*15.7*
Chicago	4.9	Los Angeles	9.5	*Bombay*	*15.4*
Moscow	4.8	*Calcutta*	*9.0*	*Beijing*	*14.0*
Calcutta	*4.4*	*Beijing*	*9.0*	Los Angeles	13.9
Los Angeles	4.0	*Rio de Janeiro*	*8.8*	*Jakarta*	*13.7*

Source: United Nations, *World Urbanization Prospects 1990* (New York, 1991); Lester Brown (ed.), *State of the World 1992.* World Watch Institute, p. 122.

Italics indicate city is in the Third World.

From Donatelle and Davis, *Access to Health*, 3/e, Allyn and Bacon, 1994.

3. How many of the cities projected to be in the top 10 in the year 2000 are Third World cities?

_____

4. What can you conclude about trends in population growth? _____

_____

Graphs and Charts

Graphs show quantitative relationships and emphasize comparisons between two or more related items. Some people prefer to use the term *graph* to refer only to line graphs, and to use the term *chart* for bar graphs and pie graphs. The pie chart or graph is probably the easiest to draw and to read. It is a circle divided into segments to show the relative portion of each part to the whole. Bar charts or graphs are found quite often in textbooks (and in magazine and newspaper articles) because they also show relative proportions in a visually effective way. Most bar graphs compare only two or three items and use color or shadings to distinguish among the items. Line graphs are ideal for showing trends or changes over time or for showing a frequency distribution—a distribution relationship of two variables, such as the number of airline passengers in various age groups.

Questions on Figure 7.4

1. What is the projected number of HIV cases worldwide by the year 2000?

   _____

2. Which area of the world is projected to have the greatest increase in cases between 1994 and 2000?

   _____

3. What conclusions can you draw from this information? (How serious is the problem? Why are some areas of the world showing a decrease? Why are some projected to have a dramatic increase in HIV cases?)

   _____

   _____

   _____

■ FIGURE 7.4

Worldwide HIV Cases, 1994–2000

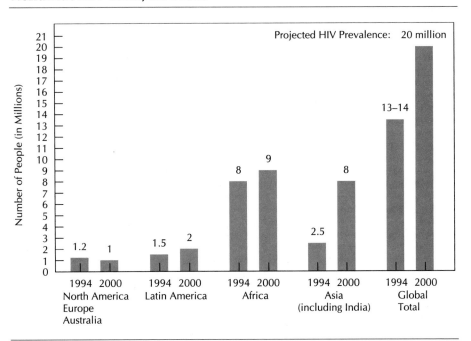

Source: World Health Organization

Questions on Figure 7.5

1. Explain how the straight line represents "perfect equality." _____

   _____

2. What percentage of people receive 31.8 percent of income? _____

3. What percentage of people receive the remaining 68.2 percent of income?

   _____

4. Does personal income distribution in 1991 seem fair to you? Why or why not?

   _____

   _____

Flowcharts

Flowcharts are a type of graph, but they show qualitative rather than quantitative relationships. Flowcharts are useful for showing the steps in a process or a sequence of events or ideas. Usually the process or sequence is explained in detail in the text, and the flowchart provides a visual summary that reinforces the textual explanation.

■ **FIGURE 7.5**

Personal Income Distribution, 1991 (Lorenz curve)

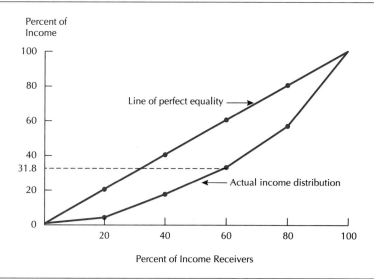

From Turley Mings, *The Study of Economics*, 5/e, Dushkin, 1995.

Questions on Figure 7.6

1. What step does the House of Representatives include that is not found in the Senate's process?

_____

■ FIGURE 7.6

How a Bill Becomes a Law: The Textbook Way

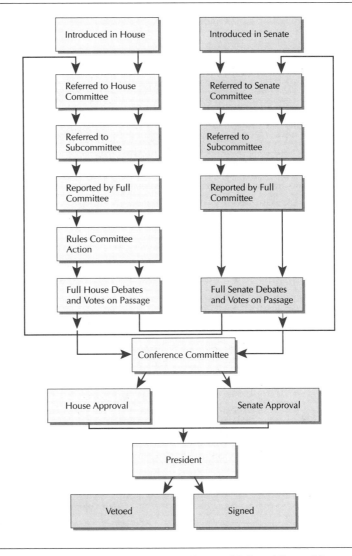

From O'Connor and Sabato, _American Government: Roots and Reform_, Allyn and Bacon, 1994.

2. If the full House votes for a bill, what must happen before the bill goes to Conference Committee?

_____

_____

3. What must happen after a bill is reconciled in Conference Committee for the bill to become law?

_____

_____

■ APPLYING READING SKILLS TO A TEXTBOOK CHAPTER

Let us assume that you are taking an introductory course in physical geography and are using *Essentials of Physical Geography* by Tom L. McKnight as your text. Applying your three-step reading strategy, you prepare by thinking about what you already know and what you expect to learn from this text and the course. Ideally, your purpose in reading extends beyond course requirements and includes a desire to learn more about the physical "landscape" of your world.

Opening the text, you read the Table of Contents to get an overview of the topics covered. Your preview of the Contents alerts you to 17 chapters, two appendices, a Glossary, and an Index. You might begin by folding down the first page of the Glossary to mark it for easy access, knowing that there will be new terms to learn. Flipping through the text after marking the Glossary, you observe that the book contains many graphics: maps, diagrams of processes, and photographs. You now turn to the Preface, a step students all too often unwisely skip. Here is the key section of McKnight's Preface:

1   This book presents the physical or environmental portion of geography in terms of its essentials. Written and designed for an introductory survey of physical geography, the text assumes that the student has little or no prior formal training in geography. The level of presentation doubles as both a survey for the liberal arts undergraduate and as a systematic overview for the student who plans to major in the subject. An informal writing style, devoid of excessive jargon, an abundance of high-quality, four-color illustrations, and the use of "focus boxes" all work together to

provide students with a solid background on which to build their future studies.

2   Written from a geographer's point of view, the text continually explores the processes of physical geography, carefully explaining the interrelationships of phenomena. There is a preliminary assessment of the Earth's planetary characteristics and a systematic presentation of the major components of physical geography with special emphasis on climate and topography. Within each chapter, focus boxes provide useful vignettes that expand on topics that are presented more briefly in the text. An innovative addition is a special series of focus boxes involving human/environmental interaction, the third of the five basic themes of geography.

3   The book begins with two chapters that are preliminary in concept and content. Chapter 1 provides an introductory look at the Earth, discussing particularly the environmental effects of its relationship with the sun. Chapter 2 deals with the concepts and practicalities of portraying and representing the Earth's surface in ways understandable and meaningful to interested humans.

4   Chapters 3 through 8 focus on the atmosphere. Emphasis is on the nature of the weather elements and the dynamics of atmospheric processes, leading to a consideration of the interaction of air masses, fronts, and storms. This section concludes with a discussion of the general subject of climatic classification and a detailed presentation of the widely used Köppen system for the world.

5   Chapter 9 is a brief introduction to the biosphere, emphasizing the significance of ecosystems and biomes. Chapter 10 is an expansive consideration of soils, dealing at some length with soil-forming factors, soil components, and soil-generating regimes. The latter half of the chapter considers soil classification in general and the United States Soil Taxonomy System in particular, outlining the world distribution pattern.

6   Chapters 11 through 17 focus on terrain analysis. These chapters proceed systematically from a conceptual introduction through a broad treatment of the internal crust-shaping processes (plate tectonics, diastrophism, vulcanism) to a more detailed consideration of the external processes of weathering, mass wasting, erosion, and deposition. The principal external land-shaping systems—fluvial, aeolian, coastal, and glacial—are discussed in detail.

7   The writer believes that a useful definition of geography is "landscape appreciation" and has prepared this book with that theme in mind. Landscape is considered to include everything that one sees when looking out a window, everything that one hears upon listening at a window, and everything that one smells upon smelling at a window, referring to every window, actual and theoretical, in the world. "Appreciation" is used in

the sense of understanding. Any proper exposition of geography should serve to heighten one's understanding of all that is seen, heard, and smelled at the window, whether an actual experience at a nearby window or a vicarious experience on the other side of the Earth. Thus it is the purpose of this book to make the environmental landscape of the world more understanding to the reader, at least at an introductory level.

As you can see, the Preface expands upon the Table of Contents. It describes both the content of chapters and the organizational plan: from introductory chapters on the Earth, to the atmosphere, with particular emphasis on climate, to the biosphere, then specifics on soil, terrain, and the effects of such dynamic elements as water, volcanoes, and weathering. The Preface also describes the author's intended audience, the style of writing for that audience, and the purpose or approach to the topic that shapes the book. Reading the Preface will give you a more complete picture of the text you are about to study from than reading the Table of Contents alone. Remember, too, that your instructor has selected this text for the course. By previewing the text you are also previewing the course you are taking.

After your initial preview of the text, you want to *preread* each chapter before reading it carefully and using some writing strategy to aid learning. As you now know, prereading is one use of skimming, skimming to get an overview rather than as an end in itself.

Let's take a closer look at Chapter 9: "The Biosphere." A skim-read preview of the chapter reveals a two-page map of the world showing the major biomes (a new term to be learned), plus small maps showing the location of each biome and at least one photograph of each biome. In addition, previewing reveals a box insert on destruction of rainforests; this insert is the first reading selection at the end of this chapter. Finally, prereading focuses attention on the key sections and the structure of the chapter. The key sections, reprinted here, have been annotated to highlight what *you* should observe and annotate in your prereading.

What is important to learn from prereading? First, in addition to the maps and photographs already mentioned, you observe Figure 9–1, a diagram of the dynamic nature of an *ecosystem*, a key term you need to learn. Second, this chapter contains, as do the others in the text, three concluding sections to aid learning: a summary, a list of key terms, and review questions. Always keep review questions in mind as you read a chapter and see if you can answer them when you are finished. Third, the basic structure and content of the chapter become clear. There are three major sections: Ecosystems and Biomes, The Major Biomes, and Biomes and Climate. The first section is subdivided to define the two terms essential to understanding the chapter: *ecosystem* and *biome*. This section also includes a list of the ten major biome types. The second, and by far the largest, section discusses each of these ten biomes in turn. The brief third section discusses the role of climate in defining the various biomes.

Chapter 9. The Biosphere

Opening paragraph

The biosphere is the least precise of the four principal components of our earthly environment. The atmosphere consists of the envelope of air that surrounds our planet, the lithosphere is the solid portion of the Earth, and the hydrosphere is composed of the various waters of the Earth; these three "spheres" are relatively distinct and easy to visualize. The biosphere, on the other hand, is an overlapping concept that impinges spatially on the other three. It consists of the incredibly numerous and diverse array of individual organisms—plant and animal—that populate our planet. Most of these organisms exist at the interface between atmosphere and lithosphere, but some live largely or entirely within the hydrosphere or the lithosphere, and others move relatively freely from one "sphere" to another. Thus it can be seen that the biosphere is more a concept of things than of space. The elements of the biosphere are very significant components of our physical environment, but only under certain circumstances, such as where there is a dense stand of trees or other planets growing together, is there a sizable spatial aspect.

Heading 1

ECOSYSTEMS AND BIOMES

In our search for meaningful organizing principles for the comprehension of the biosphere, two concepts seem to be of particular value—*ecosystem* and *biome*.

Subheading

ECOSYSTEM: A CONCEPT FOR ALL SCALES

Key term

The term (ecosystem) is a contraction of the phrase *ecological system*. An ecosystem is considered to include all the organisms in a given area, but it is more than simply a community of plants and animals existing together. The ecosystem concept is functional and encompasses the totality of interactions among the organisms and between the organisms and the nonliving portions of the environment in the area under consideration. The nonliving portion of the environment includes soil, rocks, water, sunlight, atmosphere, etc., but it essentially can be considered as nutrients and energy.

An ecosystem, then, is fundamentally a biological community, or an association of plants and animals, expressed in functional terms. The concept is built around the flow of energy among the various components of the system, which is the essential determinant of how a biotic community functions. See Figure 9–1.

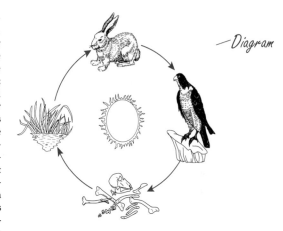

Diagram

Figure 9–1. The flow of energy in a simple ecosystem. Energized by the sun, grass feeds a rabbit, which is eaten by a hawk, whose decaying remains furnish nutrients for the grass.

This functional, systematic concept is very attractive as an organizing principle for the geographic study of the biosphere. It must, however, be approached with caution because of the variable scales at which it can be applied. There can be almost infinite variety in the magnitude of ecosystems that we might recognize. At one extreme, for example, we can conceive of a planetary ecosystem that encompasses the entire biosphere; at the other end of the scale, it would be possible to consider the ecosystem of a fallen log, or of the underside of a rock, or even of a drop of water. There is endless variety in the possibilities.

Therefore, if we are going to try to identify and understand broad distributional patterns within the biosphere, we must focus only on ecosystems that can be recognized at a useful scale.

Subheading

BIOME: A SCALE FOR ALL BIOGEOGRAPHERS

Among terrestrial ecosystems, the type that provides the most appropriate scale for understanding world distribution patterns is called a (biome) A biome is a large, recognizable assemblage of plants and animals in functional interaction with its environment. It is usually identified and named on the basis of its dominant vegetation association, which normally comprises the bulk of the *biomass* (the total weight of all organisms—plant and animal) in the area under

Key term

consideration, as well as being the most obvious and conspicuous visible component of the landscape.

There is no universally recognized classification of the world's biomes, but scholars commonly accept about ten major biome types:

list of 10 biomes

Tropical rainforest
Tropical deciduous forest
Tropical scrub
Tropical savanna
Desert
Mediterranean woodland and shrub
Midlatitude grassland
Midlatitude deciduous forest
Boreal forest
Tundra

A biome is composed of much more than merely the plant association that gives it its name. A variety of other kinds of vegetation usually grows among, under, and occasionally over the dominant association. Diverse animal species also occupy the area. Often, significant and even predictable relations are seen between the biota (particularly the flora) of the biome and the associated climate and soil types.

As one peruses the map showing major biome types of the world (Figure 9–2) the arbitrary nature of regional boundaries should be noted. The major biotic communities do not occupy sharply defined areas in nature, no matter how sharp the demarcations may appear on a map. Normally the communities merge more or less imperceptibly with one another through *Key term* ecotones—transition zones of competition in which the typical species of one community intermingle or interdigitate with those of another. In Figure 9–2, as in any small-scale map of biomes, the boundaries are drawn rather arbitrarily through the ecotones.

Heading 2 THE MAJOR BIOMES

As a summation of the geography of the biosphere, it is logical to identify and describe the major terrestrial ecosystems, or biomes, of the world. Most biomes are named for their dominant vegetation association, but the biome concept also encompasses fauna as well as inter- relationships with soil, climate, and topography.

Subheading TROPICAL RAINFOREST

• • •

Heading 3 BIOMES AND CLIMATE

One of the truly striking relationships in physical geography is the notable correlation between the gross global pattern of distribution and biomes and that of major climatic types. This correlation is readily apparent when one compares the maps of Figures 8–4 and 9–2. The interrelationships of climate, flora, and fauna are exceedingly complex, but a reasonable generalization is to note that broad vegetation patterns are generally dependent on broad climatic and vegetational milieu. An understanding of the world pattern of biomes requires consideration of many factors, but clearly a comprehension of the climatic patterns is the starting point.

Summary SUMMATION

The biosphere consists of all life forms, plant and animal, on Earth. Because it contains nearly 2 million species of organisms, the biosphere is a daunting challenge for analysis. Useful organizing concepts for its study by geographers include the *ecosystem* (the totality of interactions among organisms and their environment in a given area) and the *biome* (a major assemblage of biota in functional interaction with its environment).

Environmental relationships are fundamental to an understanding of broad biotic distributions. Clearly, the climatic influence on general vegetation distributions is stronger than that of any other environmental factor. On a broad-scale basis, the major terrestrial biomes include tropical rainforest, tropical deciduous forest, tropical scrub, tropical savanna, desert, mediterranean woodland and shrub, midlatitude grassland, midlatitude deciduous forest, boreal forest, and tundra.

KEY TERMS

arboreal	grassland
biome	prairie
boreal forest (taiga)	savanna
ecosystem	steppe
ecotone	woodland

terms to learn

REVIEW QUESTIONS

1. Explain the difference between *ecosystem* and *ecotone*.
2. Explain the difference between *biome* and *biomass*.
3. Select one biome and describe its location and principal characteristics.
4. Discuss the distribution and characteristics of the *selva*.

study questions

What does your previewing tell you that you need to study and learn from reading this chapter? Using the review questions and your prereading, make a list of what you need to learn.

_____

_____

_____

_____

_____

Did you include definitions of *ecosystem, biome, ecotone,* and also *biomass* and *selva?* Clearly you should, in addition, be able to describe the chief characteristics of each of the ten biomes—since you cannot know which one or ones will appear on a test. Remember as well that this is a geography course; you should be able to give the location of each of the biomes.

What writing-to-learn method would you use as a study tool with this chapter? Highlighting and annotating probably would not be sufficient. Either outlining or note-taking (the Cornell Method) would be more helpful. If you were to choose outlining, you would need to include subsections on characteristics and location for each of the ten biomes.

Exercise 7-4 **Learning from a Textbook Chapter**

Read the portion of the chapter presented above and the section on the tropical rainforests given below. Then complete the exercises that follow.

The Tropical Rainforest

1   The rainforest of the low latitudes, also called a **selva,** is probably the most complex of all terrestrial ecosystems. It contains a bewildering variety of trees growing in close conjunction. Mostly they are tall, high-crowned, broadleaf species that never experience a seasonal leaf fall because the concept of seasons is unknown in this environment of continual warmth and moistness. The selva has a layered structure; the second layer usually forms a complete canopy of interlaced branches that provides continuous shade to the forest floor. Bursting through the canopy to form the top layer are the forest giants, tall trees that sporadically rise to great heights above the general level. Beneath the canopy is an erratic third layer of lower trees that is able to survive in the shade. Sometimes still more layers of increasingly shade-tolerant trees grow at lower levels.

2   Undergrowth is normally sparse in the selva because the lack of light precludes the survival of most green plants. Only where there are gaps in

the canopy, as alongside a river, does light reach the ground, resulting in the dense undergrowth associated with a "jungle." Epiphytes such as orchids and bromeliads hang from or perch on the tree trunks and branches. Vines and lianas often dangle from the arching limbs.

3   The interior of the selva, then, is a region of heavy shade, high humidity, windless air, continual warmth, and an aroma of mold and decomposition. As plant litter accumulates on the forest floor, it is acted upon very rapidly by plant and animal decomposers, which find optimal conditions for their activities. The upper layers of the forest are areas of high productivity, and there is a much greater concentration of nutrients in the vegetation than in the soil. Indeed, most selva soil is surprisingly infertile.

4   Rainforest fauna is largely **arboreal** (tree-dwelling) because the principal food sources are in the canopy rather than on the ground. Large animals are generally scarce on the forest floor, although there are vast number of invertebrates. The animal life of this biome is characterized by creepers, crawlers, climbers, and flyers—monkeys, arboreal rodents, birds, tree snakes and lizards, and multitudes of invertebrates.

5   The distribution of this biome is closely related to specific climatic conditions—consistent rainfall and relatively high temperatures. Thus there is an obvious correlation with the location of Af* and some Am* climatic regions.

*Designation of climatic regions explained in Chapter 8.

A. Prepare either an outline or a page of notes of the chapter, based on that portion which you have. List all ten biomes, but provide details only for the tropical rainforests.

B. Define the following:

1. selva _____

2. arboreal _____

C. Explain the difference between *ecosystem* and *ecotone*.

_____

_____

_____

Selection 1 **Rainforest Removal**

Tom L. McKnight

Tom McKnight is a professor of geography at U.C.L.A. where he served as Chair of the Geography Department from 1978 to 1983. He has also spent a number of years living and teaching in Australia. The following article is a box insert in Chapter 9 ("The Biosphere") of his textbook *Essentials of Physical Geography* (1992).

Prepare

1. From what you know about the author and the selection, what can you predict about purpose and format or style?

   _____

   _____

2. State briefly what you expect to read about. _____

   _____

3. What do you already know about the topic? Respond using *one* of the methods described in Chapter 2.

   _____

   _____

   _____

4. Use the title to pose questions about the reading selection. _____

   _____

5. **Scan** the article to answer the following questions.

   a. Which country's rainforest has been reduced by more than 50 percent?

   _____

   b. What is one solution to preserving rainforests? _____

   _____

6. Preread the selection. Then read and annotate the article. Finally, complete the comprehension and vocabulary checks that follow and answer the questions for discussion and reflection.

1 Tropical rainforests comprise the climax vegetation over an area of nearly 3 billion acres (1.2 billion ha), or about 8.3 percent of the Earth's total land surface. These remarkable forests are shared by some 50 countries on five

continents. This vegetative association represents a biome of extraordinary diversity. Biologists believe that rainforests are the home of perhaps half the world's biotic species, about five-sixths of which have not yet been described and named.

2   Throughout most of history, rainforests were considered to be remote, inaccessible, unpleasant places, and as a consequence they were little affected by human activities. In the present century, however, rainforests have been exploited and devastated at an accelerating pace, and in the last decade or so, tropical deforestation has become one of the Earth's most serious environmental problems. The rate of deforestation is spectacular—51 acres (21 ha) per minute; 74,000 acres (30,000 ha) per day; 27 million acres (11 million ha) per year. More than half of the original African rainforest is now gone; about 45 percent of Asia's rainforest no longer exists; the proportion in Latin American is approaching 40 percent.

3   The current situation varies in the five major rainforest regions:

1. The rate of deforestation is highest in *southern* and *southeastern Asia*, primarily associated with commercial timber exploitation.

2. The current rate of deforestation is relatively low in *central Africa.*

3. Timber harvesting and agricultural expansion are responsible for a continuing high rate of forest clearing in *West Africa.* Nigeria has lost about 90 percent of its forests; Ghana, 80 percent.

4. Deforestation of the *Amazon region* as a percentage of the total area of rainforest has been moderate (about 5 percent of the total has been cleared), but it continues at an accelerating pace.

5. Very rapid deforestation persists in *Central America*, mostly due to expanded cattle ranching.

4   As the forest goes, so goes its animal life. In the early 1990s it was estimated that tropical deforestation was responsible for the extermination of one species per hour. Moreover, loss of the forests contributes to accelerated soil erosion, drought flooding, water quality degradation, declining agricultural productivity, and greater poverty for rural inhabitants. In addition, atmospheric carbon dioxide continues to be increased because there are fewer trees to absorb it and because burning of trees for forest clearing releases more to the air. Other broad-scale climatic alterations have been postulated, but these are still speculative.

5   The irony of tropical deforestation is that the anticipated economic benefits are usually illusory. Much of the forest clearing, especially in Latin America, is in response to the social pressure of overcrowding and poverty in societies where most of the people are landless. The governments throw open "new lands" for settlement in the rainforest. The settlers clear the land for crop growing or livestock raising. The result almost always is an initial "nutrient pulse" of high soil productivity, followed in only two or three years by a pronounced fertility decline as the nutrients are quickly leached and cropped out the soil, weed species rapidly invade,

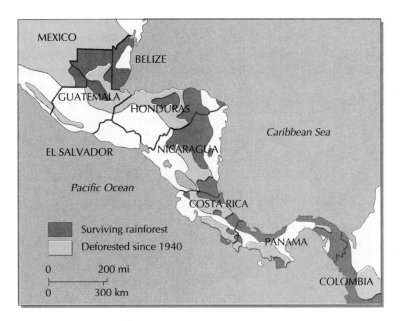

The shrinking Central American rainforest in the last half-century. This region has one of the fastest rates of deforestation in the world.

and erosion becomes rampant. Sustainable agriculture generally can be expected only with continuous heavy fertilization, a costly procedure.

6   The forests, of course, are renewable. If left alone by humans, they can regenerate, providing there are seed trees in the vicinity and the soil has not been stripped of all its nutrients. The loss of biotic diversity, however, is much more serious. Extinction is an irreversible process. Valuable potential resources—pharmaceutical products, new food crops, natural insecticides, industrial materials—may disappear before they are even discovered. Natural genotypes that could be combined with agricultural crops or animals to impart resistance to disease, insects, parasites, and other environmental stresses may also be lost. Last but not least is the possibility that many small, isolated, vulnerable groups of indigenous people may be wiped out.

7   Much concern has been expressed about tropical deforestation, and some concrete steps have been taken. The development of agriforestry (planting crops with tress, rather than cutting down the tress and replacing them with crops) is being fostered in many areas. In Brazil, which has by far the largest expanse of rainforest, some 46,000 square miles (119,000 km^2) of reserves have been set aside, and Brazilian law requires that any development in the Amazon region leave half the land in its natural state. In 1985 a comprehensive world plan, sponsored by the World Bank, the World Resources Institute, and the United Nations Development Programme, was introduced. It proposes concrete, country-by-country strategies to combat tropical deforestation. It is an $8 billion, five-year project,

dealing with everything from fuel-wood scarcity to training extension foresters. Its price tag makes its implementation unlikely.

8   Meanwhile, the sounds of the axe and the chainsaw and the bulldozer continue to be heard throughout the tropical forest lands.

Comprehension Check ·

Answer the following with a T (true) or F (false).

	T	F
1. Tropical rainforests are found in many countries across five continents.	___	___
2. Rainforests have always been exploited by humans.	___	___
3. Rainforest depletion is highest in Asia.	___	___
4. Tropical deforestation is a serious environmental problem.	___	___
5. Rainforests are destroyed in West Africa for timber and land for farming.	___	___
6. Deforestation usually brings new wealth to the land's farmers.	___	___

Fill in the blanks to complete each of the following statements.

7. Deforestation in Central America is the result of expanded _____ .

8. Problems that result from deforestation include _____ and

_____ .

9. Because of its cost, the 1985 worldwide plan to save tropical rainforests is

_____ to be successful.

10. When the forests are cut down, many _____ become extinct.

Expanding Vocabulary ·

Review the following words in their contexts and then write a brief definition or synonym for each word based on what you can learn from context clues.

biome (1) _____

exploited (2) _____

extermination (4) _____

postulated (4) _____

speculative (4) _____

irony (5) _____

leached (5) _____

erosion (5) _____

rampant (5) _____

genotypes (6) _____

indigenous (6) _____

Analysis of Content and Strategies

1. Study the map included in the article.
   a. Which country shown on the map has lost the greatest amount of rainforest since 1940?

   _____

   b. About how much of its rainforest has Honduras lost? _____

2. What is the article's primary writing pattern or strategy? _____

3. What is the article's main idea? _____

   _____

4. How does identifying the writing pattern help you recognize the main idea?

   _____

5. What kinds of details are provided in paragraphs 2 and 3?

   _____

6. What kinds of details are provided in paragraphs 4 and 6?

   _____

7. What is the purpose of paragraph 7? How does it contribute to the writing pattern?

   _____

For Discussion and Reflection

1. Look again at paragraph 1. What are the author's feelings about tropical rainforests? What words express his attitude?

2. What is the effect on you of McKnight's closing paragraph?

3. Are you concerned about deforestation of the rainforests? Should you be?

4. What solutions would you propose?

5. Compose an essay test question that would draw on a student's knowledge of this article.

Selection 2 — How Large Were the Biggest Dinosaurs?

Mark A. Norell, Eugene S. Gaffney, and **Lowell Dingus**

Paleontologists Norell and Gaffney are co-curators of the dinosaur exhibits in New York City's American Museum of Natural History. Dr. Dingus, also a paleontologist, is director of the Museum's renovation of their entire fossil exhibit. They have all done both laboratory and field work. Their book, *Discovering Dinosaurs,* from which this excerpt comes, was published in 1995 to coincide with the reopening of the dinosaur rooms at the Museum.

Prepare

1. From what you know about the authors and the selection, what can you predict about purpose and format or style?

   _____

   _____

2. State briefly what you expect to read about. _____

   _____

3. What do you already know about the topic? Respond using *one* of the methods described in Chapter 2.

   _____

   _____

4. **Scan** the article to answer the following questions.

   a. The "largest land animal ever" belongs to what dinosaur group?

      _____

   b. What is the estimated length of *Seismosaurus*? _____

   c. What is the estimated weight of *Apatosaurus*? _____

5. Preread the selection. Then read and annotate the article. Finally, complete the comprehension and vocabulary checks that follow and answer the questions for discussion and reflection.

1   Some dinosaurs reached extraordinary size. These land leviathans were the largest terrestrial animals ever to have lived. Determining which dinosaur was the biggest and how huge it was is difficult because many of the largest dinosaurs are known only from fragmentary remains. For others only a few skeletons have been completely excavated. Nonetheless, the title of "largest land animal ever" undoubtedly belongs to a member of the Sauropoda (the group containing *Apatosaurus*).

2   To discuss size, we need to establish what "large" means. Does it mean the longest dinosaur, the tallest, or the heaviest? Estimating the length and height of an animal is easy, if a fossil skeleton is reasonably complete. Weight is another matter. Consider two people: an average middle-aged out-of-shape paleontologist, and a professional athlete. If we had only their skeletons we would have difficulty estimating their weights accurately because the amount of flesh on any given skeleton may vary by a factor of two. The same is true of fossil animals. From skeletons, we know that some weighed more than others (*Apatosaurus* and *Diplodocus* were nearly the same length, but *Apatosaurus* probably weighed more, because its bones were much more robust), but because we don't have a good idea of how much soft tissue hung on the fossilized skeletons, we have no real empirical data with which to determine the exact weight of the animal.

3   We estimate the weights of fossil animals by one of two methods, both woefully inadequate. The first is an experimental procedure: We construct a small scale model of a particular dinosaur in its live state, using the fossil skeleton as a guide. Then we measure its volume. Because the densities of almost all vertebrate animals are fairly uniform (nearly equal to water, at 1 gram per cubic centimeter), we can calculate the weight. The problem with this approach is that the resulting estimate of weight depends entirely on the construction of the fleshed-out model. Because we cannot test how accurate these models are, our results are only very rough estimates.

4   The second approach relies on comparisons between fossil and living animals and is more empirical. The general idea is that there is a relationship between the width and length of limb bones and the weight of an adult animal. From thousands of measurements taken from all sorts of living animals, we can develop a general predictive mathematical model about these relationships. We can test the accuracy of this model by taking the same measurements from living animals whose weight is known. If the model performs well, we can take identical bone measurements on nonavian dinosaur fossils. Plugging the values into the model gives us the extrapolated weights. Although perhaps more reliable than the first method, this is not a real test because no terrestrial animals that exist today even approach the size of the biggest dinosaurs. Hence we do not know how accurate the estimates from these models are at the extreme scale of the largest dinosaurs.

5   We might have confidence in the weights estimated for nonavian dinosaurs if different methods produced congruent (similar) results, no matter which method was used. Scientific investigators often employ congruence tests to evaluate whether the values they are getting are reasonable. Unfortunately, the weight values for nonavian dinosaurs estimated by these different methods are incongruent. For example, *Diplodocus carnegei* has been estimated to weigh 18.5, 11.7, or 5.8 metric tons, depending on the method used. These calculated estimates for the same animal vary by a factor of three!

6   So what is the biggest dinosaur? In terms of length we do not need experiments with models or sophisticated mathematics to figure this one out, just a very long tape measure. Even though only part of its vertebral column, pelvis, and hind limbs have been excavated, *Seismosaurus* is estimated to have been 39 to 52 meters long, making it the longest dinosaur yet discovered. Although its weight has not been calculated, its close relative *Apatosaurus* (with a length of about 26 meters) has been estimated to weight around 35 metric tons. *Seismosaurus* was undoubtedly heavier, probably even heavier than the old heavyweight champion, *Brachiosaurus*. *Brachiosaurus* is not very long (only about 22 meters) but has a scale-crunching weight of between 31.6 (bone measurement) and 87 (model dinosaur) tons. Considering that an adult male African elephant weighs 5.4 metric tons, these were truly earthshaking animals.

■   **Comprehension Check** ·

Fill in the blanks to complete each of the following statements.

1. Deciding on the size of dinosaurs is difficult because we have only partial

   _____ .

2. The "largest" dinosaur can mean the _____ , the

   _____ , or the _____ .

3. One way to estimate a dinosaur's weight is to make a scale model and measure its _____ .

4. The longest dinosaur is the _____ .

5. The strategies for estimating the weights of dinosaurs are not _____ .

Answer the following with a T (true) or F (false).

	T	**F**
6. The largest land animal ever to live was the *Apatosaurus*.	____	____
7. Among dinosaurs of the same length, those with bigger bones will have weighed more.	____	____

	T	F
8. An adult male elephant weighs 5.4 metric tons.	___	___
9. All dinosaurs were bigger than the elephant.	___	___

Expanding Vocabulary

Review the following words in their contexts and then write a brief definition or synonym for each one. Use your dictionary only after seeing what you can learn from context clues (and word parts).

leviathans (1) _____

terrestrial (1) (4) _____

excavated (1) _____

paleontologist (2) _____

robust (2) _____

vertebrate (3) _____

empirical (4) _____

nonavian (4) _____

extrapolated (4) _____

Analysis of Content and Strategies

1. What is the section's main idea? _____

   _____

2. What is important to learn from this passage in addition to the actual lengths and weights of some of the dinosaurs?

   _____

3. Why is estimating weight difficult? _____

   _____

4. Explain briefly the two ways to estimate weight. _____

   _____

   _____

5. What is the problem with each method? _____

_____

_____

6. Explain what it means to say that the "weight values" are "incongruent."

_____

For Discussion and Reflection

1. Approximately how much heavier was the *Apatosaurus* than today's elephant? Can you imagine animals of such size?

2. Dinosaurs are everywhere, from Barney to the movie *Jurassic Park*. How do you account for their continued popularity? Why do they fascinate us so much?

3. What can you learn about the scientific method from reading this excerpt?

Selection 3 What TV Could Do for America

Carl Sagan

Perhaps the best-known contemporary scientist, Carl Sagan is a professor of Astronomy and Space Sciences at Cornell University. Sagan is author or editor of more than a dozen books, including the best-selling *Cosmos,* the book form of his television series. The following article appeared in *Parade* magazine on June 4, 1995.

Prepare

1. From what you know about the author and the selection, what can you predict about purpose and format or style?

_____

_____

2. State briefly what you expect to read about. _____

_____

3. What do you already know about the topic? Respond using *one* of the methods described in Chapter 2.

_____

_____

_____

4. Use the title to pose questions about the reading selection. _____

_____

5. **Skim** the article and then mark each of the following statements as True or False.

	T	F
a. Sagan's topic is the portrayal of science on television.	___	___
b. Sagan is happy with the way TV presents science.	___	___
c. In today's world, we need a better understanding of science and technology.	___	___
d. One way to put more science on TV would be a program that points out the fakery in pseudoscience.	___	___

6. Preread the selection. Then read and annotate the article. Finally, complete the comprehension and vocabulary checks that follow and answer the questions for discussion and reflection.

1   "Scientist, yes—mad, no," giggles the mad scientist on _Gilligan's Island_ as he adjusts the electronic device that permits him to control the minds of others for his own nefarious purpose.

2   "I'm sorry, Dr. Nerdnik," says the cartoon superhero, "the people of Earth will not appreciate being shrunk to 3 inches high, even if it _will_ save room and energy . . ." He is patiently explaining an ethical dilemma to a typical scientist portrayed on Saturday-morning children's television.

3   Many of these so-called scientists are moral cripples driven by a lust for power or endowed with a spectacular insensitivity to the feelings of others. The message conveyed to the young audience is that science is dangerous, and scientists are worse than weird: They're crazed.

4   The applications of science, of course, _can_ be dangerous. Virtually every major technological advance in the history of the human species—back to the invention of stone tools and the domestication of fire—has been ethically ambiguous. These advances can be used by ignorant or evil people for dangerous purposes or by wise and good people for the benefit of the human species. But, too often, only one side of the ambiguity seems to be presented in many TV offerings to our children.

5   Where, in such programs, are the joys of science? The delights in discovering how the universe is put together? The exhilaration in knowing a deep thing well?

6   What about the contribution that science and technology have made to human well-being, of the billions of lives saved or made possible by medical and agricultural technology—more than all the lives lost in all the wars since the beginning of time? There's hardly a glimpse.

7   We live in a complex age where many of the problems we face, whatever their origins, can only have solutions that involve a deep understanding of science and technology. Modern society desperately needs the finest minds available to devise solutions to these problems. I do not think that many youngsters will be encouraged toward a career in science or engineering by watching Saturday morning TV—or much of the rest of the available American video menu.

8   Over the last 10 years, a profusion of credulous, uncritical TV series and "specials" have been spawned—on ESP, channeling, the Bermuda Triangle, UFOs, ancient astronauts, Big-Foot and the like. The style-setting series *In Search Of* . . . begins with a disclaimer disavowing any responsibility to present a balanced view of the subject. You can see a thirst for wonder here untempered by even rudimentary scientific skepticism. Pretty much whatever anyone says on camera is presented as true. The idea that there might be alternative explanations, decided upon by the weight of evidence, never surfaces.

9   *In Search Of* . . . frequently takes an intrinsically interesting subject and systematically distorts the evidence. If there are both a mundane scientific explanation and one requiring the most extravagant paranormal or psychic explanation, you can be sure which will be highlighted.

10   A popular series called *The X-Files*, which pays lip service to skeptical examination of the paranormal, is in fact skewed heavily toward a reality of alien abductions, strange powers and government complicity in covering up just about everything interesting. Almost never does the paranormal claim turn out to be a hoax or a psychological aberration or a misunderstanding of the natural world. Much closer to reality, as well as a much greater public service, would be a series in which paranormal claims are systematically investigated, and every case is found to be explicable in prosaic terms.

11   Other shortcomings are evident in television science-fiction programming. *Star Trek*, for example, despite its charm and strong international and interspecies perspective, often ignores the most elementary scientific facts. The idea that Mr. Spock could be a cross between a human being and a life form independently evolved on the planet Vulcan is genetically far less probable than a successful cross of a man and an artichoke.

12   There must be dozens of alien types on the various *Star Trek* TV series and movies. Almost all we spend any time with are minor variants of humans. This may be driven by economic necessity, costing only an actor and a latex mask, but it flies in the face of the random nature of the evo-

lutionary process. If there are aliens, almost all of them, I think, will look devastatingly less human than Klingons and Romulans. *Star Trek* doesn't come to grips with evolution.

13   In many TV programs and films, even the casual science—the throwaway lines that aren't essential to a plot already innocent of science—is done incompetently. It costs little to hire a graduate student to read the script for scientific accuracy. But this is almost never done. As a result, we have such howlers as "parsec" mentioned as a unit of speed instead of distance in *Star Wars*—a film in many other ways exemplary.

14   There's a great deal of pseudoscience for the gullible on TV, a fair amount of medicine and technology, but hardly any science—especially on the big commercial networks. There are network employees with the title "Science Correspondent" and an occasional news feature said to be devoted to science. But we almost never hear any science from them, just medicine and technology. In all the networks, I doubt if there's a single employee whose job it is to read each week's issue of *Nature* or *Science* to see if anything newsworthy has been discovered. When the Nobel Prizes in science are announced each fall, there's a superb news "hook" for science: a chance to explain what the prizes were given for. But, almost always, all we hear is something like ". . . may one day lead to a cure for cancer. And today in Belgrade . . ."

15   How much science is there on the radio or TV talk shows, or on those dreary Sunday-morning programs in which middle-aged white males sit around agreeing with each other? When is the last time you heard an intelligent comment on science by a President of the United States? Why in all America is there no TV drama that has as its hero someone devoted to figuring out how the Universe works? When a highly publicized murder trial has everyone casually mentioning DNA testing, where are the prime-time network specials devoted to nucleic acids and heredity? I can't even recall seeing an accurate and comprehensible description on television of how *television* works.

16   By far the most effective means of raising interest in science is television. But this enormously powerful medium is doing close to nothing to convey the joys and methods of science, while its "mad scientist" engine continues to huff and puff away.

17   Often there's a good science program in the *Nova* series on the Public Broadcasting System, and the Discovery Channel or The Learning Channel, and occasionally on the Canadian Broadcasting Company. Bill Nye's *The Science Guy* programs for young children, which began on PBS, are fast-paced, range over many realms of science and sometimes even illuminate the process of scientific discovery. But the depth of public interest in science engrossingly and accurately presented—to say nothing of the immense good that would result from better public understanding of science—is not yet reflected in network programming.

18   How could we put more science on television? Here are some possibilities:

- Present the wonders—and, more important, the methods—of science routinely on news and talk shows. There's real human drama in the process of discovery.
- Create a series called "Solved Mysteries," in which tremulous speculations have rational resolutions, including puzzling cases in forensic medicine and epidemiology.
- Organize a series on fundamental misunderstandings and mistakes made by famous scientists, national leaders and religious figures.
- Run regular exposés of pernicious pseudoscience. One way might be audience-participation "how to" programs: how to bend spoons, read minds, appear to foretell the future, perform psychic surgery, do cold reads. Show how we're bamboozled: Let people learn by doing.
- Establish a state-of-the-art computer graphics facility to prepare in advance scientific visuals for a wide range of news contingencies.

19   There is a pressing national need for more public knowledge of science. Television cannot provide it all by itself. But if we want to make short-term improvements in the understanding of science, television is the place to start.

Comprehension Check

Fill in the blanks to complete each of the following statements.

1. Most technological advances are ethically _____ .

2. American TV often portrays scientists as not only weird but _____ .

3. Sagan wants television to present the _____ of science.

4. Sagan accuses several popular shows of generally choosing extreme and bizarre explanations of events rather than _____ explanations.

5. The most effective means of increasing interest in science is _____ .

Answer the following with a T (true) or a F (false).

	T	F
6. The contributions of science and technology have saved more lives than those lost in all wars.	____	____
7. Young people will be eager to pursue careers in science and engineering after watching Saturday-morning television.	____	____
8. Mr. Spock's parentage is scientifically possible.	____	____
9. On the major networks, most science news is really about either medicine or technology instead of science.	____	____

Expanding Vocabulary

Match each word in the left column with its definition in the right column by placing the correct letter in the space next to each word.

_____ nefarious (1)   a. disavowal, denial of connection with

_____ endowed (3)   b. joyessness, gaiety

_____ ambiguous (4)   c. abundance

_____ exhilaration (5)   d. outside the norm

_____ profusion (8)   e. harmful, detrimental

_____ credulous (8)   f. deception, practical joke

_____ disclaimer (8)   g. can be explained

_____ disavowing (8)   h. timid, fearful

_____ intrinsically (9)   i. regions within which something prevails

_____ paranormal (9)   j. equipped

_____ skewed (10)   k. study of epidemic diseases

_____ hoax (10)   l. repudiating, disclaiming knowledge

_____ aberration (10)   m. application of medicine to criminal law

_____ explicable (10)   n. illusion, mental disorder

_____ prosaic (10)   o. wicked, vile

_____ realms (17)   p. revelations of what is discredible

_____ tremulous (18)   q. trustful, naive

_____ forensic (18)   r. unclear, equivocal

_____ epidemiology (18)   s. distorted

_____ exposes (18)   t. commonplace, ordinary

_____ pernicious (18)   u. a part of by its very nature

Analysis of Content and Strategies

1. What is Sagan's topic? _____

_____

2. What is the primary writing pattern used? _____

_____

3. What is Sagan's thesis? _____

_____

4. What other writing pattern does the author use a great deal? _____

_____

5. Summarize the problems Sagan sees with television's handling of science.

_____

_____

_____

_____

_____

_____

For Discussion and Reflection

1. Do you agree with Sagan's analysis of the problem? Is TV, on the whole, not providing much instruction in science, or presenting science in a positive way? Explain your answer.

2. Would you like to see more science on television? Why or why not?

3. Comment on each of Sagan's proposals. Which do you think are good ideas? Why? Why not the others?

CHAPTER 8

Studying For College Classes

In this chapter you will learn:

- How to prepare for class

- How to participate in class

- How to retain information and prepare for testing

- How to take tests

The cartoonist Jules Feiffer did a clever cartoon some years ago showing a student, in baggy sweater and unlaced high tops, telling us that he wanted to become a successful writer and hang out with movie stars, so he signed up for a creative writing class. The writing instructor talked about how much writers have to read, read, read, but that sounded too hard for the student, so he switched to a major in accounting. Of course the creative writing instructor was right about good writers needing to read, but can our student avoid reading, or writing, by changing his major? Not really. He will have accounting and other business texts to read, and reading in other required courses. To be successful in college and the workplace, you need to develop confidence in all language uses. After reading and writing to prepare for class, you will need to participate in class by listening, by more writing, and by speaking as well.

■ PREPARING FOR CLASS

One of the best methods for becoming successful in some activity is to find out what other successful people have done and then to copy their methods. Fortunately, we do know the methods of successful students. Good students almost never miss class. Further, they go to class *prepared*. In addition to having written assignments completed the day they are due, what else is involved in preparing for class? First, always keep up with the reading assignments. Reading the assigned chapter gives you a *learning context* for the class period. Some students go to class hoping that the instructor will teach them everything they need to know so that they will not have to read. These students have the process backwards. The class lecture or discussion is designed to clarify and expand on the reading assignment. No instructor can *clarify* what you have not yet read. You may want to think of reading the assignment as your way of previewing the class. Even if the reading is difficult, you will gain some knowledge that will prepare you to follow the lecture or participate in class discussion. Students who are unprepared for class end up wasting much of the class time. Without a learning context, they are uncertain of what notes to take.

Second, be ready to personalize each class. If you have completed your reading, you can ask questions on the particular parts of the chapter you found confusing. This is also why you need to be in class, not relying on someone else's notes. If you are absent, you pass up the chance to learn what you need to know to do well. Prepare by writing down the questions you have on the reading, either in your reading notes or as part of your annotations of the text. Include page numbers so that you can direct your instructor to those passages about which you have questions.

Many good students establish a reading schedule that actually keeps them *ahead* of the class schedule. This allows them to understand how an instructor is preparing the class for the upcoming material, and it allows for schedule problems that would otherwise leave them unprepared for class.

■ PARTICIPATING IN CLASS

Good students participate. They choose to be *actively engaged* in each class. Active engagement includes the following activities.

1. **Sit on the front row.** From here you can see the board clearly. You also signal to the instructor that you are motivated to learn, and you are less likely to talk when you should be listening or to doze with your head against the back wall.

2. **Come with the appropriate materials** and have them assembled *before* the instructor begins class. Have whatever texts you need plus your notebook and pens. (Good students do not walk in late and then further disrupt class by asking a neighbor what's happening.)

3. **LISTEN.** Intend to learn. Pay attention to the signal words that announce a list or definition or contrast or analysis of a process. Listen for signal words that announce a shift in topic (e.g., "moving on," "Let's turn our attention now." "The next topic"), or those that make clear the instructor's view of student comments. (Some students automatically stop listening when other students are talking. If the instructor says, "That's an excellent

example of the principle, Mr. Jones," you will wish that you had listened to the example.) And really pay attention to the words that signal important material (because it will be on the next test!). Some of these signals include: "This is really important," "I want you all to be clear on this," and "Let me emphasize. . . ."

4. **Participate in class discussions,** question periods, and group activities. You need to speak up in class even if you are shy, for two reasons. First, if you never speak, you will never conquer your shyness. Second, the more strategies you use to learn, the better you will learn the material. Reacting to what others are saying and voicing your views, or answering the instructor's questions, engage your attention and lead you to think about the subject matter. Remember that the best way to test your knowledge and understanding is to see if you can put the material into your own words. Class discussion allows you to test yourself orally, with help from others as needed. When the instructor asks if there are any questions, take advantage of the opportunity. (The chance to learn is the reason you are sitting in the classroom; seize the moment.) Try to take the lead in small group discussions or group projects. Keep your focus on what you need to learn, not on those few students who see these activities as occasions for not working. If you are shy in class, make yourself speak up at least once each class period beginning with the second class meeting. After a few weeks, participating will become easier and more fun.

5. **Take notes.** In Chapter 6 you learned how to use the Cornell Method for taking notes to reinforce reading. This method is also ideal for class notes. Take your notes in the space to the right of the line on each page and leave the 2½ inches to the left of the line for the key words and phrases you will add. Some of these can be added while you are in class, but others may be added when you review your notes after class. Use a 3-ring binder notebook and keep your reading notes together with your class notes on the same material. Just be sure to mark each page at the top either "class notes" or "reading notes." Also date each page of notes.

When taking notes, do not try to write down everything the instructor says. Listen for main ideas, just as you read for main ideas. Follow the examples and try to grasp their point as they are presented and then take notes only on main ideas and key supporting details. Do try to get down complete definitions of key terms. And be certain to take down *everything* that is put on the board. (If it is written on the board, it is important.) Include signal words in your notes: for example, the *causes* of the Civil War or the *differences between* (contrast) the first and second World Wars.

Some students prefer to tape class lectures. Taping should be a last resort, used only if you have great difficulty following the instructor's presentation. Taping can make you passive; note taking will keep you active in class.

6. **Review notes immediately.** To fix in your memory as much of the class discussion as possible, review your notes right away. Even if you have another

class in the next hour, try to review. Get to your next class and then go over your notes while waiting for the class to begin. If you do not have another class, go to your room or the library to complete and review your class notes. As you read through your notes, add points that were left out or complete thoughts left unfinished. Then annotate your notes and put key terms in the left margin. Think carefully about what you put down the left side of the paper, because these words and phrases will be your primary way to review for tests.

EXERCISE 8-1 Preparing for Class

Read and annotate the following textbook section. Then answer the questions that follow.

Biological Theories On Aging

Of the various theories about the biological causes of aging, the following are among the most commonly accepted.

- *The wear-and-tear theory* states that, like everything else in the universe, the human body wears out. Inherent in this theory is the idea that the more you abuse your body, the faster it will wear out. A great deal of controversy exists today regarding the relative benefits and disadvantages of various exercise programs for middle-aged and elderly people. Proponents of the wear-and-tear theory argue that activities such as jogging may actually predispose people to premature bone and joint injuries in later years, particularly in the lower back, hip, and knee areas.

- *The cellular theory* states that at birth we have only a certain number of usable cells, and these cells are genetically programmed to divide or reproduce only a limited number of times. Once these cells reach the end of their reproductive cycle, they begin to die and the organs they make up begin to show signs of deterioration. The rate of deterioration varies from person to person, and the impact of the deterioration depends on the system involved.

- *The autoimmune theory* attributes aging to the decline of the body's immunological system. Studies indicate that as we age, our immune systems become less effective in fighting disease. Eventually, bodies that are subjected to too much stress, especially if this is coupled with poor nutrition, begin to show signs of disease and infirmity. In some instances, the immune system appears to lose control and turn its protective mechanisms against the host, actually attacking the person's own body. Although this type of disorder may occur in all age groups, some gerontologists believe that the condition increases in frequency and severity with age.

- *The genetic mutation theory* proposes that the number of cells exhibiting unusual or different characteristics increases with age. Proponents of this theory believe that aging is related to the amount of mutational damage within the genes. The greater the mutation, the greater the chance that cells will not function properly, leading to eventual dysfunction of body organs and systems.

1. Prepare a page of reading notes on this section (or select one of the other writing-to-learn methods).

2. List two questions that an instructor might ask to produce discussion of this passage.

   1) _____

   _____

   2) _____

   _____

3. What would you want clarified, or what related questions occur to you, from reading this section? List the questions that you would want to ask in class.

   1) _____

   _____

   2) _____

   _____

   3) _____

   _____

■ STRATEGIES FOR RETENTION

This chapter examines some of the "nuts and bolts" of college study, ways to get the job done. One important step in the process is testing. To assign grades in courses, instructors must measure student knowledge and understanding of the course content. If you have been doing the reading and participating in class, tests should not be a cause of undue anxiety.

Some students who attend class and complete assigned reading still have trouble getting good grades on tests. Perhaps these students panic during tests; perhaps they are not prepared. The easiest way to eliminate the first cause—panic—is to be prepared and do well. Success breeds success: once you start to test well you will be less anxious and then testing well will become your usual pattern.

Learning the material really well is the key to initial and continued good test performance. Here are some suggestions for learning and retaining information so that you are prepared for testing.

1. **Commit to learning.** Remember the 3Cs from Chapter 1. Attitude counts. You demonstrate your intention to learn first by completing assigned readings on schedule and then by attending and participating in class. You will be better prepared for tests if you have been learning all along instead of trying to cram before the exam.

2. **Concentrate when reading and studying.** Do not forget to monitor your concentration while reading and to stop to refocus your attention when you lose concentration.

3. **Focus on tasks, not on anxieties.** You are not concentrating on learning when you are thinking about the test instead of the subject matter. Successful students spend their time and energy doing the work of the course. Unsuccessful students spend more time thinking about themselves, about their anxieties and past performances, rather than thinking about the subject of the course. Plan to model yourself after the successful students.

4. **Use several senses.** To become as fully engaged as possible, do not try to learn only by using your eyes. Annotate as you read. Also as you read, visualize what you are reading about. When studying your physical geography text, place the tropical rainforests on the map in your head, naming specific countries or areas of continents where most of the rainforests are located. Then, as you read the description, picture the rainforests, the dense foliage overhead, the semidarkness on the forest floor, the endless chatter of the monkeys swinging through the trees.

   Finally, discuss what you are learning with others. Find a study partner or a group from each class that gets together to review periodically. But don't limit your discussion to those in your classes. Introduce your new information into conversation with friends and family, not to sound like a big shot but because new knowledge and new ideas are exciting and worth sharing.

5. **Organize information.** Disconnected pieces of information are difficult to remember because they seem to lack meaning. Only when facts and concepts and ideas are organized into meaningful patterns do they make sense and give us a reason to learn. Furthermore, even if you can memorize long lists of unrelated details from a chapter, you will not do well on tests that ask for conclusions or applications of the facts. Remember that the various

writing-to-learn strategies (mapping, summary, outlining, note taking) are all designed to reveal a pattern of main ideas and supporting details. To organize material for studying, select a writing strategy that best helps you to see patterns and understand connections. Also listen in class for clues to organizing the information.

6. **Reflect; make connections.** First, put each chapter in the larger reading context of the entire text. Again in your physical geography text, as you move from a study of the atmosphere to the biosphere, you are reminded of the important role of climate in defining the world's ecosystems. Review the previous chapter on climate, if necessary, to give context to your study of the large ecosystems. In addition, connect your study to other courses you are taking or have taken. Academic disciplines overlap; knowledge in one area enriches study in another. Think, for instance, about the role of physical geography in the shaping of different societies (sociology) or different nation-states (history/government). Also connect your study to your own life. Reflect on the part of the world in which you live; think how your life would change if you lived in a tropical rather than a temperate climate, or if you lived north of the Arctic circle.

7. **Review, review, review.** Reviewing is a critical step in your reading strategy. Just as you need to review class notes as soon after class as possible, so you need to review your reading assignments as soon as you complete them. Reviewing should be both immediate and periodic. If you take notes or write a summary of each chapter or article, then your writing provides an immediate review. If you are only annotating what you read, then you need to review your annotations and test yourself on the material as soon as you finish reading. Do not just reread key definitions, for example; close the chapter to see if you can define each term in your own words. Then reread the definitions in the chapter to see if yours were correct. Finally, review your annotations or notes (both reading notes and class notes) each week or so until it is time for a final review before an exam.

■ PREPARING FOR TESTING

Most instructors describe the format of tests either in class or on the course syllabus, so you should know if a given test will be multiple choice, fill in the blanks, short answer, or essay format. You may find that instructors will vary the format from one test to another, or use a combination of formats to make one test. If an instructor does not describe the text's format, ask.

If you know that a particular test will be one of the first three, or a combination of the first three, then you know the importance of concentrating on details. The short-answer forms of testing do not allow for drawing broad connections or analyzing in depth. They also do not reward "shooting the breeze" or personal responses to the material. They demand knowledge, but the knowledge may include ideas and inferences drawn from reading. For example, the comprehension quizzes in your reading course may include selecting the best main-idea statement, or writing a one-sentence thesis. To produce the right selection or short answer, you may need to infer the main idea from your reading.

Preparing for Short-Answer Forms of Testing

Use the following guidelines to prepare for short-answer forms of testing.

Guidelines for Short-Answer Testing

1. **Study from thorough notes.** Before reviewing for a test, make certain that both class notes and reading notes are detailed and complete. Be certain to include key terms and their definitions, or make 3"×5" flash cards (See Chapter 4) to study from. Remember that if definitions are tested through multiple choice or matching terms and definitions, all you have to do is recognize the correct definition, but if the test requires short answers, you will have to write out definitions for the words on the test.

2. **Concentrate on material the instructor has emphasized in class.** Your class notes should indicate what your instructor has stressed in class, stressed by putting the material on the board, by repeating, or by using signal words such as "This is really important."

3. **Use chapter review questions or study problems as ways to prepare.** Make certain that you can answer all the review questions, and work the additional problems at the chapter's end as a way to review and test yourself.

4. **Do not overlook historical elements in your texts.** Many instructors care about the history of their field of study and expect students in introductory courses to learn some of that history along with the subject matter of the course. Be prepared to answer such questions as "Who was the father of psychoanalysis?" or "Who discovered the atom?" in your psychology or chemistry class. Questions of this sort are not likely to appear on essay exams, but are quite common on tests with short-answer formats.

5. **Practice naming parts, reciting steps in processes, recounting key examples.** Talk through the material, either to yourself or with a study partner. Cover a page of notes and recite the material. Then check yourself for accuracy before proceeding to the next page.

6. **Be able to spell key terms correctly.** If the test is fill in the blank or short answer, you will need to practice the spelling of key terms along

· with learning their definitions. Instructors will forgive misspellings of minor words more readily than misspellings of key terms. As an aid to learning, divide words into syllables on flash cards: Ne-an-der-thal.

7. **Anticipate the questions.** As you study, ask yourself what questions you would use to test someone on the material. Listening in class and using the text's review questions should help you figure out most of what's coming on the test.

Let's apply these guidelines to the following excerpt from *Biology! Bringing Science to Life* (John H. Postlethwait et al., McGraw, 1991).

1   *Homo sapiens* During the million years that early humans inhabited the Old World, their faces and teeth slowly decreased in size, and their brains enlarged from a volume of 800 cc around 1.5 million years ago to 1200 cc by 500,000 years ago. These gradual changes led imperceptibly from *Homo erectus* to **Homo sapiens** by about 400,000 years ago.

2   Two groups of humans have occupied the earth in the millennia since that time: archaic *Homo sapiens* (including Neanderthals and others) and modern *Homo sapiens* (including the Cro-Magnons and all the current races of people). Archaic humans dominated the Old World from about 400,000 years ago until they were superseded by modern humans between 30,000 and 100,000 years ago.

3   Neanderthal fossils, first discovered in Germany's Neander Valley in 1856, were the first hominid remains to be studied scientifically. Neanderthals have been much maligned as brutish, ignorant savages, but the accumulated facts speak quite differently. Living in Europe and the Middle East, Neanderthals were short, stocky, powerfully built people able to move with a strength and speed surpassing that of today's best Olympic athletes. They had large protruding faces and characteristic projecting brow ridges. Their brains were similar in organization to a modern human's, but *larger* (1400 cc) on average. The tools and other artifacts they left behind suggest an ability to deal with the environment through learned cultural behavior rather than brute, physical force. They made spears and spearheads for hunting large game and scrapers for cleaning animal hides. They routinely built shelters, and their large front teeth were often worn, perhaps from chewing hides, as the Eskimo did traditionally, to make clothing. The skeletons of old and crippled Neanderthals showed that the strong cared for the elderly and infirm, and they buried their dead ceremoniously with fine stone tools, servings of game meat, and even flowers—evidence of belief in an afterlife.

4   Modern humans did not descend from Neanderthals but rather arose elsewhere (fossil evidence suggests Africa), migrated northward, and eventually outcompeted the archaics on their own turf. The two types

may have coexisted for thousands of years, but by 34,000 years ago, the Neanderthals had died out.

5   The Cro-Magnons looked distinctly different from their archaic cohorts. Their faces were smaller, flatter, and less projecting than the Neanderthals', the heavy brow ridges had all but disappeared, and their skulls were higher and rounder. Their limbs were more slender (but still stoutly athletic compared to our own), their teeth were smaller, and most important, their culture was vastly more complex. Their tool kits contained knives, chisels, scrapers, spearheads, axes, and tools for shaping other tools of rock, bone, and ivory. They left dozens of cave paintings, engravings, and sculptures, suggesting a major development of symbolic forms of communication, probably accompanied by increased language abilities. Their living sites and shelters became larger and more complex, and human burials became more common and elaborate, indicating the establishment of religion.

6   The success of these cultural developments spurred a population expansion. Modern humans followed the herds of mammoths, woolly rhinoceroses, reindeer, and other game into the arctic regions of Eurasia and across the Bering land bridge into the Americas. They also built boats to carry them across uncharted waters to New Guinea and Australia. By 15,000 to 20,000 years ago, people had occupied virtually all the inhabitable regions of the earth.

Here is a sample page of reading notes on the passage. Notice that the pattern for Neanderthals is repeated for Cro-Magnons. The terms down the left column emphasize the parallel information.

	Homo sapiens – Evolved 400,000 years ago
time of evolution	*archaic H.S.* *modern H.S.*
	Neanderthals *Cro-Magnons & all current races*
	400,000 —to *30,000 to 100,000 years ago*
	34,000
	years ago
Neanderthals	*Neanderthals*
location of fossils	*location of fossils first studied: Neander Valley, Germany, 1856*
characteristics	*short, stocky, strong, fast, large protruding faces, ridged brows, brain organization similar to ours*
learned cultural behavior–tools	*Made spears and spearheads*
	scrapers—to clean hides
	also chewed hide

belief in afterlife	*built shelters; buried dead—afterlife*
<u>*Cro-Magnons*</u>	<u>*Cro-Magnons*</u>
location	*arose in Africa—spread across Europe, Asia, & into Americas. Everywhere by 15,000 to 20,000 years ago.*
characteristics	*faces smaller, flatter, less protruding, no brow ridges. Rounder skulls. Smaller teeth. Thinner than Neanderthals but still athletic.*
culture-tools, art, religion	*made many tools, and tools for making tools. Cave paintings—symbolic communication increased language abilities shelters more complex burials more elaborate—religion*

You have thorough—and organized—notes from which to study. You know from class that your instructor wants students to have a good sense of the "time line," of the stages of evolution, so you know to learn the dates. In your review, you practice the spelling of: *Homo sapiens*, Neanderthal, and Cro-Magnon. You will learn the locations, characteristics, and details of culture to answer questions on both groups and to be able to contrast archaic and modern *Homo sapiens*. Here are some possible test items.

Multiple Choice

_____ 1. Neanderthals lived in

    a. Africa.

    b. Europe and the Middle East.

    c. North and South America.

    d. Alaska.

_____ 2. Modern *Homo sapiens* are related to

    a. Cro-Magnons.

    b. Neanderthals.

    c. Gorillas.

    d. Whales.

_____ 3. Cave paintings were produced by

    a. Neanderthals.

    b. modern man.

    c. Cro-Magnons.

    d. monkeys.

Often with multiple choice tests, you can eliminate two of the four possible answers immediately. (It is difficult to prepare tests with four "good" answers. Be aware that instructors sometimes just "fill in the spots" with unlikely choices.) After eliminating some of the choices, take another look at the remaining choices before rushing to answer. Sometimes there is a trick in the wording that makes only one the right answer. When the wording seems to make more than one answer right, think about the subject matter of the test. In this context, what is the answer the instructor expects you to choose?

The answer to the first question is "b." Notice that "c" parallels "b" and "d" parallels "a." The only real debate is between "a" and "b." In the second question, any answer is correct, in some sense (whales and humans are both mammals), but clearly the material for testing tells you that you are to choose "a." In other words, which term applies to ancient and which to modern *Homo sapiens.* In the third question, the instructor either became tired or decided to have some fun and included monkeys as a choice. Once again the real choice is between Neanderthals and Cro-Magnons.

Fill in the blank

1. The _____ had protruding faces with ridged brows.

2. The elaborate burials of the Cro-Magnons suggest the development of

   _____ .

3. The first Neanderthal fossils studied came from _____ .

Observe that these test items are more difficult than the multiple choice items. You have to write the answer, not just recognize the answer. Now you will be glad that you practiced the spelling of key terms, for you will need Neanderthal for the first item. Notice that the second item asks for an inference made in the text. Do not assume that fill-in-the-blank tests only test facts. The third item is a reminder to you to pay attention to details of history in your biology text. It is a good question because it reinforces the origin of the term *Neanderthal* from the Neander Valley.

With some fill-in-the-blank tests, the words or phrases to be inserted are listed at the top of the test page. Unless the directions specify that each word or phrase is to be used, and used only once, do not assume that this is what you should do. Often some items will be needed more than once, and others are not used at all. Instead of trying to second-guess the test itself, concentrate on reading each sentence and then selecting the word or phrase that best fits in each blank.

True/False

	T	F
1. The first Neanderthal fossils to be studied were found in Africa.	___	___
2. Cro-Magnons were the first to use learned cultural behavior.	___	___
3. Both ancient and modern *Homo sapiens* were religious.	___	___

When taking True/False tests keep in mind that a statement must be *completely* true to be marked true. If some element of the statement is not true, then you must mark the statement false. This means that you must read each statement carefully before deciding how to mark it. The first statement above is false; the fossils came from the Neander Valley in Germany. Some of the oldest fossils have been uncovered in Africa, but that is not what the statement says. The second statement is also false; the Neanderthals were the first. That item tests your knowledge of the time line of evolution. You could make the third item complicated if you started debating the meaning of the word *religious.* How elaborate do burial rituals have to be to label a people religious? Are you religious if you believe in an afterlife? Most people would say yes to this last question. So the answer to the third item is "True." If the statement had said something about organized religion or churches, then the statement would be false. Do not make True/False testing more complicated than it needs to be.

Short Answer

1. Contrast the physical characteristics of the Neanderthals and the Cro-Magnons.
2. When and where did archaic *Homo sapiens* live?

With short-answer topics, write to the point. The first topic does not ask about tools or shelters, only about physical characteristics. The second tests your knowledge of the time line, but it does so with just one time period. You should be able to answer each of the questions in two or three sentences if you stay on the topic. If you have trouble finishing a short-answer test, either you do not know the material well enough or you are writing more than the topic requires.

Essay Tests

Most students consider essay tests to be more difficult than any other kind, and with good reason. To write a good essay answer, you need the same information required to score well on short answer tests, but you also need several other skills. First, you need to make connections and understand larger issues. Second, you need to organize your thoughts in a relatively short time. Third, you need to compose clear and complete sentences. Combining these skills to produce an effective essay answer under time pressure is not easy. You can cope, however, if you prepare properly for essay testing. Here are some guidelines.

1. **Follow the seven guidelines given above for short-answer testing.** (See pp. 288–289.) Some students unwisely believe that essay testing is the easiest because you can "write off the top of your head," so you don't have to study. Wrong! You still need to study from good notes, concentrate on what

the instructor has stressed in class, use the text's review guides, practice until you know the details cold, and be able to spell terms.

2. **Anticipate essay questions.** Once you feel confident with the basic information to be covered, you need to focus on larger elements. Make up some essay questions that you would ask about the material. What essay questions would you compose about ancient and modern *Homo sapiens?* One possibility is "Contrast the Neanderthals and the Cro-Magnons." Such abrupt topics, offering little direction, are quite common on tests. Do not assume that your answer can be as casual as the topic. Most instructors have a list (in their heads) of a certain number of items they expect the "A" essay to include. In this case, the instructor expects you to contrast the two in terms of time, location, physical traits, and cultural advances. If you leave out any one of the major areas of contrast, you will lose points. If you confuse any of the details, such as making the Neanderthals the cave painters, you will lose points. Be sure to organize your contrast by points of difference (location, physical traits) rather than writing first about the Neanderthals and then the Cro-Magnons.

    Another possible topic is "Explain why the Cro-Magnons were more advanced than the Neanderthals." This is a good essay topic because it requires both facts and inferences about the significance of those facts. Be sure to avoid cluttering your essay with details that do not show advancement (e.g., location, most physical traits).

3. **Read the essay topics carefully and understand what you are asked to write about before you begin to compose.** Too many students have essay tests returned to them with comments such as: "This is an interesting discussion but it does not respond to the topic." Such essays are not given high marks. Here are two strategies for understanding essay topics that you may find useful.

    (a) Turn the topic statement into a question. If you are asked "to discuss the rock cycle," pose this as a question: what are the steps in the rock cycle? The question helps you see that you need to explain steps in a process.

    (b) Pay attention to the direction words. "Examine," "discuss," and "explain" call for an organized presentation of information, as one would find in a textbook. "Interpret" and "evaluate" require that you make judgments and include your views. "Relate" calls for making connections, "compare" for noting similarities or differences, "trace" for the use of time sequence to examine causes or developments or effects over time.

4. **Organize your answer before writing.** Take a moment to collect your thoughts on the topic and to select an organization. If you are asked to examine the effects of the automobile on modern society, you need to list. You might want to put the most important effect last. If you are asked to examine the recipes for living in the writings of Ben Franklin and Henry Thoreau,

then a contrast structure is needed. Think of specific points of difference between the two writers' views and organize by those differences. Remember that as you studied, you anticipated essay topics and thought about how you would respond, so you have already considered various ways of organizing the material.

5. **Learn from doing.** Study each test when it is returned to you. Note in particular the questions you did not anticipate. Compare a classmate's A paper with yours. Try to see why your response lost points whereas the classmate's response did not. Did you leave out one key point of contrast? Did your essay jump around rather than maintaining a clear organization? Apply the knowledge you gain to your study for the next test.

EXERCISE 8-2 **Practicing with Various Kinds of Test Questions**

Read the following excerpt from Jackson J. Spielvogel's Western Civilization *(2nd ed., vol. 1. 1994) and then complete the test questions that follow.*

The Reformation in England

1   At one time, a Reformation in England would have been unthinkable. Had not Henry VIII penned an attack against Martin Luther in 1521, the *Defense of the Seven Sacraments,* and been rewarded for it by the pope with the title "Defender of the Faith"? Nevertheless, there were elements of discontent in England. Antipapal feeling ran high since many of the English resented papal influence in English affairs, especially in matters of taxation and justice. Anticlericalism (opposition to and criticism of the activities of the clergy) was rife as people denounced greedy clerics who flaunted their great wealth in ostentatious extravagance. One layman charged that "These [the clergy] are not the shepherds, but the ravenous wolves going in shepherds' clothing, devouring the flock."

2   Anticlericalism and antipapal feelings were not the only manifestations of religious sentiment in early sixteenth-century England. A craving for spiritual expression fostered the spread of Lutheran ideas, encouraged in part by two different traditions of dissent. Heretical Lollardy, stressing the use of the Bible in the vernacular and the rejection of papal supremacy, continued to exert influence among the lower classes, while Christian humanism, with its calls for reform, influenced the English middle and upper classes. People influenced by Lollardy and Christian humanism were among the first to embrace Lutheran writings when they began to arrive in England in the 1520s.

3   Despite these factors, there might not have been a Reformation in England if it had not been for the king's desire to divorce his first wife Catherine of Aragon. Henry VIII's reasons were twofold. Catherine had produced no male heir, an absolute essential if his Tudor dynasty were to flourish. At the same time, Henry had fallen in love with Anne Boleyn, a lady-in-

waiting to Queen Catherine. Her unwillingness to be only the king's mistress, as well as the king's desire to have a legitimate male heir, made a new marriage imperative. The king's first marriage stood in the way, however.

4   Henry relied upon Cardinal Wolsey, the highest ranking English church official and lord chancellor to the king, to obtain an annulment of his marriage from Pope Clement VII. Normally, the pope might have been willing to oblige, but the sack of Rome in 1527 had made the pope dependent upon the Holy Roman emperor Charles V, who happened to be the nephew of Queen Catherine. Discretion dictated delay in granting the English king's request. Impatient with the process, Henry dismissed Wolsey in 1529.

5   Two new advisers now became the king's agents in fulfilling his wishes. These were Thomas Cranmer (1489–1540), who became archbishop of Canterbury in 1532, and Thomas Cromwell (1485–1540), the king's principal secretary after the fall of Wolsey. They advised the king to obtain an annulment of his marriage in England's own ecclesiastical courts. The most important step toward this goal was the promulgation by Parliament of an act cutting off all appeals from English church courts to Rome, a piece of legislation that essentially abolished papal authority in England. Henry no longer needed the pope to attain his annulment. He was now in a hurry, since Anne Boleyn had become pregnant and he had secretly married her in January 1533 to legitimize the expected heir. Now, as archbishop of Canterbury and head of the highest ecclesiastical court in England, Thomas Cranmer ruled in May that the king's marriage to Catherine was "null and absolutely void," and then validated Henry's marriage to Anne. At the beginning of June, Anne was crowned queen. Three months later a child was born. Much to the king's disappointment, the baby was a girl, the future Queen Elizabeth.

6   In 1534, Parliament completed the break of the Church of England with Rome by passing the Act of Supremacy, which declared that the king was "taken, accepted, and reputed the only supreme head on earth of the Church of England." This meant that the English monarch now controlled the church in all matters of doctrine, clerical appointments, and discipline. In addition, Parliament passed a Treason Act making it punishable by death to deny that the king was the supreme head of the church. The Act of Supremacy and the Treason Act went beyond religious issues in their implications, for they asserted that there could be no higher authority over England than laws made by the king and Parliament.

7   Few challenged the new order. One who did was Thomas More, the humanist and former lord chancellor, who saw clearly to the heart of the issue: loyalty to the pope in Rome was now treason in England. More refused to publicly support the new laws and was duly tried for treason. At his trial, he asked, rhetorically, what the effect of the actions of the king and Parliament would be: "Therefore am I not bound . . . to conform my conscience to the Council of one realm [England] against the general Council of Christendom?" Because his conscience could not accept the

victory of the national state over the church, nor would he, as a Christian, bow his head to a secular ruler in matters of faith, More was beheaded in London on July 6, 1535.

8   Thomas Cromwell worked out the details of the Tudor government's new role in church affairs based on the centralized power exercised by the king and Parliament. Cromwell also came to his extravagant king's financial rescue with a daring plan for the dissolution of the monasteries. About four hundred religious houses were closed in 1536, and their land and possessions confiscated by the king. Many were sold to nobles, gentry, and some merchants. The king received a great boost to his treasury, as well as creating a group of supporters who now had a stake in the new Tudor order.

9   Although Henry VIII had broken with the papacy, little change occurred in matters of doctrine, theology, and ceremony. Some of his supporters, such as Archbishop Thomas Cranmer, wished to have a religious reformation as well as an administrative one, but Henry was unyielding. To counteract a growing Protestant sentiment, the king had Parliament pass the Six Articles Act of 1539, which reaffirmed transubstantiation, clerical celibacy, and other aspects of Catholic doctrine. No doubt, Henry's conservatism helped the English accept the basic changes he had made; since religious doctrine and worship had changed very little, most people were indifferent to the transformation that had occurred. Popular acceptance was also furthered by Henry's strategy of involving Parliament in all the changes.

10   The last decade of Henry's reign was preoccupied with foreign affairs, factional intrigue, and a continued effort to find the perfect wife (he ended up with six). In religious affairs, Henry managed to hold the Church of England in line with Catholic doctrine. After his death the movement toward Protestantism grew much stronger under his successor, the under-age and sickly Edward VI (1547–1553), the son of Henry's third wife, Jane Seymour.

Multiple Choice

Circle the letter that indicates the best way to complete the statement.

_____ 1. Sir Thomas More was beheaded because he

    a. would not bow to a secular ruler on matters of faith.

    b. opposed Henry's desire to marry Anne Boleyn.

    c. wanted to improve his relations with the pope.

    d. wanted to marry Anne Boleyn himself.

_____ 2. Henry VIII was given the title "Defender of the Faith" because he

    a. divorced his wife Catherine.

    b. secretly married Anne Boleyn.

    c. attacked Martin Luther in a treatise written in 1521.

    d. destroyed the monasteries.

True/False

Answer with a T (true) or F (false).

	T	F
3. The reformation in England was the result of anticlerical and antipapal feelings.	___	___
4. Henry VIII was succeeded by Edward VI, son of Anne Boleyn.	___	___

Fill In The Blanks

Fill in the blanks to complete each of the following statements.

5. When Henry VIII dissolved the Catholic monasteries, he took both_____

_____ and _____ .

6. Criticism of the behavior of clerics (priests) is called _____ .

7. Henry VIII had _____ wives.

Short Answer

Briefly answer each of the following questions.

8. Why did Henry want to divorce Catherine of Aragon?

_____

_____

_____

_____

_____

9. How did Henry VIII increase his treasury and add to his supporters?

_____

_____

_____

_____

■ **Essay Topics**

Respond, in an essay, to one of the following topics.

10. Explain the steps Henry VIII took to bring about the Church of England's split with the Roman Catholic Church.
11. Discuss the causes of the Reformation in England.

Selection 1 **The Basis of Moral Judgment**

Vincent Ryan Ruggiero

Vincent Ruggiero is a professor of humanities at the State University of New York at Delhi, a writer, and an education consultant. His work has focused on encouraging the teaching of thinking skills in all subject areas at all levels of education. The following excerpt is from his textbook *The Art of Thinking* (2nd ed., 1988).

■ **Prepare**

1. From what you know about the author and the selection, what can you predict about purpose and format or style?

   _____

   _____

2. State briefly what you expect to read about. _____

   _____

3. What do you already know about the topic? Respond using *one* of the methods described in Chapter 2.

   _____

   _____

4. Use the title to pose questions about the reading selection. _____

   _____

5. Preread the selection. Then read and annotate the article. Finally, complete the comprehension and vocabulary checks and answer the questions for discussion and reflection.

1   On what basis should moral judgment be made? Certainly not the majority view—that is too unreliable. Hitler enjoyed the support of a majority of the German people. The American people at one time supported slavery. And more recently, the majority first opposed abortion, then approved it. Nor should the basis of moral judgments be feelings, desires, or preferences. If it were, then we would be forced to conclude that every rapist, every murderer, every robber is acting morally. Conscience provides a better basis for judgment, but it too can be uninformed or insensitive. (After all, the most heinous criminals sometimes feel no remorse.)

2   The most reliable basis for moral judgment, the basis that underlies most ethical systems, is the principle that people have rights existing independently of any government or culture. The most fundamental is the right to be treated with respect and left undisturbed as long as one does not infringe on others' rights. Other rights—such as "life, liberty, and the pursuit of happiness"—extend from that right.

3   The basic principle, of course, is not itself adequate to judge complex moral questions. Additional working principles are needed. The following four are found in most ethical systems and provide common ground for the discussion of issues, even among people of very different ethical perspectives.

1. Relationships with other people create *obligations* of various kinds, and these should be honored unless there is compelling reason not to do so. There are, for example, formal agreements or contracts, obligations of family membership (parent to child, child to parent, husband to wife, and vice versa), obligations of friendship, employer-employee obligations, and business and professional obligations.

2. Certain *ideals* enhance human life and assist people in fulfilling their obligations to one another. These should be served whenever possible. Among the most important ideals are: tolerance, compassion, loyalty, forgiveness, peace, brotherhood, justice (giving people their due), and fairness (being impartial, as opposed to favoring selected people).

3. The *consequences* of some actions benefit people, while those of other actions harm people. The former actions should be preferred over the latter. Consequences, of course, can be emotional as well as physical, momentary as well as lasting, and subtle as well as obvious.

4. Circumstances alter cases. Generalizations have their place, but too often they are used as a substitute for careful judgment. "Taking a human life is wrong" is useful as a general moral outlook, but it provides little help in deciding real cases. It blurs important distinctions. A hit man for the mob takes a life when he completes a contract. So does

a police officer when he kills a robber in self-defense. And so does a small child when he mistakes a real pistol for a toy and accidentally shoots his sister. But all three acts are very different from one another. Good thinking about issues means getting beyond generalizations and examining the particulars of the case.

4   To achieve depth in your examination of moral issues and wisdom in your judgment, you must deal effectively with complexities. The presence of two or more conflicting obligations or ideals creates complexity. So does the likelihood of multiple consequences, some beneficial and some harmful. Here is an easy-to-follow guide for dealing with such complexities.

1. Where two or more obligations are in conflict, decide which is the most serious obligation or which existed first.
2. Where two or more ideals are in conflict, ask which is the highest or most important ideal.
3. Where multiple consequences exist, some good and some bad, ask which are most significant—and whether the good effects outweigh the bad, or the reverse.

5   Let's look at an actual moral issue and see how these considerations apply. Ralph is a middle-aged man. In his youth he was a good athlete, and his son Mark grew up sharing his father's enthusiasm for sports. In seventh grade Mark went out for three sports but was rather poor in two of them. Basketball was his best sport; in that he was fair but not outstanding. Ralph decided that Mark could only be a first-string player if he received some assistance. So Ralph struck up a friendship with the junior varsity and varsity basketball coaches. He invited them and their wives to his house for dinner, opened his personal sports library to them, and got them tickets to professional games through his business contacts.

6   Through his friendship with the coaches, Ralph was able to help his son. He spoke to them often about Mark's intense desire to excel in basketball, and asked whether they would mind giving Mark some tips to improve his game. The coaches were happy to help Mark; their help was an expression of their friendship with Ralph. They opened the gym to him on weekends and took personal responsibility for developing his skills.

7   Soon Mark was playing junior varsity basketball. Ralph took every opportunity not only to remind the coach of Mark's dedication, but also to point out other players' weaknesses and apparent lack of dedication. Mark received more playing time in each game than his skills alone justified, and in time he became the team's scoring leader. When he moved up to varsity, Mark received further special treatment. He was almost never benched, even when his team was far ahead; instead, he was kept in to raise his point total. During his senior year, most of the team's plays were designed for him. And Ralph persuaded the coaches to write letters praising Mark's playing to a number of college coaches.

8   Did Ralph behave morally? Let's apply the principles we discussed earlier and see.

9   There are three important obligations involved in this case: Ralph's obligation to guide his son responsibly to manhood, through teaching and example; obligations of friendship between Ralph and the coaches; and the coaches' obligation to help all their players develop their potential and learn the values associated with sports.

10 The ideals that should be considered are sensitivity to others' needs, justice, and fairness. The first applies to Ralph: He should have appreciated the other players' needs for encouragement, support, and equal opportunity. The other two ideals, justice and fairness, apply to the coaches: They should have considered giving each player on the team the attention and help he deserved, rather than concentrating their attention on one player. (This, of course, does not mean that it would be an injustice to give special attention to an outstanding player; Mark, remember, was only a fair player at the outset.) And the coaches should have considered treating players impartially (fairness). One way they could have done this was by opening the gym on weekends to all players who wished to practice, instead of only to one.

11 The clearest and most certain consequence was that Mark's skills were developed and the other players were shortchanged because they did not have the same opportunities. Other probable consequences were that Mark's teammates developed a feeling of bitterness and cynicism over the coaches' favoritism and that Mark acquired the attitude that it was permissible, even desirable, for him to disregard other people's rights and needs in order to achieve his own goals.

12 It is clear that though Ralph's actions achieved some good (the development of his son's skills), they also caused a great deal of harm to a number of people. The obvious harm was to the players. But they also caused the coaches to put friendship over responsibility to their players and to violate the ideals of justice and fairness. (The main responsibility for the coaches' actions is, of course, their own. They could have resisted Ralph's influence.) Moreover, Ralph's actions probably even harmed his son. The self-serving attitude created in him far outweighs the development of his modest athletic skill

13 In light of these considerations, we would find Ralph's actions morally wrong. Further, the fact that he knew what he was doing and actually *planned* it makes him even more blameworthy.

Comprehension Check ·

Fill in the blanks to complete each of the following statements.

1. The best basis for moral judgment is the principle that people _____

_____ .

2. That people should be given respect is considered a _____

_____ .

3. Additional working principles include the idea that we need to think about the _____ of our actions.

4. Moral complexity exists when there are two or more conflicting _____

_____ .

5. The coaches did not act according to the ideals of _____

and _____ .

Answer the following with a T (true) or F (false).

	T	F
6. Moral judgments should rely on the majority view.	___	___
7. Moral judgments should be based on personal feelings.	___	___
8. Relationships with people establish obligations.	___	___
9. Ralph's actions did not cause harm.	___	___

Expanding Vocabulary

Review each of the following words in their context and then write a definition or synonym for each one.

conscience (1) _____

heinous (1) _____

infringe (2) _____

impartial (3) _____

potential (9) _____

cynicism (11) _____

Analysis of Content and Strategies

1. Ruggerio begins by stating what ought *not* to be the basis for moral judgments. What are the three bases that Ruggerio dismisses?

_____

_____

_____

2. Explain each of the four principles that support the fundamental principle of human rights.

_____

_____

_____

_____

3. Explain Ruggerio's guide to dealing with complex situations. Will these help you apply basic moral principles?

_____

_____

4. What two primary writing strategies does Ruggerio use to develop his main idea?

_____

5. Prepare a page of reading notes on this selection. In the space below, write two short-answer questions on this selection that might appear on a test.

_____

_____

6. Write an essay test topic that draws on this selection.

_____

For Discussion and Reflection

1. Do you agree that moral judgment should not be based on majority view, feelings, or conscience alone? Does Ruggerio give good reasons for his position? Why or why not?

2. Do you accept the idea of obligations? Do you agree with Ruggerio's list of obligations? Are there others you would add to the list? Explain.

3. Do you agree that the coaches and Ralph were morally wrong? Are you willing to make this moral judgment? Why or why not?

Selection 2 | Legalization of Drugs

J. Ross Eshleman, Barbara G. Cashion, and **Laurence A. Basirico**

The following selection comes from the text *Sociology: An Introduction*, published in its fourth edition in 1992. The three authors are all sociology professors: Eshleman at Wayne State University, Cashion at Shippensburg University of Pennsylvania, and Basirico at Elon College.

Prepare

1. From what you know about the author and the selection, what can you predict about purpose and format or style?

   _____

   _____

2. State briefly what you expect to read about. _____

   _____

3. What do you already know about the topic? Respond using *one* of the methods described in Chapter 2.

   _____

   _____

4. Use the title to pose questions about the reading selection. _____

   _____

5. Preread the selection. Then read and annotate the article. Finally, complete the comprehension and vocabulary checks and answer the questions for discussion and reflection.

1   Debates still rage about the best way to win the war on drugs. The most controversial policy, which has not been enacted in the United States, is legalization of drugs (also referred to as "decriminalization" or "narcotics-by-regulation"). There are strong arguments for and against this idea.

The Argument for Legalization

2   According to supporters of legalization, drug prohibition does not and cannot work and causes more harm than good (Melville, 1989). Treating

drug use as a crime rather than a health issue has created problems that cannot be solved through enforcement (Church, 1988). These problems include the inability to control the flow of illegal drugs, violent drug wars, drug-related crime, and the creation of highly dangerous drugs.

3   Supporters of legalization contend that the high prices resulting from drug prohibition make it impossible to stop or control drug traffic. The sale of illegal drugs generates over $20 billion annually (Melville, 1989). This kind of profit, legalization supporters assert, provides such an incentive for gangs, organized crime, and other drug dealers that criminal prosecution is seen simply as a "business expense." To maintain their share of the profits, drug traffickers engage in violent turf wars. The casualties of these wars include not only drug dealers and users but innocent bystanders also. In addition, addicts often commit crimes such as prostitution, mugging, and burglary in order to support their expensive drug habits. Supporters of legalization feel that the lower price and accessibility of drugs that would come with decriminalization would eliminate the incentive for criminals (thus allowing the flow of drugs to be better controlled), eliminate violent turf wars, and reduce the crime committed by addicts.

4   The enormous profit from the sale of illegal drugs has led to the creation of more dangerous drugs, such as "crack" cocaine. Drug dealers are interested in selling whatever is easiest to smuggle and whatever produces the highest profit. Marijuana, usually the first drug that people buy, is bulky, relatively easy to detect in transit, and does not command as high a price as other drugs. However, crack, a cocaine derivative, is inexpensive to produce, easy to transport, highly addictive, and thus very profitable (Melville, 1989). The profit motive also leads dealers to adulterate all drugs by adding other ingredients—often harmful—in order to stretch the amount they can sell. Thus, users have no assurance of what they get when they purchase drugs on the street (Melville, 1989). Supporters of legalization believe that if drugs were legal and controlled by the government, they would be less dangerous.

5   There are other reasons for legalization. Most important, the money spent on enforcement substantially reduces the amount that could be spent on antidrug education and treatment. In 1990, the federal drug-war budget was nearly $8 billion, 75% of which was for interdiction and enforcement (King, 1990). Legalization would permit the entire drug-war budget, plus billions more generated from government taxes on these drugs, to be used for powerful antidrug education and treatment programs that would deter drug use more effectively than prohibition (Church, 1988). These kinds of programs work, as evidenced by the steady decline in use of alcohol and tobacco in recent years (Melville, 1989).

6   Another reason that the drug war budget is misallocated, according to legalization supporters, is that drug use in itself—that is, the mere act of taking drugs—is a victimless crime. The type of interdiction that would be necessary to eradicate the personal use of drugs would be so vast that

it would violate all rights to privacy guaranteed by the U.S. Constitution (Dennis, 1991).

7   Finally, supporters of legalization say that the ineffectual enforcement of drug laws encourages disrespect for the law and, thus, decreases the effectiveness of antidrug education by labeling behavior practiced by more than 20 million Americans as criminal activity (Melville, 1989). Inconsistencies with regard to substance policies also encourage disrespect for the law. Alcohol and tobacco are legal but kill more people than illegal drugs do (Colson, 1990). However, because these substances are legal and controllable, they do not lead to the violence and crime that illegal drugs do, and their use is declining.

The Argument Against Legalization

8   While it is true that drug prohibition has not yet ended the drug problem, opponents of legalization note that prohibition works to some extent. Drug use has declined in recent years. Recent studies by the National Institute on Drug Abuse (NIDA) found that in 1978, only 35 percent of high school seniors believed that marijuana posed a great risk to health. By the late 1980s, 77 percent felt that way. Daily use of marijuana by seniors fell from 10.7 percent to 2.7 percent—a drop of 75 percent in the same period. In the general population, use of marijuana fell 28 percent in a year. Use of cocaine also declined. Thus, say opponents of legalization, this is precisely *not* the time to surrender to legalization (Gold, 1990). The fact that the drug problem still exists means that prohibition strategies must be strengthened, not eradicated (Colson, 1990). Prohibition of drugs will work if given a chance, just as the federal Prohibition of alcohol effectively reduced drinking (Gold, 1990).

9   Surveys sponsored by the Partnership for a Drug Free America indicate that the greatest deterrents to drug use are fear of getting caught, fear of punishment, and fear of harm (Gold, 1990). Opponents of legalization argue that decriminalizing drugs would decrease this fear by sending the message that drug use has the approval of the government and is socially acceptable, thereby decreasing the effectiveness of any stepped-up educational efforts (Melville, 1989). Accordingly, the number of drug users—and addicts—would increase.

10   Opponents of legalization maintain that the increased drug use that would come with legalization would *increase* crime, not decrease it. While it is true that crimes associated with heroin are usually committed while the patient is in withdrawal and in need of a fix, cocaine-related crimes are committed while the user is in the drugged state. In the first quarter of 1989, 76 percent of all people arrested in New York City had cocaine in their urine, even though cocaine is quickly eliminated from the body (Gold, 1990). Further, opponents insist that the legalization would not eliminate the crime associated with underworld drug dealers. Another black market for new, exotic, more powerful—possibly more addicting and dangerous—drugs would be created (Colson, 1990).

11   Opponents of legalization claim that besides the increase in crime, the death and illness caused by substance abuse would also increase. Opponents reason that the higher rate of destruction caused by alcohol and tobacco, when compared to illegal drugs, clearly demonstrates that dangerous substances are abused more if they are legal. The problem would be even greater with some drugs that are currently illegal. Only 10 percent of alcohol users become addicts, yet 70 percent of cocaine users do (Colson, 1990). The fact that alcohol and tobacco are dangerous yet legal should not be used as an argument in support of drug legalization but is a substantial reason *not* to *add* to the number of dangerous substances legally available. The accessibility of alcohol and tobacco to minors, however illegal they may be, also illustrates that legalization does not necessarily create control over dangerous substances.

12   Finally, opponents of legalization disagree that drug use is a victimless crime; they therefore hold that prohibition should be enforced at all costs. They suggest that it would be wrong to place the individual freedoms of drug users above the freedom of their families that may be abused through violence, molestation, neglect, and in countless other ways, and the freedom of babies born addicted to drugs because their mothers are drug users. They are all innocent victims that need to be protected.

13   The debate over legalization is likely to continue for some time. It is important, therefore, that you become familiar with the arguments for and against legalization.

Comprehension Check

Circle the appropriate letter.

_____ 1. The best statement of the main idea is
   a. Drug prohibition does not work.
   b. There are strong arguments for and against legalization.
   c. Since the debate over legalization will probably continue, you should know the arguments for and against legalization.
   d. Legalization will increase drug use.

Fill in the blanks to complete each of the following statements.

2. Supporters of legalization argue that keeping drugs illegal results in a heavy

   flow of drugs, _____ , _____ , and

   _____ .

3. Illegal drugs earn _____ each year.

4. Crack cocaine is cheap to make, easy to ship, addictive, and therefore

   _____ for drug dealers.

Answer the following with a T (true) or F (false).

	T	F
5. Those opposing legalization argue that if drugs were legal, drug use would increase.	___	___
6. Opponents of legalization argue that drug use is not a victimless crime.	___	___
7. If drugs are legalized, money used in the anti-drug war could be used for drug treatment instead.	___	___
8. Drug use has declined recently.	___	___
9. Increased drug use, if drugs were legal, would increase crime, say opponents of legalization.	___	___

Expanding Vocabulary

Match each word in the left column with its definition in the right column by placing the correct letter in the space next to each word.

_____ controversial (1) a. encouragement, stimulus

_____ contend (3) b. make impure

_____ turf (3) c. incorrectly allocated

_____ incentive (3) d. assert, argue

_____ derivative (4) e. erase, remove

_____ adulterate (4) f. preventions or hindrances to a particular action

_____ interdiction (5) g. prohibition

_____ misallocated (6) h. open to debate

_____ eradicate (6) i. substance derived from another

_____ ineffectual (7) j. not effective

_____ deterrents (9) k. neighborhood area controlled by a gang

Analysis of Content and Strategies

1. Prepare an outline of this section. Make the article's two subheadings your major divisions: "I." and "II."

_____

_____

_____

_____

_____

_____

_____

_____

_____

_____

2. What can you infer to be the authors' position on legalizing drugs?

_____

How do you know? _____

3. Make four questions from material in this section. Try to make one of each
   type: multiple choice, true/false, fill in, and short answer.

_____

_____

_____

_____

_____

_____

4. Write one essay question to test students on this material.

_____

_____

For Discussion and Reflection

1. Which position has the most convincing arguments? Why? Are they based
   more on facts? Or on an understanding of human experience?

2. Is your response to question one based on evaluating the arguments or on your previously held views? Has reading the selection changed your thinking in any way?

3. Are your views on drugs based on moral judgments, personal experience, emotions, or some combination? Explain.

Selection 3	**The Unheeding Addict**

Abigail Trafford

Abigail Trafford has a syndicated weekly column, "Second Opinion," and is Health Editor of the *Washington Post*. She is also the author of *Crazy Time: Surviving Divorce and Building a New Life* (1992). The following column appeared August 1, 1995.

Prepare

1. From what you know about the author and the selection, what can you predict about purpose and format or style?

_____

_____

2. State briefly what you expect to read about. _____

_____

3. What do you already know about the topic? Respond using *one* of the methods described in Chapter 2.

_____

_____

4. Use the title to pose questions about the reading selection. _____

_____

5. Preread the selection. Then read and annotate the article. Finally, complete the comprehension and vocabulary checks and answer the questions for discussion and reflection.

1   In the lazy afternoons of vacation, after excursions to the swimming hole, or a walk along the beach, there is always Sherlock Holmes. Part of my vacation tradition is to dive into old books, in this case the adventures of the greatest detective of all and his sidekick, the modest and amiable Dr. Watson. I pick up "The Sign of the Four," published in 1889. To my surprise, I find Dr. Watson in a very modern predicament.

2   He is confronting Holmes about a substance abuse problem—his own private "intervention" in the argot of today's treatment approach to drug addiction and alcoholism. Holmes has just taken his bottle of cocaine from the mantelpiece and with his hypodermic needle has plunged the sharp point into his left arm, already scarred by previous injections.

3   "But consider!" says Dr. Watson to Sherlock Holmes. "Count the cost! Your brain may, as you say, be roused and excited, but it is a pathological and morbid process, which involves increased tissue-change, and may at last leave a permanent weakness."

4   Brain damage. Doctors know that cocaine releases a surge of the chemical dopamine, changing metabolic pathways in the brain. Though not damaging long-term, cocaine can constrict blood vessels, blocking off needed oxygen to the brain and in rare cases causing stroke or heart attack. Alcohol can cause permanent brain damage. Called a "neurotoxin," a chemical that kills nerves, alcohol affects the cortex and limbic structures in the brain.

5   "You know, too, what a black reaction comes upon you," continues Dr. Watson.

6   Change of personality. One of the key signs that a person has a substance abuse problem. The cocaine addict who after the high enters a period of depression, agitation and craving. The alcoholic who alternates between being snarly and being depressed and withdrawn.

7   "Surely the game is hardly worth the candle," says Dr. Watson. "Why should you for a mere passing pleasure, risk the loss of those great powers with which you have been endowed?"

8   Interferes with work. Another sign that the addiction has gotten out of hand. Drug addicts and alcoholics risk losing the ability to work at all. Cocaine addicts become so focused on getting more hits of the drug that work and family no longer matter. In alcoholics, doctors have documented loss of memory, difficulty with abstract thinking and even dementia.

9   "Remember," continues Dr. Watson, "that I speak not only as one comrade to another, but as a medical man to one for whose constitution he is to some extent answerable."

10   Friend and physician, the double punch. Watson is not blaming the addict, here. Instead, he's using words of caring and support that could come straight from a manual from Alcoholics Anonymous or Narcotics Anonymous.

11   Millions of Americans find themselves in the same predicament as the fictional Dr. Watson. They are the ones who live or work with an estimated 14 million Americans who abuse alcohol and another 4 million addicted to illegal drugs, of whom 2.5 million are addicted to cocaine. Sometimes these friends, companions, co-workers, or spouses are called "enablers" because they rearrange the home or the workplace to accommodate the person who drinks or takes drugs.

12   Often that seems easier to do than confront the addict or the alcoholic. Yet, according to Hazelden, the pioneer center in drug and alcohol treatment in Minnesota, 70 percent of people who seek treatment do so because of the intervention and help of family and friends. Even so, only about 15 percent of those with a substance abuse problem get into treatment.

13   Hazelden and other centers have published guidelines for modern Dr. Watsons on how to talk to someone who abuses drugs or alcohol. Most people who live or work with an addict agonize months or even years before confronting the user, saying to themselves, "It's none of my business. . . . I wouldn't want anyone telling me what to do," in the words of the Hazelden brochure. Or, as Dr. Watson puts it, "I had lacked the courage to protest. . . . [Holmes was] the last man with whom one would care to take anything approaching a liberty."

14   Besides, interventions don't always work. Dr. Watson is completely unsuccessful. Sherlock Holmes essentially blows him off, saying: "I abhor the dull routine of existence. I crave for mental exaltation." In other words, lesser mortals like Watson might be able to get along without an addiction, but not a genius. As the Hazelden brochure advises people who fail to get through to someone who's addicted, denying there is a problem is part of the problem of addiction.

15   "There's no way to force a person into treatment," says Enoch Gordis, director of the National Institute on Alcohol Abuse and Alcoholism, who for many years ran a treatment program in New York City. "You can't force him to go to the hospital unless he's having convulsions, or he's violent and you can call the cops."

16   This leaves the friend, the co-worker, the spouse in the lurch. When the confrontation fails, what's next for the "enabler"? As Gordis says, echoing the principles of Al-Anon, the support group for friends and families of alcoholics: "You have to take care of yourself. Your life is valuable. You are not put on the planet to be a spouse of an alcoholic."

17   Once again, Dr. Watson shows the way. After the confrontation, the two go on to solve the next murder mystery. In the process, Dr. Watson falls in love with the beautiful Mary Morstan. In the end, he marries her and moves out of Holmes's apartment, where he had been recuperating from the Afghan war. In other words, Watson, the enabler moves on. What is left for the addict?

18   "For me," says Sherlock Holmes, "there still remains the cocaine bottle."

19   That's a typical comment by an addict. As Alan I. Leshner, director of the National Institute on Drug Abuse, says: "That's what happens with addiction. The only issue is the drug."

Comprehension Check

Circle the appropriate letter.

_____ 1. The best statement of the main idea is
   a. Reading should be part of any vacation.
   b. Alcohol causes brain damage.
   c. Reading Sherlock Holmes mysteries can teach us about the problems of addiction.
   d. There are basic problems with addiction that most addicts and their family and friends will face.

Fill in the blanks to complete each of the following statements.

2. Cocaine use can cause _____ or _____ .

3. Alcohol can cause _____ .

4. Friends and family who accommodate the addict are called _____ .

5. For addicts, the only issue is _____ .

Answer the following with a T (true) or F (false).

	T	F
6. The famous detective is Dr. Watson.	___	___
7. Addiction can destroy the ability to work.	___	___
8. There are an estimated two hundred thousand cocaine addicts in the United States.	___	___
9. Dr. Watson's attempt at intervention did not work.	___	___

Expanding Vocabulary

Match each word in the left column with its definition in the right column by placing the correct letter in the space next to each word.

_____ amiable (1)   a. especially gloomy

_____ argot (2)   b. sharp or quarreling manner of speech

_____ pathological (3)   c. recovering from illness

_____ morbid (3) .   d. friendly, gracious

_____ snarly (6)   e. severe mental deterioration

_____ endowed (7)   f. abnormal

_____ dementia (8)   g. hate, despise

_____ abhor (14)   h. gifted

_____ recuperating (17)   i. vocabulary

Analysis of Content and Strategies

1. What is the occasion that the author presents to introduce the Holmes mystery "The Sign of the Four"?

   _____

2. How does Trafford use the mystery story as an organizing device? _____

   _____

   _____

3. At what point in your reading are you aware that the essay is not primarily about Holmes and Watson?

   _____

4. The author begins paragraphs 4, 6, 8, and 10 with the same type of writing. What do the opening sentences of these paragraphs have in common?

   _____

   _____

   What makes this an effective writing strategy? _____

   _____

5. Why does Trafford tell us that Watson married and moved out of Holmes's house? What is her point?

   _____

   _____

For Discussion and Reflection

1. Are you surprised by the number of alcohol and cocaine addicts in the United States? Why or why not?

2. Why do you think so few addicts get into treatment?

3. Have you been a friend or family member of an addict? If so, would you describe yourself as an enabler? Or did you try intervention? How do you feel about the situation?

4. Suppose that you were assigned this article as additional reading in your psychology class. Prepare a page of reading notes on the article. Then write three short-answer questions and one essay question that might appear on a test.

CHAPTER 9

Reading Expressive Writing

In this chapter you will learn:

- The characteristics of expressive writing

- To recognize connotation and figurative language

- To read descriptive and narrative essays

- To read fiction

- To read poetry

- To draw inferences from implied writing

In previous chapters you have practiced reading selections from textbooks plus essays and newspaper articles that could be supplementary course readings. These are not, however, the only kinds of works you will read in college and in your adult lives. In this chapter we will examine some other kinds of writings, works that enrich our lives in different ways than do textbooks and other expository writing. To begin, read and compare the following passages.

I. MIDLATITUDE DECIDUOUS FOREST: Extensive areas on all Northern hemisphere continents, as well as more limited tracts in the Southern hemisphere, were originally covered with a forest of largely broadleaf deciduous trees. . . . Except in hilly country, a large proportion of this forest has been cleared for agriculture and other types of human use, so that very little of the original natural vegetation remains. . . .

This biome generally has the richest assemblage of fauna to be found in the midlatitudes, although it does not have the diversity to match that of most tropical biomes. It has (or had) a considerable variety of birds and mammals, and in some areas, reptiles and amphibians are well represented. Summer brings a diverse and active population of insects and other arthropods. All animal life is less numerous (partly due to migrations and hibernation) and less conspicuous in winter.

McKnight, *Essentials of Physical Geography*

II. Abreast of the schoolhouse the road forked, and we dipped down a lane to the left, between hemlock boughs bent inward to their trunks by the weight of the snow. I had often walked that way on Sundays, and knew that the solitary roof showing through bare branches near the bottom of the hill was that of Frome's saw-mill. It looked exanimate enough, with its idle wheel looming above the black stream dashed with yellow-white spume, and its cluster of sheds sagging under their white load. Frome did not even turn his head as we drove by, and still in silence we began to mount the next slope. About a mile farther, on a road I had never travelled, we came to an orchard of starved apple-trees writhing over a hillside among outcroppings of slate that nuzzled up through the snow like animals pushing out their noses to breathe. Beyond the orchard lay a field or two, their boundaries lost under drifts; and above the fields, huddled against the white immensities of land and sky, one of those lonely New England farm-houses that make the landscape lonelier.

Edith Wharton, *Ethan Frome*

The first passage, part of the textbook's description of the biome that includes New England, is straightforward, detailed, and objective. The writer provides information; his purpose is *expository.* The second passage, although it also provides details about the New England area, is different. In this passage Wharton is more interested in our "feeling" this place. She wants us to be aware of the loneliness of the winter landscape. The details provide information, but they do more. They make us feel Frome's loneliness and pain and silent endurance. Wharton does not wish to be objective. Her writing is not expository but *expressive.* We can learn more about expressive writing by considering how it differs from both expository and persuasive writing.

■ CHARACTERISTICS OF EXPRESSIVE WRITING

Expressive writing appeals to the senses. As you can see from the passages above, both expressive and expository writing contain information: details and examples. The difference is that in expository writing details are used to help explain ideas, whereas in expressive writing details help us see and feel—and sometimes even taste and smell—the person or object or place under discussion.

Expressive writing evokes feelings. Wharton not only makes us *see* the landscape around Starkfield, the setting of her story, she makes us *feel* something in response to her description. Most of the time in textbooks, authors strive for a lively, engaging presentation, but one that stops short of appealing to feelings. Rather, the liveliness is an intellectual one. In expressive writing ideas may be important, too, but they are developed through the awakening of feelings.

Expressive writing invites reflection on what it means to be human. Certainly students reading, for example, a biology or psychology text, are given much to think about. How do we participate in the carbon cycle, how does memory work: we want to understand the role of these processes in our lives. Expressive writing, by contrast, invites us to reflect on both broader and more basic issues: on the delight of springtime flowers, on betrayal and loss, on the pain of unfulfilled desire, on the joys and heartaches of childhood.

Expressive writing is often subtle and indirect—imaginative—in its presenting of ideas and attitudes. Certainly expository writers want us to "care" about their subjects, to acquire not only new ideas but new ways of seeing some part of the world. And surely persuasive writers arguing such issues as abortion or capital punishment, for example, appeal to our feelings and ask us to reflect on some key issues. How, then, can we really separate these three kinds of writing? Clearly it is better to think of the three types of writing along a continuum with some overlap than to think of three distinct categories, but still there are some differences that we have noted.

Perhaps, finally, there is the use of imagination, or creativity, on the part of the expressive writer, that results in a more indirect suggestion of ideas and attitudes. Textbooks are organized around specific topics, a body of information and strategies for studying. The persuasive essayist presents a thesis, examines the arguments of others, and takes a stand on a public issue. But the expressive writer paints a picture, creates a character, tells a story. The subject matter that engages us is either made up or drawn from personal experience, and the first task of the writer is to paint a compelling picture or tell an interesting story. The thoughts and feelings for reflection come indirectly, through the created vehicle of description or narration.

When reading expository prose, you actively seek a main idea statement or thesis, and you observe the writing strategy used to organize and develop the main idea. What, specifically, are the indicators of expressive writing to which you should be alert? There are several important elements of expressive writing to pay attention to as you read.

■ CONNOTATION

Words with similar meanings have similar *denotations*. Their formal definitions are similar; one can be substituted for the other as a synonym. Some words with similar denotations do not, though, have similar connotations. A word's *connotation* is what the word suggests, what we associate the word with, what goes beyond its formal definitions. For example, the words *house* and *home* both refer to a structure in which people live; these words have the same denotation. But the word *home*, for most people, suggests or is associated with concepts and feelings of family and security and comfort. Thus the word *home* has a strong positive connotation. By contrast, the word *house* has little, if any, connotative significance. *House* brings to mind a picture of a physical structure but little else because the word doesn't carry any "emotional baggage." Many words do not have connotations, but those that do often carry powerful associations.

We learn the connotative significance of words the same way we learn the denotative meanings of words: as we repeatedly hear or read them in context. Most of us, living in the same culture, share the same connotative associations of words. Most of us respond to the positive associations of the word *home*, even though our own home life may have been unpleasant. We know, from how others use the word, that the culturally shared response is positive, not negative.

Sometimes the context in which a word is used will determine the word's connotation. For example, the word *sister* usually has positive associations. We think of a kid sister or sorority sister or the sisterhood of those identifying with feminist values. But when an unfriendly person who thinks a woman may have pushed in front of him says "Better watch it, *sister*," the word has a negative connotation. Specific social and language contexts will control the connotative associations of some words. Studying the context in which a writer uses emotionally charged words is the only way to be sure that we understand the writer's attitude.

Because we are familiar with the connotations of common words, we sometimes read past emotionally charged words without being aware of the writer's choice of language to shape our perceptions and engage our feelings. As you read expressive language, try to be especially sensitive to a writer's choice of words.

Exercise 9-1 Becoming Alert to Connotation

A. For each of the following pairs of words, check the one that has the more positive connotation. The first has been done for you.

1. quiet   _____ withdrawn
2. _____ miserly   _____ economical
3. _____ stubborn   _____ persistent
4. _____ naive   _____ trusting
5. _____ child   _____ brat
6. _____ hard   _____ brittle
7. _____ laid back   _____ lazy
8. _____ female parent   _____ mom

9. _____ pushy   _____ assertive
10. _____ goal oriented   _____ overachiever

B. Select one of the two words suggested to complete each of the following sentences with a positive connotation. Briefly explain why you did not select the other word.

1. Some of the events in my brother's life have been quite _____ .
(remarkable/bizarre)

_____

2. Tony's plan to buy out his chief competition showed a _____
business sense. (shrewd/cunning)

_____

3. Madonna has become _____ for her sexual openness.
(notorious/famous)

_____

4. The first Rockefeller was known to be _____ in his
handling of money. (prudent/cheap)

_____

5. The party boss and his _____ discussed the next election.
(associates/cronies)

_____

■ SENTENCE STYLE

Writers of textbooks usually avoid using connotative words because they try to write with objectivity. They also avoid complicated sentences with numerous qualifiers and modifiers. Adding a lot of details onto the main parts of a sentence, especially when the added material is placed in the middle of the sentence, makes the point of the sentence harder to find, to grasp. (Notice that the last sentence is harder to read than the first two sentences of this section. Why? Primarily because of all the material between the two commas that is not essential to the point of the sentence.) Textbook authors are not trying to be fancy; they are trying to be clear, even though their subject may be complex.

Expressive writers want to be clear, of course, but they also want to evoke feelings, and to suggest meanings through their choice of sentence style. Having an expressive style does not always mean writing long, complex sentences. It does mean selecting sentence patterns that do more than state ideas or details.

Look again at the two passages at the beginning of the chapter. Observe that most of McKnight's sentences begin with subject and verb: "It has," "Summer brings," "All animal life is." Compare these patterns to Wharton's. Most of her sentences are longer. Three begin with a phrase instead of the subject of the sentence: "Abreast of the schoolhouse," "About a mile farther," and "Beyond the orchard." Notice how the last sentence piles up details to create her picture, much as the snow has piled in drifts to create the landscape of Starkfield.

To see how shorter sentences can be used to present details and to suggest ideas, study this passage from Ernest Hemingway's *The Sun Also Rises:*

> There were lighted bars and late open shops on each side of the street. We were sitting apart and we jolted close together going down the old street. Brett's hat was off. Her head was back. I saw her face in the lights from the open shops, then it was dark, then I saw her face clearly as we came out on the Avenue des Gobelins. The street was torn up and men were working on the car-tracks by the light of acetylene flares.

First the narrator can see Brett; then he can't. The torn up street seems an unnecessary detail. We conclude that this taxi ride is not beautiful and romantic. Hemingway's stringing together of details in short sentences with few connecting words captures the sense of dislocation and lack of connectedness in his characters.

■ FIGURATIVE LANGUAGE

Sometimes the most effective way to express an idea is to take ordinary words but put them together in ways that do not make sense *literally*. When you encounter an expression that seems to make no sense, you are probably reading a *figure of speech.* Figurative language is actually quite common, especially in ordinary speech. We are on pins and needles over a test grade, complain about the rat race, and flip out over a new love. Now these figures of speech, worn out from overuse, are called *clichés,* but they illustrate the point that figurative language isn't found only in poetry. They also make the point that you do recognize the difference between literal language and figurative language. When someone comes in saying that it's raining cats and dogs outside, you do not rush to call the animal shelter. You know not to take the expression literally and understand that the speaker means that it is raining quite hard. What is challenging about the figurative language in expressive writing is that the figures of speech are fresh and original. We have to think about the author's meaning and appreciate the new way of looking at the subject.

From ordinary speech to descriptive essays to sonnets we find figurative language in the form of metaphors. A *metaphor* is a comparison of two things that are not really alike but seem, in the writer's mind, to be alike in some significant way. There are several ways to express a metaphor, and some of these ways have their own names, but they all fit the basic definition of a metaphor. If the comparison is stated directly or implied, it is called a metaphor. If the comparison is given with connecting words such as *like, as,* or *resembles,* then it is called a *simile.* Consider the following simile:

Simile: A leader is like a mirror.

Think of the expression as having two terms, one literal and one figurative, as if it were an equation: X (leader) = Y (mirror). (Because a leader is a person, not an object with a reflective surface, the comparison is not literal but figurative.) In a simile the "equals" sign is spelled out with like or as; in a metaphor the equals sign is missing. For example:

Metaphor: A leader mirrors the desires of his or her followers.

A simile is easier to recognize because the equation is more completely spelled out for us. Some metaphors are expressed with only one of the two terms. For example:

Metaphor (figurative term implied):   A leader reflects the desires of his or her followers.

Even though the term "mirror" is not stated, the *idea* of a mirror is there in the word "reflects."

Another type of metaphor is called *personification.* When an idea, animal, or object is personified, it is given human qualities. When Wordsworth writes of daffodils "tossing their heads in sprightly dance," he is personifying the daffodils because humans dance but daffodils literally do not. (They are blown by the wind and appear, to the poet, to be dancing.) With personification, the Y of the equation is always a person.

To read and respond to metaphors, you need to do three things. First, you need to recognize the writer's use of figurative language. Next, you need to understand the two terms being compared; what is the X and what is the Y of the equation. Finally, you need to reflect on the point of the comparison and the emotional impact of the comparison. Metaphors gain some of their power through compression. To be certain that we understand, we need to expand them in our minds, to explore the ideas, values, and emotions compressed in the few words of the metaphor. For example, to speak of the English king as Richard the Lionhearted is to say that Richard was brave and courageous as the lion is. Since the lion is the king of the beasts—the lion has no predators—and we admire bravery and courage, the comparison is a positive one, a compliment to the king. We have expanded the metaphor, opened it up to more fully understand it.

EXERCISE 9-2 Reading Metaphors

Identify the type of metaphor (simile, metaphor, personification) in each of the following passages. Then explain each one by stating the items being compared and the point of the comparison. The first one has been done for you.

1. "The best mirror is an old friend."
   (George Herbert)

   A metaphor. The two terms are mirror and friend. Just as a mirror shows us our physical selves, so an old friend can show us our character, because the friend is not afraid to tell us of our strengths and our faults.

2. "One hundred years later, the Negro lives on a lonely island of poverty in the midst of a vast ocean of material prosperity."
   (Martin Luther King, Jr.)

   _____

   _____

   _____

   _____

3. "Go, lovely rose,
   Tell her that wastes her time and me,
      That now she knows,
   When I resemble her to thee,
      How sweet and fair she seems to be."
   (Edmund Waller)

   _____

   _____

   _____

   _____

4. "When I go away from you
   The world beats dead

Like a slackened drum."
(Amy Lowell)

_____

_____

_____

_____

5. "I have measured out my life with coffee spoons."
(T. S. Eliot)

_____

_____

_____

_____

6. "Life's but a walking shadow, a poor player
That struts and frets his hour upon the stage
And then is heard no more. . . ."
(William Shakespeare)

_____

_____

_____

_____

■ READING DESCRIPTIVE ESSAYS

Writers would be lost without details. The facts and examples that fill a paragraph give ideas a concreteness, a grounding that readers can understand. Sometimes a writer's purpose is to describe, not just to provide details for clarity and support. Descriptive essays paint a picture in words, bringing to life people, places, even objects. In descriptive essays, words are used to appeal to our senses, and we are likely to find connotation and figurative language.

Since essayists have a thesis or main idea to present and develop, we need to be alert to the descriptive essay's purpose as we read. Ask yourself, "Why are you showing me this scene?" or "Why are you describing this person to me?" Pay close attention to opening and concluding paragraphs of descriptive essays, because if the thesis is stated, it will probably appear at the beginning or the end of the essay. Remember, though, that in expressive writing ideas are often suggested rather than stated. We may need to infer (draw conclusions) from the details provided some, if not all, of the ideas the writer wants us to reflect upon. Recognizing ideas that are implied rather than directly stated is often not as difficult as you may think. Through connotative word choice and metaphors and telling details, the descriptive essayist shapes our emotional and intellectual responses to the person or place described. The paragraph below provides an example.

In an essay in *Time* magazine, Lance Morrow describes his experiences on safari in East Africa. Read the following paragraph from that essay, reflect on the picture Morrow creates, and then answer the questions that follow.

> In Masai Mara [in Kenya], vultures wheel dreamily in the air, like a slow motion tornado of birds. Below the swirling funnel, a cheetah has brought down a baby wildebeest. The cheetah, loner and fleet aristocrat, the upper-class version of the hyena, has opened up the wildebeest and devoured the internal organs. The cheetah's belly is swollen and its mouth is ringed with blood as it breathes heavily from the exertion of gorging. A dozen vultures flap down to take their turn. They wait 20 yards away, then waddle in a little toward the kill to test the cheetah. The cheetah, in a burst, rushes the vultures to drive them off, and then returns to the baby wildebeest. The vultures grump and readjust their feathers and wait their turn, the surly lumpen-carrion class.

1. What simile is used to describe the vultures? _____

    _____

2. Is this a positive or negative figure of speech? _____

    _____

3. What image do you get of the vultures in the concluding sentence? _____

    _____

4. Are the vultures presented in a positive or negative light? _____

    _____

5. What is Morrow's attitude toward the cheetah? _____

    _____

6. How do you know? _____

7. The details of the kill are vivid. What seems to be the author's purpose in this paragraph? What does Morrow want us to see and understand about wildlife in East Africa?

_____

_____

_____

Reading essays describing people is similar to reading about character in novels and short stories. We need to get a sense of the person by adding up the details that are given. Details give us a picture of the physical characteristics, but they also provide insight into lifestyle and into character. In an essay on her father, the British novelist Doris Lessing, describing his boyhood, writes:

> They ate economically, but when he got diabetes in his forties and subsisted on lean meat and lettuce leaves, he remembered suet puddings, treacle puddings, raisin and currant puddings, steak and kidney puddings, bread and butter pudding, "batter cooked in the gravy with the meat," potato cake, plum cake, butter cake, porridge with treacle, fruit tarts and pies, brawn, pig's trotters and pig's cheek and home-smoked ham and sausages. And "lashings of fresh butter and cream and eggs."

What a wonderful descriptive paragraph! What does Lessing accomplish with her long list of foods? Are we surprised that someone growing up on a diet of such foods would develop adult-onset diabetes? Not only do we learn of the origin of his diabetes, we also conclude that, even though his family was not wealthy, he came from a home rich in comfortable, country eating with a devoted mother in the kitchen.

EXERCISE 9-3 Drawing Inferences from Descriptive Details

Read each of the paragraphs and answer the questions that follow. Try to picture what the writer describes and sense how the writer wants you to feel.

I. My favorite place in the whole world was a big rock in the backyard that looked like the back of a buried elephant. . . . I would squat on that rock, my stick legs poking through the openings of my dirt-stained bloomers, my birdlike head turning from side to side, my gaze, unblinking, focusing up, down, in front of me, in back of me, now zooming in on the lower yard, then penetrating deeper into the garden, then rising up ever so slightly to where the corn was planted on the hill. I was in the center of life and I didn't miss a thing; nothing slipped by unobserved or unnoted.

From Mary E. Mebane, *Mary: An Autobiography*, 1981

1. List and explain two metaphors from the passage.

   _____

   _____

   _____

   _____

2. What can you conclude about Mary's childhood? Where did she live? What kind of youngster was she?

   _____

   _____

II. There are photographs of him. The largest is of an officer in the 1914–18 war. A new uniform—buttoned, badged, strapped, tabbed—confines a handsome, dark young man who holds himself stiffly to confront what he certainly thought of as his duty. His eyes are steady, serious, and responsible, and show no signs of what he became later. A photograph at sixteen is of a dark, introspective youth with the same intent eyes. But it is his mouth you notice—a heavily-jutting upper lip contradicts the rest of a regular face. His moustache was to hide it: "Had to do something—a damned fleshy mouth. Always made me uncomfortable, that mouth of mine."

   From Doris Lessing, "My Father," London *Sunday Telegraph,* 1963.

1. What elements of personality are suggested by the young man's eyes?

   _____

2. What is the most telling detail in the photos? _____

   _____

3. How did her father feel about his mouth? _____

   _____

4. What characteristic or trait is suggested by the mouth?

   _____

III. The world stills, for the longest time. Then, at the edge of sleep, the hyenas come to giggle and whoop. Peering from the tent flap, one catches in the shadows their sidelong criminal slouch. Their eyes shine like evil flashlight bulbs, a disembodied horror-movie yellow, phosphorescent, glowing like the children of the damned. In the morning, one finds their droppings: white dung, like a photographic negative. Hyenas not only eat the meat of animals but grind up and digest the bones. The hyenas' dung is white with the calcium of powdered bones.

From Lance Morrow, "Africa," *Time*, February 23, 1987

1. In the second and third sentences, what words are used to describe the hyenas?

_____

_____

2. Is the connotation of the words positive or negative? _____
How, then, are we to view the hyenas?

_____

3. List and explain three similes. _____

_____

_____

_____

_____

4. How does the figurative language add to the description of the hyenas?

_____

5. Why does Morrow include the details of the hyenas' white dung? How do these details contribute to our view of this animal?

_____

_____

■ READING NARRATIVE ESSAYS

A narrative relates a series of events in chronological order or time sequence. If the narrative relates events that are made up, that come from the writer's imagination, then the narrative is fiction. If the narrative relates events that have taken place, it is nonfiction. Nonfiction narratives are found in histories, biographies, newspapers articles, and essays. Narration, then, can be used as an organizing strategy in both expository (histories, biographies, newspapers) and expressive (novels, short stories, narrative essays) writing.

In some writing, distinction between fiction and nonfiction blurs. The historical novel, for example, is fiction bound by the author's research of a particular time and place. Many feature articles in newspapers and magazines reveal the use of some literary devices such as conflict and point of view (discussed on pp. 335–336). Generally, the narrative essay draws on experiences of the author to develop a main idea or thesis. The thesis may be stated, but often it is implied in the events recounted in the essay. The good essayist may also have taken some liberties with the actual event. That is, the writer may leave out some details or in other ways alter the story somewhat in order to focus the essay on the ideas the writer wants to suggest. Just as the descriptive essayist concentrates on telling details, so the narrative essayist focuses on those telling events that help us understand the significance of the narrative.

As you read narrative essays, think about the writer's purpose. Ask yourself: "Why is the writer telling me about these events?" Pay close attention to any general statements that seem to sum up the ideas suggested by the narration. Also think about the perspective from which the narrative is told. In many narrative essays, writers use the first person ("I"), but in some cases, even though they are writing about what happened to themselves, writers use the third person ("he," "she"). Also consider whether or not the narrator seems to be telling of the events as they happen or recounting events from the past. Do you hear, for example, the voice of a young person, or the voice of an adult retelling and reflecting on events from an earlier time? Think about how the narrator seems to feel about the events and how the narrative makes you feel. Mike Rose's use of autobiography in his book on teaching, *Lives on the Boundary* (1989), provides an example.

All the hours in class tend to blend into one long, vague stretch of time. What I remember best, strangely enough, are the two things I couldn't understand and over the years grew to hate: grammar lessons and mathematics. I would sit there watching a teacher draw her long horizontal line and her short, oblique lines and break up sentences and put adjectives here and adverbs there and just not get it, couldn't see the reason for it, turned off to it. I would hide by slumping down in my seat and page through my reader, carried along by the flow of sentences in a story. She would test us, and I would dread that, for I always got Cs and Ds. Mathematics was a bit different. For whatever reasons, I didn't learn early math very well, so when it came time for more complicated operations, I couldn't keep up and started daydreaming to avoid my inadequacy. This was a strategy I would rely on as I grew older. I fell further and further behind. A memory: The teacher is faceless and seems very far away. The voice is faint and is discussing an equation written on the board. It is raining, and I am watching the streams of water form patterns on the windows.

1. What is the perspective from which the events are told?

   _____

2. Why did the writer turn to daydreaming? _____

   _____

3. What is significant about the memory Rose describes?

   _____

   _____

4. What can you conclude about the writer's attitudes toward school when he was in school?

   _____

   _____

5. What might be Rose's purpose is telling about his school experiences?

   _____

   _____

EXERCISE 9-4 Responding to Narrative Essays

Read each of the paragraphs and answer the questions that follow. Try to become engaged in the event and reflect on what it means.

I. He was almost crying now as he turned and walked out of the big command bunker. There was sand all over the place outside and a cold monsoon wind was blowing. He looked out into the darkness and heard the waves of the China Sea breaking softly far away.

   There was a path made of wooden ammo casings that led back to his tent. He walked on it like a man on a tightrope, it was so dark and so very hard to see. A couple of times he stumbled on the wooden boxes. It was quiet as he opened the tent flap, as quiet and dark as it had been outside the major's bunker. He dragged in carrying his rifle in one hand and the map case in the other. They were all asleep, all curled up on their cots, inside their mosquito nets. He walked up to his rack and sat down, his head sinking down to the floor. Panic was still rushing through him like a wild train, his heart still raced through his chest as he saw over and over again the kid from Georgia running toward him and the crack of his rifle killing him dead.

From Ron Kovic, *Born on the Fourth of July,* 1976

1. List and explain two similes in the passage. _____

   _____

   _____

   _____

2. What has the "He" in the story recently done? _____

   _____

3. What can you conclude from the passage about where these events took place?

   _____

   _____

4. How does "He" feel about what has happened? What details support your conclusion?

   _____

   _____

   _____

5. What is the writer's purpose? What does he want us to understand and to feel from reading this narrative?

   _____

   _____

   _____

II. We set out for the gallows. Two warders marched on either side of the prisoner, with their rifles at the slope; two others marched close against him, gripping him by arm and shoulder, as though at once pushing and supporting him. The rest of us, magistrates and the like, followed behind. Suddenly, when we had gone ten yards, the procession stopped short without any order or warning. A dreadful thing had happened—a dog, come goodness knows whence, had appeared in the yard. It came bounding among us with a loud volley of barks and leapt round us wagging its whole body wild with glee at finding so many human beings together. It was a large woolly dog, half Airedale, half pariah. For a moment it pranced around us, and then, before anyone could stop it, it had made a dash for the prisoner, and jumping up tried to lick his face. Everybody stood aghast, too taken aback even to grab the dog.

From George Orwell, "A Hanging," 1950

1. What is about to take place? _____

2. What is the perspective from which the events are told? Is the narrator a part of the scene or not? How do you know?

_____

_____

3. What does *pariah* mean? _____

4. Why is it significant that the dog is half pariah?

_____

5. Why does the narrator say that the dog's appearance was "a dreadful thing"? Why was everybody "aghast"?

_____

_____

6. What does this narrative comment on? What does Orwell want us to understand?

_____

_____

_____

▪ READING FICTION

As we have observed, fiction (short stories and novels) is similar to narrative essays, except that in fiction the characters and the story line are mostly made up rather than drawn from actual experience. Additionally, stories usually contain dialogue (the characters speak directly) as well as narration, whereas in many narrative essays there is no dialogue. In most fiction you are not likely to find a direct statement of a main idea, but, as with all expressive writing, there are ideas, either stated or implied, about human life and experience. A good story engages our attention, involves us emotionally in the characters, but it also tells us something about life through the characters' responses to the events in their lives. We refer to the cluster of ideas suggested by fiction as the story's *theme* or *themes*.

Since a work's theme comes to us indirectly through all the details of the story, we want to think carefully about those details before drawing inferences about theme. The first step needs of course to be careful reading so that you know what happens. To help you remember the specific events in a complex story, a good writing-to-learn strategy is the summary. To prepare for class discussion and to review easily for tests, you can write a one-paragraph summary of the story line—what happens—as soon as you finish reading. *But you need to go beyond a knowledge of events to be comfortable with your understanding of the story's theme(s).* You need to look specifically at the various elements that make up a work of fiction.

Narrative Structure

Stories tell of a series of events, occurring in time, that happen to one or more characters. Still, there are many ways to tell a story. Consider the following two stories:

    I. The king died and then the queen died.

    II. The king died and then the queen died of grief.

Although these stories are really short, they do reveal a difference in structure, what we call the story's *plot*. In some stories, events are loosely connected, joined mostly by chronology (the king dies first and then the queen dies) and sometimes unified around a dominant main character. Most stories present events that are to some extent connected by causation in addition to time sequence. That is, action A by the main character leads to event B which requires action C by another character. In the second story above, the queen's death is a result of the king's death. His death causes her so much grief that she dies. This kind of plot structure can be diagramed, as in Figure 9.1.

Figure 9.1 introduces some terms and concepts that help us understand fiction. The story's *exposition* refers to the background details needed to get the story started. These include the time and place of the story (the *setting*) and

■ FIGURE 9.1

Plot Structure

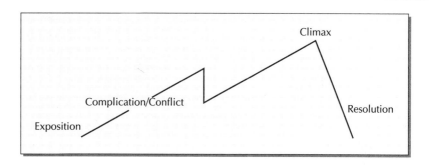

relationships of characters. A *complication* is an event; something happens to get the story started. In the second story above, the king's death becomes a complication for the queen because of her love for him. (If the queen wanted the king dead so that she could rule the land, then his death would not be a complication for her but an opportunity.) If this mini story were more developed, we would see the queen in some *conflict* in response to the complication of the king's death. Her conflict would be the tension within her between the normal will to survive and her grief which makes her feel that life is not worth living.

In stories as in real life, people try to resolve conflicts and solve complications. In long stories there will be a series of complications and attempted resolutions of them, with each new action leading to another complication instead of the sought-for resolution. At some point we reach the high point of tension in the story, its *climax*. This may be a moment of decision or insight for the main character, or it may be a failure to act. The climax then generates the story's *resolution* and ending. (The queen resolves her conflict by choosing death over life without her king.) Many modern stories end rather abruptly, without seeming to have much resolution. Such endings are part of the writer's comment on life, that life goes on, with problems remaining unresolved.

Character

An analysis of plot structure shows us that the queen is the more troubled character. She is not in conflict *with* the king; she is in conflict *over* him, or rather over life without him. Characters may have internal conflicts or conflicts with other characters, or with their society or environment. A story's plot weaves together complication and conflict and shows us that fiction requires both plot and character, events and players. In serious literature, the greater emphasis is, usually, on character, on what we learn about human life through the interplay of character and event. So we need to think about how writers present characters to us. What should we look for to understand a story's characters?

Writers use several strategies to present character. They can provide descriptive details: how a character sits or walks, how a character dresses or talks. Writers also reveal character through dramatic scenes, showing us rather than telling us. We need to listen carefully to the dialogue between characters. Having more than one character in a story establishes the possibility of contrast between characters. Often writers use minor characters who, by contrast, help reveal traits of the main character. Finally, characters can be connected to other elements in the story that provide indirect, sometimes subtle, information about character. Characters can be associated with objects that are in the story, often with ones they own (e.g., an old fur wrap, or the house they live in). Or, their names can be significant (e.g., Daisy for a young woman and Winterbourne for a withdrawn, disengaged person). Thinking about the writer's options for developing character will keep you from overlooking important details.

Point of View

Just as there is no story without events and characters, so there is no story until the author selects a *point of view,* the perspective from which the story is told. The author of the story addresses us through a created voice that sees the events and characters in a particular way. If an author changes from one created voice to another, then the story will change, just as you will get a different story of a car accident, depending on who (one of the drivers, the police officer, a witness) you ask about it.

Writers have several basic choices of point of view. One choice is to tell the story from the perspective of a character in the story, who speaks in the first person (I, we). The views of the character may or may not represent the views of the author. Sometimes writers let a character tell the story to reveal that character's lack of perception or innocence. Always remember that characters must speak and act in character; that may be different from what the author would say or do.

Authors can also tell the story in the third person (she, he, they). With a third-person narrator they can range from an all-knowing perspective to one restricted to what can be seen or heard at a specific time. An all-knowing narrator can tell us what characters are thinking and feeling, and can comment on the characters. This was a popular choice of narrator in nineteenth-century fiction, but is less popular today. Many contemporary writers choose to tell a story as if the narrator is standing by the shoulder of one of the characters. This limited point of view is similar to the first-person point of view, but gives the author the chance to use language that the character would not use and to give a bit more background or perspective than a character-narrator would be able to do. As you begin to read a story, look for clues to point of view. The sooner you identify point of view, the sooner you can start thinking about how to evaluate what you are being told.

Style and Tone

Word choice, sentence structure, and figurative language are important in all forms of expressive language. Remember Hemingway's short sentences and use of disconnected events in the example on page 322, or Edith Wharton's sweeping sentences and use of metaphors to describe the setting of Starkfield. Hemingway's style in *The Sun Also Rises* and Wharton's setting in *Ethan Frome* offer symbolic comments that help us understand each novel's themes.

 EXERCISE 9-5 **Reading Fiction**

Read the following story by the late nineteenth-century American writer Kate Chopin and then answer the questions that follow. Try to use the guidelines for reading fiction that you have just studied.

The Story of an Hour

1   Knowing that Mrs. Mallard was afflicted with a heart trouble, great care was taken to break to her as gently as possible the news of her husband's death.

2   It was her sister Josephine who told her, in broken sentences; veiled hints that revealed in half concealing. Her husband's friend Richards was there, too, near her. It was he who had been in the newspaper office when intelligence of the railroad disaster was received, with Brently Mallard's name leading the list of "killed." He had only taken the time to assure himself of its truth by a second telegram, and had hastened to forestall any less careful, less tender friend in bearing the sad message.

3   She did not hear the story as many women have heard the same, with a paralyzed inability to accept its significance. She wept at once, with sudden, wild abandonment, in her sister's arms. When the storm of grief had spent itself she went away to her room alone. She would have no one follow her.

4   There stood, facing the open window, a comfortable, roomy armchair. Into this she sank, pressed down by a physical exhaustion that haunted her body and seemed to reach into her soul.

5   She could see in the open square before her house the tops of trees that were all aquiver with the new spring life. The delicious breath of rain was in the air. In the street below a peddler was crying his wares. The notes of a distant song which some one was singing reached her faintly, and countless sparrows were twittering in the eaves.

6   There were patches of blue sky showing here and there through the clouds that had met and piled one above the other in the west facing her window.

7   She sat with her head thrown back upon the cushion of the chair, quite motionless, except when a sob came up into her throat and shook her, as a child who has cried itself to sleep continues to sob in its dreams.

8   She was young, with a fair, calm face, whose lines bespoke repression and even a certain strength. But now there was a dull stare in her eyes, whose gaze was fixed away off yonder on one of those patches of blue sky. It was not a glance of reflection, but rather indicated a suspension of intelligent thought.

9   There was something coming to her and she was waiting for it, fearfully. What was it? She did not know; it was too subtle and elusive to name. But she felt it, creeping out of the sky, reaching toward her through the sounds, the scents, the color that filled the air.

10   Now her bosom rose and fell tumultuously. She was beginning to recognize this thing that was approaching to possess her, and she was striving to beat it back with her will—as powerless as her two white slender hands would have been.

11   When she abandoned herself a little whispered word escaped her slightly parted lips. She said it over and over under her breath: "free, free, free!" The vacant stare and the look of terror that had followed it went from her eyes. They stayed keen and bright. Her pulse beat fast, and the coursing blood warmed and relaxed every inch of her body.

12   She did not stop to ask if it were or were not a monstrous joy that held her. A clear and exalted perception enabled her to dismiss the suggestion as trivial.

13   She knew that she would weep again when she saw the kind, tender hands folded in death; the face that had never looked save with love upon her, fixed and gray and dead. But she saw beyond that bitter moment a long procession of years to come that would belong to her absolutely. And she opened and spread her arms out to them in welcome.

14   There would be no one to live for her during those coming years; she would live for herself. There would be no powerful will bending hers in that blind persistence with which men and women believe they have a right to impose a private will upon a fellow-creature. A kind intention or a cruel intention made the act seem no less a crime as she looked upon it in that brief moment of illumination.

15   And yet she had loved him—sometimes. Often she had not. What did it matter! What could love, the unsolved mystery, count for in face of this possession of self-assertion which she suddenly recognized as the strongest impulse of her being!

16   "Free! Body and soul free!" she kept whispering.

17   Josephine was kneeling before the closed door with her lips to the keyhole, imploring for admission. "Louise, open the door! I beg; open the door—you will make yourself ill. What are you doing, Louise? For heaven's sake open the door."

18   "Go away. I am not making myself ill." No; she was drinking in a very elixir of life through that open window.

19   Her fancy was running riot along those days ahead of her. Spring days, and summer days, and all sorts of days that would be her own. She

breathed a quick prayer that life might be long. It was only yesterday she
had thought with a shudder that life might be long.

20   She arose at length and opened the door to her sister's importunities.
There was a feverish triumph in her eyes, and she carried herself unwit-
tingly like a goddess of Victory. She clasped her sister's waist, and together they descended the stairs. Richards stood waiting for them at the
bottom.

21   Some one was opening the front door with a latchkey. It was Brently
Mallard who entered, a little travel-stained, composedly carrying his grip-
sack and umbrella. He had been far from the scene of accident, and did
not even know there had been one. He stood amazed at Josephine's pierc-
ing cry; at Richards' quick motion to screen him from the view of his wife.

22   But Richards was too late.

23   When the doctors came they said she had died of heart disease—of joy
that kills.

1. Analyze the story's plot by applying the terms shown in Figure 9.1. That is,
   what do you learn in the exposition? What is the first complication? And so
   on.

   _____

   _____

   _____

   _____

2. What is Mrs. Mallard's conflict? Explain it in terms of opposing forces, a
   tension within her.

   _____

   _____

3. When Mrs. Mallard goes to her room, she gazes out of the window. What
   does she see? List the details.

   _____

   _____

4. What do these details have in common? _____

   _____

5. Why is it inaccurate to say that Mrs. Mallard does not love her husband? Give evidence from the story.

_____

_____

6. What decision does Mrs. Mallard make while in her room?

_____

7. What is the story's point of view? _____

_____

8. Are we to agree with the doctor's explanation of Mrs. Mallard's death? Explain.

_____

_____

9. What does Chopin want us to understand from reading her story?

_____

_____

■ READING POETRY

Some readers enjoy all forms of expressive language—except poetry. These readers insist that only English teachers can understand a poem, so they wait for the teacher to tell them what to think. When faced with the task of saying, or writing, something about a poem, these readers usually read one or two lines and then start making wild guesses. Why not guess, if you have already decided that you cannot possibly make sense of poetry? Let's agree that some poetry is challenging to read, but let's also agree that you can understand and appreciate poetry if you have a reading strategy and apply it faithfully to your poetry reading. Here are the steps to take for an effective reading strategy.

1. **Prepare** by learning as much as you can about the reading context. Think about whatever information is given about the poet. If you learn that the poet lived in an earlier century, be prepared for old-fashioned spellings or words we don't normally use today.

2. **Prepare** by looking at the poem. Poems are arranged differently than prose. Are you looking at *continuous* lines of poetry, or have the lines been structured into *stanzas* (same number of lines with the same meter—pattern of beats in the line—and rhyme scheme)?

3. **Prepare** by reading and reflecting on the title and then read the poem through once. Annotate the poem, underlining words you need to look up, circling a phrase that catches your fancy, putting a question mark next to a difficult line. Then look up unknown words or references to people or places you are not familiar with.

4. **Read** the poem a second time. Be sure to read to the end of sentences, not just to the end of lines. For example, in the poem "Promise" by Paul Dunbar, the opening line reads: "I grew a rose within a garden fair." The last two lines of the first stanza are:

> And, watching, ever smiled to see the lusty bud
> Drink freely in the summer sun to tinct its blood.

If you stop at the end of the first of these lines, the sense you get is that the speaker smiled when he looked on the healthy bud. However, if you do this, then there is no subject for the next line; *who* "drink[s] freely" in the sun? Suddenly you are confused. But if you read the two lines together, as the poet intended (there is no punctuation at the end of the first line), then the idea of both lines is clear. The speaker watches and smiles to see his rose bud take in the summer sun and develop its color (tinct its blood).

5. **Check comprehension** by writing a paraphrase of the poem. Poetry gains much of its power through compression. Sometimes we can understand a poem better by turning it into a prose statement that puts words in normal sentence order and opens up the figurative language. For example, another line of Dunbar's poem begins: "Then hasted I with smiles." This is not how we normally speak or write. Paraphrase the line to read: "Then smiling, I hurried."

6. **Check comprehension** by reviewing the facts of the poem and the situation in the poem. You are not ready to comment on what a poem *means* until you know what it *says* and in what context the words come to you. Consider the basic situation. Who is "speaking" the lines? Do you hear a narrator telling a story in verse? If so, the poem is a *narrative* poem, and you would analyze its narrative structure. Do you hear the words spoken by someone to another person who is in the scene? If the words are spoken to a listener, then the poem is a *dramatic* poem, and you need to identify the "characters" and the scene in some detail. Finally, do the words seem to be someone's thoughts? Then you are reading the most typical kind of poem, a *lyric* poem. The speaker in Dunbar's poem isn't talking to another person. He is reflecting on the growing of his rose, and we, the readers, listen in on his thoughts.

Now apply these first six steps to the following poem by seventeenth-century British poet Robert Herrick. The discussion and questions that follow will guide you through the steps.

To Daffodils

Fair daffodils, we weep to see
   You haste away so soon;
As yet the early-rising sun
   Has not attained his noon.
     Stay, stay,   5
   Until the hasting day
     Has run
But to the even-song;
And, having prayed together, we
   Will go with you along.   10

We have short time to stay, as you;
   We have as short a spring,
As quick a growth to meet decay,
   As you, or anything.
     We die   15
   As your hours do, and dry
     Away
Like to the summer's rain,
Or as the pearls of morning's dew,
   Ne'er to be found again.   20

Although this is a seventeenth-century poem, the language is simple and familiar. Even-song is a traditional late-afternoon church service that focuses mostly on music and meditation. How would you classify the poem based on its appearance?

_____

Which lines in the first stanza must be read together as one thought?

_____

Here is a possible paraphrase of the poem:

Pretty daffodils we are distressed to see your brief life. It is not yet noon. Do stay until after evensong and then, after prayer together, we will go along with you. For we also have a brief time here, as brief a spring, as short a time of growth before we decay, just like you and other living things. We die, as you do, and dry up just like the summer rain or the morning dew, and we will not, like them, ever be seen again.

How are the words of the poem coming to us? Is this a narrative, dramatic, or lyric poem?

_____

_____

Since we do not normally speak to flowers, you should recognize that this is a lyric poem and that the flowers have been personified by the speaker of the poem who then figuratively addresses the flowers. Now we can continue the steps to reading poetry.

7. **Analyze the poem's pattern of development.** Poets use various writing patterns, just as prose writers do. A poet can describe, or explain, or argue. Many poems seek to clarify an idea or feeling, to explain what love is, for example. Such a poem might use contrast and listing: love is not a, b, or c, but rather 1, 2, and 3. Poems can be organized in a question and answer pattern, or can present examples. In some poems the point of the example(s) is stated in a concluding line or two, but in many poems the idea is implied rather than stated.

8. **Analyze the poem's figurative language.** Study all of the poem's metaphors, making sure that you recognize the two items being compared, the point of the comparison, and the emotional impact of each comparison.

9. **Reflect on the poem's meaning or theme.** After your reading and analysis, you should be ready to make some general statements about the ideas of the poem and the poet's attitude toward the poem's subject.

Let's apply the final three steps to Herrick's "To Daffodils." How is the poem developed? In the first stanza the speaker, using "we" to include us all, speaks directly to the daffodil, lamenting its short life. In the second stanza, the speaker makes a connection between daffodils and humans; we, too, "haste away so soon." The poem moves from a particular example to a general application.

What figure of speech do you find in the last three lines of the poem? Explain the comparisons.

_____

_____

Finally, what is the poem's meaning or theme? The poet reminds us that human life is also short. While it may not be as brief as the daffodils, it does end. The poem's tone seems one of quiet sadness rather than anger or frustration. What is the implication? To live the life we have fully, to enjoy the spring because fall is not far behind.

The following exercise will give you practice using a specific reading strategy to understand and appreciate poetry.

EXERCISE 9-6 **Applying a Strategy to Reading Poetry**

Use your 9-step reading strategy to understand each of the following poems and then answer the questions that follow.

Dream Deferred

by **Langston Hughes** (African-American; 1902–1967)

What happens to a dream deferred?

Does it dry up
like a raisin in the sun?
Or fester like a sore—
And then run?   5
Does it stink like rotten meat?
Or crust and sugar over—
like a syrupy sweet?

Maybe it just sags
like a heavy load.   10

Or does it explode?

1. In what ways can you classify the poem? _____

   _____

2. What writing pattern does the poem use? Describe its organization.

   _____

3. What does Hughes mean by "deferred dreams"? What is another way to state the poem's subject?

   _____

4. Identify and explain each simile. What feeling do they share? _____

   _____

   _____

   _____

   _____

   _____

5. Which line is a metaphor? Explain the metaphor. _____

_____

6. What is the poem's meaning or theme? What is the poet's attitude toward deferred dreams?

_____

_____

7. What social comment might the poem be making? _____

_____

Taxi

by **Amy Lowell** (American; 1874–1925)

When I go away from you
The world beats dead
Like a slackened drum.
I call out for you against the jutted stars
And shout into the ridges of the wind.   5
Streets coming fast,
One after the other,
Wedge you away from me,
And the lamps of the city prick my eyes
So that I can no longer see your face.
Why should I leave you,   10
To wound myself upon the sharp edges of the night?

1. What kind of poem do you see on the page? _____

_____

2. Is this a narrative, dramatic, or lyric poem? That is, how are the words coming to us?

_____

3. Explain the simile in the opening lines. _____

_____

4. Explain the metaphor in the last line. _____

_____

5. What is the tone of the poem? How do the details and the emotional impact of the metaphors help create tone?

_____

_____

_____

6. What is the poem's meaning or theme? What does the poet want us to understand from reading her poem?

_____

_____

_____

Is My Team Ploughing
by **A.E. Housman** (British; 1859–1936)

"Is my team ploughing,
  That I was used to drive
And hear the harness jingle
  When I was man alive?"

Ay, the horses trample,   5
  The harness jingles now;
No change though you lie under
  The land you used to plough.

"Is football playing
  Along the river shore,   10
With lads to chase the leather,
  Now I stand up no more?"

Ay, the ball is flying,
  The lads play heart and soul;
The goal stands up, the keeper   15
  Stands up to keep the goal.

"Is my girl happy,
  That I thought hard to leave,
And has she tired of weeping
  As she lies down at eve?"   20

Ay, she lies down lightly,
   She lies not down to weep:
Your girl is well contented.
   Be still, my lad, and sleep.

"Is my friend hearty,   25
   Now I am thin and pine,
And has he found to sleep in
   A better bed than mine?"

Yes, lad, I lie easy,
   I lie as lads would choose;   30
I cheer a dead man's sweetheart,
   Never ask me whose.

1. What kind of poem do you see on the page? _____

   _____

2. Is this a narrative, dramatic, or lyric poem? That is, how are the words coming to us?

   _____

3. What is the situation of the speaker in the first stanza?

   _____

4. What were the activities of the person who speaks in the first stanza?

   _____

5. Who is the speaker in the second, fourth, sixth, and eighth stanzas?

   _____

6. What is the speaker's situation in the last stanza? Whose sweetheart does he "lie" with?

   _____

7. What "bed" is being referred to in the line "A better bed than mine?"

   _____

After we read the last stanza, what other meaning can we get from the line?

_____

8. What is the surface tone of the two speakers, and what is the underlying attitude of the poet? Explain the poem's theme.

_____

_____

_____

Selection 1   Mrs. Zajac

by **Tracy Kidder**

Tracy Kidder is a contributing editor to *Atlantic* magazine and the author of several nonfiction books, including *Among Schoolchildren* (1988), a compassionate study of a year he spent observing Mrs. Zajac's fifth-grade classroom. The following excerpt is from the first few pages of his book on Mrs. Zajac.

Prepare

1. From what you know about the author and the selection, what can you predict about purpose and format or style?

_____

_____

2. State briefly what you expect to read about. _____

_____

1   *Mrs. Zajac wasn't born yesterday. She knows you didn't do your best work on this paper, Clarence. Don't you remember Mrs. Zajac saying that if you didn't do your best, she'd make you do it over? As for you, Claude, God forbid that you should ever need brain surgery. But Mrs. Zajac hopes that if you do, the doctor won't open up your head and walk off saying he's almost done, as you just said when Mrs. Zajac asked you for your penmanship, which, by the way, looks like who did it and ran. Felipe, the reason you have hiccups is, your mouth is always open and the wind rushes in. You're in fifth grade now. So, Felipe, put a lock on it. Zip it up. Then go get a drink of water. Mrs. Zajac means business, Robert.*

The sooner you realize she never said everybody in the room has to do the work except for Robert, *the sooner you'll get along with her. And . . . Clarence. Mrs. Zajac knows you didn't try. You don't just hand in junk to Mrs. Zajac. She's been teaching an awful lot of years. She didn't fall off the turnip cart yesterday. She told you she was an old-lady teacher.*

2   She was thirty-four. She wore a white skirt and yellow sweater and a thin gold necklace, which she held in her fingers, as if holding her own reins, while waiting for children to answer. Her hair was black with a hint of Irish red. It was cut short to the tops of her ears, and swept back like a pair of folded wings. She had a delicately cleft chin, and she was short—the children's chairs would have fit her. Although her voice sounded conversational, it had projection. She had never acted. She had found this voice in classrooms.

3   Mrs. Zajac seemed to have a frightening amount of energy. She strode across the room, her arms swinging high and her hands in small fists. Taking her stand in front of the green chalkboard, discussing the rules with her new class, she repeated sentences, and her lips held the shapes of certain words, such as "home-work," after she had said them. Her hands kept very busy. They sliced the air and made karate chops to mark off boundaries. They extended straight out like a traffic cop's, halting illegal maneuvers yet to be perpetrated. When they rested momentarily on her hips, her hands looked as if they were in holsters. She told the children, "One thing Mrs. Zajac expects from each of you is that you do *your* best." She said, "Mrs. Zajac gives homework. I'm sure you've all heard. The old meanie gives homework." *Mrs. Zajac.* It was in part a role. She worked her way into it every September.

4   At home on late summer days like these, Chris Zajac wore shorts or blue jeans. Although there was no dress code for teachers here at Kelly School, she always went to work in skirts or dresses. She dressed as if she were applying for a job, and hoped in the back of her mind that someday, heading for job interviews, her students would remember her example. Outside school, she wept easily over small and large catastrophes and at sentimental movies, but she never cried in front of students, except once a few years ago when the news came over the intercom that the Space Shuttle had exploded and Christa McAuliffe had died—and then she saw in her students' faces that the sight of Mrs. Zajac crying had frightened them, and she made herself stop and then explained.

5   At home, Chris laughed at the antics of her infant daughter and egged the child on. She and her first-grade son would sneak up to the radio when her husband wasn't looking and change the station from classical to rock-and-roll music. "You're regressing, Chris," her husband would say. But especially on the first few days of school, she didn't let her students get away with much. She was not amused when, for instance, on the first day, two of the boys started dueling with their rulers. On nights before the school year started, Chris used to have bad dreams: her

principal would come to observe her, and her students would choose that moment to climb up on their desks and give her the finger, or they would simply wander out the door. But a child in her classroom would never know that Mrs. Zajac had the slightest doubt that students would obey her.

6   The first day, after going over all the school rules, Chris spoke to them about effort. "If you put your name on a paper, you should be proud of it," she said. "You should think, This is the best I can do and I'm proud of it and I want to hand this in." Then she asked, "If it isn't your best, what's Zajac going to do?"

7   Many voices, most of them female, answered softly in unison, "Make us do it over."

8   *"Make you do it over,"* Chris repeated. It sounded like a chant.

9   "Does anyone know anything about Lisette?" she asked when no one answered to that name.

10   Felipe—small, with glossy black hair—threw up his hand.

11   "Felipe?"

12   "She isn't here!" said Felipe. He wasn't being fresh. On those first few days of school, whenever Mrs. Zajac put the sound of a question in her voice, and sometimes before she got the question out, Felipe's hand shot up.

13   In contrast, there was the very chubby girl who sat nearly motionless at her desk, covering the lower half of her face with her hands. As usual, most of their voices sounded timid the first day, and came out of hiding gradually. There were twenty children. About half were Puerto Rican. Almost two-thirds of the twenty needed the forms to obtain free lunches. There was a lot of long and curly hair. Some boys wore little rattails. The eyes the children lifted up to her as she went over the rules—a few eyes were blue and many more were brown—looked so solemn and so wide that Chris felt like dropping all pretense and laughing. Their faces ranged from dark brown to gold, to pink, to pasty white, the color that Chris associated with sunless tenements and too much TV. The boys wore polo shirts and T-shirts and new white sneakers with the ends of the laces untied and tucked behind the tongues. Some girls wore lacy ribbons in their hair, and some wore pants and others skirts, a rough but not infallible indication of religion—the daughters of Jehovah's Witnesses and Pentecostals do not wear pants. There was a lot of prettiness in the room, and all of the children looked cute to Chris.

Comprehension

Fill in the blanks to complete each of the following statements.

1. Although Mrs. Zajac is thiry-four, she describes herself to her students as

    an _____ teacher.

2. Mrs. Zajac was _____ but her voice had _____ .

3. Mrs. Zajac emphasized to her students that she gives _____

and expects them to do their _____ .

4. Many of Mrs. Zajac's students qualified for _____ .

5. If Mrs. Zajac didn't think you had done your best work, she would _____

_____ .

Answer the following with a T (true) or F (false).

	T	F
6. Mrs. Zajac never wore jeans.	___	___
7. Mrs. Zajac cried easily at home but never in front of her students.	___	___
8. Mrs. Zajac never doubted that her students would obey her.	___	___
9. Mrs. Zajac dressed for class as if she were on a job interview.	___	___

Expanding Vocabulary

Review the following words in their contexts and then write a brief definition or synonym for each word based on what you can learn from context clues.

projection (2) _____

karate (3) _____

maneuvers (3) _____

perpetrated (3) _____

holsters (3) _____

unison (7) _____

pretense (13) _____

infallible (13) _____

Analysis of Content and Strategies

1. Why is the first paragraph in italics? What is it designed to represent?

_____

2. What is effective about Kidder's choice to begin the way he does?

_____

3. What are three details about Mrs. Zajac that you would consider *telling* details? Why are they especially telling?

_____

_____

_____

_____

4. List and explain two metaphors found in paragraph 2. _____

_____

_____

_____

5. What can you infer about the Kelly School neighborhood from the details provided about the children?

_____

6. What does the last line tell us about Mrs. Zajac's attitude toward teaching?

_____

7. What is Kidder's attitude toward his subject? Does he present Mrs. Zajac in a positive or negative way? As a good or bad teacher? Explain.

_____

_____

For Discussion and Reflection

1. Would you have enjoyed being in Mrs. Zajac's fifth-grade class? Why or why not?

2. Mrs. Zajac emphasizes being proud of work you sign your name to. Is it ever too early to teach this idea? Is it ever too late?

3. Mrs. Zajac believes in dressing properly for her job. Should students have a dress code or wear uniforms? How can clothes make a difference in school or on the job?

4. On a scale of 1 (not very important) to 4 (extremely important), how would you rate the following skills or traits in teachers? Energy? High standards for student work? Love of teaching? Knowledge of subject matter?

Selection 2   **The Secret Life of Walter Mitty**

by James Thurber

A graduate of Ohio State University, James Thurber (1894–1962) became well-known as a humorist and cartoonist while on the staff of *The New Yorker* magazine. He is probably most famous for the following short story, first published in *The New Yorker* in 1939, made into a movie in 1947, and now reprinted in collections the world over.

Prepare

1. From what you know about the author and the selection, what can you predict about purpose and format or style?

   _____

   _____

2. State briefly what you expect to read about. _____

   _____

1   "We're going through!" The Commander's voice was like thin ice breaking. He wore his full-dress uniform, with the heavily braided white cap pulled down rakishly over one cold gray eye. "We can't make it, sir. It's spoiling for a hurricane, if you ask me." "I'm not asking you, Lieutenant Berg," said the Commander. "Throw on the power lights! Rev her up to 8,500! We're going through!" The pounding of the cylinders increased: ta-pocketa-pocketa-pocketa-*pocketa-pocketa*. The Commander stared at the ice forming on the pilot window. He walked over and twisted a row of complicated dials. "Switch on No. 8 auxiliary!" he shouted. "Switch on No. 8 auxiliary!" repeated Lieutenant Berg. "Full strength in No. 3 turret!" shouted the Commander. "Full strength in No. 3 turret!" The crew, bending to their various tasks in the huge, hurtling eight-engined Navy hydroplane, looked at each other and grinned. "The Old Man'll get us through," they said to one another. "The Old Man ain't afraid of Hell!" . . .

2   "Not so fast! You're driving too fast!" said Mrs. Mitty. "What are you driving so fast for?"

3   "Hmm?" said Walter Mitty. He looked at his wife, in the seat beside him, with shocked astonishment. She seemed grossly unfamiliar, like a strange woman who had yelled at him in a crowd. "You were up to fifty-five," she said. "You know I don't like to go more than forty. You were up to fifty-five." Walter Mitty drove on toward Waterbury in silence, the roaring of the SN202 through the worst storm in twenty years of Navy flying

fading in the remote, intimate airways of his mind. "You're tensed up again," said Mrs. Mitty. "It's one of your days. I wish you'd let Dr. Renshaw look you over."

4   Walter Mitty stopped the car in front of the building where his wife went to have her hair done. "Remember to get those overshoes while I'm having my hair done," she said. "I don't need overshoes," said Mitty. She put her mirror back into her bag. "We've been all through that," she said, getting out of the car. "You're not a young man any longer." He raced the engine a little. "Why don't you wear your gloves? Have you lost your gloves?" Walter Mitty reached in a pocket and brought out the gloves. He put them on, but after she had turned and gone into the building and he had driven on to a red light, he took them off again. "Pick it up, brother!" snapped a cop as the light changed, and Mitty hastily pulled on his gloves and lurched ahead. He drove around the streets aimlessly for a time, and then he drove past the hospital on his way to the parking lot.

5   . . . "It's the millionaire banker, Wellington McMillan," said the pretty nurse. "Yes?" said Walter Mitty, removing his gloves slowly. "Who has the case?" "Dr. Renshaw and Dr. Benbow, but there are two specialists here, Dr. Remington from New York and Mr. Pritchard-Mitford from London. He flew over." A door opened down a long, cool corridor and Dr. Renshaw came out. He looked distraught and haggard. "Hello, Mitty," he said "We're having the devil's own time with McMillan, the millionaire banker and close personal friend of Roosevelt. Obstreosis of the ductal tract. Tertiary. Wish you'd take a look at him." "Glad to," said Mitty.

6   In the operating room there were whispered introductions: "Dr. Remington, Dr. Mitty. Mr. Pritchard-Mitford, Dr. Mitty." "I've read your book on streptothricosis," said Pritchard-Mitford, shaking hands. "A brilliant performance, sir." "Thank you," said Walter Mitty. "Didn't know you were in the States, Mitty," grumbled Remington. "Coals to Newcastle, bringing Mitford and me up here for a tertiary." "You are very kind," said Mitty. A huge, complicated machine, connected to the operating table, with many tubes and wires, began at this moment to go pocketa-pocketa-pocketa. "The new anesthetizer is giving way!" shouted an intern. "There is no one in the East who knows how to fix it!" "Quiet, man!" said Mitty, in a low, cool voice. He sprang to the machine, which was now going pocketa-pocketa-queep-pocketa-queep. He began fingering delicately a row of glistening dials. "Give me a fountain pen!" he snapped. Someone handed him a fountain pen. He pulled a faulty piston out of the machine and inserted the pen in its place. "That will hold for ten minutes," he said. "Get on with the operation." A nurse hurried over and whispered to Renshaw, and Mitty saw the man turn pale. "Coreopsis has set in," said Renshaw nervously. "If you would take over, Mitty?" Mitty looked at him and at the craven figure of Benbow, who drank, and at the grave, uncertain faces of the two great specialists. "If you wish," he said. They slipped a white gown on him; he adjusted a mask and drew on thin gloves; nurses handed him shining . . .

7   "Back it up, Mac! Look out for that Buick!" Walter Mitty jammed on the brakes. "Wrong lane, Mac," said the parking-lot attendant, looking at Mitty closely. "Gee. Yeh," muttered Mitty. He began cautiously to back out of the lane marked "Exit Only." "Leave her sit there," said the attendant. "I'll put her away." Mitty got out of the car. "Hey, better leave the key." "Oh," said Mitty, handing the man the ignition key. The attendant vaulted into the car, backed it up with insolent skill, and put it where it belonged.

8   They're so damn cocky, thought Walter Mitty, walking along Main Street; they think they know everything. Once he had tried to take his chains off, outside New Milford, and he had got them wound around the axles. A man had had to come out in a wrecking car and unwind them, a young, grinning garageman. Since then Mrs. Mitty always made him drive to a garage to have the chains taken off. The next time, he thought, I'll wear my right arm in a sling; they won't grin at me then. I'll have my right arm in a sling and they'll see I couldn't possibly take the chains off myself. He kicked at the slush on the sidewalk. "Overshoes," he said to himself, and he began looking for a shoe store.

9   When he came out into the street again, with the overshoes in a box under his arm, Walter Mitty began to wonder what the other thing was his wife had told him to get. She had told him, twice, before they set out from their house for Waterbury. In a way he hated these weekly trips to town—he was always getting something wrong. Kleenex, he thought, Squibb's, razor blades? No. Toothpaste, toothbrush, bicarbonate, carborundum, initiative and referendum? He gave it up. But she would remember it. "Where's the what's-its-name?" she would ask. "Don't tell me you forgot the what's-its-name." A newsboy went by shouting something about the Waterbury trial.

10   . . . "Perhaps this will refresh your memory." The District Attorney suddenly thrust a heavy automatic at the quiet figure on the witness stand. "Have you ever seen this before?" Walter Mitty took the gun and examined it expertly. "This is my Webley-Vickers 50.80," he said calmly. An excited buzz ran around the courtroom. The judge rapped for order. "You are a crack shot with any sort of firearms, I believe?" said the District Attorney, insinuatingly. "Objection!" shouted Mitty's attorney. "We have shown that the defendant could not have fired the shot. We have shown that he wore his right arm in a sling on the night of the fourteenth of July." Walter Mitty raised his hand briefly and the bickering attorneys were stilled. "With any known make of gun," he said evenly, "I could have killed Gregory Fitzhurst at three hundred feet *with my left hand.*" Pandemonium broke loose in the courtroom. A woman's scream rose above the bedlam and suddenly a lovely, dark-haired girl was in Walter Mitty's arms. The District Attorney struck at her savagely. Without rising from his chair, Mitty let the man have it on the point of the chin. "You miserable cur!" . . .

11   "Puppy biscuit," said Walter Mitty. He stopped walking and the buildings of Waterbury rose up out of the misty courtroom and surrounded him again. A woman who was passing laughed. "He said 'Puppy

biscuit,' " she said to her companion. "That man said 'Puppy biscuit' to himself." Walter Mitty hurried on. He went into an A. & P., not the first one he came to but a smaller one farther up the street. "I want some biscuit for small, young dogs," he said to the clerk. "Any special brand, sir?" The greatest pistol shot in the world thought a moment. "It says 'Puppies Bark for It' on the box," said Walter Mitty.

12   His wife would be through at the hairdresser's in fifteen minutes, Mitty saw in looking at his watch, unless they had trouble drying it; sometimes they had trouble drying it. She didn't like to get to the hotel first; she would want him to be there waiting for her as usual. He found a big leather chair in the lobby, facing a window, and he put the overshoes and the puppy biscuit on the floor beside it. He picked up an old copy of *Liberty* and sank down into the chair. "Can Germany Conquer the World Through the Air?" Walter Mitty looked at the pictures of bombing planes and of ruined streets.

13   . . . "The cannonading has got the wind up in young Raleigh, sir," said the sergeant. Captain Mitty looked up at him through touseled hair. "Get him to bed," he said wearily. "With the others. I'll fly alone." "But you can't, sir," said the sergeant anxiously. "It takes two men to handle that bomber and the Archies are pounding hell out of the air. Von Richtman's circus is between here and Saulier." "Somebody's got to get that ammunition dump," said Mitty. "I'm going over. Spot of brandy?" He poured a drink for the sergeant and one for himself. War thundered and whined around the dugout and battered at the door. There was a rending of wood and splinters flew through the room. "A bit of a near thing," said Captain Mitty carelessly. "The box barrage is closing in," said the sergeant. "We only live once, Sergeant," said Mitty, with his faint, fleeting smile. "Or do we?" He poured another brandy and tossed it off. "I never see a man could hold his brandy like you, sir," said the sergeant. "Begging your pardon, sir." Captain Mitty stood up and strapped on his huge Webley-Vickers automatic. "It's forty kilometers through hell, sir," said the sergeant. Mitty finished one last brandy. "After all," he said softly, "what isn't?" The pounding of the cannon increased; there was the rat-rat-tatting of machine guns, and from somewhere came the menacing pocketa-pocketa-pocketa of the new flame-throwers. Walter Mitty walked to the door of the dugout humming "Auprés de Ma Blonde." He turned and waved to the sergeant. "Cheerio!" he said. . . .

14   Something struck his shoulder. "I've been looking all over this hotel for you," said Mrs. Mitty. "Why do you have to hide in this old chair? How did you expect me to find you?" "Things close in," said Walter Mitty vaguely. "What?" Mrs. Mitty said. "Did you get the what's-its-name? The puppy biscuit? What's in that box?" "Overshoes," said Mitty. "Couldn't you have put them on in the store?" "I was thinking," said Walter Mitty. "Does it ever occur to you that I am sometimes thinking?"

She looked at him. "I'm going to take your temperature when I get you home," she said.

15   They went out through the revolving doors that made a faintly derisive whistling sound when you pushed them. It was two blocks to the parking lot. At the drugstore on the corner she said, "Wait here for me. I forgot something. I won't be a minute." She was more than a minute. Walter Mitty lighted a cigarette. It began to rain, rain with sleet in it. He stood up against the wall of the drugstore, smoking. . . . He put his shoulders back and his heels together. "To hell with the handkerchief," said Walter Mitty scornfully. He took one last drag on his cigarette and snapped it away. Then, with that faint, fleeting smile playing about his lips, he faced the firing squad; erect and motionless, proud and disdainful, Walter Mitty the Undefeated, inscrutable to the last.

Comprehension

Write a summary of the story, using no more than seven sentences.

_____

_____

_____

_____

_____

_____

_____

_____

Expanding Vocabulary

Review the following words in their contexts and then write a brief definition or synonym for each word based on what you can learn from context clues.

rakishly (1) _____

hydroplane (1) _____

distraught (5) _____

craven (6) _____

insolent (7) _____

insinuatingly (10) _____

pandemonium (10) _____

bedlam (10) _____

derisive (15) _____

inscrutable (15) _____

Analysis of Content and Strategies

1. What is the story's exposition? _____

   _____

2. What is the main activity that Mitty and his wife are engaged in during the course of the story?

   _____

3. The story does have a typical plot structure (see Figure 9.1), but what other structure does Thurber use to develop Mitty's character? What is happening in the passages that do not take place in Waterbury?

   _____

   _____

4. How do the details of Mitty's real life help reveal his character? What kinds of problems does he have?

   _____

   _____

5. What do the dream passages have in common? What do they tell us about the person Mitty would like to be?

   _____

   _____

   _____

6. What are Mitty's dominant traits? Describe his character, including his central conflict and his ways of coping with complications.

_____

_____

_____

7. What details or situations in the story are humorous? Could these situations also be viewed as serious? As sad? Explain.

_____

_____

_____

_____

_____

8. How does Thurber want us to feel about his character? Are we to relate to him? Laugh at him? Feel sorry for him? To what extent is Mitty like many people?

_____

_____

_____

_____

For Discussion and Reflection

1. Walter Mitty has particular problems with the modern marvel of his time: the car. If you were to update Thurber's story, how might you show Mitty's clumsiness or incompetence in the 1990s?

2. Can you relate to Mitty's feelings of incompetence? What advice would you give to him?

3. When you dream about a different life, what do you imagine doing or becoming? How does your dream life differ from your actual life? What can you learn about yourself by analyzing your dreams?

Selection 3   **Science and the Sense of Wonder**

by **Isaac Asimov**

A writer of more than 200 books, and many more articles and short stories, Isaac Asimov (1920–1992) is famous both as a science-fiction writer and as a scientist who wrote about science for nonspecialists. The following article first appeared in the *Washington Post* on August 12, 1979.

■ **Prepare**

1. From what you know about the author and the selection, what can you predict about purpose and format or style?

   _____

   _____

2. State briefly what you expect to read about. _____

   _____

3. Preread the selection.

4. In prereading, you discover that the article begins with a poem by Walt Whitman. Use your nine-step reading strategy for poetry and then answer the following questions just about the poem.

   a. What kind of poem is this? _____

   b. What is the situation in the poem? Where is the speaker? What does the speaker eventually do?

      _____

      _____

   c. What is the speaker's attitude toward science? Toward nature?

      _____

      _____

      _____

d. List words about science that are negative and words about nature that are positive.

_____

_____

_____

5. Now read the article and respond to the questions and exercises that follow.

1   One of Walt Whitman's best-known poems is this one:

When I heard the learn'd astronomer,
When the proofs, the figures, were ranged in columns before me,
When I was shown the charts and diagrams, to add, divide and measure them,
When I sitting heard the astronomer where he lectured with much
    applause in the lecture-room,
How soon unaccountable I became tired and sick,
Till rising and gliding out I wander'd off by myself,
In the mystical moist night-air, and from time to time,
Look'd up in perfect silence at the stars.

2   I imagine that many people reading those lines tell themselves, exultantly, "How true! Science just sucks all the beauty out of everything, reducing it all to numbers and tables and measurements! Why bother learning all that junk when I can just go out and look at the stars?"

3   That is a very convenient point of view since it makes it not only unnecessary, but downright aesthetically wrong, to try to follow all that hard stuff in science. Instead, you can just take a look at the night sky, get a quick beauty fix, and go off to a nightclub.

4   The trouble is that Whitman is talking through his hat, but the poor soul didn't know any better.

5   I don't deny that the night sky is beautiful, and I have in my time spread out on a hillside for hours looking at the stars and being awed by their beauty (and receiving bug-bites whose marks took weeks to go away).

6   But what I see—those quiet, blinking points of light—*is not all the beauty there is.* Should I stare lovingly at a single leaf and willingly remain ignorant of the forest? Should I be satisfied to watch the sun glinting off a single pebble and scorn any knowledge of a beach?

7   Those bright spots in the sky that we call planets are worlds. There are worlds with thick atmospheres of carbon dioxide and sulfuric acid; worlds of red-hot liquid with hurricanes that could gulp down the whole earth; dead worlds with quiet pock-marks of craters; worlds with volcanoes puffing plumes of dust into airlessness; worlds with pink and desolate deserts—each with a weird and unearthly beauty that boils down to a mere speck of light if we just gaze at the night sky.

8   Those other bright spots, which are stars rather than planets, are actually suns. Some of them are of incomparable grandeur, each glowing with the light of a thousand suns like ours; some of them are merely red-hot coals doling out their energy stingily. Some of them are compact bodies as massive as our sun, but with all that mass squeezed into a ball smaller than the earth. Some are more compact still, with the mass of the sun squeezed down into the volume of a small asteroid. And some are more compact still, with their mass shrinking down to a volume of zero, the site of which is marked by an intense gravitational field that swallows up everything and gives back nothing; with matter spiraling into that bottomless hole and giving out a wild death-scream of X-rays.

9   There are stars that pulsate endlessly in a great cosmic breathing; and others that, having consumed their fuel, expand and redden until they swallow up their planets, if they have any (and someday, billions of years from now, our sun will expand and the earth will crisp and sere and vaporize into a gas of iron and rock with no sign of the life it once bore). And some stars explode in a vast cataclysm whose ferocious blast of cosmic rays, hurrying outward at nearly the speed of light reaching across thousands of light years to touch the earth and supply some of the driving force of evolution through mutations.

10   Those paltry few stars we see as we look up in perfect silence (some 2,500 or more on even the darkest and clearest night) are joined by a vast horde we don't see, up to as many as three hundred billion—300,000,000,000—to form an enormous pinwheel in space. This pinwheel, the Milky Way galaxy, stretches so widely that it takes light, moving at 186,282 miles each *second*, a hundred thousand *years* to cross it from end to end; and it rotates about its center in a vast and stately turn that takes two hundred million years to complete—and the sun and the earth and we ourselves all make that turn.

11   Beyond our Milky Way galaxy are others, a score or so of them bound to our own in a cluster of galaxies, most of them small, with no more than a few billion stars in each; but with one at least, the Andromeda galaxy, twice as large as our own.

12   Beyond our own cluster, other galaxies and other clusters exist; some clusters made up of thousands of galaxies. They stretch outward and outward as far as our best telescopes can see, with no visible sign of an end—perhaps a hundred billion of them in all.

13   And in more and more of those galaxies we are becoming aware of violence at the centers—of great explosions and outpourings of radiation, marking the death of perhaps millions of stars. Even at the center of our own galaxy there is incredible violence masked from our own solar system far in the outskirts by enormous clouds of dust and gas that lie between us and the heaving center.

14   Some galactic centers are so bright that they can be seen from distances of billions of light-years, distances from which the galaxies themselves

cannot be seen and only the bright starlike centers of ravening energy show up—as quasars. Some of these have been detected from more than ten billion light-years away.

15   All these galaxies are hurrying outward from each other in a vast universal expansion that began fifteen billion years ago, when all the matter in the universe was in a tiny sphere that exploded in the hugest conceivable shatter to form the galaxies.

16   The universe may expand forever or the day may come when the expansion slows and turns back into a contraction to re-form the tiny sphere and begin the game all over again so that the whole universe is exhaling and inhaling in breaths that are perhaps a trillion years long.

17   And all of this vision—far beyond the scale of human imaginings—was made possible by the works of hundreds of "learn'd" astronomers. All of it; *all* of it was discovered after the death of Whitman in 1892, and most of it in the past twenty-five years, so that the poor poet never knew what a stultified and limited beauty he observed when he "look'd up in perfect silence at the stars."

18   Nor can we know or imagine now the limitless beauty yet to be revealed in the future—by science.

Comprehension Check ·

Fill in the blanks to complete each of the following statements.

1. In Whitman's poem, the speaker listens to an _____ lecture.

2. The speaker leaves the lecture to go outside and gaze at the _____ .

3. Asimov states that Whitman's view is _____ because it means you don't have to learn any science.

4. Some spots in the night sky, "giving out a wild death-scream," are actually

   _____ .

5. The three hundred billion Pinwheel of lights is called the _____ .

Answer the following with a T (true) or F (false).

	T	F
6. Asimov disagrees with the attitude toward science expressed by Whitman.	___	___
7. Some of the stars in the sky are actually planets or suns.	___	___
8. We live in the Andromeda galaxy.	___	___
9. Currently, the many galaxies are moving inward toward each other.	___	___
10. Some of what Asimov describes was discovered after Whitman's death.	___	___

■ Expanding Vocabulary

Review the following words in their contexts and then write a brief definition or synonym for each word based on what you can learn from context clues.

aesthetically (3) _____

incomparable (8) _____

asteroid (8) _____

pulsate (9) _____

sere (9) _____

cataclysm (14) _____

stultified (17) _____

■ Analysis of Content and Strategies

1. Asimov agrees with Whitman that the night sky is beautiful; why then does he disagree with the ideas in the poem?

   _____

   _____

2. What is the essay's thesis? _____

   _____

   _____

3. Explain the point of the two questions Asimov asks in paragraph 6.

   _____

   _____

4. List two new facts you learned about the universe from reading this essay.

   _____

   _____

5. Find, state, and explain the metaphor in paragraph 3.

_____

_____

_____

6. Asimov's description of the universe is developed in part by an underlying metaphor. What is the metaphor? Find at least three words or phrases that develop the metaphor.

_____

_____

_____

For Discussion and Reflection

1. Have you ever contemplated the universe in the exciting way that Asimov does? If not, have you been moved by Asimov's description? Why or why not?

2. Has Asimov convinced you that Whitman didn't know how much he was missing? Why or why not?

3. Whose view of nature most closely resembles your own?

4. Can you think of other situations in which it may be true that the person who knows and understands more actually sees what is more exciting, more beautiful, more meaningful?

CHAPTER 10

Reading—and Thinking—Critically

In this chapter you will learn:

- What it means to read and think critically

- The difference between fact and opinion

- To distinguish among kinds of opinions

- To recognize the writer's stance

- To evaluate arguments and take a stand

What does it mean to read—and think—critically? To begin to answer that question, examine the cartoon in Figure 10.1 and then use the questions that follow as a guide to critically reading the cartoon.

1. What are the important details? Who are the two men? Where are they? What has happened?

   _____

   _____

2. From studying the details, what conclusion do you draw? What is the idea of the cartoon?

   _____

   _____

FIGURE 10.1

"Hey, this is *my* résumé...Oh! Very good!"

3. Is the cartoon amusing? Why or why not? _____

_____

_____

The personnel director in the cartoon has been through a process similar to yours. First, he *examines* the evidence: he is holding a résumé that turns out to be his, not the job applicant's. Two questions come to mind: How? and Why? The director *infers* that the applicant obtained the résumé in a clandestine (or spy-like) manner to demonstrate his skills as an intelligence agent so that he will be hired. Once he figures out the situation, the director *evaluates* it, in this case deciding that he is pleased with the job applicant's cleverness.

In a similar pattern, you look at the facts of the cartoon: the two men, the CIA logo (sign) on the wall, the "personnel" sign on the desk, and the cartoon's caption. From these details you infer the idea or point of the cartoon, since it is not stated. Then you evaluate: if you are amused you smile or chuckle; if you are not amused you frown or think "that's a dumb cartoon."

These are some of the key steps to reading—and thinking—critically. We need to understand the facts, grasp the ideas (stated or implied) that connect to the details, and then evaluate those ideas. If you choose to learn from a text-book, presumably you have decided that the text's information is organized, current, and reliable. You judge reliability based on the author's credentials and your instructor's endorsement of the text. When reading literature, you want to evaluate the creativity and effectiveness of the work and to judge the quality of the insights offered by the work. When reading persuasive writing, you first want to evaluate the writer's argument: do the facts and the reasons build a convincing case for the writer's position? Then you need to determine your own position on the issue.

Although we talk about reading or thinking critically as somehow different from "ordinary" reading or thinking, many experts argue that active reading—or reading well—is the same thing as thinking critically. Remember: you read with your brain, not with your eyes; reading is a thinking activity. Perhaps when we speak of reading *critically*, we are emphasizing the important role of evaluating or judging ideas, not just passively taking them in. How can you develop critical reading skills? Let's begin by reviewing some basics about critical readers and then develop additional reading skills that will enable you to read critically.

Characteristics Of The Critical Reader

A critical reader is:
- **skeptical**
(Just because it's in print doesn't mean its right.)
- **fact-oriented**
(Give me the facts and convince me that they are the relevant ones.)
- **analytic**
(How has the work been organized? What strategies has the writer used?)
- **open-minded**
(Prepared to listen to different points of view.)
- **questioning**
(What other conclusions could be supported by the evidence presented?)
- **creative**
(What are some entirely different ways of looking at the problem or issue?)
- **willing to take a stand**
(Are the insights valuable? Is the argument convincing? What is my position on the issue?)

■ DISTINGUISHING FACT FROM OPINION

What do these statements have in common?

My reading class meets in 116 Gray Hall.

Up to age 44, injury is the leading cause of death.

The Earth is in the Milky Way galaxy.

These statements are all facts. *Facts* are verifiable. Factual statements refer to what can be counted or measured or confirmed through observation or by turning to trusted sources. If you want to find your reading class, you check the schedule of classes and then confirm the location by going to the room and meeting the class. You might find the second fact in a magazine article and learn the third fact from your astronomy textbook.

In a dispute over the facts, one person has the facts, the other does not. Some people think they have the facts, but they have misinformation, false facts. When reading statements that sound like facts, we need to be alert to the possibility that the "facts" are incorrect. Why would anyone communicate false facts? Sometimes the "facts" change as we learn more about the world we live in. Sometimes people pass on what they have been told without confirming the facts. And, unfortunately, sometimes writers present facts in such an incomplete or distorted way that the total impression of their writing is not factual. False facts of this variety are found all too often in product advertising and negative political ads or speeches.

Exercise 10-1 Distinguishing Between Facts and False Facts

Mark each of the following statements as either F (fact) or FF (false fact). If you are unsure, indicate how you could verify the fact.

	F	FF
1. To have a healthy diet, you should eat plenty of meat and eggs to get lots of protein.	___	___
2. The earth is 5,000 years old.	___	___
3. Egg whites contain no cholesterol.	___	___
4. HIV-infected mothers may give birth to infected babies.	___	___
5. You can become HIV-infected by attending class with an HIV-infected person.	___	___
6. The Andromeda galaxy is larger than our galaxy.	___	___
7. The Saab 900 is a *Consumer's Digest* 1995 Best Buy.	___	___
8. The Ukraine is a member of the Soviet Republic.	___	___
9. Sacramento is the capital of California.	___	___

Critical readers remain skeptical of the "facts." If a statement doesn't sound quite right to you, perhaps because of something you have read or heard, then check it out.

Now, what do these statements have in common?

My reading instructor is cool.

We need to restrict handguns to reduce the number of fatal injuries among young people.

The Milky Way galaxy was formed about 10 billion years ago.

These statements are not facts. They are all opinions, and as such they are open to debate. Most writing combines facts and opinion, sometimes even in the same sentence. You need to be able to tell the difference so that you can question the opinions and judge if the facts support them adequately. Keep in mind that conclusions (opinions) are found in expository writing as well as in argumentative writing. Often the main idea in a paragraph or a section is opinion. Authors sometimes (but not always) use signal words to distinguish between facts and opinion, so be alert to these as guides to statements of opinion. The following are some of the words and phrases signalling opinions:

consequently	in conclusion
as a result	this suggests
in my view	most experts agree that

 EXERCISE 10-2 Distinguishing Fact from Opinion

Mark each of the following statements as either F (fact) or O (opinion).

                                                            F   **O**

1. About 400,000 people die each year from smoke-related health problems. ___ ___
2. Smoking is prohibited on all flights in the continental United States. ___ ___
3. Many Americans have lost confidence in their elected officials. ___ ___
4. The best way to lose weight is to reduce the amount of fat in one's diet and to exercise regularly. ___ ___
5. It is discourteous to talk during a movie or lecture. ___ ___
6. *Adventures of Huckleberry Finn* was written in the nineteenth century. ___ ___
7. Americans are fascinated by movie stars and sports figures. ___ ___
8. I would rather eat frozen yogurt than ice cream. ___ ___
9. Taking another person's life is wrong. ___ ___

Did this exercise help you to see that there are several different kinds of opinions? The category is too large to be helpful. We need to make distinctions among several types of opinions and then respond differently depending upon the type of opinion we are facing.

"Just" an Opinion

Some people use the word *opinion* to assert that a statement has little value. They say, "That's just your opinion," as if that is a sufficient reason to reject the statement. In this context, opinion seems to mean bias or prejudice. Since it is a view I disagree with, I can reject it by putting it down, by sending it off to the dust bin of personal opinion. Now, suppose that the opinion just rejected is the statement that secondhand smoke is a health hazard. Is this "just" personal opinion, or is this a view widely held by scientists and medical personnel? Smokers may wish to dismiss the idea as prejudice against them, but if they have children they should think seriously about the health risks to which they are exposing them. As we shall see, many opinions have strong factual support and cannot be easily dismissed just because someone prefers not to accept them.

Personal Preferences

Others—sometimes students—have been known to say, "Well, that's *my* opinion," as if that is a sufficient reason to justify the statement. If it's *your* opinion, it has little worth. If it's *my* opinion, I can believe it if I want to, and I don't have to defend it in a debate. Are there some opinions that you are entitled to hold without having to defend them? Yes, you are entitled to your *personal preferences*. If you prefer frozen yogurt to ice cream, that's fine. You eat what you choose, and I will eat what I prefer. You can prefer your biology class, and I can prefer my English class. You would rather study in the morning; I like to study at night. The problem comes when we try to turn personal preferences into debatable opinions but then refuse to defend them. If you prefer rock and roll to jazz music, that's fine, until you assert that rock and roll is a better kind of music than jazz. Now you have shifted to a debatable opinion, and you can expect jazz fans to challenge your statement.

Judgments

Your assertion about music is a *judgment*, an opinion based on values and beliefs. Judgments can be challenged and must be defended with facts and reasons. If you say that you like to watch the Dallas Cowboys play, that is a statement of personal opinion. If you say that the Cowboys are the best football team, then you must give evidence in support of your judgment. Writers need to defend judgments, too, and as critical readers we must evaluate their argument and decide if we agree with their position. Judgments concern right and wrong, good and bad, should and should not. The following statements are judgments:

Jack Nicklaus is the best golfer ever to play the game.

The sunrise was beautiful.

Congress should balance the federal budget.

Capital punishment is wrong.

Inferences

There is one more type of opinion that we need to identify: inferences. An *inference* is an opinion based on evidence, on facts or on a combination of facts and less debatable inferences. You have already learned to draw inferences when you read a paragraph with an unstated main idea. You infer the main idea from the details, the "facts" in the paragraph. You also draw inferences from the telling details, the stories, the figurative language that you read in expressive writing.

Inferences vary from those closely tied to facts to those that are highly debatable. Here are four inferences.

Jack Nicklaus has been one of golf's most consistent players.

The sun will rise tomorrow.

Balancing the federal budget will result in either cutting or abolishing many popular programs.

Capital punishment in the U.S. has been applied in a racist manner.

Notice that the four inferences are about the same subjects as the four judgments given above, but the statements in each case are quite different. If we read the inference about Nicklaus, we expect to read facts given in support of the statement. We expect to find out not just how many tournaments he has won in his career, but how often he made the cut, or finished in the top ten, in the tournaments he did not win. Repeated evidence of good play can be found in golf records to support the inference.

You may think that the second inference is a fact, but until the sun actually rises, we can only assume (and hope) that it will do what it has consistently done in the past. In the third inference, notice first that no judgment is made about whether it is good or bad to cut or eliminate popular programs. The sentence merely asserts what the facts seem to indicate. The last inference is also a conclusion drawn from facts, not an assertion based on values. If more blacks receive the death penalty than whites for the same type of crime, then the death penalty has not been applied in a colorblind way. Legal scholars have studied the court records and have drawn the inference stated above. (This inference has then been used as a reason to defend the judgment that capital punishment is wrong.)

The first two inferences are simpler, more closely tied to facts, either facts we know or can understand if they are presented to us. Look again at the third inference. What assumption does the writer make when writing the statement? Can you think of a way to balance the budget and not cut programs? Of course. We can raise taxes. The writer assumes a consistent tax base. Remember: critical readers ask, "What other conclusions can be drawn? What is another way to look at the issue?" You may not think that raising taxes is a good idea, but you can recognize that it is an alternative to the idea in the third inference.

Inferences are found in all kinds of writing. They are often used, along with facts, to develop arguments in defense of judgments. (Nicklaus's consistency is one reason to judge him the best golfer; an unfair application of the death penalty is one reason to oppose capital punishment.) How do we, as critical readers, distinguish between reasonable inferences and those that seem to have little or no factual support? Evaluating a writer's argument is not always easy; here are some guidelines for accepting or questioning inferences.

Guidelines for Evaluating Inferences

1. **Evaluate the writer's expertise.** People without expertise can have good ideas, and experts can be wrong. However, in general, writers with reputations to protect are likely to present facts to support opinions and are likely to label opinions as such. In textbooks and scholarly writing, experts usually indicate the issues over which the experts disagree.

2. **Compare the experts.** Read more than one book or article on a topic to see if similar views are expressed. In a course, compare your instructor's discussion with the textbook's. The more you know about a subject, the less likely you are to accept questionable statements.

3. **In science, distinguish between hypotheses and theories.** Remember that a hypothesis is a tentative idea, a possible inference based on some observation, but one that needs testing. A theory, on the other hand, is an inference based on many facts and reasoning from those facts. And theories are supported by most experts in a field. (Most physicists accept some version of the "Big Bang" theory of the beginning of the universe; most biologists accept the theory of evolution.)

4. **Be skeptical of generalizations.** There are many laws in science, but there are few laws in the social sciences. That is, there are few generalizations about *all* human beings that are true statements. Consider, for example, this generalization: Teenagers are reckless drivers. Is this a sound inference? Of course not. There are many safe and cautious teenaged drivers. What is true is that drivers between the ages of 16 and 24 have the greatest number of accidents. (That is why their insurance rates are the highest.) It is incorrect to infer, from this fact, that *all* teenagers are reckless drivers. Also be cautious about generalizations that are only slightly qualified. For example: Most Americans believe in fair play. (If this is a fact, why do so many cheat on their taxes?)

5. **Don't trust inferences based on studies that are not identified by the writer.** Sometimes you will read "Studies show that . . ." something or other is true. Don't buy it. Writers who have studied their subject will identify the sources of their information.

6. **Analyze and evaluate the evidence provided.** Question and debate with yourself as you read. Does the inference follow from the facts? Is it the only logical conclusion? If other facts were considered, would the inference have to be changed? Consider this argument:

   Mr. Bradshaw's students all received As and Bs. He must be a great teacher.

Does the inference follow from the facts? Is it the only possible inference? No. Mr. Bradshaw could be an easy grader. The students could have been above-average students to begin with. We do not have enough facts to decide among the possible explanations.

To evaluate arguments, we need to do more than distinguish between fact and opinion. We need to recognize the type of opinion(s) presented and then decide if the support is appropriate.

EXERCISE 10-3 Recognizing Types of Opinion

Read each of the following paragraphs and underline all statements of opinion (sentences or parts of sentences). Then answer the questions that follow.

I. American society has become increasingly violent in the last twenty-five years. People of many ages and backgrounds seem more ready to use violence to solve problems. According to Adam Smith, each year in America now about 10,000 people die from gun deaths, in contrast to 3 in Great Britain and 17 in West Germany. An increasing number of victims are children and teenagers who are settling quarrels over drug territories or girlfriends by shooting. Sometimes the victims are parents, the murderers their children who are ending arguments over money or the use of the car. According to the *Washington Post,* in the first three months of 1989 in Washington, DC, over 100 people were murdered. Also, a youngster in a Maryland community shot both parents in a quarrel over money. And a Virginia teenager shot his stepmother and left her body in a truck. The conclusion that "average" citizens, not crooks, are increasingly resorting to violence seems inescapable.

1. What is the main idea of the paragraph? _____

_____

2. What type of opinion is the main idea of the paragraph? _____

_____

3. Do the facts, in your judgment, support the writer's opinion? _____

_____

4. If you do not find the argument convincing, explain why.

_____

_____

II. Consciously or unconsciously, human activity has often had an extremely negative effect on the environment. From the outset of human history, our species's need for basic resources, such as wood for fuel, ran counter to the preservation of the natural habitat. But while our ancestors did pose a threat to the environment, the damage inflicted was insignificant in comparison to the current level of destruction. Some experts would argue that if current conditions continue, we are headed toward a collision with nature: this disaster can only be averted if international priorities on resources are thoroughly overhauled.

Curran & Renzetti, *Social Problems*, 3rd. ed., 1993

1. Is the paragraph mostly fact or opinion? _____

2. What type of opinion is found in the conclusion? _____

_____

3. If there were no signal words for the opinion, what other words would help you identify the sentence as opinion?

_____

4. Have the authors persuaded you to their position? Why or why not? ____

_____

III. Jennifer: "I just read an interesting study showing that people who watch a lot of TV are more fearful, think there is more violence in the world, and are more suspicious of other people than those who don't watch much TV."

Jim: "Oh, you can't believe all those studies. They're just used to try to take all the good cop shows off TV. I watch lots of TV, and I'm not violent."

Jennifer: "But this study wasn't just about violence making us more violent. It was about TV distorting our view of reality. That's serious. Maybe we should demand more realistic programming."

Jim: "Oh, don't be a wimp. And don't believe everything you read."

Jennifer: "You're the one who's being close-minded."

Jim: "Well, that's your opinion. I can have my opinion, too."

1. What type of opinion was the study's conclusion (expressed by Jennifer)?

_____

2. What type of opinion is expressed by Jim at the end of the dialogue?

_____

3. Who is the better critical thinker? Why? _____

_____

_____

IV. Despite the laws restricting minors from buying alcohol, liquor is widely used by the nation's youth. More than one-fourth of children 12 to 13 years old said they have had at least one drink of alcohol, rising to two-thirds of the mid-teens, and nearly 90 percent of the young adults. Males and females were equally likely to have tried alcohol, but males 18 and older were more likely to be current or binge drinkers. —From a study of the National Center for Health Statistics

> Christine Russell, "Do You Know What Your Kids Are Doing?"
> *Washington Post*, July 11, 1995

1. What is the paragraph's main idea? _____

_____

2. What type of opinion is the main idea of the paragraph?

_____

3. What kind of support is provided for the main idea?

_____

4. Are you surprised by the paragraph, or are the details consistent with your knowledge of teens?

_____

■ RECOGNIZING YOUR BIASES

Some writers develop and defend their inferences or judgments with reasoned discussions of the relevant facts. Others, believing strongly in their opinions, write passionately but not always with reason or the facts. Readers are no different. With some topics you may not have much experience or hold strong feelings. You are more open to following the writer's argument and perhaps agreeing with his or her position. On other topics, however, you hold strong opinions that can affect the way you read material on those topics. You may get angry when you read, or want to dismiss the argument as "just the writer's opinion." Critical thinkers, though, are open-minded; they can "listen and learn" and perhaps be persuaded by facts and good reasons to change their views. One way to become a better critical reader is to be aware of your strongly held positions or attitudes. Then use your self-knowledge to keep your biases and emotions from interfering with your ability to read critically. The following exercise will help you identify some of your biases.

EXERCISE 10-4 Recognizing Your Biases

Complete each of the following sentences by writing what you think of first. Finish the entire exercise as quickly as you can, and then read over and reflect on what you have written.

1. Politicians are _____ .

2. Hispanics are _____ .

3. Teachers are _____ .

4. Jews are _____ .

5. Parents are _____ .

6. Teenagers are _____ .

7. Welfare recipients are _____ .

8. Football players are _____ .

9. Alcoholics are _____ .

10. Vegetarians are _____ .

Compare your responses with classmates and discuss the class's various reactions. Do you have strongly positive or strongly negative opinions about some of the groups listed? Do you have good evidence to justify your generalizations? Do others in the class have experiences that contradict your point of view? Are sweeping generalizations about entire groups of people more likely to be accurate or inaccurate?

■ THE WRITER'S STANCE

In all types of writing, we need to recognize the writer's stance, that is, the writer's subject and purpose and attitude toward the subject and characteristics of writing that create tone. Where does the writer "stand" on the subject? What does the writer want to "do" with the topic—or what does the writer want readers to do after reading about the topic? When we understand the answers to these questions, we create a meaningful reading context.

Consider Tom McKnight's *Essentials of Physical Geography*, for example. You identify this as a textbook, so you expect the purpose to be primarily expository: the author wants to explain this subject to readers. McKnight's preface makes us aware, though, that he has a deep appreciation of the topic and that he hopes students will develop that same appreciation. Because his stance is primarily to explain, however, he chooses a straightforward writing style and tone. He holds his emotions in check and concentrates on a clear explanation of the subject matter.

When the writing purpose changes to persuasion, there are a variety of stances that writers can take. A group of social scientists reporting the results of their studies of television violence to colleagues may select a straightforward, objective style to present their facts and conclusions (inferences). In a magazine article for general readers, they may change their stance to express their concern for the effects of TV violence on viewers. They may even recommend controls on TV's or ratings of shows. That is, they want readers to do something after reading their article.

Other persuasive writing relies more on strongly worded opinion than facts. The writer may express anger, or seek to shock readers into thinking about a current problem. The writer is convinced that the best way to reach readers is through the stirring of emotions. These are all possible approaches to presenting an argument. One is not necessarily better than another; each has its place. Our task as readers is to identify the writer's stance and understand the strategies that have been used to develop that stance.

Attitude

Identifying the writer's subject is only the first step to understanding stance. You also need to identify the writer's attitude toward the subject. To begin, consider the following paragraph on city life:

> The city energizes the people who live there. The noises wake them and urge them to get going. There is excitement "pounding the pavement" with all the others forming that energetic force of workers heading for offices. The tall buildings, the honking of taxis, the dense crowds, the opportunities for fulfilling ambitions all contribute to the euphoria that is city life.

What is the writer's attitude toward life in the city? The city provides excitement, energy, and opportunity. The words have positive connotations. Clearly the writer expresses a positive attitude toward city life. Now read this paragraph on the city:

> The stress of city life is nearly unbearable. Day and night the noises of the city never stop pounding into one's head. Each day brings another struggle

to push through the hordes of workers stampeding to their offices. The buildings hover overhead, ready to crush those who cannot survive the struggle to get ahead.

What is this writer's attitude toward city life? Many of the same details are noted about the city: the noises, the crowds going to work, the tall buildings, the competition. Here, though, the attitude is entirely negative. How are two such different attitudes toward the same subject created? The answer is primarily through word choice, through both connotation and figurative language.

You learned in Chapter 3 that when you combine topic and attitude (what the writer wants to say about the topic) into a complete sentence, you have a main idea or thesis statement. We can say that the main idea of the first paragraph on city life is: Living in the city is an exciting, invigorating experience. The main idea of the second paragraph can be expressed thus: City life is a demanding, stressful experience. The following exercise provides practice in identifying the writer's attitude—and in identifying your attitude toward the topic.

EXERCISE 10-5 Identifying Attitude

Read and answer the questions for each of the following passages.

I. In a nation of 40 million handguns—where anyone who wants one can get one—it's time to face a chilling fact. We're way past the point where registration, licensing, safety training, waiting periods, or mandatory sentencing are going to have much effect. Each of these measures may save some lives or help catch a few criminals, but none—by itself or taken together—will stop the vast majority of handgun suicides or murders. A "controlled" handgun kills just as effectively as an "uncontrolled" one.

From Josh Sugarmann, "The NRA Is Right, but We Still Need to Ban Handguns"

1. What is the writer's subject? _____

2. What is the writer's attitude toward his subject? _____

   _____

3. What words have alerted you to the writer's attitude?

   _____

4. Does the writer's position seem reasonable to you? _____

5. Is your answer to question 4 influenced by opinions you hold strongly?

   _____

II. Even technological developments seem to be isolating. Television has for decades reduced opportunities for interaction, dialogue, and plain talk. In recent years millions of youngsters have turned to play with computerized games, both in arcades and at home, instead of with each other (although some of the games—actually surprisingly few—involve more than one player). The symbol of the age may become a teenager with his ears plugged with earphones, eyes riveted to a Pac-Man, fingers manipulating a joy-stick.

From Amitai Etzioni, *An Immodest Agenda:
Rebuilding America Before the Twenty-First Century*

1. The first sentence establishes the topic: the isolating characteristics of technology. Is this, in the writer's view, good or bad?

   _____

2. How did you determine the writer's attitude? _____

   _____

3. Do you share the writer's attitude? Why or why not?

   _____

   _____

III. Today the world is threatened simultaneously by social and political conflict, impoverishment, resource depletion, and environmental deterioration on a level that few would have expected at the beginning of the twentieth century. These problems arise at global, national, and local levels and are so serious that the future of humanity and the biosphere itself is a risk for the first time in human existence. It would not be too dramatic to say that a global crisis exists. Major cultural adjustments will be required to see us through the twenty-first century.

From John H. Bodley, *Cultural Anthropology*

1. What is the writer's topic? _____

   _____

2. What is the writer's attitude toward his topic? _____

   _____

3. What words have alerted you to the writer's attitude?

   _____

4. Do you share the writer's attitude? Why or why not?

_____

_____

Tone

Closely related to the writer's attitude is the writer's tone. Attitude is the writer's position on the subject. The way that attitude is expressed—the "voice" we hear and the feelings conveyed through that voice—is the writer's _tone_. When talking with friends, you can hear the seriousness or teasing in the voice, and you can also observe body language and facial expressions. When responding to the written word, readers have to work a bit harder. You can't see if the speaker is smiling or about to cry; you have to "hear" the jovial or sad tone in the words on the page and by recognizing writing strategies that help shape tone.

Writers can express attitude through a variety of tones. A positive attitude toward the topic can be expressed in an enthusiastic, serious, sympathetic, light, or admiring tone. A negative attitude can be revealed through an angry, somber, sad, serious, sarcastic, mocking, or ironic tone. We cannot be sure that the writer's attitude is positive just because the tone is light. One way to create a mocking, ironic stance is to use a light tone with a very serious subject. When the tone seems inappropriate for the subject, the writer is probably ridiculing the issue.

The following paragraphs represent different responses to the same issue. Read and respond to the questions following each paragraph.

How can you even think about restricting smoking on your flights to Europe and Asia? Don't you know how long those flights are? What do you think us smokers are going to do all those hours without a cigarette? Whether you like it or not, smoking is an addiction; we _have_ to have a cigarette—and we will, damn it! What are you going to do about it? Throw us out of the plane?

1. What is the writer's attitude? _____

2. What tone has been used? _____

3. What has helped you recognize tone? _____

_____

I do understand the attitude of nonsmokers. I appreciate their desire not to have to be closed in with smoke for the length of a flight to Europe. I just wish that they could also understand the needs of smokers. Many of us feel guilty that we can't seem to quit the habit, but we know that as long as we continue to smoke we will need a cigarette before a seven-hour flight is over. If smoking is prohibited, many smokers will abide by the rules, but, I'm afraid, not all. I would be worried that some smokers would use the lavatories to sneak a smoke, and then we would all be in grave danger.

1. What is the writer's attitude? _____

2. What tone has been used? _____

3. What has helped you recognize tone? _____

_____

I just want to say thank you for finally making a decision for health, the health not only of customers but of your crew members as well. I have loved every trip I've taken to Europe—except for the going and coming on the plane. It's been so awful having to put up with seven hours of a smoke-filled plane. But now, thank goodness, we are free of that one difficult part of travel to Europe. I am so excited by your decision I am already planning my next trip. Thank you, thank you!

1. What is the writer's attitude? _____

2. What tone has been used? _____

3. What has helped you recognize tone? _____

_____

As you learned in Chapter 9, three important elements of style that create feeling and thus help to shape a work's tone are *connotation* in word choice, *sentence patterns,* and *figurative language.* These strategies are used in persuasive writing as well as in expressive writing. They are the primary tools writers have to shape tone and reveal attitude. Here are three additional strategies that are important tone indicators.

Hyperbole, Understatement, and Irony

These three strategies are similar in that all create a discrepancy between what the writer *says* and what the writer actually *means* for the reader to understand. Hyperbole is probably the easiest to recognize. Here the writer so overstates the case that we hear the joking or satiric intent. When an exasperated parent says to a five-year-old,"I've told you a million times to brush your teeth," we recognize that humor, created by exaggeration, is being used to get the youngster to the bathroom. Overstatement (hyperbole) often creates a lightly joking tone, but it can also be used to create an angry, mocking, or sarcastic tone.

Understatement can be used for a light touch, but often creates a more serious or biting tone. When you come in dripping wet and say, "It's a bit damp outside," you are using understatement for light humor. To play down what is important is to give emphasis to the issue's seriousness. In one of her columns, journalist Ellen Goodman writes about society's addictions this way:

> Hi, my name is Jane and I was once a bulimic but now I am an exercise guru. . . . Hi, my name is Oprah and I was a food addict but now I am a size 10.

The simple, child-like statements play down the difficulties of curing addictions in order to emphasize the actual complexities of eating disorders.

Hyperbole expresses more than is meant; understatement expresses less. *Irony,* the third option, expresses the opposite of what is meant. When your friend sees you in your grubbiest clothes and comments: "Wonderful outfit!" you know the friend really means that you look awful. Recognizing verbal irony in writing takes careful attention to the entire context of the passage. In her study of college sports, journalist Grace Lichtenstein chose the title: "Playing for Money." In one sense the title is without irony, because college athletes do play a game. In another sense, though, the title is ironic, for Lichtenstein makes clear in her article that college sports are not "play." They have become big business for the athletes, the coaches, and the schools. Bringing together the words "play" and "money" in the title ironically underscores a problem in college athletics.

You will find writers of serious articles using one, or perhaps several, strategies for shaping tone. For example, you may find several negative connotations, some metaphors, and one ironic statement. Writers of humor—whose purpose is to ridicule or satirize something in society, not just make us laugh—may blend most of these strategies in one essay. When you read the delightful columns of the humorists, after you stop laughing, try to analyze the various strategies that are used and understand at what, exactly, the writers are poking fun. Also think about why they are calling attention to that issue. Humorists want us to see problems in ourselves or in our society. Dave Barry's weekly syndicated columns are a good example.

Exercise 10-6 Recognizing Tone and Understanding the Writer's Stance

A humor columnist for the Miami Herald *since 1983, Dave Barry is now syndicated in more than 150 newspapers. The following column appeared July 16, 1995. Read it and then answer the questions that follow.*

Unplugged

1   RECENTLY I WAS IN MY OFFICE, with a lot to do, including write a column, when I got a phone call informing me that the electric company had cut off my power.

2   Years ago, I would have responded to this petty annoyance with a pointless, immature outburst of anger. But since then I have learned that

stress management is vital to health. So I hung up the phone, took a deep breath, exhaled slowly, then punched my desk so hard that I could not make a fist for three days.

3   Then, using my other hand, I called the electric company, which has one of those automatic call-routing systems, designed by escaped Nazis with the aid of the Educational Testing Service, wherein you must use your touch-tone phone to pass a lengthy multiple-choice test (". . . If you know your first name but NOT your last name, press . . ."). This is the electric company's way of testing your worthiness as a customer; it's similar to the way knights of old had to prove themselves by slaying dragons, except that instead of winning the hand of a fair maiden, you get put in line to speak with an actual Customer Service Representative.

4   While waiting, I kept my stress level down by calmly going over the points I planned to make, as follows:

1. You stupid idiots.
2. Give me back my electricity THIS INSTANT.
3. What are you people using for brains?
4. Pez?

5   While I was refining these points, a Customer Service Representative came on the line and immediately irritated me by—I believe this was a deliberate tactic on her part—being polite. She explained to me that my electricity had been turned off because—get a load of THIS excuse—I had not paid my bill.

6   I was furious. The only thing that prevented me from hiring the entire O.J. Simpson defense team and suing the electric company for every last volt it owns was the realization that I had not, in fact, paid my electric bill. You know how you sometimes make a pile of papers that you Definitely Have to Get to Soon, and then you avoid making eye contact with the pile for several weeks, secretly hoping—you crazy optimist—that a giant comet will strike the Earth and wipe out all human life and you won't have to deal with it? My electric bill was in a pile like that.

7   The irritatingly polite woman told me that they could turn my electricity back on that day, but only if I paid the bill in person before 2 P.M. She told me to pay at a drugstore near where I live. (I don't know why she didn't have me pay at the electric company; probably they don't want anybody to find out their secret method for generating electricity, which I suspect involves a carpet being scuffed by a giant pair of mechanized shoes.)

8   So I had to rush home to get my electric bill, and naturally my car chose that exact moment to be low on gas, so I had to stop at one of those all-purpose gas stations that also sell beer, cigarettes, magazines, hats, beef jerky and hot dogs the same age as Strom Thurmond. Naturally I wound up standing in line behind some moron who was investing his family's grocery money in some kind of state lottery transaction so complex as to require the full attention of ALL THREE store clerks for about 15 minutes, during which time I controlled my stress level by staring laser holes into the back of the moron's neck and shrieking silently, inside my head, WHY

NOT SAVE YOURSELF SOME TIME? WHY NOT JUST SET YOUR MONEY ON FIRE?

9   So as you can imagine I was feeling very nonstressed when, with 2 P.M. rapidly approaching, I finally got back out onto the highway and immediately got stuck in severe traffic behind a driver with ears the size of pie plates who had just this moment arrived here from the year 1937 and had therefore never seen a left-turn arrow. You could see him studying it, trying to figure it out—A green arrow! Pointing left! Here in the left-hand lane! Whatever could it MEAN?—while those of us behind him controlled our stress levels by pounding our horns and then yelping with pain because we had accidentally used the same hand that we had used, in an earlier stress-control effort, to punch our desk.

10   Finally, with only minutes to go, I got to the drugstore—a cramped and dingy place selling unattractive housewares on layaway—and found myself at the end of a long, Soviet-style line of people paying their utility bills in cash, which they pulled out of their wallets one dollar at a time in slow motion, pretending that they couldn't hear my brain shrieking at them HURRY UP YOU FOOLS but of course they knew exactly what they were doing because they were ALL PART OF THE PLOT, along with the electric company and the big-eared driver and the lottery moron and the black federal helicopters constantly monitoring my movements, all of them working together to RAISE MY STRESS LEVEL BUT I KNOW WHAT THEY'RE TRYING TO DO AND IT'S NOT GOING TO WORK HAHAHAHAHAHAHAHAHA HEY GET AWAY FROM ME YOU

Editor's Note: There will be no Dave Barry column this week. Dave is taking the week off.

1. Barry's opening sentences appear to be serious. At what point in your reading did you decide that Barry was not writing in a serious tone?

   _____

2. The title and opening sentences could suggest that Barry's subject is the electric company. What details in the essay lead you to conclude that Barry's subject is something else?

   _____

   _____

3. What is Barry's subject? _____

4. What is his purpose in writing? What does he want to accomplish in this essay?

   _____

5. How would you describe the essay's tone? Serious? Humorous? Ironic? Angry? Something else?

_____

6. What do you conclude to be the author's thesis? Does he have more than one main idea? You may have to write a couple of sentences to state his thesis.

_____

_____

7. List several examples of hyperbole. _____

_____

_____

8. Find an example of understatement in paragraph 3. _____

_____

9. When Barry writes, in paragraph 10, that "they were ALL PART OF THE PLOT," does he mean what he says? If not, what does he mean? What strategy is he using?

_____

_____

_____

10. Explain the ending of the essay. What apparently happens to the narrator, the "I" of the essay? Why is the Editor's note included? How are we to read the note?

_____

_____

_____

11. What parts of the essay did you find the funniest? Why? _____

_____

_____

■ EVALUATING ARGUMENTS AND TAKING A STAND

Evaluating arguments does not mean reading only until you discover a position different from yours and then closing the book. When you read an argument that takes a stand you disagree with, try to stay open-minded while you are reading. You may come away with a better understanding of those with whom you disagree. You may find some common ground and also discover that there are not just two sides to the issue but many "sides."

Reading critically does mean making informed judgments, revising old ideas if necessary, and taking a stand—every time you read. It is a "cop-out" to hold the view that one opinion is as good as another. If you really believed this, you would have to say that decisions to murder, rape, or kidnap are just as valuable as decisions to do your job, be helpful to neighbors, and honest in your dealings with others. Surely you would not try to support such a viewpoint. To be open-minded *while* you read is not the same thing as saying that all positions have equal merit. With some complicated public policy issues, you may feel that you do not know enough to judge someone's argument and take a stand. Try at least to have a position on those parts of the issue that you do understand. For example, you may not know exactly how the tax code should be changed. Still, you could embrace the basic value that there should not be loopholes that allow rich people to avoid paying taxes. When you decide on some basic ideas, you develop guidelines for understanding and evaluating debates on the specifics.

We have already established guidelines for evaluating arguments supporting inferences. Evaluating arguments that support judgments can be more difficult because judgments involve values—and therefore strong emotions. Still, these arguments usually contain some facts, inferences, and reasons in addition to value statements. We can make judgments about the reliability of the facts, the soundness of the inferences, and the logic of the reasons. Many bad arguments can be spotted because they use one or more patterns of illogic that we call *logical fallacies.* These patterns are so common they have been given names. You can find the weaknesses in some arguments by recognizing that they contain logical fallacies.

Recognizing Logical Fallacies

Overstatement: An overstatement is an error in generalizing. The inference, if properly qualified, may be sound, but when stated as a sweeping generalization, it is illogical. Overstatements are frequently signaled by such words as *all, every, always, never,* and *none.* Remember that a statement such as "Children love clowns" is understood to mean "*All* children love clowns." This is an overstatement; some young children are afraid of clowns. Challenge overstatements by thinking of exceptions. For example:

Lawyers are only interested in making money.

(What about Ralph Nader who works to protect consumers?)

Non Sequitur: This Latin term means, literally, "it does not follow." In this type of argument, the "glue" that connects evidence to conclusion is missing. It can be missing because whatever connection the writer sees is not made clear to the reader. It can also be missing because there is no logical connection. The writer has made some false assumptions. You challenge the *non sequitur* by pointing out the false assumptions. For example:

Bill will definitely get a good grade in physics; he loved biology.

(If Bill is not good in math, he will not "love" physics. The illogic comes from assuming that success in one science course predicts success in other science courses. The skills needed are not always the same.)

Slippery Slope: This argument says that we should not take step *A* because if we do so, then the terrible consequences *X*, *Y*, and *Z* will follow. This type of argument oversimplifies by assuming, without evidence and often by ignoring existing laws or traditions, that *X*, *Y*, and *Z* will follow inevitably from *A*. Arguments that project into the future may be sound—based on evidence and logic. For example, economists study present trends to predict future inflation or recessions. The illogic of the slippery slope fallacy occurs when current events and some reasonableness in people are ignored because the writer desperately wants to keep the first step (*A*) from happening. One of the best contemporary examples is found in the gun-control debate:

If we allow the government to control handgun purchases, next is will restrict rifles and then ban all guns, at which point only criminals will have guns.

(Handgun control will not necessarily lead to banning. We restrict and register cars and boats and planes. We have never considered banning them. The United States is a democracy with free elections.)

False Dilemma: A false dilemma occurs when one argues that there are only two choices to deal with a problem, when there are clearly more than two. The either/or thinking of this kind of argument can be effective if we fail to recognize the tactic. If the writer gives us only two choices, and one of those is unacceptable, then the writer can push us toward the preferred choice. You challenge a false dilemma by showing that there are other possibilities. Here is an example:

Either we legalize drugs, or we will never get rid of the country's drug problem.

(Although this argument is appealing, we need to recognize its flawed logic. The anti-drug program has made a difference. We can also get tougher with countries supplying the drugs.)

Post Hoc **Fallacy:** This term (literally, "after this") refers to an error in arguments about causation. The error is confusing a time relationship with a causal relationship. Just because *B* occurs after *A* does not mean, necessarily, that *A* caused *B* to happen. You can challenge illogical causal arguments by explaining more likely causes. For instance:

> Teenage pregnancy is on the increase. It must be the result of all those sex education classes in the high schools.

> (The sex education classes were started to try to address the problems of teenage pregnancies; they are not the cause but an attempted solution to the problem. The classes may not be having much impact on the problem because the real causes remain powerful influences: poverty, history of single parenting in the family, social and psychological needs.)

Straw Man: The straw man fallacy argues that opponents hold views they do not hold. Usually these views are ridiculous and thus easier for the opposition to attack. You point out the weakness in such an argument by explaining that the arguer's opponents do not hold such views, or by demanding that the arguer provide proof that they do hold those views.

> Bilingual education is a mistake because it encourages students to use only their native language.

> (Supporters of bilingual education see it as a way to keep students learning subjects while they also learn English.)

Bandwagon: To argue that an action should be taken or a position accepted because "everyone is doing it" is illogical. The majority is not always right. This is a desperate argument by someone who knows the action or position isn't ethical and can't be defended any other way.

> There's nothing wrong with fudging on your income taxes. Everybody does it, and the government expects everyone to cheat a little.

> (First, not everyone cheats on taxes. Second, if it is wrong, it is wrong no matter how many people do it.)

EXERCISE 10-7 **Recognizing Logical Fallacies**

After reading each passage, explain what is illogical about the argument. Then identify the type of fallacy.

I. We should stop giving handouts to the homeless. The poor of this world, of which we have all been a part at one time in our lives, have pride and work hard to improve themselves. The homeless have no pride and don't try to work.

_____

_____

_____

II. The basic freedoms of America's smokers are at risk today. Tomorrow, who knows what personal behavior will become socially unacceptable, subject to restrictive laws and public ridicule? Could travel by private car make the social engineers' hit list because it is less safe than public transit? Could ice cream, cake and cookies become socially unacceptable because their consumption causes obesity? What about sky diving, mountain climbing, skiing and contact sports? How far will we allow this to spread?

Stanley S. Scott, *New York Times*, December 12, 1984

_____

_____

_____

III. College doesn't seem to make people better. In fact, it seems to make them worse. Think of the "unabomber." Although he is a college graduate and was a college professor, he sent bombs through the mail to kill people. And then there are the lawyers, using all that education to defraud clients by overcharging them. Maybe we should close down the colleges so they can't do any more harm.

_____

_____

_____

Taking a Stand

You may have been cautioned not to "rush to judgment." That is good advice. Decisions should be based on study and thoughtful consideration. Still, at some point, you need to make decisions. As you continue to read for this course and in all your other courses, listen and learn, reflect, and then take a stand.

In the following exercise are excerpts from two long essays on capital punishment. At the beginning of his essay, Ernest van den Haag reminds us that "the death penalty is our harshest punishment. . . . Further, although not intended to cause physical pain, execution is the only corporal punishment still applied to adults. These singular characteristics contribute to the perennial, impassioned controversy about capital punishment." Indeed, the debate continues and it evokes passion, as debates on serious moral issues should. As you read these excerpts, observe the writers' tones that blend high seriousness and emotion.

Exercise 10-8 Taking a Stand

Read each passage and answer the questions related to it. Then answer the questions on the issue. The first excerpt is from "The Ultimate Punishment: A Defense." written by psychoanalyst Ernest van den Haag and published in 1986 in the Harvard Law Review. *The second excerpt is from "Capital Punishment," written by law Professor Anthony G. Amsterdam and published in the 1977 issue of* Stanford Magazine.

From "The Ultimate Punishment: A Defense"

1   We threaten punishments in order to deter crime. We impose them not only to make the threats credible but also as retribution (justice) for the crimes that were not deterred. Threats and punishments are necessary to deter and deterrence is a sufficient practical justification for them. Retribution is an independent moral justification. Although penalties can be unwise, repulsive, or inappropriate, and those punished can be pitiable, in a sense the infliction of legal punishment on a guilty person cannot be unjust. By committing the crime, the criminal volunteered to assume the risk of receiving a legal punishment that he could have avoided by not committing the crime. The punishment he suffers is the punishment he voluntarily risked suffering and, therefore, it is no more unjust to him than any other event for which one knowingly volunteers to assume the risk. Thus, the death penalty cannot be unjust to the guilty criminal.

2   There remain, however, two moral objections. The penalty may be regarded as always excessive as retribution and always morally degrading. To regard the death penalty as always excessive, one must believe that no crime—no matter how heinous—could possibly justify capital punishment. Such a belief can be neither corroborated nor refuted; it is an article of faith.

3   Alternatively, or concurrently, one may believe that everybody, the murderer no less than the victim, has an imprescriptible (natural?) right to life. The law therefore should not deprive anyone of life. I share Jeremy Bentham's view that any such "natural and imprescriptible rights" are "nonsense upon stilts."

1. What is the purpose of punishing a criminal, according to van den Haag?

   _____

2. Explain, in your own words, the author's justification of legal punishment, including the death penalty.

   _____

   _____

3. To argue that the death penalty is always excessive, what must one believe? Does the author believe this?

_____

_____

From "Capital Punishment"

1   Capital punishment is a dying institution in this last quarter of the twentieth century. It has already been abandoned in law or in fact throughout most of the civilized world. England, Canada, the Scandinavian countries, virtually all of Western Europe except for France and Spain have abolished the death penalty. The vast majority of countries in the Western Hemisphere have abolished it. Its last strongholds in the world—apart from the United States—are in Asia and Africa, particularly South Africa. Even the countries which maintain capital punishment on the books have almost totally ceased to use it in fact. In the United States, considering only the last half century, executions have plummeted from 199 in 1935 to approximately 29 a year during the decade before 1967, when the ten-year judicial moratorium began.

2   Do you doubt that this development will continue? Do you doubt that it will continue because it is the path of civilization—the path up out of fear and terror and the barbarism that terror breeds, into self-confidence and decency in the administration of justice? The road, like any other built by men, has its detours, but over many generations it has run true, and will run true. And there will therefore come a time—perhaps in 20 years, perhaps in 50 or 100, but very surely and very shortly as the lifetime of nations is measured—when our children will look back at us in horror and unbelief because of what we did in their names and for their supposed safety, just as we look back in horror and unbelief at the thousands of crucifixions and beheadings and live disembowelments that our ancestors practiced for the supposed purpose of making our world safe from murderers and robbers, thieves, shoplifters, and pickpockets.

3   All of these kinds of criminals are still with us, and will be with our children—although we can certainly decrease their numbers and their damage, and protect ourselves from them a lot better, if we insist that our politicians stop pounding on the whipping boy of capital punishment and start coming up with some real solutions to the real problems of crime. Our children will cease to execute murderers for the same reason that we have ceased to string up pickpockets and shoplifters at the public crossroads, although there are still plenty of them around. Our children will cease to execute murderers because executions are a self-deluding, self-defeating, self-degrading, futile, and entirely stupid means of dealing with the crime of murder, and because our children will prefer to be something better than murderers themselves. Should we not—can we not—make the same choice now?

1. What has been the history of capital punishment? _____

   _____

2. What does Amsterdam predict about its future? _____

   _____

3. What is Amsterdam's position on capital punishment, and what are the reasons for his position?

   _____

   _____

On the Issue:

Amsterdam argues that capital punishment is, among other things, futile. Here he is referring to the issue of deterrence, which he discusses earlier in his essay. Legal scholars have found no evidence that capital punishment deters crimes that would get the death penalty. Van den Haag argues that the threat is appropriate if there is any possibility of deterrence, but that retribution is a sufficient reason for the death penalty. What do you think?

1. Which writer makes the more convincing argument in the excerpt that you have read? Why?

   _____

   _____

2. What view on the death penalty did you hold before reading these excerpts?

   _____

3. Has your view influenced your evaluation of these two arguments? Has your view changed at all from having read the two arguments? Explain.

   _____

   _____

The goal of critical thinking is to solve problems. We need to make decisions about where to attend school or what kind of career goals are best for us. As responsible citizens we need to understand the issues of political debate and prepare ourselves to vote in elections. As humans we need to develop a moral code, to think about how we want to live with family, friends, co-workers, and strangers. We need to think about the kind of person we want to be and to become. That's a long list of problems to solve and decisions to make. We don't make them all at once, or only once. Learning is a lifetime activity. As we read and talk to others and listen and learn, we continually revise our plans and goals and values. Sometimes we make mistakes; sometimes we have to get rid of bad habits, false facts, and misguided codes. The key is to seize every opportunity to learn, to think, and to reevaluate who we are and what we believe. College offers you many opportunities to learn and grow. Seize them.

Selection 1 **Stranger-Danger**

by **Ellen Goodman**

Ellen Goodman has been a feature writer for the *Boston Globe* since 1967 and a syndicated columnist since 1976. Several collections of her columns have been published, and she has won a Pulitzer Prize for distinguished commentary. The following column appeared on July 15, 1995.

Prepare

1. From what you know about the author and the selection, what can you predict about purpose and format or style?

   _____

   _____

2. State briefly what you expect to read about. _____

   _____

3. What do you already know about the topic? Respond using *one* of the methods described in Chapter 2.

   _____

   _____

4. Use the title to pose questions about the reading selection. _____

   _____

5. Preread the selection. Then read and annotate the article. Finally, complete the comprehension and vocabulary checks and answer the questions for discussion and reflection.

1   Casco Bay, Maine—I pass the children every day now as they walk and bike down the island roads by themselves. They are off on their own errands or adventures.

2   The parents who come here from the mainland have finally shed their anxieties like three-piece suits. Sometimes, it takes days for city folks to let a 4-year-old out of their grasp and an 8-year-old out of their sight. It takes days for parents to feel safe and for children to be set free.

3   Gradually the summer adults ratchet down the level of warnings they routinely deliver to their children. They go from "beware of strangers" to "watch out for poison ivy." Gradually the children, unleashed, grow sturdy with independence. And trust.

4   Just this morning, a small girl I don't know stopped me on my walk to point out an injured swallowtail. We talked for a minute about the fragility of a butterfly's wings and then went our separate ways.

It was a passing event but one that might never have happened on a city street. In cities, suburbs, even small towns, children are now carefully taught to be afraid of people they don't know. Their wariness is worn like a shield. A stranger becomes reluctant to penetrate that defense.

5   Far south of here, in Union, S.C., Susan Smith has gone on trial for drowning her two small children. As the cameras return to that little town, I remember how this saga began—not as a horror story of two children buckled into their death seats by their mother but as a classic, mythic tale of the stranger.

6   Susan Smith came to national fame as a distraught mother, a self-described victim of carjacking and kidnapping. When it all unraveled, and she was taken to court for arraignment, many people lined the streets shouting epithets at her. One woman said it all: "We believed you!" It was strikingly easy to play upon the fear of the stranger.

7   Far west of here, in Petaluma, Calif., another murder trial has begun this week. This defendant is indeed the stranger, a man named Richard Allen Davis, who confessed to abducting 12-year-old Polly Klaas at knife-point from a slumber party while her sister and mother slept nearby.

8   Nearly two years later, another Petaluma mother of kids 11 and 13 says, "I'm still very leery when my kids go out. I won't let them go out by themselves. I say, 'Remember Polly Klaas.' "

9   In vastly different ways, these two horrifying trials are evidence of what has become a national obsession with the fear of strangers. As fact and fantasy, they are evidence of our terror about the abduction of our children.

10 It was only a decade ago that missing children became as common on milk cartons as nutritional labels. It wasn't until then that we began to

fingerprint and toothprint children. But by 1991 a study in Clinical Pedi-atrics showed that parents had more frequent worries about abduction than about anything else, even car accidents. That was before Polly Klaas's death.

11   In fact, there are 200 to 300 kidnappings a year by non-family members out of 63 million American children. The missing children on the milk cartons have most likely been taken by a noncustodial parent.

12   However bone-chilling the idea of stranger-danger, more children are murdered by parents than are kidnapped by strangers. Susan Smith is more the norm than Richard Allen Davis.

13   Yet every magazine has had its cover stories on stranger danger, every television show its scare segments, every school its lessons. In every home, parents wrestle with their terrors and with how to warn their children away from the unfamiliar.

14   I'm not surprised that we have become so protective of children. It isn't just the broadcasting of such tales. We live in a time when neighborhoods and families are less stable. As our children spend more time out of our care, we worry more. As we know fewer people in our communities, there are, by definition, more outsiders.

15   But at some point in time, we must also begin to acknowledge the risks of protectiveness. Risks that come when children are taught to be afraid. Risks that come to a diverse society when kids grow up suspicious of "others."

16   Somewhere along the tortuous way, somewhere between the reality of Richard Allen Davis and the fantasy of Susan Smith, the freedom to ride a bicycle and the independence to walk up the road by yourself is becoming a sometime, summertime thing. These days, even the ease of talking with a grown-up about butterflies can, and maybe has, become as rare as a July day on an island road.

Comprehension Check ▪

Circle the appropriate letter.

_____ 1. The best statement of the main idea is:
   a. Be wary of strangers.
   b. Children need vacations to learn independence.
   c. We need to find a balance between warning children about strangers and letting them become independent and trusting.
   d. The Susan Smith story teaches that children are more at risk from parents than from strangers.

Fill in the blanks to complete each of the following statements.

2. A swallowtail is a _____ .

3. Children are being taught to be _____ .

4. Teaching children to be suspicious of people who are different has social

_____ .

Answer the following with a T (true) or F (false).

	T	F
5. No one believed that Susan Smith's children were killed by a stranger.	___	___
6. Polly Klaas's murderer was a family friend.	___	___
7. Missing children have most likely been taken by a noncustodial parent.	___	___
8. Today, in many communities, there are more strangers.	___	___

Expanding Vocabulary

Review the following words in their contexts and then write a brief definition or synonym for each word based on what you can learn from context clues.

ratchet (3) _____

wariness (5) _____

saga (6) _____

mythic (6) _____

epithets (7) _____

leery (9) _____

Analysis of Content and Strategies

1. How seriously do we perceive the danger from strangers to be?

_____

2. How serious is the danger from strangers? _____

_____

3. The greatest risks to children come from what group?

_____

4. What does Goodman use, or draw on, as a way to begin her essay?

_____

How does she use this material later in the piece?

_____

_____

What makes this an effective strategy? _____

_____

5. What two examples does Goodman use from recent news events?

_____

6. What do the examples illustrate? _____

_____

7. What is Goodman's thesis? _____

_____

For Discussion and Reflection

1. Were you surprised by Goodman's statistics? If so, why? What has been your source of information about the dangers to children?

2. If you were a parent, how would you try to balance appropriate warnings about strangers with independence and trust?

3. Do you think the media are to blame for increasing fear, and for misdirecting our fears? What, if anything, should be done?

4. Should Susan Smith's father be prosecuted for rape and child abuse? Why or why not? Take a stand on the issue.

Selection 2   Ban the Things. Ban Them All.

by **Molly Ivins**

Molly Ivins is a journalist with the *Fort Worth Star-Telegram* and a syndicated columnist. She also writes articles for magazines, including the *Nation* and *Ms.* The following column, displaying her well-known wit and irreverent style, was published March 16, 1993.

■ **Prepare**

1. From what you know about the author and the selection, what can you predict about purpose and format or style?

_____

_____

2. State briefly what you expect to read about. _____

_____

3. What do you already know about the topic? Respond using *one* of the methods described in Chapter 2.

_____

_____

4. Use the title to pose questions about the reading selection. _____

_____

5. Preread the selection. Then read and annotate the article. Finally, complete the comprehension and vocabulary checks and answer the questions for discussion and reflection.

1   AUSTIN—Guns. Everywhere guns.

2   Let me start this discussion by pointing out that I am not anti-gun. I'm pro-knife. Consider the merits of the knife.

3   In the first place, you have to catch up with someone to stab him. A general substitution of knives for guns would promote physical fitness. We'd turn into a whole nation of great runners. Plus, knives don't ricochet. And people are seldom killed while cleaning their knives.

4   As a civil libertarian, I of course support the Second Amendment. And I believe it means exactly what it says: "A well-regulated militia being necessary to the security of a free state, the right of the people to keep and bear arms shall not be infringed." Fourteen-year-old boys are not part of a well-regulated militia. Members of wacky religious cults are not part of a well-regulated militia. Permitting unregulated citizens to have guns is destroying the security of this free state.

5   I am intrigued by the arguments of those who claim to follow the judicial doctrine of original intent. How do they know it was the dearest wish

of Thomas Jefferson's heart that teenage drug dealers should cruise the cities of this nation perforating their fellow citizens with assault rifles? Channeling?

6   There is more hooey spread about the Second Amendment. It says quite clearly that guns are for those who form part of a well-regulated militia, i.e., the armed forces including the National Guard. The reasons for keeping them away from everyone else gets clearer by the day.

7   The comparison most often used is that of the automobile, another lethal object that is regularly used to wreak great carnage. Obviously, this society is full of people who haven't got enough common sense to use an automobile properly. But we haven't outlawed cars yet.

8   We do, however, license them and their owners, restrict their use to presumably sane and sober adults and keep track of who sells them to whom. At a minimum, we should do the same with guns.

9   In truth, there is no rational argument for guns in this society. This is no longer a frontier nation in which people hunt their own food. It is a crowded, overwhelmingly urban country in which letting people have access to guns is a continuing disaster. Those who want guns—whether for target shooting, hunting or potting rattlesnakes (get a hoe)—should be subject to the same restrictions placed on gun owners in England—a nation in which liberty has survived nicely without an armed populace.

10   The argument that "guns don't kill people" is patent nonsense. Anyone who has ever worked in a cop shop knows how many family arguments end in murder because there was a gun in the house. Did the gun kill someone? No. But if there had been no gun, no one would have died. At least not without a good footrace first. Guns do kill. Unlike cars, that is all they do.

11   Michael Crichton makes an interesting argument about technology in his thriller "Jurassic Park." He points out that power without discipline is making this society into a wreckage. By the time someone who studies the martial arts becomes a master—literally able to kill with bare hands—that person has also undergone years of training and discipline. But any fool can pick up a gun and kill with it.

12   "A well-regulated militia" surely implies both long training and long discipline. That is the least, the very least, that should be required of those who are permitted to have guns, because a gun is literally the power to kill. For years, I used to enjoy taunting my gun-nut friends about their psychosexual hangups—always in a spirit of good cheer, you understand. But letting the noisy minority in the National Rifle Association force us to allow this carnage to continue is just plain insane.

13   I do think gun nuts have a power hangup. I don't know what is missing in their psyches that they need to feel they have the power to kill. But no sane society would allow this to continue.

14   Ban the damn things. Ban them all.

15   You want protection? Get a dog.

Comprehension Check

Fill in the blanks to complete each of the following statements.

1. The Second Amendment says that guns are for those in _____ .

2. Ivins believes that guns, like _____ , should be registered and restricted.

3. People should not have power without _____ .

4. People who want protection should get a _____ .

Answer the following with a T (true) or F (false).,

	T	F
5. Because she supports the Second Amendment, Ivins is opposed to gun control.	___	___
6. Ivins believes that guns do kill.	___	___
7. People should not be allowed to have guns for hunting or target shooting.	___	___
8. Gun-nuts have, according to Ivins, psychosexual hang-ups.	___	___

Expanding Vocabulary

List the words for which you need a definition. Look them up in your dictionary and write down the definition that works in this context.

Word	**Definition**
_____	_____
_____	_____
_____	_____
_____	_____
_____	_____

Analysis of Content and Strategies

1. What is Ivins's thesis? _____

_____

2. Where does she state it?

_____

_____

3. What, according to Ivins, does the Second Amendment mean?

_____

_____

4. What, at a minimum, does the author want? _____

_____

5. List words that have negative connotations. _____

_____

6. What type of sentence does Ivins use frequently, particularly at the beginning and end of the essay?

_____

7. What tone is created by her style? _____

8. When the author says that she is "pro-knife," in what way is she serious?

_____

What else does she accomplish by her paragraph on the knife?

_____

_____

For Discussion and Reflection

1. Pro-gun groups use the Second Amendment as a strong part of their argument. Has Ivins effectively challenged their argument? Does she effectively challenge the "guns don't kill" argument? Be prepared to explain and defend your evaluation of her argument.

2. What readers might be offended by this column? Then, to what readers is Ivins writing?

3. How might Ivins defend her "in your face" approach to the topic? Why does she think this approach is necessary?

4. Where do you stand on the issue of gun control? Has your position affected the way you have read and responded to this argument?

Selection 3   **Why Women Are Paid Less Than Men**

by **Lester C. Thurow**

Lester Thurow is a professor at MIT and a consultant both to government and private companies. He has written books and articles on economics and public-policy issues. The following article was published in the *New York Times* on March 8, 1981.

Prepare

1. From what you know about the author and the selection, what can you predict about purpose and format or style?

_____

_____

2. State briefly what you expect to read about. _____

_____

3. What do you already know about the topic? Respond using *one* of the methods described in Chapter 2.

_____

_____

_____

4. Use the title to pose questions about the reading selection. _____

_____

5. Preread the selection. Then read and annotate the article. Finally, complete the comprehension and vocabulary checks and answer the questions for discussion and reflection.

1   In the 40 years from 1939 to 1979 white women who work full time have with monotonous regularity made slightly less than 60 percent as much as white men. Why?

2   Over the same time period, minorities have made substantial progress in catching up with whites, with minority women making even more progress than minority men.

3   Black men now earn 72 percent as much as white men (up 16 percentage points since the mid-1950s) but black women earn 92 percent as much as white women. Hispanic men make 71 percent of what their white counterparts do, but Hispanic women make 82 percent as much as white women. As a result of their faster progress, fully employed black women make 75 percent as much as fully employed black men while Hispanic women earn 68 percent as much as Hispanic men.

4   This faster progress may, however, end when minority women finally catch up with white women. In the bible of the New Right, George Gilder's "Wealth and Poverty," the 60 percent is just one of Mother Nature's constants like the speed of light or the force of gravity.

5   Men are programmed to provide for their families economically while women are programmed to take care of their families emotionally and physically. As a result men put more effort into their jobs than women. The net result is a difference in work intensity that leads to that 40 percent gap in earnings. But there is no discrimination against women—only the biological facts of life.

6   The problem with this assertion is just that. It is an assertion with no evidence for it other than the fact that white women have made 60 percent as much as men for a long period of time.

7   "Discrimination against women" is an easy answer but it also has its problems as an adequate explanation. Why is discrimination against women not declining under the same social forces that are leading to a lessening of discrimination against minorities? In recent years women have made more use of the enforcement provisions of the Equal Employment Opportunities Commission and the courts than minorities. Why do the laws that prohibit discrimination against women and minorities work for minorities but not for women?

8   When men discriminate against women, they run into a problem. To discriminate against women is to discriminate against your own wife and to lower your own family income. To prevent women from working is to force men to work more.

9   When whites discriminate against blacks, they can at least think that they are raising their own incomes. When men discriminate against women they have to know that they are lowering their own family income and increasing their own work effort.

10 While discrimination undoubtedly explains part of the male-female earnings differential, one has to believe that men are monumentally stupid or irrational to explain all of the earnings gap in terms of discrimination. There must be something else going on.

11   Back in 1939 it was possible to attribute the earnings gap to large differences in educational attainments. But the educational gap between men and women has been eliminated since World War II. It is no longer possible to use education as an explanation for the lower earnings of women.

12   Some observers have argued that women earn less money since they are less reliable workers who are more apt to leave the labor force. But it is difficult to maintain this position since women are less apt to quit one job to take another and as a result they tend to work as long, or longer, for any one employer. From any employer's perspective they are more reliable, not less reliable, than men.

13   Part of the answer is visible if you look at the lifetime earnings profile of men. Suppose that you were asked to predict which men in a group of 25-year-olds would become economically successful. At age 25 it is difficult to tell who will be economically successful and your predictions are apt to be highly inaccurate.

14   But suppose that you were asked to predict which men in a group of 35-year-olds would become economically successful. If you are successful at age 35, you are very likely to remain successful for the rest of your life. If you have not become economically successful by age 35, you are very unlikely to do so later.

15   The decade between 25 and 35 is when men either succeed or fail. It is the decade when lawyers become partners in the good firms, when business managers make it onto the "fast track," when academics get tenure at good universities, and when blue collar workers find the job opportunities that will lead to training opportunities and the skills that will generate high earnings.

16   If there is any one decade when it pays to work hard and to be consistently in the labor force, it is the decade between 25 and 35. For those who succeed, earnings will rise rapidly. For those who fail, earnings will remain flat for the rest of their lives.

17   But the decade between 25 and 35 is precisely the decade when women are most apt to leave the labor force or become part-time workers to have children. When they do, the current system of promotion and skill acquisition will extract an enormous lifetime price.

18   This leaves essentially two avenues for equalizing male and female earnings.

19   Families where women who wish to have successful careers, compete with men, and achieve the same earnings should alter their family plans and have their children either before 25 or after 35. Or society can attempt to alter the existing promotion and skill acquisition system so that there is a longer time period in which both men and women can attempt to successfully enter the labor force.

20   Without some combination of these two factors, a substantial fraction of the male-female earnings differentials are apt to persist for the next 40 years, even if discrimination against women is eliminated.

Comprehension Check ·

Fill in the blanks to complete each of the following statements.

1. From 1939 to 1979, white women made _____ percent as much as white men.

2. Conservatives (the New Right) explain the difference in income as the result of _____ , not _____ .

3. Women are more _____ workers than men.

4. Men who are not successful by the time they are _____ are not likely to become successful.

5. Women need to remain _____ between the ages of twenty-five and thirty-five to compete equally with men.

Answer the following with a T (true) or F (false).

		T	F
6.	Hispanic women earn more than Hispanic men.	___	___
7.	Thurow believes that the income difference is explained by biological differences.	___	___
8.	Thurow believes that discrimination against women is not the primary cause of the income gap.	___	___
9.	The income gap is the result of differences in education.	___	___

Expanding Vocabulary ·

Review the following words in their contexts and then write a brief definition or synonym for each word.

monotonous (1) _____

counterparts (3) _____

differential (10) _____

monumentally (10) _____

acquisition (17) _____

extract (17) _____

Analysis of Content and Strategies

1. What is Thurow's subject? _____

2. What writing strategy does he use? (When he asks "Why?" at the end of paragraph 1, what strategy does that signal?)

_____

3. List each of the arguments that Thurow examines and his reason for dismissing each one.

_____

_____

_____

_____

4. What is Thurow's explanation for the difference in income between men and women?

_____

_____

5. Evaluate Thurow's two solutions. If he is right about the cause of the problem, are his solutions good ones?

_____

_____

6. Thurow says that most people who are going to be successful will be so by age thirty-five. Is this statement fact or opinion? _____ Do you agree with the statement? _____ If you do not agree, what evidence would you need to challenge the assertion?

_____

7. The author's figures are based on the total earnings of all full-time workers; they are not comparisons by job category. What facts about the jobs that men and women hold may account for some of the difference in pay?

_____

_____

8. Do you think that Thurow underestimates the degree of discrimination against women? _____ Why or why not?

_____

For Discussion and Reflection: Take a Stand on the Following Issues.

1. Should women be able to take time out for children without this hurting their careers? Why or why not?

2. How can women be encouraged to enter well-paying fields such as engineering?

3. Should men be favored over women in advancement? Should affirmative action be continued to help women and minorities gain access to jobs?

4. Should all workers receive equal pay for equal work?

CHAPTER 11

Living and Working in the Twenty-First Century

A new century is almost upon us. The year 2000: all those zeros give us pause and suggest that we reflect on where we are headed and where we may want to go. The nineteenth century took us into the Industrial Age, the twentieth century into the Information Age or the Age of Technology—take your choice. Modern communications technology has changed the world. Indeed, the former Soviet Union and Eastern bloc countries could not keep out Western ideas and images from freedom and human rights to Levis and rock and roll. Modern communications helped bring down the Berlin Wall and break apart the Soviet regime.

Modern technology has also changed our individual lives. Television brings the world into 98 percent of American homes. Classes are now taught through television and tele-conferencing programs. And there are few jobs, from sales clerks to CEOs, not dependent upon a worker's computer literacy.

Have we been given more than we bargained for? Liesl Schillinger thinks so. In "Who's Afraid of the Year 2000?" Schillinger writes:

> It would be possible to go on endlessly chronicling the changes in this century that have left us so jaded: the transformation of narcotics from rare vice to international youth pastime; the decline of heterosexual romance and rise of unconsidered sexuality; the loss of leisure time; the end of the large family; the death of the notion that technology must bring social progress—and so on.

These are sobering thoughts. Schillinger might have added the isolating nature of much technology. Television separates us from community—even from family members as each one tunes into a different channel in a separate room in the house. We used to write letters, long newsy letters that expressed feelings. Now we leave messages on machines, or we e-mail. Some banks actually charge customers who want to transact business the old-fashioned way: with a live teller. We are supposed to grow up and use the machine outside the bank. The microwave not only frees "Mom" from cooking; it frees the entire family from having to eat together.

In the process of making progress, we extended life, decreased infant mortality, vaccinated away deadly diseases, and cured others with antibiotics. However, we now face a population explosion that places heavy demands on the environment, pollution of the air and water from both industry and "modern" farming, the stresses of crowded urban living, a projected 20 million HIV-positive cases by the year 2000, and an aging population counting on a Social Security system that will run out of funds. Is this really progress? What are the answers to today's problems? And how do we plan for a new century in the hope that we will not repeat some of the mistakes of this one?

These are tough questions. The writers in this chapter examine the present and explore the future, focusing primarily on problems in the environment, education, and the world of work. Underlying their discussions are questions of values. How do we choose between industry and the environment? How do we balance economic growth with preserving our Earth and our traditions? How do we exercise justice, promote tolerance, maintain freedoms, and cherish community? What do you think? Read and reflect. Learn and then act on your knowledge.

Environmental Health

Rebecca J. Donatelle and Lorraine G. Davis

The following selection is part of a chapter from the third edition of the textbook *Access to Health*. Dr. Donatelle is a professor and Coordinator of Graduate Studies in the Oregon State University Department of Public Health. Dr. Davis is a professor of health education at the University of Oregon. Both authors are well-known health educators.

This excerpt will give you practice in reading graphs and charts, in addition to learning about the key problems that put the health of the environment—and ourselves—at risk.

Questions for Discussion and Reflection:

1. What environmental health issues are examined by the authors?
2. Which ones are new to you?
3. Which problem do you think is the most serious for the twenty-first century? Why?
4. What do you think are the best ways to deal with this problem?

Environmental Health

Thinking Globally, Acting Locally

WHAT DO YOU THINK?

The chaotic, unplanned cities of the Third World are often dangerous places. In Calcutta, the Metropolitan Development Authority has been filling in fragile marshlands for new development on the periphery of the city while land in parts of the central city is underused. Many Asian cities have serious housing shortages even though vast tracts of vacant land lie nearby. In Dakar, Senegal, a municipal dump will soon be completely surrounded by housing whose residents will draw their drinking water from nearby wells. The most deadly automobile-caused air pollution and the worst traffic jams are often found in Third World cities even though they have much smaller vehicle fleets than do large cities in the developed world.

■ What responsibility do those of us in the developed world have to help reduce population growth and curb pollution in developing nations? Would you be willing to pay 1 percent of your tax dollars to help other nations develop environmental programs?

In 1985, one environmental activist, Pat Bryant, began focusing attention on the poor people living in the lower Mississippi Valley's "Cancer Alley," so-called because one-fourth of the nation's chemicals are produced in this area. Bryant worked with groups to improve housing conditions in the area and then focused on the industrial pollution in the region. Within a year, he had mobilized people from several environmental groups to stage a 10-day demonstration known as the Great Louisiana Toxics March, after which he became the director of the Louisiana Toxics Project. As a result of Bryant's efforts, the Louisiana legislature passed the state's first air quality act in 1989.

■ What can we as individuals do to stop pollution and its attendant problems? What factors put environmental groups and big business at odds with each other?

Human health, well-being, and survival are ultimately dependent on the integrity of the planet on which we live. Today the natural world is under attack from the pressure of the enormous numbers of people who live in it, and the wide range of their activities (see the Health Headlines box). Even though the United States has made measurable environmental progress in recent years, our environmental achievements allow no room for complacency. An informed citizenry having a strong commitment to care for the environment is essential to the survival of our planet.

Americans' concern about the environment has intensified since the initial outpouring on the first Earth Day in April 1970. Public opinion polls show that concern for the environment has become a core value for virtually every sector of our society. The number of people who view pollution as a pressing personal concern has tripled in the 1990s. A 1991 study by Environment Opinion Study found that 71 percent of Americans agree that "improving the quality of the environment can create jobs and help the national economy." And a Gallup poll reported that 78 percent of Americans now consider themselves environmentalists.[1]

OVERPOPULATION

Our most challenging environmental problem is population growth. The anthropologist Margaret Mead wrote, "Every human society is faced with not one population problem but two: how to beget and rear enough children and how not to beget and rear too many."[2]

The world population is increasing at unprecedented numbers. In early 1990, it was nearly 5.3 billion and 23 babies were born every 5 seconds: that's 397,440 new people every day, or 145 million every year. This rate gives the planet an annual net population gain of 93 million people. Population experts believe that unless current birth and death rates change radically, 10.4 billion people will be competing for the world's diminishing resources by the year 2029.[3] Table 23.1 shows world population growth by decade, with projections through the year 2029.

The population explosion is not distributed equally around the world. The United States and western Europe have the lowest birth rates. At the same time, these two regions produce more grain and other foodstuffs than their populations consume. Countries that can least afford a high birth rate in economic, social, health, and nutritional terms are the ones with the most rapidly expanding populations.

The vast bulk of population growth in developing countries is occurring in urban areas. Third World cities' populations are doubling every 10 to 15 years, overwhelming their governments' attempts to provide clean water, sewage facilities, adequate transportation, and other basic services. As early as 1964, researcher Ronald Wraith described the Third World giant city plagued by pollution and shantytowns as, "megalopolis—the city running riot with no one able to control it."[4] In 1950, only 3 of the world's 10 largest cities were in the Third World; by 1980, 7 of them were, and this trend is expected to continue into the next century (see Table 23.2).

As the global population expands, so does the competition for the earth's resources. Environmental degradation caused by loss of topsoil, pesticides, toxic residues, deforestation, global warming, air pollution, and acid rain seriously threatens the food supply and undermines world health.

In China, the goal of one child per family is promoted by the government in its effort to reduce the birth rate and gain control of the many problems associated with overpopulation.

Environmental Facts

■ An assessment of urban air quality jointly undertaken by the World Health Organization and the United Nations Environment Programme reports that 625 million people around the globe are exposed to unhealthy levels of sulfur dioxide resulting from fossil fuel burning. More than 1 billion people—a fifth of the planet's population—are exposed to potentially health-damaging levels of air pollutants of all kinds.

■ At the end of the International Drinking Water Supply and Sanitation Decade (1981–1990), 1 billion people were without a safe water supply and almost 1.8 billion did not have adequate sanitation facilities.

■ The United Nations Conference on Environment and Development—the Earth Summit—met in Rio de Janeiro, Brazil, in June 1992. Perhaps the most remarkable achievement of this conference was Agenda 21, a 900-page action plan for protecting the atmosphere, the oceans, and other global resources. The Earth Summit marked the arrival of environmental concerns as a major new international consideration.

■ In the United States, 70 monitoring stations have identified crop-damaging concentrations of ground-level ozone in every part of the country. A joint study by the EPA and the U.S. Department of Agriculture indicates that crops are affected in varying degrees, depending on their sensitivity to air pollutants. Applying these proportions to the annual harvest, which has a market value of around $70 billion, this amounts to a loss of $3 billion to $7 billion caused by air pollution.

■ Until cholera broke out in Peru in 1991, there had been no epidemics of that disease in Latin America or the Caribbean for almost a century. Yet, since January 1991, cholera has invaded 19 countries. Over 600,000 cases and more than 6,000 deaths have been reported. The siege of cholera has revealed appalling inadequacies and inequalities in the provision of clean water, sanitation, and health care.

■ Lead is a silent hazard in many American homes: 74 percent of all private housing built before 1980 contains some lead paint; one of nine children under the age of six has enough lead in his or her blood to be at risk for serious health problems; children with high lead levels are six times more likely to have reading disabilities.

■ An Oregon woman founded Deja, Inc. to manufacture Eco Sneakers from used textiles, rubber products, and other consumer waste. Turtle Plastics in Cleveland, Ohio, turns used swimming pool liners and scrap automobile trim into industrial floor matting and urinal screens. Earth Partners, also based in Oregon, plans to make newsprint into floor paneling material and molded panels for hollow-core doors.

■ Refilling bottles, once a common practice in this country, has virtually disappeared. In the early 1960s, 89 percent of all packaged soft drinks and nearly 50 percent of all packaged beer were sold in refillable bottles. Today only about 6 percent of all packaged beer and soft drinks combined is sold in refillables. By comparison, Germany mandates that 72 percent of beverages must be sold in refillable containers.

■ Helped by the U.S. Customs Service, the EPA has filed administrative actions, seeking a total of $9.8 million in fines, against 21 companies for illegal import or export of chemicals and hazardous wastes. A number of these cases involve shipments across the Canadian and Mexican borders.

Nowhere are these threats more visible than in Third World countries in Africa, Asia, and Latin America. The combination of falling economic levels and rising grain prices due to grain scarcity has frequently led to famine in these areas. An estimated 40,000 children under the age of five die each day in these countries from severe nutritional deprivation and related infectious diseases.[5] Drought in the late 1980s reduced world grain stocks to their lowest levels since the 1950s. Grain harvests in 1989 were 18 million tons below the projected consumption level, and grain stores were further depleted.[6]

Harvests are directly affected by the state of the environment. Air pollution and acid rain affect crops, as do global warming, deforestation, soil erosion, and toxic waste disposal. The ways in which these environmental issues specifically relate to human health and survival will be discussed throughout this chapter.

At first examination, it may seem that there is little we can do as individuals to alleviate these conditions in Third World countries. We can begin to do our part, however, by recognizing that the United States consumes far more energy and raw materials per person than does any other nation on earth. Many of these resources come from other countries, and our consumption is depleting the resource balances of those countries. Therefore, we must start by living environmentally conscious lives.

Perhaps the simplest course of action we can take is to control our own reproductivity. The concept of zero population growth (ZPG) was born in the 1960s. Proponents of this idea believed that each couple should produce only two offspring. When the parents die, the two offspring are their replacements, and the population stabilizes.

The continued preference for large families in many developing nations is caused by such factors as high infant

RATE YOURSELF

It's Not Easy Being Green

Circle the number of each item that describes what you have done or are doing to help the environment.

1. When walking or camping I never leave anything behind.

2. I ride my bike, walk, carpool or use public transportation whenever possible.

3. I have written my representative in the state or federal government about environmental issues.

4. I avoid turning on the air conditioner or heat whenever possible.

5. My shower has a low-flow shower head.

6. I do not run the water while brushing my teeth, shaving, or handwashing clothes.

7. I take showers instead of baths.

8. My sink faucets have aerators installed in them.

9. I have a water displacement device in my toilet.

10. I snip or rip plastic six-pack rings before I throw them out.

11. I choose recycled and recyclable products.

12. I avoid noise pollutants (I sit away from speakers at concerts, select an apartment away from busy streets or airports, and so on.)

13. I make sure my car is tuned and has functional emission control equipment.

14. I try to avoid known carcinogens such as vinyl chloride, asbestos, benzene, mercury, X-rays, and so on.

15. I don't buy products that contain CFCs or methylchloroform.

16. When shopping, I choose products having the least amount of packaging.

17. I dispose of hazardous materials (old car batteries, used oil, or used antifreeze) at gas stations or other appropriate sites.

18. If I have children or when I have children, I will use a diaper service as opposed to disposable diapers.

19. I store food in glass jars and waxed paper rather than in plastic wrap.

20. I use as few paper products as possible.

21. I take my own bag along when I go shopping.

22. I avoid products packaged in plastic and unrecycled aluminum.

23. I recycle newspapers, glass, cans, and other recyclables.

24. I run the clothes dryer only as long as it takes my clothes to dry.

25. I turn off lights and appliances when they are not in use.

Scoring and Interpretation

Count how many items you have circled. Ideally, you can be doing all these things, but if you are trying to do at least some, you can score yourself as follows:

20–25	Good contributions to maintaining the environment.
14–19	Moderate contributions to maintaining the environment.
Below 13	Need to consider the recommendations made in this chapter to help the environment.

---

mortality rates; the traditional view of children as "social security" (they not only work from a young age to assist families in daily survival but also support parents when they are too old to work); the low educational and economic status of women; and the traditional desire for sons that keeps parents of several daughters reproducing until they get male offspring. Moreover, some developing nations feel that overpopulation is not as great a problem as the inequitable distribution of wealth and resources, both within their countries and worldwide. For all these reasons, demographers contend that broad-based social and economic changes will be necessary before a stabilization in population growth rates can occur.

Sulfur dioxide: A yellowish-brown gaseous by-product of the burning of fossil fuels.

Particulates: Nongaseous air pollutants.

Carbon monoxide: An odorless, colorless gas that originates primarily from motor vehicle emissions.

Nitrogen dioxide: An amber-colored gas found in smog; can cause eye and respiratory irritations.

WHAT DO YOU THINK?

How would you react to governmentally imposed restriction on family size? Do you favor imposed mandatory limitations in developing nations? What do you think we, as a world community, ought to do about population growth?

TABLE 23.1 ■ World Population Growth by Decade, 1950–1990, with Projections to 2029

Year	Population (billion)	Increase by Decade (million)	Average Annual Increase (million)
1950	2.5		
1960	3.0	504	50
1970	3.7	679	68
1980	4.5	752	75
1990	5.3	842	84
2000	6.3	959	96
2029	10.4	not available	

Source: Information from Lester R. Brown, "The Illusion of Progress," in *State of the World, 1990,* ed. Lester R. Brown (New York: Norton, 1990), 5; Ruth Caplan, *Our Earth, Ourselves* (New York: Bantam, 1990), 248.

AIR POLLUTION

As our population has grown, so have the number and volume of the environmental pollutants that we produce. Concern about air quality prompted Congress to pass the Clean Air Act in 1970 and to amend it in 1977 and again in 1990. The object was to develop standards for six of the most widespread air pollutants that seriously affect health: sulfur dioxide, particulates, carbon monoxide, nitrogen dioxide, ozone, and lead.

Sources of Air Pollution

Sulfur Dioxide.   **Sulfur dioxide** is a yellowish-brown gas that is a by-product of burning fossil fuels. Electricity generating stations, smelters, refineries, and industrial boilers are the main source points. In humans, sulfur dioxide aggravates symptoms of heart and lung disease, obstructs breathing passages, and increases the incidence of such respiratory diseases as colds, asthma, bronchitis, and emphysema. It is toxic to plants, destroys some paint pigments, corrodes metals, impairs visibility, and is a precursor to acid rain, which we discuss later in this chapter.

Particulates.   **Particulates** are tiny solid particles or liquid droplets that are suspended in the air. Cigarette smoke releases particulates. They are also by-products of some industrial processes and the internal combustion engine. Particulates can in and of themselves irritate the lungs and can additionally carry heavy metals and carcinogenic agents deep into the lungs. When combined with sulfur dioxide, they exacerbate respiratory diseases. Particulates can also corrode metals and obscure visibility.

Carbon Monoxide.   **Carbon monoxide** is an odorless, colorless gas that originates primarily from motor vehicle emissions. Carbon monoxide interferes with the blood's ability to absorb and carry oxygen and can impair thinking, slow reflexes, and cause drowsiness, unconsciousness, and death. When inhaled by pregnant women, it may threaten the growth and mental development of the fetus. Long-term exposure can increase the severity of circulatory and respiratory diseases.

Nitrogen Dioxide.   **Nitrogen dioxide** is an amber-colored gas emitted by coal-powered electrical utility boilers and by motor vehicles. High concentrations of

TABLE 23.2 ■ Population of World's 10 Largest Metropolitan Areas, 1950 and 1980, with Projections for 2000 (in Millions)

City	1950	City	1980	City	2000
New York	12.3	Tokyo	16.9	Mexico City	25.6
London	8.7	New York	15.6	São Paulo	22.1
Tokyo	6.7	Mexico City	14.5	Tokyo	19.0
Paris	5.4	São Paulo	12.1	Shangai	17.0
Shangai	5.3	Shangai	11.7	New York	16.8
Buenos Aires	5.0	Buenos Aires	9.9	Calcutta	15.7
Chicago	4.9	Los Angeles	9.5	Bombay	15.4
Moscow	4.8	Calcutta	9.0	Beijing	14.0
Calcutta	4.4	Beijing	9.0	Los Angeles	13.9
Los Angeles	4.0	Rio de Janeiro	8.8	Jakarta	13.7

Source: Information from *World Urbanization Prospects 1990* (New York: United Nations, 1991); Lester R. Brown et al., *State of the World 1992: A Worldwatch Institute Report on Progress toward a Sustainable Society* (New York: Norton, 1992), 122.

Italics indicate city is in the Third World.

nitrogen dioxide can be fatal. Lower concentrations increase susceptibility to colds and flu, bronchitis, and pneumonia. Nitrogen dioxide is also toxic to plant life and causes a brown discoloration of the atmosphere. It is a precursor of ozone, and, along with sulfur dioxide, of acid rain.

Ozone. Ozone is a form of oxygen that is produced when nitrogen dioxide reacts with hydrogen chloride. These gases release oxygen, which is altered by sunlight to produce ozone. In the lower atmosphere, ozone irritates the mucous membranes of the respiratory system, causing coughing and choking. It can impair lung functioning, reduce resistance to colds and pneumonia, and aggravate heart disease, asthma, bronchitis, and pneumonia. This ozone corrodes rubber and paint and can injure or kill vegetation. It is also one of the irritants found in smog. The natural ozone found in the upper atmosphere, however, serves as a protective membrane against heat and radiation from the sun. We will discuss this atmospheric layer, called the ozone layer, later in the chapter.

Lead. Lead is a metal pollutant that is found in the exhaust of motor vehicles powered by fuel containing lead and in the emissions from lead smelters and processing plants. It also often contaminates drinking water systems in homes that have plumbing installed before 1930. Lead affects the circulatory, reproductive, and nervous systems. It can also affect the blood and kidneys and can accumulate in bone and other tissues. Lead is particularly detrimental to children and fetuses. It can cause birth defects, behavioral abnormalities, and decreased learning abilities.

Hydrocarbons. Although not listed as one of the six major air pollutants in the Clean Air Act, hydrocarbons encompass a wide variety of chemical pollutants in the air. Sometimes known as *volatile organic compounds* (VOCs), **hydrocarbons** are chemical compounds containing different combinations of carbon and hydrogen. The principal source of polluting hydrocarbons is the internal combustion engine. Most automobile engines emit hundreds of different types of hydrocarbon compounds. By themselves, hydrocarbons seem to cause few problems, but when they combine with sunlight and other pollutants, they form such poisons as formaldehyde, various ketones, and peroxyacetylnitrate (PAN), all of which are respiratory irritants. Hydrocarbon combinations such as benzene and benzopyrene are carcinogenic. In addition, hydrocarbons play a major part in the formation of smog.

Photochemical Smog

Photochemical smog is a brown, hazy mix of particulates and gases that forms when oxygen-containing compounds of nitrogen and hydrocarbons react in the presence of sunlight. Photochemical smog is sometimes called *ozone pollution* because ozone is created when vehicle exhaust reacts with sunlight. Such smog is most likely to develop on days when there is little wind and high traffic congestion. In most cases, it forms in areas that experience a **temperature inversion,** a weather condition in which a cool layer of air is trapped under a layer of warmer air, preventing the air from circulating. When gases such as the hydrocarbons and nitrogen oxides are released into the cool air layer, they cannot escape, and thus they remain suspended until wind conditions move away the warmer air layer. Sunlight filtering through the air causes chemical changes in the hydrocarbons and nitrogen oxides, which results in smog. Smog is more likely to be produced in valley regions blocked by hills or mountains—for example, the Los Angeles basin, Denver, and Tokyo.

The most noticeable adverse effects of exposure to smog are difficulty in breathing, burning eyes, headaches, and nausea. Long-term exposure to smog poses serious health risks, particularly for children, the elderly, pregnant women, and people with chronic respiratory disorders such as asthma and emphysema. According to the American Lung Association, continued exposure accelerates aging of the lungs and increases susceptibility to infections by hindering the functions of the immune system.

Despite local efforts to reduce the problem, smog and other air pollutants repeatedly surge above federal safe standards. The Clean Air Act Amendments of 1990 are designed to reduce smog levels, as well as those of other air pollutants, significantly.[7] The Air Toxics program established by the Clean Air Act Amendments of 1990 is designed to curb 189 toxic air pollutants produced by industry that are carcinogens, mutagens, or reproductive toxins.[8]

Acid Rain

Acid rain is precipitation that has fallen through acidic air pollutants, particularly those containing sulfur dioxides

---

Ozone: A gas formed when nitrogen dioxide interacts with hydrogen chloride.

Lead: A metal found in the exhaust of motor vehicles powered by fuel containing lead and in emissions from lead smelters and processing plants.

Hydrocarbons: Chemical compounds that contain carbon and hydrogen.

Photochemical smog: The brownish-yellow haze resulting from the combination of hydrocarbons and nitrogen oxides.

Temperature inversion: A weather condition occurring when a layer of cool air is trapped under a layer of warmer air.

Acid rain: Precipitation contaminated with acidic pollutants.

and nitrogen dioxides. This precipitation, in the form of rain, snow, or fog, has a more acidic composition than does unpolluted precipitation. When introduced into lakes and ponds, acid rain gradually acidifies the water. When the acid content of the water reaches a certain level, plant and animal life cannot survive. Ironically, lakes and ponds that are acidified become a crystal-clear deep blue, giving the illusion of beauty and health.

Sources of Acid Rain. More than 95 percent of acid rain originates in human actions, chiefly the burning of fossil fuels. The single greatest source of acid rain in the United States is coal-fired power plants, followed by ore smelters and steel mills.

When these and other industries burn fuels, the sulfur and nitrogen in the emissions combine with the oxygen and sunlight in the air to become sulfur dioxide and nitrogen oxides (precursors of sulfuric acid and nitric acids, respectively). Small acid particles are then carried by the wind and combine with moisture to produce acidic rain or snow. Because of higher concentrations of sunlight in the summer months, rain is more strongly acidic in the summertime. Additionally, the rain or snow that falls at the beginning of a storm is more acidic than that which falls later.

The ability of a lake to cleanse itself and neutralize its acidity depends on several factors, the most critical of which is bedrock geology. Bedrock and topsoil that contain high concentrations of carbonates, bicarbonates, and hydroxides have the greatest neutralizing abilities. Lakes located in areas with low concentrations stand a small chance of remaining unacidified. Figure 23.1 shows those areas in North America that are most vulnerable to acid

rain because of their bedrock geology and proximity to industries that produce sulfur and nitrogen oxides.

Effects of Acid Rain. The damage caused to lake and pond habitats is not the worst of the problems created by acid rain. Each year, it is responsible for the destruction of millions of trees in forests in Europe and North America. Scientists have concluded that 75 percent of Europe's forests are now experiencing damaging levels of sulfur deposition by acid rain. Forests in every country on the continent are affected.[9]

Doctors believe that acid rain also aggravates and may even cause bronchitis, asthma, and other respiratory problems. People with emphysema and those with a history of heart disease may also suffer from exposure to acid rain. In addition, it may be hazardous to a pregnant woman's unborn child.

Acidic precipitation can cause metals such as aluminum, cadmium, lead, and mercury to **leach** (dissolve and filter) out of the soil. If these metals make their way into water or food supplies (particularly fish), they can cause cancer in humans who consume them.

Acid rain is also responsible for crop damage, which, in turn, contributes to world hunger. Laboratory experiments showed that acid rain can reduce seed yield by up to 23 percent. Actual crop losses are being reported with increasing frequency. In May 1989, China's Hunan Province lost an estimated $260 million worth of crops and seedlings to acid rain. Similar losses have been reported in Chile, Brazil, and Mexico.[10]

A final consequence of acid rain is the destruction of public monuments and structures. Damage to buildings in the United States alone is estimated to cost more than $5 billion annually.[11]

Air pollution is obviously a many-faceted problem. Because we breathe approximately 15,000 to 20,000 liters of air per day (compared to drinking 2 liters of water), we are more likely to be exposed to pollutants by breathing than in any other way.

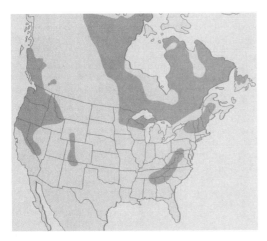

FIGURE 23.1

Areas of North America Most Vulnerable to Acid Rain

Ozone Layer Depletion

We earlier defined *ozone* as a chemical that is produced when oxygen interacts with sunlight. Close to the earth, ozone poses health problems such as respiratory distress. Farther away from the earth, it forms a protective membrane-like layer in the earth's stratosphere—the highest level of the earth's atmosphere, located from 12 to 30 miles above the earth's surface. The ozone layer in the stratosphere protects our planet and its inhabitants from ultraviolet B (UV-B) radiation, a primary cause of skin cancer. Ultraviolet B radiation may also damage DNA and may be linked to weakened immune systems in both humans and animals.

In the early 1970s, scientists began to warn of a depletion of the earth's ozone layer. Special instruments developed to test atmospheric contents indicated that specific chemicals used on earth were contributing to the rapid depletion of this vital protective layer. These chemicals are called **chlorofluorocarbons** (CFCs).

Chlorofluorocarbons were first believed to be miracle chemicals. They were used as refrigerants (Freon), as aerosol propellants in products such as hairsprays and deodorants, as cleaning solvents, and in medical sterilizers, rigid foam insulation, and Styrofoam. But, along with halons (found in many fire extinguishers), methyl chloroform, and carbon tetrachloride (cleaning solvents), CFCs were eventually found to be a major cause of depletion of the ozone layer. When released into the air through spraying or outgassing, CFCs migrate upward toward the ozone layer, where they decompose and release chlorine atoms. These atoms cause ozone molecules to break apart.

In 1979, a satellite measurement showing a large hole in the ozone layer over Antarctica shocked scientists. Since then, satellite measurements of the ozone layer have regularly shown increases in the size of the hole.

In the early 1970s, the U.S. government banned the use of aerosol sprays containing CFCs in an effort to reduce ozone depletion. But CFCs are still used in various foam products, refrigerators, and air conditioners. In fact, the United States still has the highest per capita use of CFCs in the world, generating approximately 30 percent of all the emissions of ozone-depleting chemicals. Japan is close behind us.

In 1987, after much international negotiation, a group of 24 nations agreed to freeze all production of CFCs immediately and to reduce CFC outputs by 50 percent by the year 2000. This agreement, called the Montreal Protocol, was strengthened in June 1990, when 81 nations signed the Helsinki Declaration, pledging to phase out completely five of the most hazardous CFCs by the year 2000.

Global Warming

More than 100 years ago, scientists theorized that carbon dioxide emissions from fossil-fuel burning would create a buildup of greenhouse gases in the earth's atmosphere and that this accumulation would have a warming effect on the earth's surface. The century-old predictions are now coming true, with alarming effects. Average global temperatures are higher today than at any time since global temperatures were first recorded, and the change in atmospheric temperature may be taking a heavy toll on human beings and crops. Climate researchers predicted in 1975 that the buildup of greenhouse gases would produce life-threatening natural phenomena, including drought in the midwestern United States, more frequent and severe forest fires, flooding in India and Bangladesh, extended heat waves over large areas of the earth, and killer hurricanes. Recently, the planet has experienced all five of these phenomena, although whether they were connected to global warming remains a matter of debate.

Greenhouse gases include carbon dioxide, CFCs, ground-level ozone, nitrous oxide, and methane. They become part of a gaseous layer that encircles the earth, allowing solar heat to pass through and then trapping that heat close to the earth's surface. The most predominant of these gases is carbon dioxide, which accounts for 49 percent of all greenhouse gases. Eastern Europe and North America are responsible for approximately half of all carbon dioxide emissions. Since the late nineteenth century, carbon dioxide concentrations in the atmosphere have increased 25 percent, with half of this increase occurring since the 1950s. Not surprisingly, these greater concentrations coincide with world industrial growth. See Figure 23.3 for more about contributions to global warming.

Rapid deforestation of the tropical rain forests of Central and South America, Africa, and Southeast Asia is also contributing to the rapid rise in the presence of greenhouse gases. Trees take in carbon dioxide, transform it, store the carbon for food, and then release oxygen into the air. As we lose forests, we are losing the capacity to dissipate carbon dioxide.

The potential consequences of global warming are dire. The rising atmospheric concentration of greenhouse gases may be the most economically disruptive and costly change set in motion by our modern industrial society. The cost to the U.S. economy of doubling greenhouse gases, which could occur as early as 2025, would amount to nearly $60 billion, or roughly 1 percent of U.S. gross national product in 1993[13] (see Table 23.3).

Reducing Air Pollution

Our national air pollution problems are rooted in our energy, transportation, and industrial practices. We must develop comprehensive national strategies to address the problem of air pollution in the 1990s in order to clean the air for the coming century. We must support policies that encourage the use of renewable resources such as solar, wind, and water power as the providers of most of the world's energy.[14]

Most experts agree that shifting away from automobiles as the primary source of transportation is the only way to reduce air pollution significantly. Many cities have taken steps in this direction by setting high parking fees, imposing bans on city driving, and establishing high road-usage tolls. Community governments should be encouraged to provide convenient, inexpensive, and easily accessible public transportation for citizens.

Auto makers must be encouraged to manufacture automobiles that provide good fuel economy and low rates of toxic emissions. Incentives given to manufacturers to produce such cars, tax breaks for purchasers who buy them, and gas-guzzler-taxes on inefficient vehicles are three promising measures in this area.

What can you do to help? Find out in the Building Communication Skills box.

TABLE 23.3 ■ Annual U.S. Economic Losses from Global Warming Caused by Doubling of Greenhouse Gases

Source of Loss	Amount of Loss ($ billion)
Agricultural losses due to heat stress and drought	18
Increased electricity for air conditioning	11
Sea level rise	7
Curtailed water supply from reduced runoff	7
Increased urban air pollution	4
Reduced lumber yield from forests	3
Other (includes hurricane and forest fire damage, and increased mortality due to heat stress)	8
Total	58

Source: Adapted with permission from William R. Cline, *Global Warming: The Economic Stakes* (Washington, D.C.: Institute for International Economics, 1992). Copyright © 1992 Institute for International Economics.

*N*OISE POLLUTION

Loud noise has become commonplace. We are often painfully aware of construction crews in our streets, jet air-

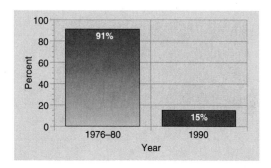

FIGURE 23.5

The graph measures EPA's estimates of the percentage of children with blood lead above 10 micrograms per deciliter of blood, the "level of concern" established by the U.S. Centers for Disease Control. The government's goal is to virtually eliminate the lead problem by the year 2000.

Source: Reprinted from U.S. Environmental Protection Agency, *Securing Our Legacy: An EPA Progress Report, 1989–1991* (EPA Publication No. 175R-92-001, 1992).

planes roaring overhead, stereos blaring next door, and trucks rumbling down nearby freeways. Our bodies have definite physiological responses to noise, and noise can become a source of physical or mental distress.

Prolonged exposure to some noises results in hearing loss. Short-term exposure reduces productivity, concentration levels, and attention spans, and may affect mental and emotional health. Symptoms of noise-related distress include disturbed sleep patterns, headaches, and tension. Physically, our bodies respond to noises in a variety of ways. Blood pressure increases, blood vessels in the brain dilate, and vessels in other parts of the body constrict. The pupils of the eye dilate. Cholesterol levels in the blood rise, and some endocrine glands secrete additional stimulating hormones, such as adrenaline, into the bloodstream.

Sounds are measured in decibels. Table 23.4 shows the decibel levels for various sounds. Hearing can be damaged by varying lengths of exposure to sound. If the duration of allowable daily exposure to different decibel levels is exceeded, hearing loss will result.

SKILLS FOR BEHAVIOR CHANGE

Reducing the Effects of Noise Pollution

Beyond giving your political support to legislation and enforcement of policies designed to reduce noise pollution, what can you do to lessen the effect of noise pollution on you? The following suggestions are only a few of the recommended approaches:

- Wear ear protectors or ear plugs when working around noisy machinery or when using firearms.
- When listening on a headset with volume settings numbered 1 through 10, keep the volume no louder than 4. Your headset is too loud if you are unable to hear people around you speaking in a normal tone of voice.

- Avoid loud music. Don't sit or stand near speakers or amplifiers at a rock concert and don't play a car radio or stereo above reasonable levels.
- Maintain your automobile, motorcycle, or lawn mower exhaust system in good working order.
- Furnish your room, apartment, home, and office with sound-absorbing materials. Drapes, carpeting, and cork wall tiles are excellent for reducing both interior and exterior noises.
- Avoid any exposure to painfully loud sounds and avoid repeated exposure to any sounds above 80 decibels.

TABLE 23.4 ■ Noise Levels of Various Activities (in Decibels)

Decibels (db) measure the volume of sounds. Here are the decibel levels of some common sounds.

Type of Sound	Noise Level (db)
Carrier deck jet operation	150
Jet takeoff from 200 feet	140
Rock concert	120 (painful)
Auto horn (3 feet)	110 (extremely loud)
Motorcycle	100
Garbage truck	100
Pneumatic drill	90
Lawnmower	90
Heavy traffic	80
Alarm clock	80
Shouting, arguing	80 (very loud)
Vacuum cleaner	75 (loud)
Freight train from 50 feet	70
Freeway traffic	65
Normal conversation	60
Light auto traffic	50 (moderate)
Library	40
Soft whisper	30 (faint)

At this point, it is necessary to distinguish between sound and noise. Sound is anything that can be heard. Noise is sound that can damage the hearing or cause mental or emotional distress. When sounds become distracting or annoying, they become noise.

Unfortunately, despite gradually increasing awareness that noise pollution is more than just a nuisance, noise control programs at federal, state, and local levels have been given a low budgetary priority. In order to prevent hearing loss, it is important that you take it upon yourself to avoid voluntary and involuntary exposure to excessive noise. Playing stereos in your car and home at reasonable levels, wearing ear plugs when you use power equipment, and establishing barriers (closed windows, etc.) between you and noise will help you keep your hearing intact. The Skills for Behavior Change box discusses more ways to reduce the effects of noise pollution.

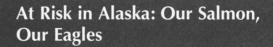

At Risk in Alaska: Our Salmon, Our Eagles

Sarah James and **Floyd Peterson**

Sarah James is a member of the Gwich'in tribe of northern Canada and a spokesperson for the tribe's Steering Committee which strives to protect the Arctic National Wildlife Refuge. Floyd Peterson is a member of the Tlingit tribe of southeastern Alaska. In the following column, published in the *Washington Post* on July 21, 1995, the authors address the issue of logging in two of Alaska's national parks. Native American tribes live in the large parks along with an abundance of wildlife, wildlife that will be threatened by large-scale logging in the area.

Questions for Discussion and Reflection

1. What, in the authors' views, are the two chief results of extensive logging in the Tongass National Forest and the Arctic National Wildlife Refuge?
2. What animals are at risk from deforestation?
3. What is the authors' thesis? What is their position on logging?
4. What arguments do they present to support their position?
5. What is your position on logging in Alaska's forests? Do you agree or disagree with the authors? If you agree with them, did they convince you or did you already share their views? If you disagree, support your position.

1   Over more than a thousand generations, Alaska Natives have mastered the art of living in the Far North. Our peoples have built flourishing cultures in remote isolation. We have survived extreme conditions by understanding our environment. As Alaska natives we are used to challenge. But this year, we face our greatest challenge ever—congressional giveaways of Alaska lands at the expense of our cultural survival.

2   Southeast Alaska's Tongass National Forest is the nation's largest. It is home to the largest remaining intact stretches of a coastal rain forest that once stretched south to California. The Tongass still supports the world's healthiest populations of salmon, grizzly bears and eagles. Scattered in this vast forest are small villages accessible only by boat or plane. The Halda, Tlingit and Tsimshlan native peoples of the Tongass learned long ago to live richly on the deer, salmon, and other bounty provided by this forest.

3   But now clear-cut logging is encroaching. The forest is being exported, mostly to Asia, from an accelerating expanse of clear-cuts. We have to travel farther from our villages, sometimes in dangerous waters, to find uncut forests. Scientists have warned us that unless the logging slows, our generation will witness the local extinction of wildlife such as grizzly

bears. They have predicted grave declines for the salmon and deer, which are the food on our table and center of our way of life. Now, Congress may radically expand the clear-cuts, further endangering our culture.

4   Far to the north, the Arctic National Wildlife Refuge hosts one of nature's true wonders. Each summer, more than 160,000 caribou migrate hundreds of miles to this coastal plain along the Arctic Ocean to bear and nurse their young. This stretch of America's most northern coast is also home to polar bear, musk ox, wolves, and millions of migratory birds earning the Arctic Refuge's reputation as "America's Serengeti."

5   At the close of each summer, the caribou leave the refuge and migrate south over the Brooks Range, passing by isolated Gwich'in Villages. For uncountable generations, our Gwich'in people have depended on the caribou for food, clothing and shelter. But in this generation, we have had to turn our attention to oil and gas drilling proposals. The drilling, predicted to produce only 150 days of oil at best, could destroy the caribou birthing grounds and threaten the survival of our children and grandchildren.

6   From the Tongass coastal rain forest to the Arctic National Wildlife Refuge, Congress is quietly considering policy that would dramatically change the face of Alaska. The proposals endanger the future of our peoples. But Alaska's federal lands belong to all Americans. The plans before Congress will also destroy your right to enjoy Alaska.

7   One proposal would transfer more than 600,000 acres of protected public lands in the Tongass National Forest to private corporations that could then clear-cut at will. A few lines slipped into the congressional budget proposal would open up the Arctic National Wildlife Refuge, the only protected stretch of Alaska's arctic coast, to oil and gas drilling. Both of these plans have the demonstrated potential to destroy the salmon, deer, and caribou that support our people and our culture.

8   Sadly enough, Alaska's own members of Congress are leading this destructive charge. For the first time in history, one state's delegation controls the two most powerful congressional committees overseeing federal public lands. Alaska's Sen. Frank Murkowski is chairman of the Senate Energy and Environment Committee, and Alaska's Rep. Don Young is chairman of the House Resources Committee. They have turned a deaf ear to our traditional native needs and to the will of all Americans who value their Alaskan natural heritage.

9   We believe that there is still room in Alaska for traditional native cultures and America's natural treasures.

10   Alaska is too important to be wasted on a few quick favors to multinational corporations. This is not some Third World country where we need to sell off every last inch of America's heritage and let our native peoples fade away. The wonders of Alaska belong to future generations of our families and yours.

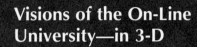

Visions of the On-Line University—in 3-D

Amy E. Schwartz

Amy Schwartz is a member of the editorial-page staff of the *Washington Post*. In her column, published June 16, 1995, Schwartz examines some of the ideas for the future of the university.

Questions for Discussion and Reflection

1. What is Schwartz's subject? Does she accept all of the futuristic ideas she presents?
2. What, then, is her thesis? Where is it stated?
3. What is the historical explanation for the current arrangements of colleges (students and faculty together on a campus)?
4. What difference between a teacher and a book does the author suggest? Is there, in your view, any difference between a teacher and a book? Would you prefer to have the best economist on 3-D CD-ROM or attend an economics class on campus? Explain your answer.

1   If you want to hear full-blown futurist rhetoric, the people to hang out with are not politicians but university administrators. Trying to find magical ways out of budgetary problems and tending by nature toward big thoughts, in the right mood they can attain a state of techno-rhapsody that outstrips anything heard from Congress or the business world. The rhapsodies make good listening. Sometimes they also demonstrate a skid in logic that shows just how hard it is to predict where technology will go.

2   Take the vision sketched recently in conversation by Donald Langenberg, chancellor of the University of Maryland system. Maryland is moderately computerized but not yet one of the hypercampuses that hold classes on-line and present every student with a laptop on entry. Like many others, Langenberg sees the electronic networks and the infinitely replicable digitized data banks as an epochal change, "the first change in the underlying technology of knowledge in 500 years." He argues that it's time to imagine a university that no longer operates in terms of "the most basic units of what faculty members do—the course, the credit unit, the semester, the library, the campus."

3   In other words, with students and faculty online, classroom discussion can take place without most students' actually being in the classroom, an innovation that could ease the problem of overcrowding. Ultimately, it could also begin to break down the whole notion of enrolling, matriculating and being charged tuition.

4   Another thoughtful visionary, Gregory Farrington, the dean of the engineering school at the University of Pennsylvania, can explain in historical terms how those concepts grew out of the once immutable physical fact of libraries. "Information was stored in books, and so universities grew up around libraries," he says. "To do research in books over a lifetime, the faculty had to sit near the books, and to learn about the research students had to come and sit in front of the faculty. And to do that, students had to be at a time of their life when they could come and sit intensively in front of the faculty for several years, which is why we developed this pattern of sending them when they were young. Now we charge students $25,000 a year to come to a campus to grow up—networking, student-to-student contacts, socialization. If we're charging them for information, they can get that from CompuServe."

5   Langenberg, though, sees greater possibilities. "It's an opportunity to return to the golden age, before the professor as lecturer," he says. "We can go back to the professor as coach, guide, mentor, tutor—but *on a mass basis.* What the Oxford colleges once gave an elite, what Philip of Macedon gave his son, we can offer to everybody."

6   This is a princely offer indeed, if you consider that Philip of Macedon's son was Alexander the Great, and Alexander the Great's tutor was Aristotle. But it also involves something of a leap. A professor conducting a computerized "bulletin board" seminar or lecturing on interactive video link, as many now do, will certainly reach more people. Students may ask questions by modem or listen to interaction in what's widely referred to now as "distance learning"; they can get on-line and have a conversation with the professor about homework and save commuter fare all the while. It could be a great improvement. But Aristotle?

7   "Oh, but that's the beauty of it," Langenberg says, when asked about the presumed scarcity of Aristotle-quality professors. "You can get wonderful packages. With the best economist in the world on 3-D CD-ROM, full color, in your living room, should you really get in your car and go sit in a room at the local community college and hear a less brilliant professor *quoting* the world's best economists?"

8   But here is where the technological sleight of hand sneaks in, the logical skid—because, while you might still be said to attend a university if you are interacting with the professor at a video distance, you are no longer doing anything of the kind once you click a canned professor into the VCR.

9   This, the effortless blurring of hardware with actual presence, may be the most frequent of all logical slips with regard to new technology. When telephones were developed, one story has it, most people expected them to be used for the one-way transmission of facts, music and entertainment; no one had any idea people would end up using them exclusively to talk to each other.

10   Similarly, recent commentators on the fortunes of computer services like CompuServe and America Online have noted that those who set the price systems for these services assumed people would use them to order plane tickets and buy merchandise—to "shop for underwear in your underwear," as one mogul exulted. Those companies began a panicky rethinking of the price structure when it became obvious that, though the commercial services get an occasional glance, the overwhelming majority of the millions on the Internet are using it to send e-mail.

11   Whatever the effect of technology on distance, one distance, or difference, can surely never be made smaller—the difference between consulting stored information and encountering the real presence of a real person. Forget full-color, 3-D CD-ROMS; no matter what form education finally takes, it will need to keep observing the difference between a teacher and a book, even if the teacher is far away and the book can talk.

Affirmative Action by Class

Richard D. Kahlenberg

Responding to challenges to affirmative action in college selection, Richard Kahlenberg is writing a book about class-based affirmative action. His article on this topic was published in the *Washington Post* in July 1995.

Questions for Discussion and Reflection

1. What three choices for student selection did the University of California consider? (Do you know what decision the University made? If not, how might you locate this information?)
2. Which approach to student selection does Kahlenberg favor?
3. Why does the author object to preferences for the purpose of "diversity"?
4. On what concept or for what purpose should preferences be awarded, according to Kahlenberg?
5. What are Kahlenberg's arguments for his position on affirmative action? Do you agree with Kahlenberg's position? Why or why not? If you disagree, what is your position on affirmative action in college selection? On affirmative action in hiring? On affirmative action in promotions?

1   This week the University of California's Board of Regents is slated to consider whether to keep its current system of race-based preferences, abolish it or adopt a third alternative—providing affirmative action preferences to the disadvantaged of all races. Defining beneficiaries by class, not race, would restore fairness to a system that has strayed far from the goals of the early proponents of affirmative action.

2   The University of California does not justify its current racial preference system as a temporary compensatory program to remedy past discrimination, but says that preferences should be part of a permanent scheme to achieve racial "diversity," irrespective of past discrimination. The divide between diversity preferences and compensatory preferences, though often ignored, is at least as significant as the divide between colorblindness and racial preference—and has profound practical consequences.

3   At the flagship Berkeley campus, the diversity policies do help blacks and Latinos vis a vis whites, as a compensatory program would. But the school's own data indicate its emphasis on diversity helps whites vis a vis Asians, turning compensation on its head. Asian Americans, who suffered egregious discrimination the first time around, are asked to suffer a second time because diversity theory says there are "too many" of them on campus.

4   Initially, liberal supporters of affirmative action were worried about this very prospect, and in the 1978 *Bakke* case, Justices Brennan, White, Marshall and Blackmun went out of their way to distance themselves from Justice Powell's embrace of "diversity" as a rationale for preferences, emphasizing that the preference program at issue was compensatory in nature. Today, the theory of diversity is sometimes used as a sword against blacks, who are overrepresented in the U.S. Postal Service and in certain city governments. Ironically, Latinos, many of them recent immigrants with no claim to compensation, receive preference over African Americans, to whom the greatest societal debt is owed.

5   Some supporters of diversity actually emphasize its amoral consequences. Last July, the Justice Department decided to support the firing of a white schoolteacher in Piscataway, N.J., to maintain faculty diversity. In defending the move, President Clinton pointed out that in a school district where blacks are overrepresented, diversity could be used to justify firing an equally qualified black teacher because of her skin color.

6   Class-based affirmative action restores the focus to equal opportunity and provides preferences on the sensible premise that a disadvantaged student who has faced obstacles—not at all of her own making—may in fact have greater long-run potential than her SAT score suggests. Because of our nation's history of discrimination, blacks are disproportionately poor and will disproportionately benefit from class preferences. A study released by Berkeley in May confirmed that blacks and Hispanics will do better under a system of class preferences than under a system where academic achievement is the sole criterion for admissions.

7   The study also found (unsurprisingly) that counting class is a less efficient way of promoting racial diversity than counting race (there is no better way to guarantee racial representation than to mandate it). But a sensitively constructed needs-based program could yield significant minority representation in a fair manner. Counting parental income or education boosts minority numbers some, and looking at additional indicators of an

applicant's disadvantage not measured in the Berkeley study—such as her parents' wealth, the concentration of poverty in her school and the number of parents she has—will raise minority numbers further. Berkeley Chancellor Chang-Lin Tien told the *Wall Street Journal* "We can come up with some tricks."

8   The new program would benefit poor students of all races, all of whom deserve a leg up, but the minorities admitted under a class-based program would generally differ from those minorities admitted to Berkeley today. The preferred students of color would themselves all be disadvantaged— the very subcategory most likely to suffer from the continuing legacy of past discrimination, though least likely to benefit from current programs. The moral underpinnings of the system would be restored, and a more genuine diversity, economic as well as racial, would naturally result.

Will Our Future Be Workable?

William Raspberry

William Raspberry began his career in journalism in Indiana before joining the *Washington Post.* He now writes one local column and two syndicated columns each week. His primary concerns are urban or race problems or issues regarding the poor, as his June 5, 1995, column on work reveals.

Questions for Discussion and Reflection

1. What, in Raspberry's view, are our conflicting ideas about work? Do you share these views? Do you think many Americans hold these conflicting views? Has Raspberry raised an interesting issue?

2. When companies "downsize" and turn to technology instead of people, what are the three economic consequences?

3. What do "we" think the solutions are to greater technology? Does Raspberry think they are going to be real solutions?

4. If Raspberry's views on the future of the workplace are accurate, what, then, should we as a society be doing? What solutions do you have?

1   There is something about us human beings that doesn't like work. We look forward to weekends and vacations and retirement. We speak disparagingly of those who love work—workaholics, we call them. Sometimes we think it almost blasphemous to like work; after all, wasn't work God's punishment for the sins of Adam and Eve? Our futuristic musings are virtual hymns to anti-work; machines run everything, make everything, do everything.

2   And yet we value work—very nearly worship it. We assign it great dignity and moral power. We look down on those who don't (or won't) work,

counting them as less than full contributing members of society. In our ideal world, *everybody* would have a job.

3   Is there any way to reconcile these two contradictory ideas?

4   The question is not merely philosophical. It has deep implications for our society, particularly as machines (robots, computers and the entire range of Information Age technology) take over more of the work that humans used to do. It's something Jeremy Rifkin has been thinking a great deal about.

5   "On the micro level," he said the other day, "every business leader and CEO is determined to replace bodies with thinking machines. The machines are more reliable and more productive; they make fewer demands and work longer hours. Using them gives a company a major advantage.

6   "But on the macro level, if everybody uses machines to replace human beings, the obvious question is: Who will buy their products?"

7   It's a point he made in his new book, "The End of Work," and in a fascinating interview. "I recently talked to the Young Presidents' Organization, and I asked these young executives how many of them are re-engineering and downsizing and letting people go, and most of them raised their hands. How many of them saw fewer employees in their corporate futures? All of them. But when I asked them what they were going to do with these people—their customer base as well as their worker pool—they had no idea.

8   "They are smart enough to see that they are building tremendous inventories in the face of falling purchasing power, but they haven't seen the connection—that both have the same source."

9   There are other similar dilemmas on the man vs. machine landscape. For example, says Rifkin: "We already have near-workerless factories in such industries as insurance and banking—and not just because the machines are more efficient. There are advantages to having a small, highly trained work force that go beyond efficiency or even health insurance costs. Pensions, for instance, are a big chunk of employer costs, and the fewer workers you have the smaller the outlays for pension plans.

10   "But as corporations let people go, the pension funds dwindle, and then you discover that it is the pension funds that have kept the economy going; they are the main form of savings for the capitalist system, a third of the bond and stock markets, worth more than the commercial assets of all the banks in America. They are, in fact, the main source of funds for the shift to the Information Age."

11   There's a third dilemma. As much as companies love low-cost production and high profits, they fear instability. But the same forces that produce the one threaten to produce the other. The incipient instability is not immediately obvious, as it might be in periods of high unemployment. But look at the nature of much of today's employment: part-time work, contingent work, sporadic work—erstwhile employees transmogrified into "independent contractors," which is to say workers without security and the fringe benefits we had come to expect.

12   Not only do insecure workers buy fewer of the goods businesses want to sell, which tends to destabilize markets, but they also tend to earn less, thereby accelerating the polarization of rich and poor. The very economic changes that make entrepreneurs rich also create the instability and uncertainty that threaten their economic survival.

13   The issues Rifkin raises seem so obvious that you wonder why we haven't spent more time talking about them. Most of our future-of-work conversations explore only the edges of his concerns. We recognize that work is becoming more technical, but take little notice of the fact that there will be less of it. We talk about the growing gap in real earnings between the elite workers and the blue-collar class, but we delude ourselves into believing that the answer lies in periodical retraining. We accept the idea that work is the solution to welfare dependency—indeed we are ready to accept two-years-and-out as a reasonable way of nudging people back into the world of work.

14   But to do *what?* It's a question worth exploring.

The New America

Michael Barone

Journalist Michael Barone has written a long but fascinating article about the issues that divide Americans and that have reorganized political alliances or groups. "The New America" appeared in the weekly newsmagazine *U.S. News and World Report* on July 10, 1995.

Questions for Discussion and Reflection

1. What is Barone's thesis, the main idea of his essay?
2. How was the poll of registered voters organized? What did it reveal? What, more than anything else, is it that divides Americans?
3. Explain the characteristics of each of the seven "tribes" or "galaxies." What are the views of each group on the key issues of crime, the economy, government, and so forth?
4. What are some of the advantages of today's diversity of views? Do you see more advantages or disadvantages?
5. Into which tribe do you best fit? If you have trouble placing yourself, is it because you have not yet decided on some of the issues? Is it time to take a stand?

1   America has always been a divided nation. *E pluribus unum* may be a national motto and the melting pot a national metaphor, but the reality has been patriots and Tories, free whites and black slaves, Philadelphia bankers and Tennessee woodsmen, Northern abolitionists and Southern

slave owners, free silver and hard currency, natives and immigrants, Wall Street and Main Street, Republicans and Democrats, hawks and doves, liberals and conservatives.

2   Today America is divided in new and different ways. There are scraps of evidence everywhere that old ties have frayed and loose new ones are being woven. The South, once solidly Democratic, is fast becoming Republican. In 1994, 40 percent of labor union votes went to Republican candidates. African-Americans and Hispanics are divided about affirmative action and welfare reform. There is a gulf between women who work outside the home and women who stay at home with their children. Politicians of both parties squabble over whether economic issues should take precedence over moral ones. "Are we a nation?" are the first words of Michael Lind's *The Next American Nation.* "Social classes speak to themselves in a dialect of their own, inaccessible to outsiders," wrote Christopher Lasch in *The Revolt of the Elites.* Republican analyst William Kristol warns of "the Balkanization of America."

3   We can sense these new divisions every day—living in geographical and cultural enclaves; sitting in walled backyards, not open front porches; listening to our own music and watching our own cable-television channels. Some of the institutions that once served as little melting pots, like the military draft and basic training, are gone. Others—public libraries and public-school systems—are in disrepair.

4   **The new divides.**   For this Independence Day, *U.S. News* has taken a fresh look at America, using polling and social science techniques to find what divides and unites Americans today. The results, based on a nationwide poll of 1,045 registered voters by Democratic pollster Celinda Lake of Lake Research and Republican pollster Ed Goeas of the Tarrance Group, indicate that culture is now more important in shaping voters' attitudes than race, geography, gender or political ideology, and they challenge all the ways in which politicians, academics, marketers and the media traditionally try to understand, describe and persuade voters.

5   Using techniques called factor analysis and cluster analysis, Lake and Goeas identified seven species of voters—not according to demographic traits such as race, gender and region or political attributes like ideology or party identification, but according to attitudes toward four cultural, two economic and one foreign dimension. The *U.S. News* poll and analysis help to illuminate the tensions in both major political parties, explain the increasing volatility of the electorate and reveal which issues are likely to be most effective in 1996. The survey, for example, found supporters of the Christian Coalition, Perot voters and African-Americans not clustered in single groups but scattered in many of them; African-Americans are present in significant numbers in six of the seven groups defined by the *U.S. News* poll.

6   Three striking messages emerge from the survey. The first is that there no longer is any center in American politics. The seven groups are not arrayed along a one-dimensional line from conservative right to liberal left;

instead, they can be thought of as seven separate galaxies, clusters of stars, some of which look close together from one vantage point but far apart when viewed from another. Second, while most Americans think they're much like most other Americans—only 17 percent said most of their fellow Americans are not like themselves—most Americans don't think the people who run the country are like them. Almost 58 percent said the nation's leaders are not very much or not at all like themselves. Finally, the country is divided largely by the fervency of religious belief.

7   **Two plus five.**   Only two of the seven tribes tilt heavily toward one political party or the other; the other five are ambivalent, drawn to one party or candidate on some issues and to the other side on others. This helps explain how the "Republican lock" on the presidency that analysts described in the 1980s was broken in 1992, how the Democrats who were thought to control Congress lost resoundingly in 1994 and why today's Republican revolution may not last.

8   Although together they account for only 35 percent of the electorate, the two most polarized groups—"Liberal Activists" and "Conservative Activists"—form the foundations of the Democratic and Republican parties and dominate the political debate. Just as geologically young mountain ranges have sharp peaks, while older ones have been softened by time, so the younger-than-average Liberal and Conservative Activists stand out from older groups that have less dramatic profiles.

9   The "Stewards" and the "Ethnic Conservatives" are the descendants of the pro-management and pro-labor blocs whose battles polarized American politics half a century ago. If many Stewards are lapsed Republicans, skeptical of the party's emphasis on abortion and other social issues, many Ethnic Conservatives are fallen Democrats.

10   Although Ethnic Conservatives are the group with the second-lowest incomes, their feelings of class conflict seem to have eroded over the years, though they still see government as an educator and protector. They are the group most often positive about banks (76 percent), lawyers (60 percent) and the news media (51 percent).

11   Two other groups perch at odd angles to the battle between Liberal Activists and Conservative Activists. "Populist Traditionalists" feel strong conflicts with gays and lesbians, welfare recipients, large corporations and the news media; they are most friendly to senior citizens, small business and the police. "Agnostics" see little conflict with any other groups; they are both pro-large corporation and pro-labor union; pluralities are friendly to gays and lesbians and Christian conservatives. The Agnostics' strongest negative feelings are toward those they see as disturbing the peace: prime-time television, the news media, talk-radio hosts, the National Rifle Association, welfare recipients and lawyers.

12   The final group, "Dowagers," is the smallest, only 7 percent of American voters. They rely heavily on the old media of network TV news and newspapers, but many recent events and arguments seem to pass them by. Two thirds are not sure whether they are friendly or in conflict with either large

corporations or labor unions; smaller majorities are unsure about Hispanics and Jews, feminists, gays and lesbians, Ivy League graduates, lawyers and immigrants.

13 These seven tribes produce no stable alliances. Rather, they line up with different groups on different issues:

14 • **Crime.** More than 55 percent of Conservative Activists and Stewards prefer punishment over prevention to stop crime; more than 60 percent of Agnostics, Liberal Activists and Ethnic Conservatives prefer prevention.

15 But when the trade-off is between faster, more certain punishment and protecting rights, the lineup is different: Liberal Activists join Conservative Activists and Stewards in preferring speedy justice; Agnostics, Ethnic Conservatives and Populist Traditionalists are split evenly. Populist Traditionalists and Conservative Activists, however, both say they're reluctant to give up some rights to control crime, while 76 percent of Ethnic Conservatives—who are most likely to fear crime in their own neighborhoods—say they would give up some rights.

16 • **Economic threats.** Conservative Activists fear federal deficits and high taxes. Liberal Activists, Ethnic Conservatives and Agnostics are most concerned about rising prices; Populist Traditionalists, about high taxes. Unemployment, for years the economic threat assumed by politicians and journalists to have the greatest political impact, was the concern of no more than 12 percent of any tribe.

17 • **Government's role.** Although most Ethnic Conservatives and Liberal Activists think government should help families achieve the American dream, large majorities of Conservative Activists, Stewards and Agnostics say government should stay out. Populist Traditionalists, the tribe identifying itself most as working class, are split down the middle.

18 • **Safety net.** Dowagers, who presumably are concerned about Social Security and Medicare, tend to prefer a federal government "safety net."

19 • **Abortion.** Most Ethnic Conservatives, Conservative Activists and Populist Traditionalists think abortion should be illegal in some or all cases. Over 70 percent of Liberal Activists and Stewards think it should be legal. In both cases, alliances cross party lines and economic divides.

20 • **Radical agendas.** Conservative Activists, Populist Traditionalists and Ethnic Conservatives worry more about the radical gay or feminist agendas; Liberal Activists, Stewards and Agnostics are more worried about the religious right.

21 • **Foreign aid and trade.** More than 70 percent of the usually antagonistic Liberal Activists and Conservative Activists agree that foreign aid is in the nation's interest. Seventy percent of Populist Traditionalists—the Perot-leaning group both Clinton Democrats and Gingrich Republicans are courting—disagree. Similarly, two thirds of Liberal Activists, Conservative Activists and Agnostics—the usually antagonistic high-education groups—favor expanding free trade with Latin America; two thirds of the Populist Traditionalists oppose it.

22   • **Military spending.**   A whopping 82 percent of Conservative Activists favor increased military spending, as do 54 percent of Populist Traditionalists; 71 percent of Agnostics and 63 percent of Liberal Activists and Stewards oppose it. In these numbers one hears echoes of 25-year-old debates over the Vietnam War.

23   • **Feminism.**   While 73 percent of Liberal Activists think the women's movement has not gone far enough, no more than 23 percent of any other tribe agrees.

24   • **Civil rights.**   A big 68 percent of Liberal Activists think the civil rights movement has not gone far enough. But only 14 percent of most other groups agree.

25   The results show how hard it is to assemble a stable political majority in the divided America of the 1990s, in which people vote social issues along cultural lines. Indeed, without the majority-forcing features written into the American political system by the faction-fearing Founding Fathers —the Electoral College and the single-member congressional district— both political parties might be fragmenting. And although conventional wisdom holds that third parties are not viable in America, the survey suggests that there is now plenty of room for serious third-party candidacies.

26   The balance on major issues—on religious beliefs and values, on the size and scope of government—favors conservatives. But if the Democrats seem an endangered species, the Republicans are also vulnerable. Voters are split on abortion, favorable to some forms of gun control and more sympathetic to labor than to management. While Populist Traditionalists, with their mistrust of institutions, seem to like political attacks, Agnostics and Stewards seem repelled by confrontational tactics. House Speaker Newt Gingrich quotes Republican pollster Fred Steeper, saying, " 'There is a large antipartisanship bloc that leans to us on issues and values, but doesn't like us to be partisan.' That's probably the group I gained most from by appearing with the president in New Hampshire."

27   Many Americans, especially Agnostics and Stewards (who together are 27 percent of voters), hunger for a political dialogue above partisan squabbles and perhaps for an above-the-fray candidate for president. Ross Perot was able to attract many consensus-minded Stewards and angry Populists in 1992. And although his views on many issues are not known and he does not seem to share the preoccupations of either Conservative Activists or Liberal Activists, Colin Powell's military success might appeal to Populist Traditionalists, his racial and immigrant background to Ethnic Conservatives, his tolerance to Agnostics and his internationalism to Stewards. Those groups contain 58 percent of the nation's voters.

28   • **Family feud.**   The conflicts in today's divided America can be overstated, and new alliances are easily overlooked. In only 22 of 217 cases does a majority of any tribe think its goals conflict with those of various controversial groups, from gays to gun owners. The two groups most often seen as hostile—the news media and prime-time television—both highlight the conflicts and divisions in American life and often take one

side to the irritation of others. And with the notable exception of the disproportionately African-American underclass, Americans today are freer than ever to join whatever tribe they choose. Race and ethnicity no longer determine one's group; nor do economic status or geography. Personal values are now the critical variable.

29   The culturally unified and much romanticized America of the 1950s, in contrast, had much less room for economic entrepreneurialism or cultural activism. And if today's elites seem disconnected from most or all of the tribes, Americans of all groups show no more deference to those who set themselves up as their betters today than the nation's founders showed to the king of England's royal governors in 1776.

30   But the things that are dividing us also may be holding us together. At America's extended family Thanksgiving dinner table, the Liberal Activist sister and the Conservative Activist brother argue one issue after another. Father, a Steward, and Mother, an Ethnic Conservative, find themselves agreeing and disagreeing, first with one side and then with the other. The Populist Traditionalist cousin relishes the clash; the Agnostic cousin wishes the siblings got along better. The Dowager grandmother tries to follow issues that were never raised when she formed most of her opinions. But all of them stay at the table. The argument keeps them together when they otherwise would have dispersed to watch their separate cable channels and listen to their different music, plug into the Internet or page through their favorite magazines. Today's America is divided, but its divisions, properly and sympathetically understood, can help hold it together.

Women, Children, and Ethics

Jill Ker Conway

Dr. Conway, a scholar of social and intellectual history, was president of Smith College for ten years. She is currently visiting scholar and professor at MIT, and she is the author of her autobiography *The Road from Coorain.* The following talk with Dr. Conway is from *Shared Values for a Troubled World,* a collection, by Rushworth M. Kidder, of conversations on ethical issues with well-known people from around the world.

Questions for Discussion and Reflection

1. What is the first problem that needs to be addressed?
2. What connects the first and second problems on Conway's list? What do they share?
3. What is one way to improve the lives of women?

4. What is the third problem on her list? How does it connect to the first two? What will happen, according to Conway, if we fail to address the third problem?

5. What is Conway's solution? In what three ways do we go about achieving her solution? Where should we look for change?

6. In your view, has Conway focused on important problems? Why or why not? If you agree to the problems, do you agree with her solutions? Why or why not? What solutions would you suggest?

1   It is snowing into the shrubbery outside her colonial living room as Jill Ker Conway ushers a visitor in. She apologizes for jet lag: she has just returned to this Boston suburb from Australia, where shooting is in progress for a film based on her autobiography. As the discussion turns to the values and ethics needed to shape a sustainable future, it is apparent that her Australian background is never far from her conversation.

2   First on her list, she says, is a need to reshape the role of women in societies around the world. "As we bring new technologies to our Western societies and undermine traditional patterns of agriculture and family and domestic life," she says, "what we see happening is an increasing exploitation of women and children and increasing violence against them—combined with a kind of international trade in women for sexual exploitation that makes Victorian prostitution look like small beer."

3   The examples she cites girdle the globe. "There is a trade in women in Saudi Arabia. Women are sold into prostitution in Thailand, Cambodia, and Burma. Everybody knows about the Japanese [sex-tourism] bonanza affecting the Philippines and many parts of Southeast Asia. That is a terrible blot on civilization."

4   She acknowledges that the problem has long historical precedent. But her conversations with Asian and African women point to a serious escalation in recent years. "As men go away to work in mines, as they do in Africa—or as women are shipped off to the city as surplus, as happens in many parts of rural Asia—the community constraints on violence against them are eroding." She notes, too, that the revival of traditional customs in the Islamic and Hindu worlds subject wives who are no longer wanted to "accidental-but-on-purpose household fires." In India, she says, "it happens with the arranged marriage: the bride is sent home to her family to bring back a transistor radio or television, and the family knows that, if she does not produce it, there will be a fire and she will die."

5   She also notes "an escalating problem of violence against women" in the developed world, but says that it is "nothing like" the scale of the problem in the developing world. In those countries, the issue takes on added significance because of its relation to global population. "There is plenty of evidence to show that, wherever women get control over the returns on their own work, they allocate them so that the health of their children increases and so they won't have to have so many [children]."

6   "That is a new problem," she insists, "which I wish I could get more feminists in the United States and the West to be concerned about."

7   The second values-driven issue on her list is concern for the global environment. "I am not of the school that blames corrupt corporate management for the degradation of the environment," she says. "I think that we each personally have to change our habits of consumption—and that if we did that, there would be an instant response from profitmaking enterprises."

8   She dismisses the argument that "we are all dupes of consumerism" who "can't change our habits [even] if we wish to." Such changes, in fact, are already beginning. Her current students at MIT, both male and female, are "willing to change their standards of consumption for two purposes: to be better environmental citizens, and to achieve greater equity between the sexes." What unites these two points of view in this post-1960s generation, she feels, is the fact that these students "see exploitation of the environment and of human beings as on a continuum of the same set of values."

9   Conway's third point centers on what she calls "north-south inequity"—the problem of the severe and growing economic imbalance between the wealthy developed nations that generally lie in the temperate northern hemisphere and the predominately tropical and southern less-developed countries. While the evidence of inequity is increasingly apparent, she says she is disturbed by the simplistic arguments used by some in the north who say that " 'those people should control their birth rate' or 'why should we be expected to invest our tax money in achieving a more stable human environment for non-Western countries?' "

10   "I just came back from a board meeting of a major international service company," she says. "Everybody knows the world is one world: they trade twenty-four hours a day in many different currencies, and you would not have to persuade anybody there that we live in a single global environment. But when I go out to dinner in a suburb like this, it is not apparent to people at all."

11   And while she acknowledges that a great deal of the West's foreign-aid contributions have "ended up in the hands of governments or corrupt contractors who are not the appropriate beneficiaries," that does not convince her that "we should slack off in the slightest in trying to achieve some global transfers of one kind or another."

12   What does she see as the risks of not doing so?

13   The danger, she says, is no longer of global warfare, since "mass warfare between nation-states" is increasingly seen as an ineffective tool of policy. The danger, instead, will come from "the kind of terrorism and sporadic but well-targeted violence that is not inspired by sinister international conspiracies but by the kind of desolation and desperation that gives you one kind of urban guerrilla army in Lima, Peru, and another terrible terrorist army in the rural areas." Peru, she says, is "a society which

has no hope—although theoretically it could be another California and feed the hemisphere."

14   How can those three broad issues—the woman's place, environmental degradation, and the north-south divide—best be addressed?

15   The problems, Conway admits, defy simple answers. The growth of technological systems—whether they are "systems of ideas or of material objects"—has produced a world "so complex and complicated that it is impossible to imagine any oversight by professionals" to assure the proper functioning of large-scale systems. "There isn't really that much supervision of how professionals in the high-tech world behave," she notes, citing as evidence "the fact that we have gone for so many years implanting various kinds of defective mechanisms into the human body" for medical reasons. The same problem applies, she says, "across the spectrum" in law, government, psychiatry, engineering, and scientific research in general.

16   Nor does she think the problem of regulation can ever be addressed simply through legal structures. "I can't imagine ever inventing the *regulated* free environment that would control how somebody builds a bridge, or the decisions those people made about the Challenger O-rings, and so on. In the long run, the only way a society can control [those issues] is ethical."

17   How, then, do you raise a society's ethical barometer?

18   "I think there are probably three ways," she says, speaking as an educator. First, she says, it is clear that "young ones learn their ethics from the adult generation. So we have to model a greater ethical concern."

19   Second, she notes, is a need for more volunteerism by the young. Educators could "broaden people's social conscience" and help impart a "stronger social service orientation in them" if they would only insist on "some form of public service between high school and college or college and graduate school" and "some exposure to society's problems."

20   Even today, she says, she still meets people whose "lives were changed by being part of the New Deal or the CCC [Civilian Conservation Corps]" and whose careers were shaped by that experience. By contrast, she says, "society demands no service from young people today. It is very meritocratic in the way it goes about things. We finance everybody's education through debt—and one of the consequences is that very early young people learn to think about themselves as an 'investment' that is going to 'pay off.' It is fascinating to see that the people who do most brilliantly in this educational system are the children of immigrants who don't think that way."

21   The third point, says Conway, centers on something approaching a religious sensibility. "It's very hard to say this without sounding like somebody from the New Right," she observes, "but I think that in some ways a totally secular education for young people may not develop a formed conscience." It doesn't matter, she says, whether you are going to be "a believer in later life" or not. The fact is, she says, that "a sense of evil and

personal guilt and the obligation to see to one's moral well-being is a religious mentality, and we do not foster that at all."

22   She recognizes that such a religious outlook can be "subject to all kinds of misuse and manipulation" in a world that is "menaced by fundamentalism of many different kinds—Muslim, Hindu, Arab, and the fundamentalist Right in our own society." But the absence of such a religious mentality "is also a terrible social hazard." And in fact, she adds, "those kinds of fundamentalism are there" because today's limited versions of moral consciousness "leave out something very important."

23   But can a genuinely broad moral consciousness be developed through a public education system, given the nature of today's pluralistic and diverse society? "The Roman Empire managed to do it," she says, noting that "until it was suddenly undermined by Christianity, it had this great structure of tolerance" for a wide variety of religious practices. So too did the Islamic empire under Akbar, who settled India and "prided himself on tolerating and supporting other religious minorities." Today, however, she worries that the trend may be moving in the opposite direction. "Many of the things that we choose to call 'ethnic tension' often have religious roots," she says.

24   What, then, is the connection between religion and ethics? Can there be ethics without faith?

25   "In my view," she says, "you probably can't have a strong ethical sense without some first principles." Some societies find those first principles in a connection to the land: Australian Aboriginals, she says, "believe the earth is sacred and that when you go to visit the place where your father's tribe walked, you kiss the ground and embrace the dust." Western cultures, too, have such first principles, although they are no longer as consciously held. In the West, she says, "we have really been living off the moral capital of the Judeo-Christian world, while the religious system that produced that set of ethical values erodes away."

26   That erosion, she believes, has laid the foundation for the growth of fundamentalism in many developing societies, where religious leaders have "often devised the most rigid and authoritarian notions of their traditional religion" in order to "expunge the West and de-Westernize the society." Islam, for instance, is nothing like the faith that "the Islamic fundamentalists are insisting upon today."

27   Where, then, does she see the future taking us?

28   Her answer begins with a backward reflection. "The old missionary world of the eighteenth and nineteenth centuries," she says, "cared a lot about what happened in other parts of the planet—especially in societies they defined as heathen. Even in the first blush of idealism after the Second World War, people looked outward from this society and felt an obligation to share some wealth and resources." But with the Vietnam War came "the total disaster of the misdirection of those concerns," leaving people feeling that "we can't do anything right in our relationship with other societies, so we will forget it."

29 Today, she says, her hope comes from "a revival of internationalism, more rooted in an environmental sense. One can't begin to care about the environment without caring about the pressures on people that lead them to damage it more than it is. So perhaps there is the possibility of a non-imperialist concern about other parts of the world."

30 Can that happen? She admits that "a quick look at the electoral politics of the United States does not give you much optimism for the future." Then her features break into a wry smile. "But not having been born here," she says, "I don't think of [the United States] as the center of the globe. It might occur elsewhere."

GLOSSARY

Analogy A comparison between two items, usually for the purpose of explaining one of the items or to support an idea or thesis.

Analysis Dividing a work or a topic into its parts.

Annotating A combination of underlining and marginal notes used to guide one's study of written material.

Bias The position or viewpoint of the author, as revealed in the way facts are presented and strategies used to create tone.

Cause and effect An organizational strategy in which one or more items are shown to produce one or more consequences.

Chronology The arrangement of events in time sequence. A narrative or historical account organizes events in chronological order. A process analysis explains steps in their appropriate chronology.

Cognition The process of knowing or learning.

Commitment An active desire to do something well.

Comparison A structuring of information to show similarities between two items.

Concentration An active attention given to a task.

Connotation The associations and emotional overtones suggested by a word.

Context clues The language environment that gives information about the meaning of words within that environment.

Contrast A structuring of information to show differences between two items.

Cornell Method A method of taking notes from reading or from lectures. A vertical line divides each page into two parts, the left part one-third of the page and the right two-thirds. Notes are taken to the right of the line and key words and topics are placed to the left.

Critical thinking An organized, purposeful study of information and ideas to evaluate their usefulness.

Definition Explanation of a word's meaning or meanings. It can be provided in a sentence or expanded into an essay.

Denotation The meanings of a word, often referred to as a word's dictionary definitions.

Description Details appealing to the five senses that help readers to "see" the writer's subject.

Details Specific pieces of information that range from descriptions of people and places to statistical data and that are used by writers to illustrate and support ideas and general points.

Evidence Facts and examples used to support the main idea of an argument.

Example A specific illustration used to develop a main idea.

Expository writing Writing primarily designed to provide information, e.g., reporting and textbook writing.

Expressive writing Writing designed to produce an emotional as well as intellectual response to the subject discussed and to generate reflection on human life and experiences.

Fact A statement that is verifiable by observation, measurement, experiment, or use of reliable reference sources such as encyclopedias.

440

Fiction An imagined narrative; a story.

Figurative language Language containing figures of speech (e.g., metaphors) that extend meaning beyond the literal.

Flowchart A type of graph best used to depict steps in a process or a sequence of events or ideas.

Graphics Methods of presenting information visually, such as graphs, maps, charts, or diagrams.

Highlighting The use of colored markers to make some lines of a text stand out, as an aid to studying the text.

Hyperbole Exaggerated writing that is designed to give emphasis through overstatement.

Inference A conclusion drawn from related information on a given subject.

Irony The expression of some form of discrepancy between what is said and what is meant, what we expect to happen and what actually happens, or what a character says and what we understand to be true.

Main idea The central point of a passage or work.

Mapping A writing-to-learn strategy that displays main ideas and shows their relationships graphically.

Metacognition The knowledge of cognition, the understanding of the process of reading and learning that allows for directing and monitoring the process.

Metaphor A figure of speech in which a comparison is either stated or implied between two basically unlike items. (E.g., Love is compared to red roses.)

Monitor Regular, purposeful checking of one's work to maintain ideal performance of a task.

Notetaking Paraphrasing and summarizing main ideas and key points in assigned readings as a strategy for studying the readings.

Opinion Statements of inference or judgment, in contrast to statements of fact.

Organization The structure or pattern of development of a work.

Outlining A strategy for summarizing and indicating the relationships of a work's main ideas, main details, and minor details by using a pattern of Roman numerals, letters, and Arabic numerals and indentation.

Paraphrase A restatement in different words of what is said in a work or passage. The purpose is to clarify rather than to condense.

Personification A comparison that gives human qualities to something not human. (E.g., "The daffodils tossed their heads.")

Persuasive writing Writing primarily designed to support a position on an issue or beliefs about a given subject.

Point of View The perspective from which a story is told.

Preread A step in preparing to read that involves getting an overview by reading only key parts of a work.

Purpose The reason or reasons a writer chooses to write a particular work.

Scanning A method of quick reading that focuses on finding just the information needed from the reading material.

Signal words Words or phrases that make clear a passage's structure.

Simile A comparison between two basically unlike things stated explicitly through a connector such as *like* or *as*. (E.g., "My love is like a red, red rose.")

Skimming A reading strategy that focuses on obtaining an overview or "gist" of a work by searching for main ideas and skipping most details.

Style A writer's choice of words and sentence patterns.

Summary A condensed, objective restatement in different words of the main points of a passage or work.

Theme The central idea or ideas that a literary work expresses.

Thesis The main idea of an essay, article, or book; what a writer asserts about his or her subject.

Tone The way the writer's attitude is expressed. (E.g., playful, sarcastic.)

Topic The subject of a piece of writing.

Topic sentence The sentence in a paragraph that states the paragraph's main idea. (In some paragraphs, the main idea is not stated but implied.)

Understatement A strategy of saying less than is meant to achieve emphasis.

Credits (continued)

Beetle Bailey. Reprinted with special permission of King Features Syndicate.

Thomas A. Bailey and David M. Kennedy, *The American Pageant,* 6th edition. Reprinted with permission of D.C. Heath and Company. Copyright 1979 by D.C. Heath and Company.

William Barklow, "Hippo Talk," Reprinted with permission from *Natural History,* May 1995. Copyright the American Museum of Natural History, 1995.

Michael Barone, "The New America," *U.S. News and World Report,* July 10, 1995. Copyright, July 10, 1995, U.S. News and World Report.

Dave Barry, "Unplugged," *Miami Herald,* July 16, 1995. Reprinted with permission: Tribune Media Services.

John H. Bodley, *Cultural Anthropology: Tribes, States, and the Global System.* Reprinted with permission of Mayfield Publishing Co. Copyright © 1994 by Mayfield Publishing Co.

Brandon Centerwall, "Television and Violent Crime." Reprinted with permission of the author and *The Public Interest,* Number III, Spring 1993, pp. 56–71, © 1993 by National Affairs, Inc.

William Cline, Table 23.3 on page 419 from *Global Warming: The Economic Stakes.* Reprinted with permission of the Institute for International Economics. Copyright 1992 by the Institute for International Economics.

Douglass Colligan, "The Light Stuff," *Technology,* Feb/March 1982. Reprinted by permission of the author.

Jill Ker Conway, "Women, Children, and Ethics." Reprinted with permission of Jossey-Bass Inc., Publishers. From *Shared Values for a Troubled World: Conversations with Men and Women of Conscience* by Rushworth Kidder. Copyright © 1994 by Jossey-Bass Inc., Publishers.

Aaron Copland, *What to Listen For In Music.* Reprinted with permission of The Aaron Copland Fund for Music, Inc. Copyright © 1939 The Aaron Copland Fund for Music, Inc.

Daniel Curran and Claire Renzetti, *Social Problems,* 3rd edition. Reprinted with permission of Allyn and Bacon, Inc. Copyright © 1993 by Allyn and Bacon, Inc.

R. J. Donatelle and L. G. Davis, *Access to Health.* Reprinted with permission of Allyn and Bacon, Inc. Copyright © 1996 by Allyn and Bacon, Inc.

J. Ross Eshleman, Barbara G. Cashion, and Laurence A. Basirico, *Sociology: An Introduction,* 4th edition. Copyright © 1993, by HarperCollins College Publishers Inc. Reprinted by permission.

Evans and Berman, *Marketing,* 6th edition. Reprinted with permission of Prentice Hall Inc. Copyright © 1994 by Prentice Hall Inc.

Ellen Goodman, "Stranger-Danger," *Boston Globe,* July 15, 1995. Copyright © 1995, The Boston Globe Newspaper Co./Washington Post Writers Group. Reprinted with permission.

Dianne Hales and Dr. Robert Hales, "Does Your Body-Talk Do You In?" *Parade,* March 12, 1995. Reprinted with permission from *Parade,* copyright © 1995.

Sydney J. Harris, excerpt from *Clearing the Ground.* Copyright © 1982, 1983, 1985, 1986 by The Chicago Sun-Times, Field Newspaper Syndicate, News-America Syndicate and Sydney J. Harris. Reprinted by permission of Houghton Mifflin Co. All rights reserved.

M. Hein and S. Arena, *Foundations of College Chemistry, 5th Alt edition.* Copyright © 1993 Brooks/Cole Publishing Company, a division of International Thomson Publishing Inc., Pacific Grove, CA 93950. By permission of the author.

James M. Henslin, *Sociology.* Reprinted with permission of Allyn and Bacon, Inc. Copyright 1995 by Allyn and Bacon, Inc.

Bunny Hoest, *Laugh Parade* cartoon © 1995. Reprinted courtesy of the artist and *Parade* Magazine.

From *The Collected Poems of A. E. Housman.* Copyright 1939, 1940 by Holt, Rinehart and Winston, Inc. Copyright © 1967 by Robert E. Symons. Reprinted by permission of Henry Holt and Co., Inc.

Langston Hughes, "Dream Deferred" from *The Panther and the Lash: Poems for Our Times,* 1951. Reprinted by permission of Random House/Knopf.

Molly Ivins, "Ban the Things. Ban Them All." *Washington Post,* March 16, 1993. Copyright © The Washington Post.

Sarah James and Floyd Peterson, "At Risk in Alaska: Our Salmon, Our Eagles," *Washington Post,* July 21, 1995. © The Washington Post.

Richard D. Kahlenberg, "Affirmative Action by Class," *Washington Post,* July 17, 1995. © The Washington Post.

Thomas H. Kean, "The Crisis Coming to Campus," *Washington Post,* May 1, 1995. © 1995 The Washington Post.

Tracy Kidder, *Among Schoolchildren.* Copyright © 1989 by John Tracy Kidder. Reprinted by permission of Houghton Mifflin Co. All rights reserved.

Charles Krauthammer, "Painless Patriotism," *Washington Post,* June 30, 1995. Copyright © 1995, Washington Post Writers Group. Reprinted with permission.

Don Lago, "Symbols of Mankind," *Science Digest,* March 1981. Reprinted with permission of the author.

Lester A. Lefton, *Psychology.* Reprinted with permission of Allyn and Bacon, Inc. Copyright 1995 by Allyn and Bacon, Inc.

Stephen Lucas, *The Art of Public Speaking,* 5th edition. Reprinted with permission of McGraw-Hill, Inc. Copyright © 1995 by McGraw-Hill, Inc.

McKnight, Tom, *Essentials of Physical Geography,* © 1992, Preface and Chapter 9. Reprinted with permission of Prentice Hall, Upper Saddle River, New Jersey.

INDEX

"Affirmative Action by Class,"
425–27

"Amish—*Gemeinshaft* Community in a *Gesellshaft* Society,
The," 105–08

Analogy, 3

Annotating, 43, 198–99

Asimov, Isaac, 360

"At Risk in Alaska: Our Salmon,
Our Eagles," 421–22

Bailey, Thomas, A., 90

"Ban the Things. Ban Them All."
398–400

Barklow, William, 30, 35–37

Barone, Michael, 429

Barry, Dave, 383–86

Basirico, Laurence A., 305

"Basis of Moral Judgment, The,"
299–304

"Behavior of the Baboon Has
Evolved in a Social
Context, The," 95–100

"Belly Up to the Bar: This
Round's On Me," 148–52

Biases, 376–77

Brainstorming, 38–39

Cashion, Barbara G., 305

Cause/Effect, 166–69

signal words for, 168

Charts, 254–58

Chopin, Kate, 337

Class participation, 282–84

Class preparation, 281–82

Cognition, 9–10

Colligan, Douglas, 20

Commitment, 5–6

Comparison/Contrast, 163–66

signal words for, 164

Concentration, 6–9, 47

guidelines for fixing, 47

steps to improved, 7–9

Connotation, 319–21

Context clues, 112–19

Conway, Jill Ker, 434

Copland, Aaron, 222

Cornell Method, 208–09,
211–13

"Crisis Coming to Campus, The,"
183–87

Critical reader, characteristics of,
368–69

Definition, 158–61

signal words for, 159

Details, 73–90

Diagrams, 250–52

Dictionary, 125–34

"Differences Between Public
Speaking and
Conversation," 78–82

Dingus, Lowell, 270

"Discovery of Short-Term
Memory, The," 44

"Does Your Body-Talk Do You
In?" 100–05

"Dream Deferred," 344–45

"Effects of the Automobile, The,"
187–93

Engaged reader, 4–10

Eshleman, J. Ross, 305

Essays, 325–33

descriptive, 325–29

narrative, 330–33

Examples, 156–58

signal words for, 157

Expository Writing, 30

Expressive writing, 317–65

Facts, 368–70

Figurative language, 322–25

Freewriting, 38

Gaffney, Eugene S., 270

Glossaries, 126

Goodman, Ellen, 383, 394

Graphics, 248–58

guidelines for reading, 248–49

Hales, Dianne, 100

Hales, Robert, 100

Harris, Sydney, 138

Henslin, James M, 105, 187

Herrick, Robert, 342

Highlighting, 195–97

"Hippo Talk," 35–38

"How Large Were the Biggest
Dinosaurs?" 270–74

"How We Listen to Music,"
222–29

"Hypnosis," 51–56

Housman, A. E., 346

Hughes, Langston, 344

Hyperbole, 382–83

Inferences, 371–74

guidelines for evaluating,
373–74

Irony, 382–83

"Is My Team Ploughing," 346–47

Ivins, Molly, 398

James, Sarah, 421

"Jeffersonian Idealism and
Idealists," 91–93

Kahlenberg, Richard D., 425

Kean, Thomas H., 183

Kennedy, David M., 90

Kidder, Tracy, 348

Krauthammer, Charles, 229

"Learning to Learn," 17

Lefton, Lester A., 17, 43–44, 51,
142

"Legalization of Drugs,"
305–11

"Light Stuff, The," 20–25

Listing, 154–56

signal words for, 155

Logical fallacies, 387–90
"Long-Term Memory; Focus on
 Retrieval," 44–45
Lowell, Amy, 345
Lucas, Stephen E., 39, 178
Lutgens, Frederick, K., 56, 177

Main idea, 67–110
 guidelines for identifying,
  72–73
Mapping, 206–08
Maps, 252–53
McKnight, Tom L., 258–60,
 263–64
Metacognition, 9–10
Metaphor, 323–25
Mings, Turley, 93, 219
Monitor, 45–48
"Mrs. Zajac," 348–52

Narration, 330–31, 334–36
 character in, 335–36
 point of view in, 336
 structure of, 334–35
"Nature of Scientific Inquiry,
 The," 56–60
"New America, The," 429–34
"New Industrial Revolution,
 The," 93–94
Norell, Mark A., 270
Note taking, 208–13

Opinions, 369–76
"Opposing Principles Help
 Balance Society," 138–42
Outlining, 200–05
Ordering, 161–63
 signal words for, 161

"Painless Patriotism," 229–34
Paraphrasing, 208–10

Persuasive writing, 30, 366–408
Peterson, Floyd, 421
Prefixes, 120–22
Prereading, 33–38
"Private Participation in Public
 Education," 219–22
Problem/Solution, 169–71
 signal words for, 170
Pronunciation guides, 128–29

"Rainforest Removal," 264–70
Raspberry, William, 427
Reading
 context, 15–17
 definition of, 11–12
 expressive writing, 317–65
 graphics, 248–58
 predicting in, 13–15
 strategy, 26–66
Reading process, 10–17
Reading profile, 3–4
Reflection, 48–50
Retention strategies, 285–87
Review, 50–51
Ricklefs, Robert E., 95
Roots, 122–23
Ruggiero, Vincent Ryan, 299

Sagan, Carl, 274
Samuelson, Robert J., 61
Scanning, 236–41
Schwartz, Amy E., 423
"Science and the Sense of
 Wonder," 360–65
"Secret Life of Walter Mitty, The,"
 353–59
Sentence style, 321–22
Simile, 323
Skimming, 241–47
"Story of an Hour, The," 337–40
"Stranger-Danger," 394–98

Suffixes, 124–25
Summary, 213–18

Tables, 253–54
Tarbuck, Edward J., 56
"Taxi," 345
Test taking, preparation for,
 287–99
Thesaurus, 127
Thurber, James, 353
Thurow, Lester C., 403
"To Daffodils," 342
Topic, 69–71, 73–74
Topic sentence, 75–78
Trafford, Abigail, 311
"Triumph of the Psycho-Fact,
 The," 61–66

Underlining, 195–97
Understatement, 382–83
"Unheeding Addict, The," 311–16
"Unplugged," 383–86

Vocabulary cards, 135–37
"Visions of the On-Line
 University—in 3-D,"
 423–25

Welsch, Roger L., 148
"What Is Prejudice?" 142–47
"What TV Could Do for
 America," 274–80
"Why Women Are Paid Less
 Than Men," 403–08
"Will Our Future Be Workable?"
 427–29
"Women, Children, and Ethics,"
 434–39
Writer's Stance, 377–86